# BUILDING
# TABLET PC
## APPLICATIONS

*Rob Jarrett*
*Philip Su*

PUBLISHED BY
Microsoft Press
A Division of Microsoft Corporation
One Microsoft Way
Redmond, Washington 98052-6399

Library of Congress Cataloging-in-Publication Data
Su, Philip, 1976-
    Building Tablet PC Applications / Philip Su, Rob Jarrett.
        p. cm.
        Includes index.
    ISBN 0-7356-1723-6
    1. Pen-based computers.  2. Application software--Development.  I. Jarrett, Rob, 1969-
II. Title.

    QA76.89 .S8 2002
    005.3--dc21

                                                                2002026540

Printed and bound in the United States of America.

1 2 3 4 5 6 7 8 9    QWE    7 6 5 4 3 2

Distributed in Canada by H.B. Fenn and Company Ltd.

A CIP catalogue record for this book is available from the British Library.

Microsoft Press books are available through booksellers and distributors worldwide. For further information about international editions, contact your local Microsoft Corporation office or contact Microsoft Press International directly at fax (425) 936-7329. Visit our Web site at www.microsoft.com/mspress. Send comments to *mspinput@microsoft.com*.

**Acquisitions Editor:** Danielle Bird
**Project Editor:** Lynn Finnel
**Technical Editor:** Brian Johnson

Body Part No. X08-81825

From Philip:

*For parents who provided sacrificially,*

*for a brother who proved dear,*

*for two friends who bore forgiveness,*

*for a woman who steadfastly loved.*

From Rob:

*For all those with a vision and the courage to try and realize that vision.*

# Table of Contents

# Foreword

Who would have thought that writing in digital ink on a computer display could be as satisfying as the real thing?

Well, I knew it *could*, but I wasn't sure when, if ever, it would become a feature of Microsoft Windows. Now it's happening, and Rob Jarrett and Philip Su were right there at the center of the activity that made it so.

When you stroke your pen across a page of Windows Journal, you're experiencing digital ink the way Rob and Philip and I think it was meant to be. Quick. Smooth. Colorful. Expressive. Strokes with these qualities help you remember what you were thinking when you wrote them. They naturally capture your thoughts, making your personal computer quite a bit more personal.

Digital ink—now a first-class data type—is just one of the many reasons that you will want to make your applications tablet-aware moving forward.

I view this and other Tablet PC capabilities in a particular light, one that has been helpful in focusing our Tablet PC development work. My dream has long been to make electronic information as handy as paper. In much that same way that ClearType (my first team at Microsoft) enabled applications to display type with paper-like quality, the Windows Ink Services Platform (WISP) enables Windows and applications to include a paper-like inking experience. With the Windows XP Tablet PC Edition, you get ClearType and WISP and many related capabilities with which you can make *your* electronic information as handy as paper.

In fact, I think the most important steps toward making electronic information as versatile as paper will come from application developers rethinking what it means for computing to be personal and for information to be handy. And this rethinking will also create the biggest opportunities.

Let the Tablet PC Platform SDK be your starting point, and let Rob and Philip be your guides. Whether you are just getting your feet wet with Web development or are experienced enough to have written your own system components, this book will give you insights you can apply to the Tablet PC Platform SDK to achieve the handiness of paper in your domain.

Rob and Philip evidently fondly remember the way I carried this torch into Microsoft and handed it to them because they have asked that before they give you their insights, I share some of my thoughts about our collective work. I'll be brief:

1.  Physically, we are creating a better paper—comfortable to hold and appealing to the eye, but better due to its interactivity, capacity, intelligence, and connectedness. The tablet's ergonomics are catching up with paper, and this has implications for application design. Specifically, consider the interaction design of paper—you can pick up papers and dash off to a meeting. You can glance at your papers while walking down the hallway, and refer to your papers off-and-on during the meeting. Such freedom of movement and casual referral in the electronic world will require that applications work well with the tablet's buttons and pen, and provide immediate feedback in response to each user event.

2.  The pointing device is catching up with the keyboard. It's not going to replace the keyboard, but it is going to be able to perform all the tasks of a keyboard when the keyboard is inconvenient to use. Handwriting recognition now supports text input tasks just as keyboard shortcuts have allowed the keyboard to accomplish pointing tasks.

3.  One of the most useful steps you can take during this catch-up phase is to support inking on any paper-like surfaces displayed by your application. Because capturing thoughts is about aiding memory, ink as ink can be valuable to users even in an application that doesn't otherwise make use of ink as a data type.

4.  The pen is useful for pointing and writing, but buttons can be even handier for tasks that can be done without picking up the pen. For example, pages are easy to flip through using a thumb or finger. Tablet PC hardware supports this by providing "Up," "Down," "Enter," and "Escape" buttons at the tablet's edge. These four buttons should be supported in as many situations as possible for scanning information and entering and rejecting choices without the pen. If you fully exploit these buttons for basic navigation within your application, you will be approaching the handiness of paper for tasks that don't require a pen.

5.  Paper's handiness is partly due to its low cognitive load. In mobile and social settings, many things are vying for the user's attention. A user needn't formulate many questions to complete a task with paper; it is always ready to be flipped through, written on, and marked for follow-up in obvious ways. Our programs should aspire to the same readiness and obviousness for common tasks. We can

simplify by offering additional tasks only when and where they are relevant. Both inductive UI and on-object UI can be helpful (the latter being close at hand when using the pen).

6.  WISP is the world's most powerful ink platform. If you create a solid foundation with the preceding items, you can use the advanced capabilities of WISP to build all manner of advanced structures.

The work you do to fine-tune your application for tablets is what will achieve handiness for users accessing your application's information. I look forward to using your products!

— *Bert*

Bert Keely
Architect
Tablet PC

# Acknowledgments

Inevitably, it ends up like the Oscars. Someone's going to wear too little. Someone's going to cry. And someone, perhaps everyone, will have a mile-long list of people to thank, with nods to producers, actors, neighboring musicians, dead musicians, soon-to-be musicians, and moms (not to mention the requisite "Shout-out to my peeps in Milwaukee—you da best!").

But it has to be this way. Too much from too many people has gone into this book for us to simply thank God and be played off the stage with the theme from our summer blockbuster. Indeed, much goes on behind the scenes. We will try our best here to acknowledge as many people as we can, in no definite order.

## Rob and Philip Thank...

Lynn Finnel, our editor, and Brian Johnson, our technical editor. Disasters were averted, readers were saved, and great suggestions were made. This book is the result of your careful guidance. Thanks for walking alongside us. Danielle Bird, for believing in this book and for standing up for us. We made it! And of course Michael Kloepfer—your incredible art establishes a delightful flavor and feel to the book. Bert Keely, Dan Altman, Evan Feldman, Greg Hullender, Michael Shilman, and Rich Grutzmacher for the insightful interviews, and Arin Goldberg, Jerry Turner, Michael Tsang, Shiraz Somji, Stephen Fisher, and Tim Kannapel for answering the many technical questions we had. Anson Horton, for solid advice on making the C# samples lucid for our readers. And what's a Tablet PC book without thanking the Microsoft Pen Windows folks? Brian Watson, Byron Bishop, Eric Berman, Keith Stutler, Lloyd Frink, Scott Hysom, and Tomas Matos—thanks for all the great discussions and insights. We really wish we could have included more. Finally, the Microsoft Tablet PC team. The reason is obvious—you made all this possible. One day we'll be able to tell our grandkids that we were there when it all happened.

## Rob Thanks...

Caitlin, for your support, understanding, and putting up with the many hours I was locked away in the den. Bert Keely, Charlton Lui, and David Jones, thank you for sharing your incredible visions of what the Tablet PC can be. My two best friends, and two thirds of "The Trio," Richard Paige and Matthew Wilson—without you guys I wouldn't have had the confidence to write a book. Sashi Ragupathy, thanks for encouraging me to stick with my idea, and for all the good karma. Cory Kitchens, thanks for the distracting IM conversations about the Microsoft Xbox during marathon writing sessions. And last but not least, thanks to Tim Horton's, Krispy Kreme, and TiVo for providing me with energy, sustenance, and entertainment, respectively—all so very desperately needed during the writing of this book.

## Philip Thanks...

My wife, Tanya. Your support has been tremendous over the past few months. Thanks for giving up weeknights and weekends, and for encouraging me through the low points. Your contribution is evident throughout. The food, folks, and fun crew: Bertrand Lee, Cory Hilke, Huey "Bubble Tea" Siah, Jonas Keating, Mary Hilke, and Neil Brench—thanks for the uplifting words and of course the "Midtown Madness." Finally, the family. Your sacrifice has given me all these opportunities. Thank you for your faith in me.

# Introduction

The year is 2015. You find yourself resting on a beach in Maui, watching nearby youngsters zip along the boardwalk on their brand-new Segway Human Transporters. The sound of the ocean, ever so soft and reassuring, fills the air with its soothing rhythm. Your early retirement has treated you well—it's not a bad lifestyle at all for having invented Cheezy Dew, the world's first and greatest caffeinated cheeze drink (the lawyers require that *cheeze* be spelled that way for reasons we won't go into here). It's a great time to continue writing your third best-selling autobiography, "Cheezy Does It." You reach down into the icebox for a refreshing can of Cheezy Dew and grab your computer.

But what does it look like? Surely you aren't holding a clumsy 3-pound laptop with a 2-hour battery life—it's 2015, for Knuth's sake! Maybe you're imagining a quad-processor 64-bit machine the size of a credit card that's capable of flawless voice recognition and responds to the affectionate name "Computer." But what if, in addition to dictation, you want to draw a self-portrait of your profile for the cover (à la Alfred Hitchcock)? What you're therefore imagining is a powerful computer the size and weight of a light clipboard that allows you to draw on it with a pen. What you're imagining is a tablet computer.

Tablet computers have been one of the Holy Grails of computing for decades. Television and movies such as *Star Trek* popularized the notion of tablet computers to a broad audience of technophiles. When we imagine the future, slate-like computers with interactive screens *just make sense*—tablet computers are the natural and expected evolution of desktop and laptop computers. In considering tablet computers, it is not a matter of *whether* they'll arrive, but *when*.

This book is specifically about Microsoft's tablet computer and the Tablet PC Platform. It explains how to best use the new Tablet PC Platform API as well as how to design your applications for pen-based users.

# A Beautiful Day

There's something about the heat of the moment that makes it easy to forget the bigger picture. In the fall of 2001, Rob and I were both on the Microsoft Tablet PC team, heavily involved in locking down the fourth development milestone. Bugs were coming in every day, and developers were fixing them as efficiently as possible. Everyone was working, head down, on his component.

One day I took a step back from all the excitement and realized that although the Tablet PC team was creating a brand-new software platform for developers, there would be no books to explore such a platform in depth when it became available. Developing software for Tablet PCs is unlike developing software for any other platform. Pen computing, in general, is a new area for most developers. The pen introduces a host of usability concerns that many developers are not aware of. And then there's the issue of the completely new APIs.

So I approached Rob about coauthoring a book specifically written to address tablet application design as well as the new APIs. He agreed, believing as I did that the success of the Tablet PC Platform lay in the development of great software. What you are now holding is the result of that day's conversation and many months' collaboration between Rob, me, and a host of our supporters.

Rob and I work in the Tablet PC division at Microsoft, but we were not part of the team that created the Tablet PC Platform SDK. Instead, we were responsible for integrating the Tablet PC Platform SDK technologies into Microsoft Windows XP Tablet PC Edition (specifically Windows Journal). Our situation gives us the best of outsider and insider experiences: as outsiders using the Tablet PC Platform SDK technologies, we share the perspective of third-party developers like you; but as insiders on the Tablet PC team, we understand many of the reasons behind the design of the SDK. We'll share our experiences with you throughout this book.

# Target Audience

We designed this book for developers, who write code to implement designs, and designers, who write specifications or lay out user interfaces for developers. In many cases, developer and designer are the same person.

Developers will get the most benefit from this book if they have working knowledge of UI development in the Microsoft .NET Framework. We venture only briefly into other parts of the .NET Framework when necessary. Because we kept the focus of the technical chapters on the Tablet PC Platform APIs, even a developer who is new to the .NET Framework should find it easy to follow along.

## Sample Code

Throughout this book, we present code samples in C#. Those of you who don't know C# but are familiar with C++ or Java should find the samples easy to understand. Developers and designers familiar with Microsoft Visual Basic .NET will find very few differences between the C# implementations and their Visual Basic .NET counterparts. We have, however, stayed away from presenting samples in C++/COM to keep the code samples clear and concise. If you want to write your tablet application in C++/COM, you'll be happy to know that the .NET interfaces of the Tablet PC Platform APIs are similar to the C++/COM interfaces.

> **Note** To keep the samples in this book as concise as possible, they were written "Petzold style," that is to say, without the use of the designers in Microsoft Visual Studio .NET.

Another great source of samples is the Tablet PC Developer Web site (*http://www.tabletpcdeveloper.com*). Developers from around the world are free to contribute code to this Web site, which aims to provide solid samples of Tablet PC applications and solutions to developers. If you have a question or need a particular sample, you should make this your first stop on the Web for Tablet PC software solutions.

## The Companion CD-ROM

This book's companion CD-ROM has been carefully formulated to enhance your Tablet PC software development experience. Here's where to find everything you need on the CD-ROM:

**StartCD Program** The StartCD program provides a graphical interface to the content that you'll find on the CD-ROM. If you have autorun enabled, this program will open by default when you insert the CD-ROM into your CD-ROM drive.

**\SDK** This is where the Tablet PC Platform SDK is located.

**\Samples**    This folder contains the samples referenced in the book. These are not the SDK samples, which come with the SDK itself; these are the samples specifically discussed in the chapters. The BuildingTabletApps utility library, developed throughout the book, is also available in this folder. The file Setup.exe in the Samples folder will copy the samples to your PC's hard drive and add a link to the folder in your Start menu in Building Tablet PC Applications. You can remove the Samples by going to Control Panel and opening Add or Remove Programs, choose Building Tablet PC Applications and click Remove.

**\Extra**    Content tangentially related to the Tablet PC and the book is placed here. Most of the items are miscellaneous and not directly addressed in the book, but you might find them useful or entertaining.

**\eBook**    The eBook folder contains the setup program that will install a searchable electronic version of this book to your hard drive.

## Using the Companion CD-ROM Samples

Using the SDK, you can compile, run, and modify the samples included on the companion CD-ROM. You can use, modify, and redistribute the samples in this book, in part or in whole, free of charge and restriction. Although great effort has been taken to ensure that these samples are safe for general consumption, they are provided as is, with no warranty expressed or implied as to their usefulness in any particular application. The samples are not designed for and may not be used with any life-sustaining or health-monitoring software. In addition, the samples may not be modified and used to disparage Rob, myself, or either of our mothers.

> **Note**    The Tablet PC Platform SDK must be installed before the book samples will compile or run.

Each sample referenced in the book is contained within its own directory under the main Samples directory on the companion CD-ROM. Standard Microsoft Visual Studio .NET solution files (.SLN) and project files (.CSPROJ) are included for your convenience. In addition, a solution file in each chapter folder contains all the projects in that particular chapter. The default settings included in the solutions should be adequate. However, you might need to adjust a few settings in the samples' solution files if your development environment or SDK installation is different from the default configuration.

# System Requirements

Following are the system requirements for building and running the samples included with this book. Some of the samples in this book require ink recognition capabilities, which are available only on Windows XP Tablet PC Edition.

## Software

- One of the following supported operating systems:
    - Microsoft Windows XP Tablet PC Edition,
    - Microsoft Windows XP Professional (see note below),
    - Microsoft Windows XP Professional with Service Pack 1 (see note below), or
    - Microsoft Windows 2000 with Service Pack 2 (see note below).

> **Note**    You can install the Tablet PC Platform SDK on Windows 2000 or Windows XP Professional, but your applications will have less functionality available to them. On these platforms, your application can collect ink with *InkCollector* and can be tested and debugged. However, no recognition is available and you cannot use the InkEdit and InkPicture controls to collect ink on these operating systems.

- Microsoft Visual Studio .NET.
- Microsoft Internet Explorer 6.0 (recommended).

## Hardware

- CD-ROM or DVD drive.
- 8 MB of hard drive space for a complete installation of the Tablet PC SDK.
- 10 MB of hard drive space for the installation of the book samples.

■ A pointing device for input, which includes a mouse, an external tablet (non-HID-compliant digitizers are treated like a mouse but have higher resolution and more metadata on strokes), or a Tablet PC with an HID digitizer.

# Chapter Overviews

We've divided this book into four parts to address the needs of developers and designers. Table 1 shows each part of the book along with its primary audience.

**Table I-1 The Four Parts of Building Tablet PC Applications**

|  | **Content** | **Primary Audience** |
| --- | --- | --- |
| Part One | Introduction to Tablet PCs and how to design software for them | Designers/Developers |
| Part Two | The Tablet PC Platform SDK in detail | Developers |
| Part Three | Advanced Tablet PC topics such as how to update existing applications | Developers/Designers |
| Part Four | Appendixes, including the Building-TabletApps library reference | Developers/Designers |

Following is a brief overview of each chapter. For those of you in a hurry to skip some chapters, we identify some of the dependencies between chapters so that you will not get confused if you miss an important concept.

# Chapter 1—The Tablet PC and Its Applications

We start by defining what a tablet computer is and is not, especially in contrast with other pen-driven devices. Then we recount the major milestone products, both hardware and software, that marked the history of tablet computing. The chapter ends with a description of the distinguishing characteristics of a Microsoft Tablet PC.

# Chapter 2—Designing Tablet PC Applications

Microsoft invested heavily in user research to bring a compelling tablet computer to market. Chapter 2 presents the results of that research as a set of recommendations to help you build easy-to-use Tablet PC applications.

## Chapter 3—The Tablet PC Platform SDK

This chapter contains an overview of the Tablet PC Platform SDK. It covers the various components that form the SDK and also introduces the managed API.

## Chapter 4—Tablet PC Platform SDK: Tablet Input

We begin our in-depth adventure into the SDK with the Tablet Input API. The two objects that collect digital ink, *InkCollector* and *InkOverlay*, form the basis of our discussion.

## Chapters 5 and 6—Tablet PC Platform SDK: Ink Data Management

We spend two chapters discussing one of the core areas of the Tablet PC Platform. The Ink Data Management API exposes the all-important *Ink* and *Stroke* objects, which we delve into extensively. We also explain how to accomplish everyday tasks with the Ink Data Management API, such as rendering ink, saving ink, and transferring ink to the clipboard.

## Chapter 7—Tablet PC Platform SDK: Ink Recognition

One of the most popular features people associate with tablet computing is handwriting recognition. Although handwriting recognition is not a major focus of the Microsoft Tablet PC Platform, the SDK nevertheless supports recognition by means of a rich set of objects. We offer a survey of the objects in the Ink Recognition API and show by example how to apply them in common scenarios.

## Chapter 8—Ink Controls

The Tablet PC Platform SDK comes with two ink controls: InkEdit and InkPicture. We explore how InkEdit is an enhancement over standard textboxes for tablet users. Finally, we end Part Two of the book by investigating how to use the InkPicture control.

## Chapter 9—Updating Existing Applications

The Tablet PC Platform poses some unique challenges for developers and designers who plan to update an existing application rather than write a new one. In this chapter we offer advice, derived from our own experience in integrating the Tablet PC Platform APIs into existing applications, regarding how best to update your application.

# Some Final Thoughts

Rob and I are not gurus or demigods, nor are we Shakespeare or Cicero. But we *are* every bit as excited about the Tablet PC as you are! We have worked with several versions of Tablet PC prototypes as well as scores of Tablet PC Platform SDK revisions over the past two years as part of Microsoft's Tablet PC team, which gives us a unique vantage point from which we can point out tips and pitfalls.

We hope that you enjoy reading this book as much as we have enjoyed writing it. In the coming months and years, as the Tablet PC picks up momentum in the industry, we look forward to hearing from you about the cool things you've done with a Microsoft Tablet PC and the Tablet PC Platform SDK.

Cans of cool, refreshing Cheezy Dew await. So does a world of innovative, yet-to-be-written Tablet PC software!

Philip Su
Rob Jarrett

# Support

Every effort has been made to ensure the accuracy of this book and the contents of the companion CD-ROM. Microsoft Press provides corrections for books through the World Wide Web at the following address:

*http://www.microsoft.com/mspress/support/*

To connect directly to the Microsoft Press Knowledge Base and enter a query regarding a question or issue that you may have, go to:

*http://www.microsoft.com/mspress/support/search.asp*

If you have comments, questions, or ideas regarding this book or the companion CD-ROM, please send them to Microsoft Press using either of the following methods:

Postal Mail:

Microsoft Press
Attn: *Building Tablet PC Applications* Editor
One Microsoft Way
Redmond, Washington 98052-6399

E-mail:

MSPINPUT@MICROSOFT.COM

Please note that product support is not offered through the above mail addresses. For support information regarding the Tablet PC please visit the Microsoft Product Support Web site at

*http://support.microsoft.com*

# Part I

# The Tablet PC and Its Applications

# 1

# Tablet Computing Comes of Age

So you want to be a Tablet PC software developer! We're encouraged by your enthusiasm, which we quite heartily share. Of late, there has been much interest in the press regarding Microsoft's Tablet PC, and indeed the interest is well deserved. There are a lot of exciting possibilities for the Tablet PC, many of which are yet to be discovered and developed by people like you.

But first we must acknowledge that tablet computing is not a new idea. In fact, it's not even new to Microsoft, which about a decade ago made its first foray into the world of tablet computing with Windows for Pen Computing (Pen Windows). Others have made excursions into the same territory in the past few years, some notable, some quickly forgotten. In this chapter we first define what a tablet computer really is, and then we follow up with the remarkable history of prior attempts in tablet computing. Finally we close with a discussion of the distinguishing characteristics of Microsoft's Tablet PC, which is both similar to and different from those that have gone before it.

The microcosm of tablet computing is filled with strong opinions, big bets, and even bigger disasters. Let's explore the past together, while getting to know the new kid on the block—Microsoft's Tablet PC.

# What Makes a Tablet Computer

Although there are many ways to describe and define a tablet computer, for this book we will stick with a slightly stricter definition:

*A tablet computer is a thin stand-alone general-purpose computer with an integrated interactive screen. It typically has a large screen and accepts a special pen (a stylus) as an input device.*

The essential characteristics that make a particular computer a tablet computer are detailed below.

## Form Factor

Indispensable to the idea of tablet computers is their hardware profile, or *form factor*. The clearest defining characteristic of a tablet computer is its size and shape. A tablet computer is relatively flat yet has a large screen (say, the size of a sheet of paper or greater). In 2002, a well-designed three-quarter-inch-thick tablet computer is considered very thin.

In addition to a large screen and a thin profile, weight (or lack of it) is also a characteristic associated with tablet computers. In general, portable computers should be lightweight; in the case of tablet computers, their usage scenarios make weight an even more important factor. The goal of making a tablet computer lightweight is offset, however, by the often conflicted goals of making its screen bigger and its battery life longer. The heaviest single item in most portable computers is the liquid crystal display (LCD). After all, it's hard to make a big sheet of glass and liquid crystal light (no pun intended). Similarly, modern batteries such as the rechargeable lithium ion (Li) or nickel metal hydride (NiMH) varieties are filled with heavy chemicals. In fact, in most portable computers the battery is the second single heaviest item.

All things considered, the form factor of a typical tablet computer is the amalgam of a series of trade-offs between thickness, screen size, battery life, and weight. The ideal tablet computer, though, is as thin as a clipboard, as big as a sheet of paper, as light as a floppy disk, and as long lasting as a TV remote.

# Pen Input

Closely associated with tablet computers is the notion of using a pen as a means of input. Although such pen-like input devices are more accurately termed *styluses* (or *styli*) or even *pen styluses*, we use the colloquial pen throughout this book when referring to input styluses.

While it is true that accepting pen input is not an essential defining characteristic of all tablet computers, most serious uses of tablet computers require some sort of pen input. The alternatives are simply not sufficient for most usage scenarios. Fingers, for instance, are too imprecise of an input mechanism for all but the simplest uses, such as clicking huge buttons. Even the best calligrapher, confined to writing with his fingers, will produce handwriting only appropriate for posting on refrigerator doors. Furthermore, fingers quickly soil what otherwise is a perfectly clear screen. Pens have all the advantages of precision targeting, increased control, familiarity, and cleanliness. They are thus typically the preferred input devices on tablet computers.

This is not at all to say that tablet computers do not, or should not, support alternative input devices such as keyboards and mice. On the contrary, most tablet computers will accept a variety of input devices appropriate for various usage scenarios. However, all tablet computers feature pen input as one of their main input methodologies.

# Stand-Alone and General-Purpose

Now we approach a potentially controversial aspect of our definition of tablet computers. We assert that tablet computers are distinguished from a variety of similar devices by the following two characteristics:

- **They are stand-alone** True tablet computers are not simply display or input devices tethered to a host machine without which they could not function. Instead, tablet computers are stand-alone computers in their own right, able to function fully without the assistance of any other computer (tethered or networked). This does not mean that tablet computers cannot or should not function as part of a larger network of computing devices. Quite the opposite, they will most likely play a central role in a grid of networked devices. However, they must be usable on their own, without the support of a network or attached hardware.

■ **They are general-purpose**  By this we mean that a tablet computer is useful in the general way that any personal computer is useful. It should not be restricted by either its processing power or its operating system (OS) to function only for specific purposes. On the contrary, it should enable its owner to do all the things that can reasonably be expected of a regular personal computer, and possibly even more. A tablet computer will ideally be able to run all the software that is available for desktop and laptop personal computers, making it truly another type of personal computer.

There are well-intentioned and highly intelligent people, both inside and outside the field of tablet computing, who may disagree with the assertion that tablet computers must be stand-alone and general-purpose. Nevertheless, when we refer to tablet computers in this book, we are specifically referring to stand-alone general-purpose computers of a certain hardware profile.

## What Isn't a Tablet Computer

For the purposes of this book, there are several types of computing devices that are not considered tablet computers:

■ **Pocket-Sized PCs**  Popular pocket-sized PCs include the PalmPilot, the Handspring Visor, and the Compaq iPAQ. These devices are indeed stand-alone computers and accept a stylus for input on their interactive screens. However, their limited processing power and screen size make them inappropriate as a primary general-purpose computer. Instead, they are optimized for a specialized set of uses.

■ **Electronic book readers**  These computers, meant to display electronic books for easy reading, are lightweight and come with large interactive screens, but they do not qualify as general-purpose computers because they typically run only electronic book software.

■ **Web pads**  These flat, stylus-driven computers were created to allow Web browsing throughout a home or office with wireless connectivity. Web pads are also not general-purpose computers.

■ **Remote access pads**  A more flexible variant of the Web pad, remote access pads are wireless devices that are essentially roaming screens for their host computer. By allowing you to see and interact with the host computer, remote access pads offer all the richness of software available on the host computer. This makes them general-purpose computers. The critical difference between a remote access pad and a tablet computer is that the remote access pad is not truly stand-alone. Without wireless connectivity or without the host, the remote access pad becomes useless.

# The Role of Tablet Computers

In the spectrum of computing devices, what niche do tablet computers occupy? What are the ideal uses for a tablet computer, and how do these uses differ from other computing devices?

First, tablet computers are full-fledged computers, not specialized hardware meant for limited purposes. Although tablet computers can be used as personal information managers (like Palm devices) or electronic book displayers, they are flexible beyond either of these uses because they can perform a variety of other functions as well. As we've said earlier, a tablet computer should be capable of running all the software available for desktop or laptop computers, thus potentially being as powerful and as useful as both.

However, a tablet computer is not a replacement for a desktop computer. The usage scenarios are vastly different between the two, creating a wide canyon of contrast that cannot, and arguably should not, be crossed. A desktop computer's portability is of little concern. Instead, desktop computers should be powerful, supporting many large profile devices such as DVD drives, subwoofers, and generous display monitors. In contrast, a tablet computer needs to be portable despite its ability to run all the software that a desktop computer can. The need for portability places restrictions on the types of hardware peripherals that a typical tablet computer will host, at least in its roaming (away-from-desk) configuration.

Laptop computers, on the other hand, share some of the same design goals as tablet computers. Both are portable versions of full-functioned computers. Both must be lightweight while supporting a comfortable screen size and battery life. Both allow the attachment of hardware peripherals, such as disk drives and mice, for increased flexibility in situations where portability is not as great of a concern. Convertible tablets are thus a superset of laptop computers because they fulfill the same design goals as laptops while adding a few features of their own.

## Convertible Tablet Computers

Tablet computers are called *convertible* when they easily convert between a laptop-like keyboard usage configuration and a slate-like tablet usage configuration. Different manufacturers of tablet computers have accomplished this polymorphic feat in various ingenious ways, usually involving a swiveling screen or a tuck-away keyboard. Figure 1-1 shows one possible convertible design in action.

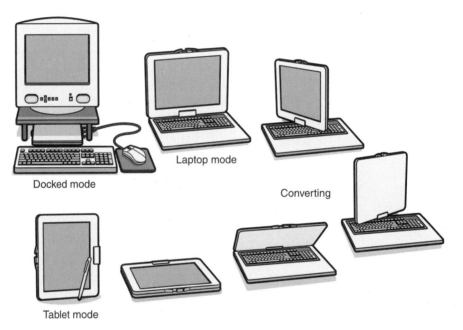

Docked mode

Laptop mode

Converting

Tablet mode

**Figure 1-1**   A convertible tablet computer supports both a laptop-like configuration and a tablet-like configuration.

Tablet computers fill an important niche in the spectrum of computing devices. In addition to the portability scenarios addressed by laptop computers, tablet computers accept the pen as a familiar alternative input methodology. The pen resolves two shortcomings of laptop computers:

- **Natural input**  Even "computer-illiterate" people are familiar with how to use pens, pencils, and paper to write. For many people, the pen is also easier to use as a direct manipulator of items on screen, whereas mice and other pointing devices are indirect manipulators requiring more focused hand-eye coordination. Support for pen input enables a variety of scenarios, such as sketching or handwriting, that are simply not practical with other input methodologies.

- **Social context**  How many times have you been in a meeting where an attendee was clicking away at a laptop while the speaker was talking? Many people are distracted by the sound of others typing during a meeting. Furthermore, some feel uncomfortable about the barriers set up by a room full of meeting attendees each with his laptop screen raised in front of him. Tablet computers address both of these social context challenges handily. Attendees are much less distracted by others taking notes on a tablet computer than they are by the sound of typing. Similarly, the design of a tablet computer allows it to be used flat on the surface of a table instead of raised in front of the face of the user.

Tablet computers are thus well positioned as a replacement for laptop computers because they target the same design goals as laptops while enabling new usage scenarios by accepting pen input and by resolving the social dilemmas posed by laptops.

## A Brief History of Tablet Computing

The next few pages present profiles of some of the pioneers of tablet computing and its related technologies. The profiled technologies mark important milestones on the road to where we are today with the Tablet PC. It is important not only to remember the past, but also, by investigating it, to learn the lessons and spot the trends that will drive us toward a successful future in tablet computing. Our coverage is far from comprehensive, though it does detail the major advances over the past decade or so in the field. Figure 1-2 is a timeline of the featured tablet pioneers.

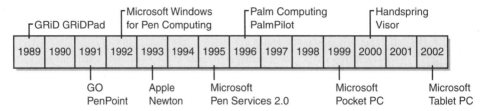

**Figure 1-2**    A timeline of milestones in tablet computing.

# GRiD GRiDPad

**GRiDPad**

| | |
|---|---|
| Release Date | 1989 |
| Dimensions | 9" × 12" × 1.4" |
| Weight | 4.4 lbs. |
| Screen | 10-inch LCD, 640 x 400 CGA |
| Processor | 10-MHz Intel 80C86 |
| Price | $2,400 |

In 1989, GRiD Computing released the GRiDPad, a portable computer with a tablet design. It came without a keyboard (although one could be attached) and used a pen as the default method of interaction. Boasting a 640 x 400 CGA display, the GRiDPad cost around $2,400 without the software. GRiDPad's software ran on top of MS-DOS 3.3. Applications for the GRiDPad were written in GRiDTask, a rapid-application development infrastructure designed specifically for the device.

Development of the GRiDPad and GRiDTask was led by GRiD Vice President of Research Jeff Hawkins, who would later play ever-increasing roles in the world of pen computing. GRiD Computing subsequently released several other tablet-like devices, with the GRiD Convertible being most notable as the first convertible tablet device. Despite its many innovations, GRiD Computing's sales were disappointing, and Tandy eventually bought the company. Gradually, its creativity and market clout faded away.

# GO PenPoint

**EO Personal Communicator**

| | |
|---|---|
| Release Date | 1991 |
| Key Manufacturers | EO (pictured), GRiD, NCR, Samsung |

The story of GO Corporation and its pen-driven operating system, GO PenPoint, is filled with drama and controversy. PenPoint was designed from the ground up to interact primarily with pens. But it was ahead of its time in many other ways as well. The PenPoint operating system supported a flat view of memory (32-bit addressed) and preemptive multitasking. It also allowed detachable networking (moving from connected to disconnected states, depending on the availability of a network). And to top it all off, PenPoint was an object-based operating system that had an entire application framework for developers.

Because of its revolutionary design, PenPoint's user model was very different from most operating systems (past and present). PenPoint had a notebook paradigm for the user's workspace. Each document was a page in the notebook that the user could flip to when necessary. Furthermore, there wasn't the concept of launching applications. Instead, to create a new document of a particular type, the user would simply create a new page using a particular stationery. Applications were implemented as stationeries, thereby completing PenPoint's notebook paradigm.

The drama with GO Corporation, however, allegedly begins with Microsoft. As former CEO and cofounder Jerry Kaplan tells it in his book, *Startup: A Silicon Valley Adventure Story*[1], representatives of Microsoft met with engineers at GO to discuss some application compatibility issues under a nondisclosure agreement—or so the representatives claimed. Lo and behold, according to the story, Kaplan discovers six months later that Microsoft had, since the meeting with GO, started its own Windows for Pen Computing project. Pen Windows, writes Kaplan, was clearly a reactionary initiative launched by Microsoft to destroy GO

---

1. *Startup: A Silicon Valley Adventure Story*, Penguin Books, 1995 (soon to be made a movie, apparently).

Corporation's PenPoint operating system. Much bitterness ensued on both sides as the pen-computing market, small as it was, became fiercely competitive.

After having difficulty raising money to develop its own hardware, GO spun off EO Inc. in 1991 to develop a tablet device. The EO Personal Communicator, as it was eventually called, ran PenPoint and Aha! Software's InkWriter, an ink software processing package. In a true act of irony, in 1993 AT&T first bought EO and then GO, reuniting the two companies under the same corporate umbrella. Unfortunately, GO suffered the same fate as GRiD after it was consumed by a large corporation. Development on PenPoint ceased soon thereafter.

## Microsoft Windows for Pen Computing

**Fijitsu Tablet**

| | |
|---|---|
| Release Date | 1992 |
| Key Manufacturers | Compaq, GRiD, Fujitsu, NCR, Toshiba |

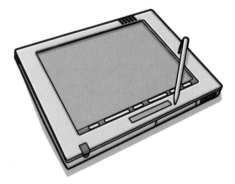

Two representatives from Microsoft visited GO Corporation early in GO's history to discuss the PenPoint operating system. According to the representatives[2], their mission was to convince GO to build on top of Windows instead of creating PenPoint as its own operating system. When GO was reluctant to do so, the representatives urged Microsoft Chairman Bill Gates to modify Windows to support the use of pens. This effort became Windows for Pen Computing, or Pen Windows.

The first version of Pen Windows was released as a modification to Windows 3.11 and was officially called Windows for Pen Computing version 1. It added several components into Windows, including a specialized video driver, pen device drivers, a handwriting recognizer, and a note-taking application. Users typically got Pen Windows when hardware manufacturers bundled it with their tablet devices. Pen Windows also had an API that developers could use to write pen-enabled applications.

---

2. We conducted an interview with the two Microsoft representatives, who no longer work at Microsoft, in May 2002.

Pen Windows tried to revolutionize computing by imbuing all parts of the Windows operating system with support for the pen. In particular, edit controls in applications were automatically replaced by enhanced edit controls that supported handwriting conversion. Similarly, a variety of gestures (specific motions of the pen) were available in applications as command shortcuts. In the end, a few factors plagued Pen Windows, which never became a successful business for Microsoft. Perhaps the most important issue is that hardware at that point in time was just not quite ready for a pen computing revolution. Memory and processing power weren't sufficient to do accurate handwriting recognition, and tablet devices were quite heavy and unwieldy. Furthermore, the many gestures included in Pen Windows were a usability nightmare, being both hard to discover and hard to remember.

By the time Windows 95 rolled around, Pen Windows was demoted from a full-blown operating system to merely an add-on. Version 2 was called Pen Services, and it was a much scaled-down effort compared to the ambitious Windows for Pen Computing version 1. In 1995, GO was already absorbed by AT&T and barely functional, while the Apple Newton (shown below) was also shown to be a commercial disaster. PalmPilot had not yet arrived. Pen computing was at an all-time low in the mid 1990s, and the reduced role of Pen Services in Windows 95 reflected the times. There was very little interest from hardware manufacturers and from consumers in the second version. After shipping Pen Services, the Pen Windows team was effectively dissolved. Some of the members went on to other pen-related Microsoft efforts, including the eventually successful Windows CE. Others, haunted by disillusionment[3], forsook the promise of pen computing altogether.

## Apple Newton

**Newton MessagePad**

| | |
|---|---|
| Release Date | 1993 |
| Dimensions | 4.5" × 7.25" × 0.75" |
| Weight | 14.4 oz. |
| Screen | 240 x 336 black-and-white pressure-sensitive LCD |
| Processor | 20-MHz ARM 610 |
| Price | $700 |

---

3. According to interviews with former Pen Windows employees Keith Stutler and Brian Watson.

The Newton MessagePad (commonly referred to simply as the Newton) was the first (and only) handheld computer produced by Apple Corporation. It was the pet project of John Sculley, then CEO of Apple, who in 1992 coined the term *Personal Digital Assistant* (PDA) in reference to the Newton. There was an entire line of Newton MessagePad models released between 1993 and 1998: 100, 110, 120, 130, 2000, and 2100. All the models had PCMCIA slots for easy expansion, and most also had internal modems for connectivity.

Unfortunately, the original Newton was plagued by a series of problems. Its note-taking application, Note Pad, would gluttonously consume all system resources when running. The device was thought by some to be too wide for smaller hands, and its unprotected glass screen was easily shattered. Furthermore, the original handwriting recognition software was word-based, not character-based, containing a dictionary of a meager 10,000 words, which was not sufficient for good recognition. The Russian-created ParaGraph recognition engine also had a severe memory fragmentation bug that would degrade recognition results after prolonged use, requiring users to reset the device frequently. As if the negative press wasn't enough, the poor handwriting recognition was lampooned in a series of Garry Trudeau's *Doonesbury* comic strips (*http:// www.doonesbury.ucomics.com*) The media latched onto the Newton's handwriting recognition woes, and sales of the original Newton were dismal.

By the end of the Newton line in 1998, the MessagePad 2100 was a truly spectacular PDA. It sported a zippy 162-MHz StrongARM processor, 8-MB RAM, a large grayscale backlit LCD, and much improved handwriting recognition. But the damage was done, and the Newton never recovered from its slow start. Apple, under its newly restored CEO Steve Jobs, ended the Newton in February of 1998. According to some critics, the Newton's high price and poor desktop connectivity were the true reasons for its demise. But in most people's minds, the underperforming handwriting recognition of the first Newton sealed its doom. This remains the main reason cited for its failure.

*Newton was intended to be a platform for wireless communications and handwriting was a very, very small part of the product.*

> — *John Sculley, Former CEO,*
> *Apple Corporation*[4]

---

4. From "Why Did Apple Kill Newton?" by David MacNeill. *Pen Computing Magazine*, June 1998.

## Palm Computing PalmPilot

**PalmPilot Professional**

| | |
|---|---|
| Release Date | 1996 |
| Dimensions | 3.2" × 4.7" × 0.7" |
| Weight | 5.7 oz. |
| Screen | 160 x 160 black-and-white LCD |
| Processor | 17-MHz Motorola DragonBall 68328 |
| Price | $300 |

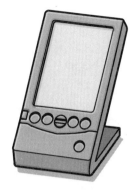

After his success releasing the GRiDPad, Jeff Hawkins was looking to produce a consumer-targeted portable computer. However, GRiD Computing had by then been relegated to producing computers for the verticals market (basically niche market computers for industries). Hawkins approached Tandy Corporation, owner of GRiD, and secured some seed money to start Palm Computing.

At first, Palm Computing was purely a software producer, making the applications that shipped on a Casio device called the Zoomer. The Zoomer was released a few months after the Newton, and sales were abysmal. However, what essentially was the first version of the Graffiti character recognition system shipped on the Zoomer, as did one-button synchronization (HotSync).

Hawkins then realized that to make a truly compelling handheld platform, Palm would have to be responsible not only for the software but for the hardware as well. He took GeoWork's operating system (GEOS), combined it with Graffiti and HotSync, and asked US Robotics (then primarily a modem manufacturer) to produce the hardware.

The PalmPilot 1000 (and others in the series, such as the 5000, Personal, and Professional) was an instant success. It succeeded where many others had failed by clearly defining the PDA niche. The PalmPilot was a handheld device that could easily fit in a shirt pocket, and it supported its four main functions very well: appointments, notes, tasks, and contacts. To top it off, it was priced brilliantly to sell for under $300. Consumers were clearly ready for such a device—PalmPilots sold in record units in the first year of release, and they still dominate the PDA market today.

Soon after Palm Computing's fledgling success, networking giant 3Com Corporation bought US Robotics, effectively gaining Palm in the deal. Hawkins and several other executives at Palm were concerned about their absorption into 3Com and lobbied for 3Com to spin off the Palm division as a separate company. As it became clear that 3Com was unwilling to do this, Hawkins and his executives left to start their own venture, called Handspring.

After a year's worth of hard work producing their new handheld device, Hawkins would receive shocking news. The day before the announcement of the new Handspring Visor, 3Com announced that Palm Computing would be spun off as a separate company. Hawkins's two start-ups, Palm and Handspring, would compete directly with one another in the same market.

## Microsoft Pocket PC

**Compaq iPAQ**

| | |
|---|---|
| Release Date | 1999 |
| Dimensions | 3.28" x 5.11" x 0.62" |
| | (all stats are for Compaq iPAQ) |
| Weight | 6.7 oz. |
| Screen | 240 x 320 color backlit LCD |
| Processor | 206-MHz Intel StrongARM |
| Price | $500 |

PalmPilot permeated the lucrative PDA market with its low price and convenient size. The Windows CE team at Microsoft had failed to grab a piece of the PDA market with the failed Windows CE version 1 family of devices, which had tiny keyboards and hard-to-use software. Version 2 made some inroads but was far from a hit. Version 3 was to be different—it would redo the user interface to address usability problems and would support hardware much more like the existing PalmPilots on the market. Dubbed the "Pocket PC," several major hardware manufacturers lined up to bring Windows CE version 3 to consumers hungry for a true second-generation PDA.

Palm had been creating devices in the lower end of the market. Although they still generated significant sales, consumers were starting to tire of the grayscale screens that were sometimes hard to read in daylight. There wasn't much happening in the PDA market.

More than any other manufacturer, Compaq and its Pocket PC device (the iPAQ) would create a stir of excitement in the handheld community. Windows CE version 3 sported a familiar interface borrowed from the Start Menu paradigm of the desktop Microsoft Windows products. Compaq's iPAQ showed Windows CE version 3 in its full glory. It also one-upped Palm by catering to the high end of the handheld market, with its beefy 32 MB of RAM and blazing fast 206-MHz processor. While Palm catered to the average consumer, the new Pocket PCs mainly targeted the corporate professional.

The success of the Pocket PC was largely due to spectacular hardware at an acceptable price. There was not much software on the Pocket PC platform that could be considered innovative, though it connected pen computing's past with its future. After all, Pocket PC's software handwriting recognizer was derived from ParaGraph's Calligrapher, an earlier version of which powered the Apple Newton. Furthermore, its note-taking application was derived from Aha! Software's InkWriter, which ran on EO's Personal Communicator and would also contribute indirectly to the Microsoft Windows XP Tablet PC Edition Journal. Despite the lack of innovative software, the Pocket PC was Microsoft's successful reentrance into the arena of tablet computing. Indeed, big things were to come.

## In a Little While

One consistent theme in our journey through tablet computing's past is the critical role that hardware plays in the success or failure of tablet devices. A key reason often sited for the failure of GRiDPad, PenPoint, and Windows for Pen Computing is that the hardware simply was not good enough to make them compelling. It was either too heavy or too bulky, battery life was too short, readability was poor, and processing power and memory couldn't support accurate handwriting recognition.

Indeed, the future success of tablet devices, including the Microsoft Tablet PC, may continue to be heavily influenced by hardware technology. Several exciting hardware developments are visible on the horizon and should become widely available over the next few years. Each of these developments could have a direct positive impact on tablet computing, making Tablet PCs even more portable and functional than they are today. Potential technologies that could revolutionize tablet technology include:

- **Organic Light-Emitting Diode (OLED) technology** This new type of display is made by layering thin films of organic material between conductors. The organic material illumines when electrical current is applied, in a process called *electrophosphorescence*. Traditional LCD screens require strong backlights that shine through the liquid crystal cells. These backlights can often consume up to half of an LCD's total power consumption. Because the organic material in OLEDs is emissive (that is, it emits its own light), OLEDs do not need backlighting. OLEDs have many other advantages over today's LCD technologies, including wider viewing angles, thinner profiles, and increased brightness.

- **Projected virtual keyboards** A company based in Jerusalem called VKB has successfully developed a virtual keyboard. The technology works by projecting an image of a keyboard onto any flat surface. Using infrared, the virtual keyboard can detect when the user has typed on the projected image. The required hardware for both projecting the keyboard and detecting the typing is relatively compact, making many roaming usage scenarios possible. There is a good chance that future cell phones, and perhaps even Tablet PCs, can leverage this technology.

- **Better batteries** Much research is being done in the field of batteries. Traditional batteries, such as nickel cadmium (NiCad) and nickel metal hydride (NiMH), were not as efficient as the current lithium ion type. However, the future of batteries may lie in lithium polymer and hydrogen fuel cells. Whereas current battery technologies require metal casing to hold their liquid electrolytes under pressure, lithium polymer batteries suspend their electrolytes in a solid polymer matrix. This greatly reduces their weight and size, making them a potential replacement for lithium ion. Hydrogen fuel cells, on the other hand, promise to pack a lot of power in an environmentally friendly battery by combining hydrogen and oxygen to form heat and water, creating electricity in the process. Both lithium polymer batteries and hydrogen fuel cells have yet to be made into viable commercial products.

The past has shown that hardware technologies can make or break the commercial success of a tablet device. The next few years will witness whether these and other technologies will significantly advance the state of tablet computing.

# The Microsoft Tablet PC

Although the failure of Pen Windows to revolutionize computing left some at Microsoft disillusioned, there was still a set of core believers within the company who championed the cause of tablet computing. Out of this coterie would eventually arise, nearly a decade later, the Microsoft Tablet PC. The new Tablet PC initiative combines a set of hardware requirements along with a software platform to deliver a rewarding user experience.

# The Birth of Microsoft Tablet PC

It was the last straw. Bert Keely, engineering director at SGI (Silicon Graphics, Inc.) in Mountain View, California, had managed the tablet computer project long enough to know that the company's ability to deliver on his tablet computing vision was waning. Although the project started out with a lot of promise, repeated decisions over the years had relegated it to its current status as a research project. And, as with most research projects at large technology corporations, the SGI tablet computer initiative seemed destined never to see the light of day. Cheap and powerful PCs were eroding the bottom end of SGI's market, forcing SGI to focus on higher-end servers. The tablet project would probably not survive.[5]

Determined to see tablets rise to the forefront of computing, Keely began to shop the idea around Silicon Valley's elite. Steve Jobs, CEO of Apple Computer, was unwilling to pursue the idea out of what many thought was spite, directed at former Apple Computer CEO John Sculley, who fronted the failed Newton project. Jeff Hawkins at Handspring was uninterested for a different set of reasons—he felt that the tablet computer proposed by Keely was halfway between the palm-sized devices that he was creating and the full-blown laptops that dominated the portable market. In separate discussions, Michael Dell, founder of Dell Computer Corporation, told Keely straight out that he would not be interested in such a device from a business point of view until a reasonable market demand was demonstrated. Although he was unwilling to expose his company to the possible market risk, Dell gave Keely a fateful parting thought—try Bill Gates's Microsoft Corporation.

Microsoft was the last company that Keely would have considered approaching, especially given his background in the sometimes heavily anti-Microsoft community of Silicon Valley. However, his commitment to tablet computing brought him to an impasse. All other likely suitors were reluctant to carry on Keely's vision. So in early 1998 Keely headed off to Seattle to propose the tablet project to Microsoft.

His proposal was well accepted by the executives in attendance. Although it had been only a few years since the failure of Pen Windows, Bill Gates was still a firm believer in tablet and pen-based computing. It was decided that the time had come for Microsoft to launch a bold new venture into tablet computing. Microsoft senior vice president Dick Brass asked Keely to work in Seattle to begin the development of electronic books, ClearType font technology, and ultimately a new tablet computer.

---

5. Interview with Bert Keely, Microsoft Corporation, May 2002.

Independent of Keely's entrance into Microsoft, many others were pulling together towards the nascent Tablet PC project. Chuck Thacker, best known as the chief designer of the Alto computer while at Xerox PARC, and Microsoft Distinguished Engineer Butler Lampson, had both worked on the DEC Lectrice reading device. Charlton Lui and Dan Altman had been foundational at Aha! Software, which produced pen-based applications for many pen computing platforms. Evan Feldman had similar relevant experience, having done usability research while at Compaq on their Concerto device. Alexandra Loeb, currently vice president of the Tablet PC division, pulled together these and other key people from various related projects throughout Microsoft in the spring of 1999. The Tablet PC team would eventually grow to more than 200 members, their efforts culminating in the fall 2002 release of the Microsoft Tablet PC.

## Microsoft Tablet PC Hardware Guidelines

In order to be called a Microsoft Tablet PC, an original equipment manufacturer (OEM) needs to meet a set of hardware guidelines. Microsoft crafted these guidelines after conducting an extensive suite of usability studies to determine what sort of features users wanted in Tablet PC hardware. The full set of guidelines is presented in Appendix B. The main guidelines are summarized below:

- **Digitizer**   The digitizer must be able to detect a hovering pen and take samples of the pen's location at least 100 times a second. It must also support a resolution of at least 600 points per inch.

- **Power states**   The Tablet PC must be able to resume from standby in less than two seconds.

- **Viewing mode**   It must support changing between landscape and portrait screen orientations without requiring a reboot.

- **CTRL+ALT+DEL equivalent functionality**   A Tablet without an attached keyboard must have a dedicated hardware button that triggers the secure authentication sequence.

## Microsoft Tablet PC Software

Meeting the hardware guidelines is the responsibility of each hardware manufacturer. Microsoft's responsibility, on the other hand, is to create and deliver a set of software features to support Tablet PCs and third-party software vendors. In order to support Tablet PCs, Microsoft created a version of Windows XP with Tablet PC features named Windows XP Tablet PC Edition. This special version of Windows XP, sold directly to hardware manufacturers, contains the following set of software features not available in any other version of Windows:

- **Digital ink applications**    Several digital ink applications were written especially for Windows XP Tablet PC Edition. The first of these is Windows Journal, a note-taking application that showcases the world of possibilities afforded by digital ink. Sticky Notes is a handy accessory designed to capture random notes and reminders similar to its physical counterpart. On the lighter side, InkBall is a game best played with a pen—the objective is to control the motion of colored balls by crafting the right digital ink strokes.

- **Tablet Input Panel**    When using a Tablet PC without a keyboard, there needs to be a way to enter text into standard applications. The tablet input panel fills this role on Tablet PCs by providing a combination of on-screen keyboards and alternative text input methodologies. It supports character-by-character text entry in a style similar to that of Pocket PCs, but it also supports free-form cursive handwriting as a way to input text.

- **Platform binary executables**    The final (and essential!) element of Windows XP Tablet PC Edition is the set of Tablet PC Platform binary executables. With the release of Tablet PC, Microsoft introduced a set of application programming interfaces (APIs) collectively referred to as the Tablet PC Platform. These APIs are provided for third-party software vendors to exploit the digital ink features made possible by the Tablet PC Platform. By including these binary executables with every copy of Windows XP Tablet PC Edition, third-party software vendors can be assured that their software will be able to leverage special digital ink features when running on Tablet PCs.

Most flavors of Windows (such as Windows 98, Windows Me, and Windows XP) have a set of requirements known as *logo requirements*. When a third-party software vendor's application meets these requirements, it is allowed to put a special logo on the software's packaging to indicate that it was written "especially for Windows *X*" (where *X* is the particular flavor of Windows whose logo requirements were met). These logos are meant to assure the end user that the software being purchased is indeed fully compatible with a certain version of Windows. In stark contrast, Windows XP Tablet PC Edition does not have its own set of logo requirements. It's quite likely that subsequent versions of Windows XP Tablet PC Edition will have logo requirements, particularly given the specialized nature of Tablet PC software and the many usability-related concerns it raises.

## Could This Be the One?

Microsoft's introduction of the Tablet PC follows a long trail of failures by a plethora of companies (including Microsoft itself!) who tried to bring pen-based computing to the masses. Some of the failed attempts were fronted by large companies with good reputations (for instance, Apple's Newton), proving Microsoft's Tablet PC initiative very bold indeed. Is there reason to believe that this attempt will be any different from those in the past? Why would Microsoft continue to invest in something that it, and many other companies, had failed at before?

Although there are no guarantees, there are a few good reasons to believe that Microsoft's latest attempt at tablet computing may succeed where others have failed. There are three major factors that favor Microsoft's Tablet PC over its competitors' prior attempts:

■ **The hardware landscape is vastly different** Hardware is continuously getting faster, lighter, and more efficient. A huge determinant of the success or failure of a tablet device is the effect of its hardware profile on its usage scenarios. There was a time when "portable" computers were 20 pounds each, rendering them essentially useless for the majority of consumers' portable scenarios. Similarly, when most users think of tablet computers, they envision certain key scenarios, such as note taking in a meeting, annotating documents, or jotting down thoughts. The current state of hardware technology makes these key scenarios more plausible because well-designed Tablet PCs should be about three-quarters-inch thick and weigh about 2.5 pounds. High dots-per-inch (dpi) displays are also on the horizon, further improving annotation scenarios. These and other technological advancements make this a more compelling time than ever to release a tablet device.

■ **Digital ink recognition technology is much improved** Closely tied to hardware improvements is the availability of improved handwriting recognition algorithms. These new algorithms make it possible, for the first time in widespread commercial software, to recognize continuous (cursive) English instead of just segmented print characters. Similarly, increased processing power has now made it possible to recognize words faster and more accurately than ever before. Much of the frustration of early tablet computing attempts arose out of poor ink recognition by the underlying software. The situation is now much improved.

- **Digital ink is treated as a native data type**    Ideal handwriting recognition, just like ideal voice recognition, is one of those technologies that has been "just five years away" for the last 20 years. The problem with this widely held expectation is that it is simply unrealistic. The fact of the matter is that sometimes even the very author of a document has trouble recognizing what he wrote—how could a computer *possibly* be expected to do a better job? Similarly, in many conversations we have to ask the speaker to repeat himself—surely a computer wouldn't be able to do better, especially without the contextual clues afforded by understanding the conversation's subject matter! We must recognize that there is, and perhaps always will be, a basal amount of error that will not be overcome by handwriting recognition algorithms. That said, the approach taken by Microsoft's Tablet PC differs from many that have gone before it because it acknowledges up-front that at least some amount of error is inevitable. Instead of putting all the effort into trying to eliminate the error, the Tablet PC treats digital ink as a native data type. By keeping ink as ink, as opposed to constantly converting ink into text as soon as it's entered, the human reader of a document is given the opportunity to recognize handwriting that the computer may otherwise have mistaken. Far from shirking responsibility, this philosophy of ink as a native data type, keeping ink as ink, supplements the technology's shortcomings with the human's strengths. The computer tries to be helpful by offering recognized text when asked, but it also preserves the author's original ink because it is equally important as a data type of its own.

There is no way to accurately predict the success of Microsoft's Tablet PC, though it has several notable advantages over those that have gone before it. Only time will bear out whether these advantages are enough to make Microsoft's Tablet PC the one to popularize tablet computing, or whether it will fade into history along with all the previous attempts. In the meantime, there are lots of exciting technologies made possible by the Tablet PC Platform, which we will in turn explore throughout the rest of this book.

## Summary

*Now this is not the end. It is not even the beginning of the end.*
*But it is, perhaps, the end of the beginning.*

*—Winston Churchill, speaking of the Battle of Egypt in 1942*

We've seen in this chapter the characteristics that define a tablet computer, as well as a brief history of notable tablet computers (and related devices) of the past. The inspiration of their innovations and the lessons from their shortcomings commingled to form what became the Microsoft Tablet PC—a collection of hardware guidelines backed by software support, which together bring the experience of tablet computing to a new generation of users.

You've come along for the ride, and we're glad to have you. The next chapter will guide you through important concerns specific to digital ink and tablet computing. It's a whole new world out there!

# 2

# Designing Tablet PC Applications

Now that you understand the basic elements of a Tablet PC, we can explore some of the considerations unique to developing applications for it. We begin by looking at some of the fundamental differences between applications targeted for desktops versus those targeted for Tablet PCs. Although you can transfer most of your Microsoft Windows development know-how to the Tablet PC world, you'll find that tablet development requires you to pay some additional attention to usability concerns.

Two factors that Tablet PCs introduce to application development are pens and digital ink. Before looking at these, we describe the key user research the Tablet PC team conducted during development of the Tablet PC. By observing users with Tablet PCs, the team discovered a set of design principles that will make your application easier to use.

## User Research

When the Tablet PC team formed at Microsoft in the fall of 1999, Microsoft Vice President Alexandra Loeb hired user research advocate Evan Feldman as one of the team's first members. Even before any software developers or testers were hired, Feldman was on the scene preparing for the host of user studies that he and his team would conduct over the next three years. Everyone recognized early on the pivotal role user research would play in developing a successful product.

From fall 1999 to the release of the Tablet PC in fall 2002, Feldman and his team conducted more than 100 user studies with a total of more than 1000 users. The studies varied in duration, but each user received and used a prototype Tablet

PC developed by Microsoft. User research discoveries contributed directly to several major design changes and many smaller refinements in what would become Windows XP Tablet PC Edition.

Let's take a look at some of the findings of the Microsoft user studies. By applying the following guidelines based on user research, you will be able to create more user-friendly applications and avoid some of the more common usability pitfalls. We'll divide our discussion into three areas: Tablet Usability, Application Usability, and Pen Usability.

## Tablet Usability

The Tablet PC team conducted its most extensive user study in the spring of 2001. The team selected participants from several companies (none directly involved in information technology) to use prototype Tablet PCs for four weeks. During the study, users shared their thoughts on the experience.

The participants perceived two major benefits of tablets over laptops. The first is that tablets overcome a social barrier that laptops pose, namely, that it is not acceptable in many workplaces to bring laptops into meetings. Tablets do not suffer the same stigma even though they are every bit as powerful as laptops in their functionality. People more readily accept the use of Tablet PCs in meetings because of their pen-based interface, which many find less disruptive than traditional laptop keyboards. The second major benefit of tablets over laptops noted by users is also due to the pen: tablets are easier to use in standing positions and confined spaces.

The study also revealed that most participants wanted to have tablets with keyboards. Convertible tablets that switched easily between tablet and traditional laptop modes clearly offered a lot of value in the users' eyes. Many users said that although the pen was great for the majority of scenarios while away from their desks, there were occasions where having a convertible tablet with a keyboard would have improved usability. Based on this feedback, Microsoft expects that the majority of tablets sold in the next few years will be convertible or will come with detachable keyboards.

The Tablet PC team began with a charter to bring pen-based tablet computing to the masses. At the time of the team's formation, the decision about which operating system to use was not a given. In fact, for a time the team pursued the idea of a new pen-centric operating system built from the ground up, akin to Palm Inc.'s PalmOS or GO Corporation's PenPoint. However, an even earlier user study helped drive the decision to use Windows XP. Users in that study liked how easy it was to use a pen-centric prototype operating system but preferred the convenience of being able to access the same applications that ran on their desktops from their tablets. From that point on, the team knew that running

Microsoft Windows instead of a custom pen-based operating system on tablets would be integral to the Tablet PC's success.

# Application Usability

User research conducted by the Tablet PC team in a series of smaller studies also yielded some general application design guidelines. The most important of these guidelines are outlined below. You can consult the "Planning Your Application" section of the Tablet PC Platform SDK documentation for additional information.

## It's Unconventional but Boy Is It Optimized

Early on, the Tablet PC team produced a lot of prototype software. The prototypes were designed specifically for pen interaction. Because pen and mice operate differently from one another, these prototypes ended up being rather unconventional Windows applications—for example, toolbars were placed on the bottom instead of the top. New UI widgets were created to be pen-accessible, and some UI elements were emphasized over others to make it easier to target them with a pen.

Pen-optimized unconventionality, however, extracted its toll on usability. While users were indeed more productive with a pen in the prototype applications, frequent switching between the prototypes and traditional Windows applications left users confused. After multiple user studies returned the same results, the team resigned themselves to the fact that users are most productive when all applications on a Tablet PC are consistent. Granted, the software prototypes were designed expressly for pen users and were often more effective than their traditional Windows counterparts, but a tablet user's day-to-day experience would benefit more from overall consistency than from a few pen-optimized applications and features. The team therefore shelved radical UI designs in favor of a more traditional Windows interface.

## Ink as Ink

In Chapter 1, we recounted Microsoft's deviation from previous tablet computers by treating ink as a native data type. Most of the Tablet PC's predecessors treated ink as an intermediary to text. Ink was merely an intuitive way by which text was entered. But Microsoft's Tablet PC attempts to give ink just as much status as text. Applications on the Tablet PC such as Windows Journal allow the user to leave ink as ink instead of assuming that conversion to text is what the user ultimately wants.

The Tablet PC wasn't always designed this way. However, extended usage studies showed that many users were content with leaving their ink notes and annotations in ink form. In fact, a majority of users preferred reviewing their own notes and annotations as ink instead of as text. Slowly, the team began to design the Tablet PC around the idea that ink is an important data type in its own right, its appearance having intrinsic value that the recognition process strips away upon conversion into text.

The application you plan to write might be one in which ink plays an important role, or it might be one in which ink is a convenient avenue on the way to text. Don't discount the value of keeping ink as ink—users often prefer to see their own handwriting!

## Visual Distinction of Inkable Regions

One usability issue that has not been fully addressed in Windows XP Tablet PC Edition is how users are to distinguish inkable regions from non-inkable regions in the UI. *Inkable regions* are the areas of the screen or application that accept ink as input. The problem is that there is no officially recommended UI guideline to make inkable regions visually distinct. Without visual distinctions, the user cannot know which parts of the application to write on. Figure 2-1 shows how serious such a problem can be.

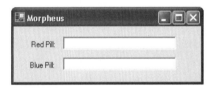

**Figure 2-1**    Two types of textboxes. The one on the top is a normal *Rich-TextBox* and the one on the bottom is an inkable *InkEdit* control.

In the extended usage study of spring 2001, it became apparent that without visual distinctions users expect to be able to write everywhere. For instance, users had difficulty transitioning between Windows Journal and Microsoft Word. After becoming familiar with the way that Windows Journal accepts digital ink anywhere on the page, users expected to be able to ink directly onto a Word document as well. Unfortunately, blank pages look like blank pages no matter what the application is.

With portrait orientation tablet and with pen in hand, the illusion of writing on paper was complete. Participants in the extended usage study found themselves trying to ink on documents in all sorts of applications, most of which were not ink-enabled. The lack of visual distinction between inkable and non-inkable regions frustrated the users' expectations to be able to ink everywhere.

Windows Journal attempts to mitigate this confusion by ruling its default stationery with lines like note-taking paper has. The intent is to have Windows Journal documents look clearly inkable. If your application presents documents on screen in a paperlike manner, users will expect to be able to write where there appears to be paper.

> **Note**   Your application ideally should support inking in the areas where a user would expect it. If that is not possible, provide visual cues that tell the user where digital ink is accepted and where it's not.

## High Screen DPI

Experienced application developers understand the importance of writing code that scales well in high-DPI environments. As tablet display technology advances, manufacturers will continue to increase the screen DPI to boost readability. Thus, it's a good idea to be proactive in both writing code that is prepared for high DPI and testing code in high-DPI environments.

High-DPI problems typically manifest themselves in user studies in two ways. The first is that some things are simply too small on high-DPI screens. Sometimes applications adjust images and programmatically sized controls in units of pixels instead of device-independent units of measure. As the DPI increases, the UI elements that are fixed in pixel size become smaller on screen. To avoid this problem, your application should not work in pixels when dealing with UI. Instead, it's better to query the system's display metrics so that your application can size UI elements in a device-independent manner. That way, your UI remains the same physical size regardless of the tablet's DPI.

The second problem is that some controls are not big enough to allow room for the optional larger font size that users may choose when using a high-DPI screen. The larger font makes it easier to read text, especially as the DPI goes above 120 or when the screen is small. However, you will need to test your application in large-font high DPI to make sure that controls are appropriately sized. The good news is that testing for high-DPI compatibility does not require fancy hardware. Simply set your Windows display settings to use a higher DPI and you're good to go. We recommend testing your application at 120 DPI on a 10.5" to 12" LCD.

> **Note**   Your application UI should work in device-independent units and be tested in high-DPI, large-font configurations.

## Input Modality

Our last concern with application usability is input modality. *Modality*, in this context, refers to the different states, or modes, in which the application accepts input. An application in one mode might accept a completely different set of commands from those available in another mode.

Not all applications have modal input interfaces. For instance, Microsoft Calculator has no input modality. Although Calculator interprets the numbers you input differently depending on the numeric base you're in (decimal, hexadecimal, or binary), a button in Calculator always retains its functionality. Now consider an application such as Microsoft Paint, an application driven by input modalities. Scribbling around when the pencil tool is active is different from doing so when the eraser tool is active. The various tools in Paint establish input modalities. While you're in pencil mode, your interactions with the canvas are interpreted one way; while in eraser mode, your interactions are interpreted in another way. Some features, such as the line thickness settings, are available only in certain modes. Thus the input mode of the application governs users' perception of what they can and can't do. The right input mode in the application must be set in order to perform a specific action.

Input modes make a small set of input possibilities mean a great deal more. By having modes, an application can make the same action (say, dragging the mouse) invoke different functionality. Input modes are therefore useful when working with a limited number of input possibilities. At the same time, input modes can reduce efficiency in some common scenarios because the user has to switch modes before performing actions.

All this talk about input modalities also applies to ink. It would be ideal if the pen, a natural input method, did not require you to explicitly change modes to know what you wanted to do. For instance, it would be useful if you could ink with the tip of the pen and invert the pen to erase without switching modes in the application. Furthermore, imagine that if after writing for a bit, you could just tap on a word and it would be selected automatically. A modeless user interface would make the process of inking on a Tablet PC even more natural, allowing you to capture and edit thoughts without any barriers.

Early in the development of the Tablet PC, application designers placed quite a bit of faith in being able to make Windows Journal a modeless application. After all, the potential efficiency gains are significant if a user does not have to explicitly change modes between inking, selecting, and erasing. However, a key discovery of the extended usage study was that, given the current technology, we won't be able to get rid of explicit mode switches entirely. Today, the back of the pen can be used as an eraser (and implementing this functionality is quite easy with the Tablet PC Platform SDK). But it's much harder to make other mode transitions accurately, such as interpreting that a tap on a word means the user wants to select that word. For that particular mode transition to be implicit, you must first decide that the tap on the word was not meant to dot an *i* or to make a diacritical mark. These sorts of decisions are hard to make correctly with a high degree of reliability. The imperfect algorithms used to make such implicit mode switches during the extended usage study ended up frustrating users more than helping them. The last thing users want is a mysterious mode switch occurring at an inopportune time.

This is not to say that all implicit mode switches are inherently unreliable. Indeed, some implicit mode switches, such as those triggered by the press-and-hold gesture in Windows Journal, work remarkably well. Good implicit mode switching requires that you use actions which the user can easily trigger intentionally but will rarely trigger accidentally.

# Pen Usability

Although pens are natural input devices, they nevertheless bring a set of usability issues to tablet computing. We outline the conclusions of Microsoft user research on pen-computer interaction here, but we will also discuss the practical implications of these findings later in the chapter.

## Targeting

Targeting of screen locations is one of the biggest challenges when interacting with a computer through a pen. Throughout a typical day of computer use, users target many areas of the screen with a mouse. Whether it's to place an insertion caret, move an object, or use the Windows desktop, it's of the utmost importance to first be able to move the mouse cursor to the relevant location on the screen. Tablet PC users must fulfill those same targeting requirements with a pen.

The Tablet PC team conducted a series of revealing user studies on targeting early in 2001. In these studies, increasingly smaller areas of the screen lit up in different locations for brief periods of time. By asking users to tap the lit areas as quickly and accurately as possible, the team determined that users can reliably target areas only 5 millimeters wide or larger.

## Selection

The final area of user research on which the Tablet PC team spent quite a bit of time is ink selection. From late 2000 to the middle of 2001, the team experimented with different ways to select digital ink. As users responded to these various prototype selection models, the team adjusted the selection models accordingly to better enable users to select the desired ink.

Neither traditional text selection tools nor rectangular area selection tools perform well when selecting the user's ink. The main problem is that few users write (or draw) in neat rows and columns. Instead, a typical user's ink notes often consist of ink written in different sizes and at various angles. This free-form nature of inking makes traditional selection tools a bad fit.

The Tablet PC team finally settled on using a free-form selection tool—the lasso tool—as the standard way by which users select digital ink. The lasso tool enables the user to enclose all the ink he or she wants to select by simply drawing a closed loop around the ink. Windows Journal and the Tablet PC Platform SDK Ink Picture control both support a lasso tool to select ink. We will return to the topic of ink selection later in this chapter.

# Of Mice and Pen

We now turn our attention to the hardware technology that pervades the Tablet PC experience and how it impacts the way we design software for tablet users.

Tablet hardware differs from traditional computer hardware in two ways: tablets often run in portrait screen orientation and tablets have pens with *digitizers*. Digitizers are the devices responsible for detecting the position, pressure, and tilt of a pen on the tablet's screen. The technology behind a pen is vastly different from the technology behind a mouse, and the pen introduces unique usability challenges. In addition, the user of a pen, by mere physiology, can inadvertently create additional usability challenges that the software has to address. We consider the challenges of screen orientation, pen technologies, and user physiology in the following sections.

## Tablet Displays

Tablet PCs run primarily in *portrait* orientation, with the height of the screen greater than its width. This arrangement models the traditional orientation of paper, which is also usually taller than it is wide. Paper's orientation is optimized for readability—because it's difficult to read long lines of text, wide paper doesn't make a lot of sense. It's better to pack more narrow lines of text onto a tall sheet of paper.

Running the display in portrait mode has a few noteworthy consequences, however, the foremost being that menus and toolbars have less space in which to display their content. This can result in menus wrapping over multiple lines or toolbars being cut off. An example of the latter is shown in Figure 2-2.

> **Note**   When designing your application, be sure that toolbar buttons fall within the usable width of a portrait screen.

You can also have your toolbars wrap into more rows to accommodate the screen's limitations. In addition, you should test all your dialog boxes in portrait mode to verify that they are not cut off. Remember to check them in large-font mode as well.

**Figure 2-2**   Microsoft WordPad in 768 × 1024 portrait mode, with its toolbar cut off on the right.

Some graphics chips don't natively support portrait mode. In these cases, the graphics chips manufacturer can implement portrait mode screen rotation by rotating everything using software. Although this approach is valid, you should be aware of the tremendous performance penalties it entails. When a device driver rotates a screen in memory, it essentially intercepts every call to draw on the screen, transforming the call parameters so that it ends up drawing in portrait mode instead of landscape mode. For certain calls, such as the popular *BitBlt* (which renders a bitmap on the screen), the consequences of software screen rotation are disastrous, requiring the driver to remap the bitmap pixel by pixel. If your application uses a lot of graphics calls, you'll want to test its performance in portrait mode to see whether software rotation is an issue. Keep in mind that not all graphics chips will have this problem.

# Digitizer Technology

Three popular types of digitizer technologies are in use today: resistive, electrostatic, and electromagnetic. The following sections describe these different technologies.

## Resistive Digitizers

The least expensive type of digitizer is resistive. Resistive digitizers can have one or two layers. A single-layer resistive digitizer is made with a transparent film of known, predictable resistance (hence the name). Voltages can be applied at the four corners of the film. Because the film introduces even resistance across its surface, applying a voltage on one edge of the film creates a gradient of voltage across the entire film. Figure 2-3 shows how applying voltage at the corners can introduce such a gradient. When a single-layer resistive digitizer is used, a pen connected to the computer reads the voltage when the pen makes contact with the film. By alternating between horizontal and vertical gradients, the computer can pinpoint the pen's position by making two readings on contact: a horizontal gradient voltage reading for the $x$ position and a vertical gradient voltage reading for the $y$ position.

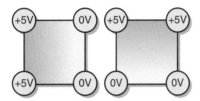

**Figure 2-3** A horizontal gradient is applied by raising the voltage of the two left corners. Similarly, a vertical gradient is applied by raising the voltage of the two top corners.

The main disadvantage of a single-layer resistive digitizer is that its pen needs to be connected back to it because voltages are read through the pen when it makes contact with the resistive film. Two-layer designs sidestep this disadvantage by means of a highly conductive film. This second film is placed below the resistive film, and the two are separated by a series of spacers usually set in a layer of polyester. A cross section of this design is shown in Figure 2-4. When a pen presses down on the resistive film, it forces the film to make contact with the conductive film beneath, which then conducts the voltage to the digitizer circuitry. Because the voltage is communicated to the digitizer directly through the conductive film, the pen does not need to be connected to the computer at all. In fact, because contact between the two films is all that's required, a pen isn't even needed! Your finger, or any blunt object for that matter, would serve just as well.

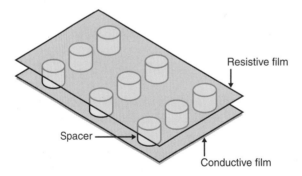

**Figure 2-4** A two-layer resistive digitizer shown in cross section. The resistive top layer is kept apart from the conductive bottom layer by a system of spacers.

Despite the innovation of two-layer resistive digitizers, all resistive digitizers still have other disadvantages. Because resistive digitizers need to be placed over the LCD screen, they greatly reduce the LCD's brightness. This reduction can be significant, in many cases over 30 percent. Although you can address the brightness issue by increasing the LCD's backlight, you cannot mitigate the cloudiness that the overlaying films introduce. Another practical concern with resistive digitizers is that they cannot detect hover, pressure, or tilt. This is a direct consequence of their design, which dictates that voltage values be read on contact. Without hover, pressure, or tilt, resistive digitizers are not practical for use in Tablet PCs. Furthermore, two-layer resistive digitizers do not handle users resting their hands on the screen while writing, a perfectly natural thing to do. The mere act of resting a hand on a two-layer resistive digitizer causes the films to meet, generating a false pen impression.

Even though resistive digitizers have many drawbacks, they are by far the dominant technology in handheld devices such as the Pocket PC. These devices use resistive technology because of its low price. The flexibility of being able to detect the user's finger is viewed as a benefit, and the small screen makes hand contact interference less of a problem. Resistive digitizers are not used on Tablet PCs because they do not supply hover and pressure information.

## Electrostatic Digitizers

Electrostatic (or capacitive) digitizers are made by bonding a thin conductive film to a sheet of glass. A pen tethered to the digitizer emits a high-frequency signal that is picked up by the conductive film. The film can sense the pen's signal even from a small distance away, giving electrostatic digitizers an important edge over resistive digitizers—electrostatic digitizers can sense pens even without direct contact. The distance of the pen to the digitizer can be determined by the relative strength of the detected signal. Because the pen is constantly emitting a signal, the digitizer can extrapolate how far away the pen is hovering by tracking the fluctuations in the signal's amplitude.

Electrostatic digitizers can also determine the tilt of a pen. Figure 2-5 shows the axes of pen movement, including hover and tilt. When the pen is tilted relative to the surface of the digitizer, it distorts the shape of the field generated by its signal. The conductive film detects this distortion, and the digitizer interprets it as a tilt measurement.

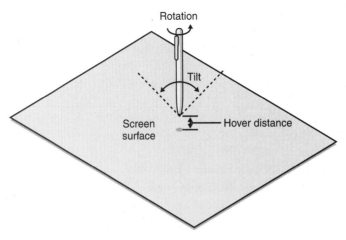

**Figure 2-5**   Hover, tilt, rotation, and pressure are the four axes of pen movement.

Conventional electrostatic digitizers require the pen to be connected to the digitizer because the pen itself needs to emit a signal. This requirement makes such digitizers less desirable for use in Tablet PCs.

## Touch Pads

A variant of electrostatic digitizers is used in touch pads that come with laptop computers. Touch pads were once built on resistive technology, which had the drawback that a small amount of pressure had to be exerted on top of the pad for it to detect a touch. Repeated applications of this pressure would eventually cause the pad to wear out. Modern touch pads use a two-layer electrostatic technology that relies on mutual capacitance between the layers. Fingers, which have different dielectric properties from air, change the mutual capacitance when they approach and touch the pad. Interacting with the touch pad requires little pressure, making electrostatic touch pads more durable than their resistive counterparts.

### Electromagnetic Digitizers

Electromagnetic digitizers work in a manner similar to their electrostatic cousins. However, they require much less power because their pens need to emit only a low-power RF (radio frequency) signal. The reduced power consumption makes it possible for electromagnetic digitizers to use pens that are not tethered to the digitizer. Instead, the pen can contain all the necessary circuitry, along with a little battery, to generate the RF signal by itself.

In addition to having pens that need not be attached, electromagnetic digitizers can be installed *below* the LCD screen. This flexibility is quite a benefit, and one that distinguishes electromagnetic digitizers from other types of digitizers. By installing below the screen, electromagnetic digitizers do not affect the screen's brightness or clarity. Because the screen's brightness is not affected, electromagnetic digitizers have lower power requirements for an equivalently bright screen. Like electrostatic digitizers, electromagnetic digitizers can detect hovering and tilt. With some additional smarts, some electromagnetic digitizers can also detect rotation. A cross section of an electromagnetic digitizer is shown in Figure 2-6.

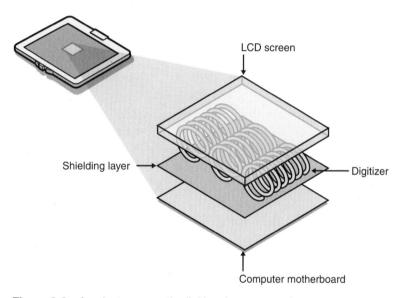

**Figure 2-6**    An electromagnetic digitizer in cross section.

Electromagnetic digitizers are the best of the existing pen technology. Low power requirements, stand-alone pens, and behind-the-screen mounting make them the clear choice for Tablet PCs.

## Digitizer Distortion

All electronic devices generate electromagnetic fields when operating. Within the confines of a computer, some devices can generate large electromagnetic fields. For instance, the hard drive is usually a significant source of such fields, as is the power supply. Other devices within a computer, such as video cards and memory chips, also generate electromagnetic fields (albeit much smaller ones). Together, the electronics within a computer create a *halo* of electromagnetic interference. The closer you get to the computer, the stronger the interference you will experience.

Electromagnetic digitizers usually have a back plane under them that is designed to shield them from electromagnetic interference. Unfortunately, these back planes aren't perfect. They might not always be able to isolate the digitizer from interference originating from below. In the case of Tablet PCs, the compact size of the computer exacerbates the problem of electromagnetic interference leaking through the protective backplane. Ultraslim tablets (which can be less than three quarters of an inch thick) have digitizers that are literally millimeters away from underlying hardware. It becomes impossible at this proximity for the backplane to do its job perfectly, so electromagnetic interference is introduced into the digitizer's readings.

What does this interference mean in practical terms for the digitizer? Figure 2-7 shows the distortion lines on a typical Tablet PC. These lines started as a series of straight, parallel lines drawn across the surface of the tablet (say, with the aid of a ruler). However, the digitizer's readings tell a completely different story. As you can see, the digitizer hardly thinks that the lines were straight. It was misled by electromagnetic signals arising from the hardware below it. These signals commingle with the signals the pen generates, resulting in an inaccurate reading by the digitizer.

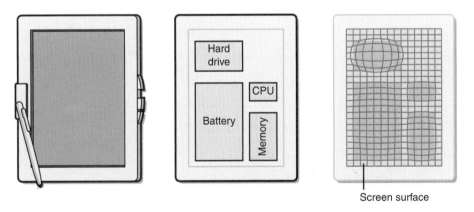

**Figure 2-7** A Tablet PC's digitizer readings of what began as straight lines drawn on its surface. Notice the strong correlation between certain parts of the underlying hardware and the visible distortion.

These distortions are present in the readings of every tablet's digitizer. If they are left uncorrected, the user who tries to draw a straight line on the tablet will instead get a curve. Tapping on a particular spot becomes a challenge because the digitizer rarely agrees with the user about where the pen is pointing. Fortunately, this rather serious problem is *not* left uncorrected! Tablet PC manufacturers carefully calibrate their digitizers by first taking a series of readings like the ones shown in Figure 2-7. Armed with these distortion lines, they then program each digitizer's device driver to account for the distortions. The digitizer's device driver acts as a filter, adjusting every reading to correct known distortions. The result is that the user typically does not perceive any problem.

Calibration to account for electromagnetic interference is never perfect, however. The main reason for varying interference patterns is that every Tablet PC has a slightly different electromagnetic halo. Even if all the hardware a particular manufacturer uses is exactly the same for each tablet it produces, minute differences still exist between each individual unit. A little spacing difference here, a little twisted cable there, and pretty soon you've got a unique electromagnetic halo.

Another reason for different interference patterns is entirely out of the manufacturer's control: the real bummer with electromagnetic interference is that it varies with the surroundings. All sorts of external factors change a tablet's interference pattern: temperature, humidity, a nearby Rolex, the user's pacemaker, and solar flares. (OK, maybe we're pushing it too far, but you get the idea.) The most you can hope for is that, under normal conditions, these external sources are somewhat random and transient, often canceling each other out. The net effect should be that the pen seems accurate most of the time. Every once in a while, though, you might find that the pen does not seem to go exactly where you point it. It is precisely at those times that you should seriously consider living farther away from the neighborhood hydroelectric power plant!

## Parallax

Even if a tablet is calibrated correctly to offset the effects of electromagnetic interference, there might still be a difference between where a user thinks the pen is pointed versus where the system thinks it's pointed. This difference is due to a phenomenon called *parallax*. Parallax is the difference between the apparent locations of an object when viewed from two angles. Although the term might sound esoteric, parallax is something you encounter in everyday life. Anyone who has looked into an aquarium through its thick glass walls understands the effects of parallax. As you change the position from which you look into the aquarium, you notice strange distortions in the appearance of what's inside. These distortions are refraction-induced parallax effects: the thick glass refracts light, which alters the apparent location of contents within the aquarium when viewed from different angles. Refraction-induced parallax is diagrammed in Figure 2-8.

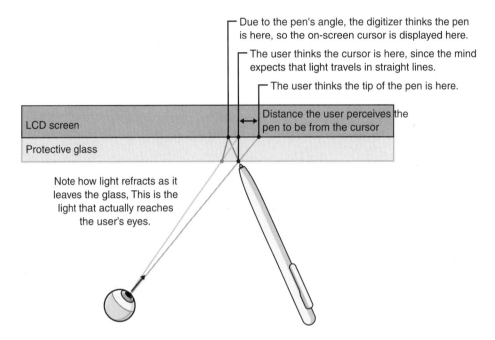

Due to the pen's angle, the digitizer thinks the pen is here, so the on-screen cursor is displayed here.

The user thinks the cursor is here, since the mind expects that light travels in straight lines.

The user thinks the tip of the pen is here.

Distance the user perceives the pen to be from the cursor

LCD screen

Protective glass

Note how light refracts as it leaves the glass, This is the light that actually reaches the user's eyes.

**Figure 2-8**   Refraction creates parallax, but even without refraction, a screen's thickness alone can create parallax.

Being an alert reader, you've by this point probably begun to suspect that the glass covering a tablet's LCD screen doesn't create enough refraction to account for all the parallax. And you're right—refraction-induced parallax is only part of the problem on a tablet. Even if there were no refraction, tablets would still have parallax problems. The second source of parallax, also pictured in Figure 2-8, comes from the distance between the surface of the LCD screen's image and the surface of the tablet. All LCD screens come with a layer of protective glass (or other material). To this, tablet manufacturers add a layer, usually made of plastic, to protect the screen from the constant rubbing of the pen's tip. These protective layers together introduce several millimeters between the surface of the tablet and the underlying screen image. When viewing the tip of a pen and its corresponding screen cursor from an angle, parallax results. Parallax affects users nearly all the time because they rarely look at the pen from directly over it. It's much more natural to look at the pen from a slight angle when writing.

Parallax is unavoidable, for the reasons just mentioned. It can lead to user confusion if not dealt with because the user may end up pointing to and tapping on the wrong things. You should take precautions to reduce the negative effects of parallax in your applications. One precaution is to make sure that controls are big enough to be easily targeted. Another equally important improvement is to offer clearly visible cursors that track pen movement so that the user can reference the cursor's position on screen as the authoritative point of interaction even if parallax is present. Without a reasonably sized cursor that can't be blocked by the pen itself, it's difficult for the user to know what to expect when tapping.

> **Note**   You can address the problem of parallax by making controls big enough and providing clearly visible cursors.

The good news is that users, after prolonged use, tend to adapt to parallax. As they come to anticipate a difference between where they think the pen points and where the system thinks it points, they become more adept at using the pen. In the meantime, it's helpful to have onscreen cursor feedback to mitigate this problem.

## Still Motion

One of the user's most immediate challenges when using a Tablet PC is the difficulty of holding the pen steady. Muscles in a human body are not wired to hold absolutely still. Instead, when you try to hold a muscle steady, in a fixed position, your brain causes alternate muscle bundles within that muscle to tense up in order to give each bundle the chance to relax. This "taking turns" within a muscle causes the muscle to vibrate just a little around that fixed position.

Make a dot on a sheet of paper and try to hover the tip of your pen about two millimeters above that dot. If you look at the tip of the pen carefully, you will see that it moves around quite noticeably (especially after that three-shot espresso). In fact, the harder you try to hold the pen still, the more it will fluctuate. Relaxing your hand helps, but it is hard to get it to stop quivering. This phenomenon carries over to when a user tries to use a tablet with a pen.

The quivering-pen syndrome does not exist with conventional pointing devices, such as a mouse or a trackball. These devices stay where you park them, making pointing and hovering easy. If you want to keep the mouse over a certain toolbar button, simply make minor adjustments to its position until it rests in the desired location. Clicking on a point is similarly easy—just make sure the mouse is positioned correctly, and then click.

Pens, however, do not work like mice. As a result of the quivering-pen syndrome, several big challenges arise, including the following:

- **Precise targeting** A tablet user cannot be expected to target too small an area on screen with a pen. The fact that the pen is always moving around a little makes it hard to land in any particular location. Parallax exacerbates the problem. These two factors make some actions a bit difficult on a Tablet PC. For instance, the typical resizing area of a window border is about 3 pixels wide. That is way too small for a pen to easily target. Some controls on toolbars or in dialog boxes are also too close together, making accidental taps inevitable. An example of controls placed too closely together is given in Figure 2-9.

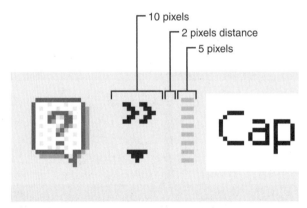

**Figure 2-9** These toolbar controls in Microsoft Word are too small and too close for a Tablet PC user to reliably target.

- **Double-Clicking** It's hard enough for the user to tap *once* on a desired location. Because the pen is constantly shifting position, tapping *twice* in the same place is even more difficult. The operating system's default settings for double-click detection require that both taps fall on the same pixel. If the two taps fail to do this, the operating system does not register a double click. In the case of a pen, those two taps are rarely on the same pixel, making double-clicking quite a challenge for the user.

- **Tap without drag**   It's easy to click a button on a mouse without moving its position on screen. Tapping on a fixed position with a pen is a lot harder. The problem is that when the tip of the pen touches the screen with some force, it inevitably tends to move a little on the screen. This tendency is exacerbated if the screen is covered with protective material that is too smooth. Imagine using a ballpoint pen to make a somewhat forceful dot on a sheet of glass. If you hold the pen at a slight angle (which is natural in the course of writing), the pen tends to slide on the glass when it makes contact, leaving a streak instead of a dot behind. The same thing happens on tablets—sometimes users inadvertently drag something they intended to tap.

- **Hovering**   Hovering, in the sense that a mouse cursor can hover over a single pixel, is impossible on a tablet device using a pen. At first, this revelation might seem insignificant. But what about features like ToolTips? *ToolTips* are the little yellow boxes that pop up with useful descriptions when you hover the cursor over a toolbar icon long enough. In general, ToolTips require that the cursor be absolutely still for a few seconds before they will appear. With a pen, this requirement simply can't be fulfilled. Hovering also triggers similar features in other applications.

You might be wondering what you can do to mitigate these challenges. Fortunately, help is available! Windows XP Tablet PC Edition contains some modifications that specifically address a few of these challenges. The first modification is in double-click detection. Instead of requiring the two taps to be on the same pixel, Windows XP Tablet PC Edition relaxes the requirement to a general *area of sensitivity*. As long as the two taps land sufficiently close to the same pixel, the system will register a double click. This modification will affect all applications that use the standard system facilities for detecting a double click (*WM_LBUTTONDBLCLK* and its family of messages), so most applications will automatically receive the benefit. Applications that do not use the standard system provisions for double click but instead implement their own double-click detection will not benefit from this change. Unfortunately, a surprising number of applications continue to implement their own double-click detection, which makes addressing this problem in a centralized manner difficult.

The second modification in Windows XP Tablet PC Edition is in toolbar hover detection for the purposes of displaying a ToolTip. Microsoft has modified the toolbar control in the common controls library (Comctl32.dll) in Windows XP Tablet PC Edition so that hovering anywhere within a toolbar button for the required amount of time will yield a ToolTip. This behavior stands in stark contrast with the unmodified version of the toolbar control, which displays a ToolTip only if the cursor does not move at all. Now, at least, the cursor can move within the area of a toolbar button and still bring up its ToolTip. As with double-click detection, applications will benefit from this modification only if they use the standard system toolbars. You'll find that some applications don't, once again diluting the benefits for the user.

You can also address these challenges when designing your applications. Perhaps most important is to make sure that controls are large enough and separated from each other by enough space so that they are easy to use on a tablet. The simplest way to know whether you've got it right is to try your user interface on a tablet device with a pen. In general, you'll find that with focus and determination, most users can stay within about a 5-by-5-millimeter area on a tablet screen. This area varies with the individual user, so try to leave generous margins for error. The second modification you can make for users is eliminating features that are accessible only through hovering. Although it is OK to have hover-triggered features, pen-based users will appreciate alternative methods of triggering the same feature. Another option is to make the hover tolerance more lenient so that hovering within a general area, rather than just over one pixel, is sufficient.

Finally, we encourage you to consider using standard system UI controls when possible. In the current version of Windows XP Tablet PC Edition, Microsoft has modified many controls for the benefit of pen users. Future versions of Windows XP Tablet PC Edition might have other enhancements to standard controls to make them even easier to use with a pen. This means that as new versions of Windows XP Tablet PC Edition are introduced, your application will automatically benefit from those enhancements. If, on the other hand, you're creating your own controls, we suggest that you take into account the issues we've discussed in this chapter concerning the design of those controls.

## Handedness

The second major user-introduced set of challenges comes from the user's hand. When writing with a pen, the user's hand ends up blocking a good portion of the screen. The key here is *which* portion of the screen gets blocked. The screen is blocked differently depending on whether the user is right-handed or left-handed. For an example of how serious the blocking effect can be, see Figure 2-10.

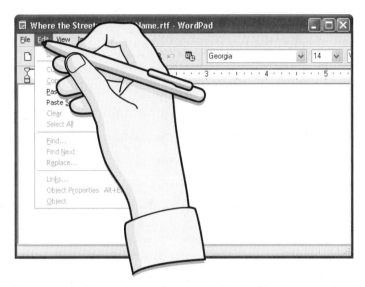

**Figure 2-10**   The majority of a menu is blocked by the user's hand.

Usually, blocking of the screen by the user's hand is not that big of a deal because the user can just move his hand to see what's obscured. In some cases, however, moving the hand is not possible or desirable. Consider the case of menus and ToolTips. By default, they both appear to the lower right of the cursor. This positioning is a problem when you consider that most people are right-handed. A right-handed user's hand is (surprise, surprise) to the lower right of the cursor as well, so when he hovers over a toolbar, the ToolTip comes up under his hand. In moving his hand to see the ToolTip, the cursor moves, thereby making the ToolTip disappear!

A partial resolution to this problem, available in Windows XP Tablet PC Edition, is that menus and toolbars respect a handedness setting. By *handedness*, we mean the hand with which a user writes. In the Tablet PC Control Panel item, you can tell the system this information. In the case of right-handed users, the system paints menus and ToolTips to the lower left of the cursor, making them clearly visible. An example of this behavior is shown in Figure 2-11.

**Figure 2-11**  The same menu as shown in Figure 2-10, this time shown for a right-handed user.

The handedness setting affects only the standard system menus and Tool-Tips, so applications that paint their own menus or implement their own toolbars will most likely not benefit from this enhancement. As long as you use the standard menus and toolbars, your application will behave according to the user's preferences on Windows XP Tablet PC Edition.

**Note**  If you do implement your own menus or toolbars, you can query the user's handedness setting by calling *SystemParametersInfo* to check the *SPI_GETMENUDROPALIGNMENT* flag.

# Thinking in Ink

Now that we've spent a little time talking about pen-related concerns, we'll move on to considering digital ink and its possible role in your application. By now, you've gotten the idea that digital ink plays a big part in the Microsoft Tablet PC vision. It's time to turn that idea into concrete examples of how both your application and the user treat digital ink. In the following sections, we explore how digital ink is modeled, manipulated, and rendered.

# Ink Modeling

One of the biggest decisions you'll make as an application developer is how to treat ink in your application. We refer to this as *ink modeling*, which is how the application models digital ink in its overall schema. Before tackling this subject, you must first decide on the purpose of digital ink in your application.

## What's Ink Got to Do with It?

Digital ink generally has two purposes in an application. The first, and perhaps most obvious, is the treatment of digital ink as ink. When ink is used for this purpose in an application, users can enter digital ink just as if they were writing on paper. The ink, once entered, is not converted or otherwise changed. When an application keeps digital ink as ink, it is in effect treating its document space like a sheet of paper. Any digital ink used in this way is *first order* ink, serving no other purpose than to be a digital version of the user's handwritten notes.

Digital ink can also serve another purpose in an application. You might want your application to have *second order* ink, or ink that exists as an intermediary for some other purpose. Second order ink doesn't stick around long; instead, it is often converted to another data type. Second order ink leverages the pen as a natural form of data entry. It is treated not as an end in itself but as a means to arrive at some other end. Here are two examples of how using second order ink as a natural form of input can make an application better:

- **Ink for spatial layout**   Any application that requires the user to create and spatially arrange items is a good candidate for second order ink. A typical example of such an application is Microsoft Visio, which is a diagramming application. Generating flowcharts and other diagrams in Visio using a mouse can sometimes be tedious. Creating, resizing, and placing shapes are often time-consuming, requiring careful and adept mouse manipulation. The typical user can probably draw a flowchart on a napkin faster than he can create one in Visio. However, imagine if Visio could accept digital ink as a form of input, converting the ink (using reasonably good shape-recognition algorithms) to a nice flowchart either as the user inks or once the user is done. It's a great example of how digital ink can be a natural form of input without being an end in itself.

- **Ink for complex scripts**   Many computer users can type English much faster than they can write it. However, this great imbalance between the throughputs of the keyboard and the pen does not hold true for all languages. In fact, many languages not based on Latin script have complex alphabets that are difficult to type. In such languages, the size of the alphabet dwarfs the number of keys available on a keyboard, requiring users to type characters by using complicated combinations of keys. Worsening the problem, typical words in some of these languages have many homonyms, making phonetic spelling difficult as well. The average inexperienced typist using such a language (Chinese, for example) enters text at a painfully slow speed. Without training, they are often unable to enter text at all. Here digital ink comes to the rescue. Ink can be used as a method of text entry when combined with a good handwriting recognizer. For the average user who wants to enter text in a complex script, digital ink is a much faster alternative to typing. This is another example of how digital ink can be not only a feature but also a significant improvement in a user's computing experience.

## Mysterious Ways

Second order digital ink has numerous other uses, limited only by your imagination and your application's needs. Instead of discussing additional uses of second order digital ink, however, we now want to turn our attention back to first order ink, whose purpose once entered is to remain as ink. First order ink can be modeled in your application in at least three ways. We cover each of these ways in the following sections. Figure 2-12 is a simple illustration of the three ink-modeling methods.

**Figure 2-12**    Three ways to model ink in an application.

**Free-Form Ink**   Perhaps the most paperlike of all the ways to model ink in an application, free-form ink lets the user ink anything anywhere in the document. Whether it is drawings, writing, or annotations, the user has complete control over what goes on the document canvas. The application treats ink just as a piece of paper would, which is to say that it places little or no restrictions on how ink is placed on it.

Although this model of digital ink might be appealing, its laissez-faire treatment of ink might not be appropriate for all applications. After all, how many applications could there be whose sole purpose is to simulate digital paper without providing many additional benefits?

You might be interested in adding a free-form inking surface as a component of your application instead of having it be the entire focus. The key to making a successful free-form inking surface is to restrict the user in as few ways as possible.

**Annotation Ink**   A more likely use of first order digital ink in your application is as a means to annotate documents, especially if you already have an application and you're considering adding some Tablet PC enhancements to it. Your existing application has a document type of its own, which likely consists of anything but digital ink. You might like to add an annotation feature to it; after all, many people print documents to annotate them with a pen. Many applications don't have a means for users to add annotations at all, much less digital ink annotations. Herein lies an opportunity for your application to shine on the Tablet PC.

Successfully modeling annotation ink requires your application to accept ink in an almost free-form manner. Users should feel that they are writing on the document just as they would write on a printed version of it.

Most annotations don't target the document in general; instead, they tend to apply to a specific word, section, page, or other portion of the document. The challenge with annotations is figuring out how to keep them anchored to what they annotate. For instance, if a user circles a sentence in a word processing application, it would be nice if the circle moved with the sentence as the user edited nearby portions of the document. Without this functionality, any edits to the document that cause its content to move around would destroy the meaning of many annotations because they would become detached from their context.

Annotation anchoring need not be difficult, particularly if your application already supports anchored non-ink annotations. If digital ink will be your application's first foray into supporting annotations, you might want to consider how you will anchor those annotations to your application's document content.

**Inline Ink**   The last way of modeling ink in an application is to treat the ink as another textual element. Putting the ink *inline*, or within the flow of document text, is a possibility for applications that deal with flowing text (such as word processors). In this model, digital ink is not much more than additional words in the document.

Microsoft Word currently puts ink inline with text, letting the ink flow with the rest of the document content. However, of the three models of digital ink, inline ink is the least compelling. Inline ink does not have a real-world analog that makes a case for common scenarios in which it would be useful. This method is the least like paper, and it is also of questionable value to the user. In your application, you're more likely to model your first order ink as free-form or as annotation.

# Ink Interaction

Regardless of how you model digital ink in your application, you will need to decide how to help the users interact with the ink they've written. Many of the well-established text interaction conventions will have analogs in the digital ink world. For the most part, the suggestions we give here are not revolutionary. Rather, they distill the conclusions of the Tablet PC team's user research down to some general guidelines that will help you design ink-enabled applications that are easy to use.

## Common Pen Actions

Before we get into the details behind ink interaction, we should establish a vocabulary of terms that denote common pen actions. In general, literature you read about pen-based computing will adhere pretty closely to the terms listed in Table 2-1. The Tablet PC Platform SDK documentation also uses some of these terms when referring to these pen actions. Table 2-1 contains the terms and definitions for pen actions that we'll be using throughout this book.

**Table 2-1   Pen Action Terminology**

| Term | Action |
|------|--------|
| Hover | The pen stays within the detection range of the digitizer without actually touching the screen. Windows XP Tablet PC Edition maps this action to a mouse movement. |
| Tap | The pen touches and lifts from the screen within a short amount of time. While touching the screen, it does not travel more than a few pixels (if at all). This action is mapped to a left mouse button click. |
| Double Tap | The pen taps twice in quick succession, traveling little or no distance between the taps. This action is mapped to a left mouse button double click. |

**Table 2-1**  **Pen Action Terminology**   *(continued)*

| Term | Action |
| --- | --- |
| Press-and-Hold | The pen touches the screen and neither lifts nor moves much distance for a set amount of time. When the pen has been held down for that amount of time (which can be adjusted in the Tablet PC Control Panel item), it is lifted from the screen. This action can be mapped to a right mouse button click, which is especially useful if a tablet pen does not have a barrel button. |
| Hold-Through | The pen begins a press-and-hold action but does not lift when the set amount of time elapses. The pen instead remains held down for even longer. This action is mapped to holding the left mouse button down. Incidentally, this explains why press-and-hold to trigger a right click requires the user to lift the pen within a certain window of time. If holding the pen down for *any* period of time always generated a right click, there would be no way for the user to simulate holding the left button down (an action required by some user interfaces). |
| Drag | The pen touches the screen, moves more than a very short distance, and eventually lifts off the screen. This action is mapped to a left mouse button drag. |
| Hold-Drag | The pen begins a press-and-hold action but then drags when the hold time is reached. This action is mapped to a right mouse button drag. |
| Lasso | A specific drag action that is meant to select objects within an application. The dragged path indicates a loop that encloses all objects that the user wants to select. |
| Gesture | Any of a set of patterns traced by the pen. If the pattern is traced without touching the screen, the gesture is said to be an *in-air gesture*. By moving the pen in a specific pattern, the user can trigger behaviors in an application that expects the gesture. In addition to the in-air variety, some gestures are performed after touching the pen to the screen. In either case, gestures are a way to interact with an application without requiring any visible user interface. They are the pen analog to keyboard shortcuts. |

## Selecting Ink

Other than creating ink on the Tablet PC, selecting ink is possibly the most important action that a user performs with digital ink. Selection, after all, is a prerequisite for all other ink manipulation actions. Many of the benefits of digital ink, such as being able to change its color and move it around, are predicated on the ink being selectable. Just as text selection in a word processor is critical to its functionality, ink selection in a Tablet PC application is core to the inking experience.

There are, however, major differences in the way that selection is performed, depending on the application and the document type. Selection methods should be based on the characteristics of the document data being selected. Several common document types and their selection methods follow.

- **Simple layout text**   Many applications deal only with simple layout text streams. By *simple layout*, we mean that given any two words in the document, it is possible to determine without ambiguity which one is first. An example of this type of application is Microsoft Notepad. In Notepad, it's pretty clear that the text is contained in one linear stream and that there is a defined order for each word. The great part about one-dimensional text streams is that their selection mechanisms are easy to learn. By choosing a beginning and an end point, it's obvious which words are selected and which aren't. Most simple layout text selection mechanisms display selection by inverting the color of the text and its background.

- **Complex layout text**   In a complex layout text document, it might not always be easy for a user to determine the relative order of any two particular words. In addition, complex layout text documents can often have mixed context, such as images and other objects interspersed with the text. An example of this type of application is a Web browser, in which text can be laid out in different frames on screen along with images. This type of layout puts clusters of words at various locations on screen. The user is often unable to guess the real order of these clusters, creating a unique kind of challenge when simple layout text selection mechanisms are applied to complex layout text documents. Try selecting a few clusters of text from a complicated Web page, and you'll quickly discover that it's rather unpredictable which clusters get selected. The problem is that the application has an internal ordering for the clusters, but this ordering isn't exposed visually to the user. The solution to this problem is to let go of the simple layout selection mechanisms, which are inadequate in this case, and instead to support a more appropriate mechanism. However, most complex layout text applications still use simple layout selection.

- **Two-dimensional canvas**   Outside the text-processing world, a host of applications use a document model that is best described as a two-dimensional canvas. A good example of this type of application is an image editor such as Adobe Photoshop. These applications present a flat canvas from which the user can select areas. The richness of their selection model varies with the type of selection tools they provide. The most basic area selection tool is the rectangular selection tool, which when dragged selects a rectangle from the canvas. More advanced tools include ellipses, polygons, and even free-form selection tools that select any closed loop area the user draws.

■ **Two-dimensional object-based**    Related to the two-dimensional canvas document is the two-dimensional object-based document. The difference is that two-dimensional object-based applications do not allow the user to select just any part of the document surface. Instead, their documents consist of individual objects laid out in two dimensions. These objects, and not the document surface itself, can be selected. The Windows desktop is an example of sorts of a two-dimensional object-based document. You can drag out a selection rectangle on it, which then selects all icons that fall within the rectangle.

Documents with digital ink in them are usually best described as being in the two-dimensional object-based category. However, traditional two-dimensional object-based selection mechanisms need to be adjusted to handle some challenges specific to digital ink.

The first and perhaps most essential deviation from traditional selection mechanisms is that digital ink often selects poorly when using a rectangular selection tool. Figure 2-13 shows a common difficulty with using a rectangular selection tool on ink. The crux of the problem is that we usually don't write perfectly straight, using exact margins. The free-form nature of ink tends to create amorphous groups of ink instead of rectangular blocks, making rectangle-based selection tools difficult to apply.

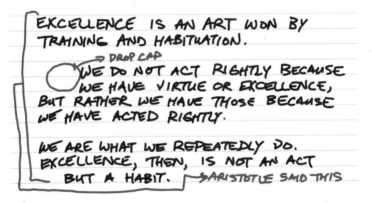

**Figure 2-13**    Using a rectangular selection tool to select digital ink is sometimes a challenge. How would you use a rectangular selection tool to select only the darker ink?

It's better to use a free-form selection tool when selecting digital ink. A free-form selection tool allows the user to draw a loop that encloses only everything that should be selected. We discuss free-form (or lasso) selection in greater detail in Chapter 4 and Chapter 6.

The second deviation from traditional selection mechanisms comes in the way the selection of an object is shown. Some two-dimensional object-based applications show that objects are selected by surrounding them with a selection box while not altering the object's original appearance. An example of selection boxes, taken from Visio, is shown in Figure 2-14. The difficulty, as apparent in the figure, is seeing exactly which objects are selected. When many objects overlap, seeing which ones are selected can sometimes be nearly impossible.

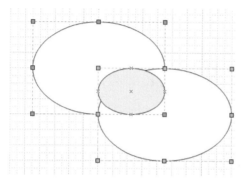

**Figure 2-14**   Is the gray oval in the middle selected as well as the two outer ellipses?

The way to avoid this problem is to make sure that selected objects are visually distinguishable from unselected objects. The Windows Desktop, for instance, indicates that an icon is selected by imbuing it with a selection color (usually blue). This visual difference makes it easier to tell whether something is selected, even if other objects are nearby or partially overlapping. Having a visual difference is even more important with digital ink because ink strokes often cross and overlap one another.

We end this section with one final note about free-form selection of ink. An issue particular to digital ink selection that comes up in usability tests is the tendency for users to be somewhat sloppy in using lasso selection tools. Instead of carefully corralling the ink in a neat little loop, users tend to quickly circle approximately what they want. If ink strokes are ruled to be in or out of the loop based on whether they are completely contained within the loop, some strokes near the edges of the loop might be inadvertently excluded from the selection. Your application can help the user select ink quickly and effectively in two ways:

■ **Establish a stroke selection threshold**   Instead of selecting those strokes that are wholly contained in the lasso (or conversely, selecting all strokes that have any part within the lasso), consider using a percentage-based selection threshold. For instance, you might say that the lasso selects all strokes that fall at least 60 percent within the lasso. The interesting part is in calculating whether a stroke meets this criterion. Because two strokes that look identical can contain a different number of points (depending on how fast the stroke was drawn), a perfect percentage-based calculation is hard to arrive at. Further complicating the issue is pressure-sensitive ink, which can be thicker in some parts and thinner in others. Fortunately, the Tablet PC Platform SDK provides a simplified algorithm for lasso selection. This algorithm, exposed through the lasso *HitTest* method, determines whether an ink stroke is selected based on the percentage of its points that fall within the lasso.

■ **Support word-based selection**   A user often will select a word and accidentally miss the dot of an *i* or some other small stroke in the word. When selecting written ink, the user most likely wants to work with whole words, not just individual strokes within a word. To help the user, you might consider offering word-based selection, in which an entire word—not the individual strokes—falls within or outside the lasso. This approach makes it easy for the user to quickly select and manipulate words, instead of having to carefully make sure that dots and dashes aren't omitted from the selection. In Chapter 7, we'll explain how the Ink Recognition API in the Tablet PC Platform SDK helps you determine which ink strokes belong to the same word.

## Other Ink Interactions

In addition to selecting ink, there are several other ink interactions that your application might support. We briefly cover a few of the more common interactions and the pitfalls to avoid when implementing them.

**Moving and Resizing**   Once ink has been selected, the user might want to move or resize it. Moving the ink is straightforward—the user should be able to directly drag the ink from one location to another, instead of, say, using the arrow keys on a keyboard to move selected ink. Dragging the ink is especially convenient because the user will most likely be holding a pen and not using a keyboard when entering ink on a tablet. If your application supports resizing of selected ink via resize handles, be sure that they are big enough to be easily targeted by a pen.

**Formatting**    There isn't an official list of recommended ink formatting settings that every application should expose. However, users will expect the most basic formatting variables (such as color and thickness) to be settable. Some of the more advanced formatting options that the Tablet PC Platform SDK supports include pressure sensitivity and the shape of the pen tip. The user might expect these, too, when writing in a Tablet PC application.  Some throwbacks from font formatting conventions include gimmicks such as bold and italic. However, while it is fairly easy to implement bold and italic by applying scale and shear transforms to the ink, the utility of such functionality is questionable. After all, the user can write bold or italicized ink fairly easily without the application's help. But in a Tablet PC application, the user should be able to set color and thickness as well as pressure sensitivity and pen tip shape.

An alternative to exposing these raw settings is to offer a set of virtual pens, each with its own implicit settings. For instance, you could offer fine blue ballpoint, medium black square-tip marker, and yellow highlighter as three virtual pens. This approach sacrifices precise control of pen formatting for the convenience of having a stash of commonly used pens. Whether you choose to offer virtual pens or to let the user control the pen settings, be sure to give the user some way to format the ink. Ink formatting adds a sense of depth and completeness to the user's perception of your application running on the Tablet PC.

**Gestures**    Pen gestures can be an effective way to interact with an application. Particularly because pen gestures can be performed anywhere, without triggering UI functions, they can be as efficient as keyboard shortcuts for the user who is familiar with them. However, gestures have some of the same usability concerns as keyboard shortcuts. For one, they are hard to discover (that is, the user might not know of their existence because they do not have associated UI elements). If an application accepts a lot of gestures, it might be hard for the user to perform the gestures distinctly and for the gesture recognizer to tell the many gestures apart.

Besides poor discoverability and gesture overload, a serious threat to successful gesture-driven features is the accidental triggering of gestures. Unlike keyboard shortcuts, which require deliberate combinations of keys to be pressed, gestures can be performed unintentionally merely by waving the pen around or by inking something that resembles a gesture. The chance of accidentally triggering a gesture increases with the number of gestures an application uses, adding to the problem. For these reasons, you must take great care when deciding whether to support gestures, and if you do, which features they should actuate.

> Tip   Consider associating gestures only with nondestructive actions
> so that unintentional gestures do not yield devastating results.

# Ink Realism

We've explained how you can model and interact with digital ink in your application. Now we'll take a look at how you can make ink more realistic. Ink realism is a key part of what Tablet PCs are all about. In trying to mimic the experience of pen and paper, the Tablet PC Platform goes to great lengths to improve the capture and appearance of digital ink. We'll see what you can do to improve the user's inking experience as well as what the Tablet PC Platform does to make digital ink realistic. We'll also give you some tips that will make your application a great one for inking in.

## Right Here, Right Now

One facet of ink realism is its immediacy. To match the utility of paper, digital ink must be captured in real time, as the user is writing. Any sort of lag will impede the user's thought process, reducing the effectiveness of inking on a tablet. Two sources of lag exist in applications:

- **Packet processing lag**   The Tablet PC Platform sends notifications of newly captured ink. These notifications are sent to an application whenever new points are captured in the middle of an ink stroke. If the application processes these new points (*packets*) on its own, it is expected to render the partially drawn stroke as well. A lag occurs if there's a noticeable time lapse between the time the notification is sent and when the partial stroke is finally drawn.

- **Application responsiveness lag**   The Tablet PC Platform also sends notifications when a user begins a new ink stroke. Applications can sometimes take a long time to respond to these notifications, creating a noticeable delay between when the pen first touches the screen and when its ink gets rendered.

There's plenty of good news when it comes to ink immediacy on a Tablet PC. By default, the Tablet PC Platform tries to take care of both these problems for you. The standard ink collection facilities available in the Platform, *InkCollector* and *InkOverlay*, process packets and new ink strokes automatically. Their default processing for packets and new strokes is reasonably fast, introducing little to no lag in typical situations. If you use them without modification, they should provide a good inking experience for the user. We will cover *InkCollector* and *InkOverlay* in more depth in Chapter 4.

At times, you might need to do some of your own processing of ink notifications sent by the Tablet PC Platform, either in addition to or in lieu of the default processing. In these cases, make sure that your packet processing code is minimal and fast so that the user will not perceive a delay in inking. Periodic delays, in which packets occasionally take much longer to process, can be even more disturbing for the user, so try to avoid them if possible.

## Curves Ahead

Another facet of ink realism is the appearance of the ink itself. On physical paper, ink strokes are smooth and continuous. Fine nuances are littered throughout, such as the thinning of a stroke as the pen lifts. These numerous and subtle nuances cause us to expect that using digital ink will be a bit more involved than simply connecting some dots on the screen.

The Tablet PC Platform provides several simple optional features to make digital ink more realistic. A brief mention of each follows.

**Bézier Curve Fitting**   One of the biggest improvements to digital ink that the Tablet PC Platform provides is support for Bézier curve fitting. If you simply took all the points captured by a digitizer and connected the dots, you would come up with an ink stroke that was fairly jagged in areas where the pen moved quickly. The reason is that the sampling rate of the digitizer is only so fast. If you move quickly enough, the digitizer will be able to sample only one point for every few pixels you move. When these sparsely sampled points are connected, they leave stretches of straight-line segments, making the ink stroke appear jagged or full of kinks.

Curve fitting is the process of taking some points and figuring out a smooth curve that passes near all the points. Instead of taking the digitizer at its word, curve fitting assumes that the user wrote fairly smoothly without sudden changes in direction. The Tablet PC Platform has an option to render ink strokes using curve-fitted points instead of the originally collected digitizer points. This option improves the overall appearance of the ink tremendously.

Rest assured that turning on curve fitting won't just round everything out. The algorithm used is smart enough to detect inflection points, or *cusps*, in the ink stroke. It preserves the natural sharpness of cusps while smoothing out the rest of the ink with curve fitting.

The Tablet PC Platform fits points onto Bézier curves. Bézier curves are only one of many types of curves that can be used for this purpose. They were chosen for their simplicity. Bézier curves are quite common in graphics software and are used heavily by digital artists and computer games designers alike. We won't go into the details of Bézier curves in this book, but for your viewing pleasure an example of an unassuming Bézier curve is provided in Figure 2-15.

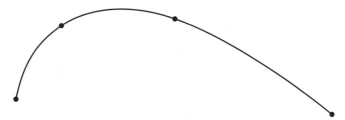

**Figure 2-15**   A Bézier curve. Bézier curves use a number of control points that affect the appearance of the curve. All four control points of the curve are shown.

**Antialiasing**   Even after fitting an ink stroke to a curve has smoothed it out, the edges of the stroke might still appear to be slightly rough. This roughness is caused by the size of the screen's pixels, which are big enough for the eye to make out individually. Because some pixels are part of the ink stroke and others (presumably the background) are not, there is a jagged steplike appearance at the edge of a stroke.

To reduce this roughness, antialiasing of ink strokes is supported in the Tablet PC Platform. *Antialiasing* is the process by which pixels on the border between two colors are set to an intermediate color somewhere between the two original colors. When viewed from a reasonable distance, this blending of colors makes for a smooth appearance. Figure 2-16 shows an example of what antialiasing can do for the appearance of a curve.

**Figure 2-16**   A circle shown both normally (left) and antialiased (right). The technique is easier to see in these magnified circles. At normal size, the antialiased circle will look smoother.

**Pen Tip Shape**    To add a subtle enhancement to the realism of digital ink, two pen tips are supported. You can ask the Tablet PC Platform to render ink as if it were drawn using either a round-tipped pen or a rectangular-tipped pen. A round-tipped pen simulates a ballpoint pen: the ends of ink strokes are semi-circular, and inflections in the stroke have rounded edges to them. A rectangular-tipped pen, on the other hand, simulates the appearance of felt-tipped markers that have rectangular tips. Edges of a stroke drawn by a rectangular-tipped pen are straight, and inflections have straight edges as well. Ink drawn with the two types of pen tips is shown in Figure 2-17.

**Figure 2-17**    Ink strokes drawn with the round tip and the rectangular tip appear markedly different from each other.

**Pressure Sensitivity**    In addition to two types of pen tips, the Tablet PC Platform can also simulate pressure-sensitive pens. The reason for this is that some pens draw differently depending on the amount of pressure applied to the pen during the stroke. Because many tablets will have hardware support for detecting the pressure used on a pen, the Tablet PC Platform exploits the opportunity to add another facet to digital ink's realism. If you ask the Tablet PC Platform to use the pressure information gathered from a digitizer that supports pressure, it will render ink strokes according to the pressure that was used to generate them. Areas in which greater pressure was applied will appear thicker, and areas in which lighter pressure was applied will appear thinner. Figure 2-18 shows a stroke that was captured with pressure sensitivity turned on.

**Figure 2-18**    A pressure-sensitive stroke. Notice how the end of the stroke appears as though the pen were lifted off the tablet in a quick motion.

**Subtractive Color Rendering**    The last enhancement to the appearance of digital ink drawn by the Tablet PC Platform affects transparent strokes. Ink can be drawn with a degree of transparency, giving it the appearance of a light-colored marker or highlighter. When two highlighters of different colors are mixed on a sheet of paper, the resulting color of the overlapping areas is different from that produced by mixing two colors on a computer screen.

The reason for this difference lies in the color model that's used. A *color model* is a system of fundamental colors that can be intermixed in various proportions to produce all other colors. An example of this is the RGB (red-green-blue) color model used on computers. When mixing colors in the RGB model, each color you mix in adds to the final color's value. Because of this, the RGB color model is said to be *additive*. In the RGB model, you get white when you mix the three fundamental colors together in equal proportions.

In stark contrast are *subtractive* color models, so called because each additional color that's mixed in subtracts from the others already present. When you mix the fundamental colors of a subtractive color model in equal proportions, you get black, not white. A popular subtractive color model is CMYK (cyan-magenta-yellow-black). The CMYK color model is commonly used when printing on paper (magazines, newspapers, ink-jet printers, and so forth). Examples of additive and subtractive color models, albeit less compelling in grayscale, are shown in Figure 2-19.

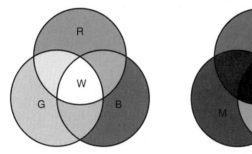

**Figure 2-19**  The RGB color model, on the left, mixes red, green, and blue to make white. The CMYK model mixes cyan, magenta, and yellow to make black.

When mixing semitransparent ink with underlying colors, the Tablet PC Platform uses a subtractive color model, yielding much more realistic results. If you mix enough colors of semitransparent ink, you'll get black, just like on real paper. This subtlety is a nice addition to the realism of the ink that's rendered.

**Note**  Black is a purely practical member of the set, with no theoretical basis for its membership. It's needed because typical printing processes don't produce a solid black when cyan, magenta, and yellow are mixed.

## Summary

We started this chapter by describing application design guidelines with regard to tablets. The Tablet PC team designed these guidelines based on user studies conducted over a number of years. Because Tablet PCs are so different from standard desktops and laptops, it's essential to consider the results of this kind of user research when designing your application.

Pen and digitizer hardware have usability implications that we investigated. The user's physiology also creates some design concerns for applications that expect pen interaction. We suggested several ways to address these usability challenges. We then considered how ink is modeled and interacted with in your application. Finally we explored how your application works with the Tablet PC Platform to create a sense of realism in the digital ink that's generated.

We have now formed the mental foundation behind designing Tablet PC applications. Starting with the next chapter, we dive right into the specifics of the Tablet PC Platform SDK, which will give you the necessary tools to write your own well-designed Tablet PC applications.

# Part II

# The Tablet PC Platform SDK

# 3

# Introduction to the Tablet PC Platform SDK

Microsoft Windows XP Tablet PC Edition comes bundled with special Tablet PC features that focus on digital ink. Many of these features can be programmatically accessed using Microsoft's Tablet PC Platform SDK. If you develop applications for the Tablet PC, you'll no doubt need to understand the SDK.

In this chapter, we first walk you through the mechanics of the SDK, its constituent parts and installation. Once you're up and running, we'll delve into the managed API, which is the heart of the Tablet PC Platform SDK. We'll introduce the main objects in the managed API and also analyze the differences between the managed API and the Ink controls. By the end of the chapter, you should understand the main components of the SDK, the reasoning behind its design, and some fundamentals about the managed API and Ink controls.

## A Sort of Homecoming

The Tablet PC Platform SDK has undergone some notable improvements since its debut in 2001, largely driven by constructive feedback from the developer community. It is now available in its final form, free to download and install from the Microsoft Developer Network (MSDN) on the Web. The Tablet PC Platform SDK is also available on this book's companion CD for easy installation.

The naming of the Tablet PC Platform SDK announces what is unique about it. Platform emphasizes that the Tablet PC platform is designed to enable and significantly enhance pen-driven computing. The entire Tablet PC experience is defined by this completely new platform. The Tablet PC Platform SDK is supported by a host of functionality available only on Microsoft Windows XP Tablet PC Edition. Together, the Tablet PC Platform SDK and Windows XP Tablet PC Edition make powerful pen-driven computing possible.

The Tablet PC Platform SDK has several major conceptual components, listed here. Details regarding some of the components are discussed in the next sections.

- **Managed application programming interfaces (APIs)**  The core of the SDK is composed of a set of APIs exposing pen and ink features that can be leveraged by Microsoft .NET applications.

- **Ink controls**  As a way of supporting simple and rapid integration of ink into applications, several .NET and Microsoft ActiveX controls are provided.

- **Component Object Model (COM) automation APIs**  COM is a core Microsoft technology that has been used widely in the world of Windows programming. These APIs are provided as an alternative to the managed APIs, for use with C/C++ and Microsoft Visual Basic 6.

- **Documentation**  The documentation for the SDK is included with the SDK and is also available on MSDN (*http://msdn.microsoft.com*).

- **Sample applications**  Several samples are included to demonstrate possible uses of the SDK.

- **Runtime libraries**  To make the development of Tablet PC applications possible on non-Tablet PC editions of Windows, the SDK installs the necessary runtime libraries.

The architecture block diagram in Figure 3-1 shows a high-level view of the Tablet PC Platform SDK architecture. The arrows in the figure represent dependencies between components. At the lowest level of the SDK are the COM automation APIs, which are implemented in C/C++ and directly use Microsoft Win32 calls. The managed APIs are built on top of the COM automation APIs, essentially providing a managed wrapper for that functionality. It's worth noting that the Tablet PC managed API is not merely a subset of the available COM automation features. The managed APIs are fully able to do all the things that the underlying COM automation APIs can, oftentimes in an easier fashion by using features made possible by the .NET architecture.

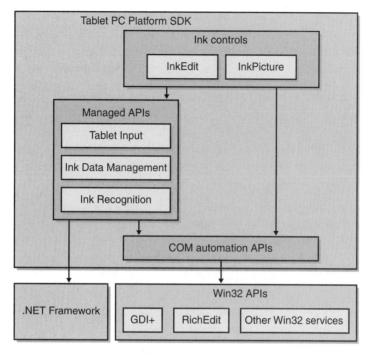

**Figure 3-1**   The Tablet PC Platform SDK architecture

The Ink controls are built with C/C++ and exposed via .NET wrappers for easy access via C#, Visual Basic .NET, and other .NET-capable languages. Unlike the managed APIs, the Ink controls expose only a subset of the available underlying functionality. For instance, the InkEdit control does not give access to the *RecognizerContext* used when the user writes in it. Instead, the control generates *RecognizerContext* objects internally, exposing only the *Recognizer* being used. This makes it impossible for you to provide a *RecognizerGuide* to influence recognition, and it also makes it difficult to control whether recognition happens in the background. The InkPicture control is less restricted, being mostly a superset of the *InkOverlay* object. The InkPicture control does not support a few properties and methods, such as *AttachMode*, *OnMouseDown*, *OnMouseUp*, and *OnMouseMove*, but overall it provides almost all the functionality available in *InkOverlay*.

Although the Tablet PC Platform SDK is designed to create applications targeting Tablet PCs, it can be installed and used on any PC running Windows XP.

This allows for development and testing of Tablet PC software on whatever computer is most convenient for you. However, developing Tablet PC applications on a standard PC has certain limitations. Here are several things to consider when developing with the Tablet PC Platform SDK on a standard PC:

- Features that rely on the Ink Recognition API will work only on computers running Windows XP Tablet PC Edition. The Ink Recognition API itself will not work, and any other features in the SDK that use the Ink Recognition API (for instance, the InkEdit control's ability to capture and convert ink into text) will be similarly disabled on computers running other versions of Windows.

- The Ink controls are severely limited when used on any computer not running Windows XP Tablet PC Edition. Most notably, the Ink controls go into what is essentially a "render-only" mode, where new ink cannot be captured and existing ink cannot be further recognized. Note that this will also severely impact development using the Ink controls on any non-Tablet PC edition of Windows XP. One exception is that InkPicture will capture ink on any computer with the SDK installed. These limitations will be discussed further in Chapter 8.

- It may be helpful to have a digitizer pad if you are developing on a desktop computer. Not having a pen-based input device makes ink entry and testing somewhat challenging. (Try writing a few words with your mouse in Microsoft Paint to get a feel for what it's like.)

## Finding the Right Operating System for the Job

Although the Tablet PC Platform SDK requires only Windows XP, control functionality is actually significantly limited when applications are not run on the Tablet PC edition of Windows XP. The two most significant limitations are that ink recognition is disabled and Ink controls do not capture ink. These limitations mean that most Tablet PC application development efforts will want to have at least one machine running Windows XP Tablet PC Edition for debugging and testing the restricted features.

We recommend that you debug and test your Tablet PC application on a Tablet PC device. One way to do this is to develop and debug entirely on a Tablet PC (with an attached keyboard and mouse, ideally!). Unfortunately, this option appeals to developers about as much as developing and debugging on a laptop would. The other way to debug and test on a Tablet PC device is to use remote debugging so that you can execute your code on a Tablet PC while writing and debugging it from a desktop computer. Regrettably, both methods result in reduced developer efficiency.

Given these restrictions, you may have to incur significant ramp-up time and some inconvenience in order to develop and test the full spectrum of features available in the Tablet PC Platform SDK on a non-Tablet PC computer.

## Managed APIs

At the heart of the Tablet PC Platform SDK is a set of managed APIs. A significant part of the Microsoft .NET Framework is the common language runtime (CLR), which controls and supports the execution of .NET-compatible applications written in various languages. The core Tablet PC Platform SDK APIs are "managed" because they are designed to run in, or be managed by, the .NET Framework's common language runtime. Because the managed APIs target the CLR, you can call them from any .NET language. Currently available .NET languages include Microsoft Visual C#, Visual Basic .NET, managed C++, and Microsoft JScript. In our discussion of the managed APIs, we will be using Visual C# in code samples.

The managed APIs are divided into three subsets, each providing a specific portion of essential Tablet PC pen and ink functionality.

- **The Tablet Input API (Pen API)**  This API is targeted at pen-specific features, such as the various buttons on a pen, and also at collecting digital ink and gestures from the movement of the pen.

- **The Ink Data Management API (Ink API)**  Once ink has been collected using the Tablet Input API, manipulation and storage of the ink is done through the Ink Data Management API. The bulk of ink-related features are exposed through this API.

- **The Ink Recognition API (Recognition API)**  This highly specialized API is used to interpret ink intelligently by grouping and recognizing written ink.

Later in this chapter we will look at the managed APIs in more detail.

## Ink Controls

Two Ink controls are included in the Tablet PC Platform SDK as a means to quickly integrate pen and ink functionality into a new or existing application. The controls can be easily dragged onto Windows Forms in languages that support forms-based development, such as C# and Microsoft Visual Basic. Although the Ink controls are presented separately from the managed API and the COM automation APIs, they actually support both. You can use the managed Ink controls from managed code or the ActiveX Ink controls from COM automation code.

- **InkEdit**   This control is an extension of the RichEdit control. It captures and optionally converts ink into text and is ideal in situations where immediate conversion of ink to text is desired.

- **InkPicture**   Meant to capture and display ink over images, this control is an eclectic amalgam of features. Its distinguishing feature is its ability to display an image underneath ink, which is automatically captured and managed by the control.

## COM Automation APIs

For developers more familiar with COM, the Tablet PC Platform SDK includes a set of COM automation APIs that are almost direct analogs of the managed APIs. The COM automation APIs allow development of Tablet PC applications in unmanaged code, using languages such as C++ and Visual Basic 6. We have omitted a separate discussion of these APIs because they behave, in almost all cases, exactly like their managed counterparts. If you are more familiar with COM, or would rather develop with the automation APIs, you should find the managed APIs in Chapters 4, 5, and 6 relevant and directly applicable. The differences between the managed APIs and the COM automation APIs can be attributed to the following:

- **Language limitations**   Whereas C# and many other .NET languages support the notion of easily registered event handlers, COM does not. So, for instance, while the managed APIs simply send events to all the attached delegates of an object, the COM automation APIs require that you call *SetEventInterest* to tell them which events you want to receive.

- **.NET Framework's enhancements**   The .NET Framework used by the managed APIs implements some data structures that are not available to the COM automation APIs. Whereas the managed APIs use the .NET Framework's *Rectangle* and *Matrix* objects, the COM automation APIs must provide their own *InkRectangle* and *InkTransform* for the same functionality.

■    **Unexplained reasons**    There are some differences between the two APIs, and these differences are not easy to understand. Why don't the managed APIs support *AddStrokes*? Why don't the COM automation APIs support the basic *ClipboardCopy*? Fortunately, these abstruse differences are relatively rare and should not get in the way of everyday use of these APIs.

More details regarding the differences between the COM automation APIs and the managed APIs are noted in the SDK documentation.

## Sample Applications

The Tablet PC Platform SDK comes bundled with quite a few sample applications that demonstrate various features of the SDK. You can access these samples by clicking the Samples and Source Code shortcut in the Tablet PC Platform SDK folder on the Start menu. Many of the samples come with source code for multiple programming languages, which is very convenient if you are particularly adept in a particular language. The included samples fall into three major categories:

■    **Ink**    These samples show how to do common things with ink, such as collecting, erasing, zooming, and saving. You may be interested in the Ink Zoom sample, which illustrates the relationship between three coordinate spaces: tablet space, ink space, and view space.

■    **Recognition**    The Ink Recognition and Advanced Recognition samples are particularly good starting points that show how the Ink Recognition API is used.

■    **Controls**    There are two controls samples, "Auto Claims" and "Scanned Paper Form," which demonstrate the InkPicture and InkEdit controls, respectively.

The SDK documentation briefly describes the samples included, but you should take a look at the source code and try some of the samples to get a more complete picture of what they demonstrate.

## A Word or Two About the Speech API

Speech recognition will play an important role in the Tablet PC experience in many applications. By nature of its portability and keyboard-free operation, the Tablet PC lends itself to many scenarios in which speech recognition is important. This is why the Tablet PC design guidelines included in the SDK documentation feature a good amount of discussion related to the role of speech on Tablet PCs. The Windows XP Tablet PC Edition has a very good built-in speech recognition engine, making it easy to integrate speech into your Tablet PC applications.

For a number of years now Microsoft has been shipping the Microsoft Speech API (SAPI) SDK. The SAPI SDK is currently in its fifth major revision, and it contains some of the best speech-recognition technology available on the market. Although the Speech API and speech recognition in general can play an important part in some Tablet PC applications, we will not be addressing SAPI in this book. The issues and considerations that go into developing a successful speech-enabled application are intricate, deserving the more thorough and comprehensive treatment available in speech recognition books as well as the SAPI SDK documentation. We encourage you to download and try the SAPI SDK from Microsoft's Web site, at *http://www.microsoft.com/speech/*. Speech recognition is an exciting world all its own!

# Installing the Tablet PC Platform SDK

This section provides an overview of how to install the Tablet PC Platform SDK. If you have already obtained and installed the SDK and have successfully verified its correct installation by compiling a few of the samples, you may wish to skim this section or skip it entirely. You can always refer back to this section if you later run into problems with your installation.

## System Requirements

The SDK does not have much in the way of hardware and software requirements. The following two items, however, are necessary and the last one is recommended in order to develop Tablet PC applications with the SDK:

- **Windows XP**   The machine on which you develop with the SDK should be running Windows XP. Ideally, you should run the Tablet PC edition of Windows XP to develop most efficiently.

- **Microsoft Visual Studio 6 Service Pack 5 or later**   For unmanaged development, you can use Visual Studio 6 or Visual Studio .NET. For managed development, you'll need to use Visual Studio .NET.

- **Digitizer pad**   Although not strictly required for development, a digitizer pad that takes pen input is highly recommended. (Try using a mouse to write "Rock Me Amadeus" three times fast and you will quickly become convinced that a digitizer pad is well worth the money.) For easy installation, consider a USB digitizer pad such as those manufactured by Wacom (*http://www.wacom.com*).

## Getting the SDK

For your convenience, the complete Tablet PC Platform SDK is included on this book's companion CD. The SDK can also be downloaded from Microsoft's Web site from the Tablet PC home page (*http://www.microsoft.com/tabletpc*). In its compressed distributable form, the SDK is under 12 MB.

To install the SDK, navigate to the directory where the Tablet PC Platform SDK's installation files are located and run Setup.exe. Be sure to read the following section for information about setting up your development environment properly. This setup is critical in order to compile programs that use the SDK.

## Setting Up Your Environment

Installing the SDK is fairly straightforward. Throughout the rest of this book, it is assumed that you installed the SDK in its default path (c:\Program Files\Microsoft Tablet PC Platform SDK), although you should feel free to choose any other path as appropriate. The only installation step that may need some explanation is the Custom Setup option, where you can choose which components to install.

The component selection step is shown in Figure 3-2. By default, all the SDK components are installed. However, the SDK samples and redistributable merge module are optional. You should install the SDK samples if you would like to view the samples that come with the SDK—most of these showcase various features available on the Tablet PC Platform. The redistributable merge module, mstpcrt.msm, contains the Tablet PC runtime components that may be redistributed with your application. You should need this only if you are building an application that might need to run on non-Tablet computers. The merge module can be included by your application's installer, thereby allowing your application to run gracefully on non-Tablet computers. Remember that when your application is not running on a Tablet PC, any Ink controls you use will not collect or recognize ink.

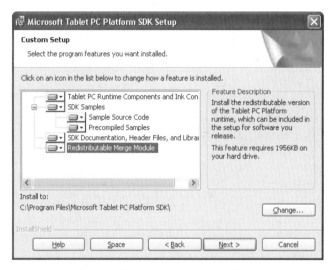

**Figure 3-2**   Custom Setup options for the SDK

## Setting Up Your Visual Studio .NET Environment

Once the Tablet PC Platform SDK is installed onto your development computer, you will need to update some settings in Visual Studio .NET to use the newly installed components. The rest of this section gives instructions on how to set up an environment for using the SDK with a .NET language such as Visual C# or Visual Basic .NET.

> **Note**   If you are using Visual Studio 6 and/or C++, please refer to the Tablet PC Platform SDK documentation for detailed instructions on setting up your development environment.

In order to use the managed API, your project should reference Microsoft.Ink.dll. To add a reference, use the Project menu's Add Reference item, as shown in Figure 3-3, which will bring up the Add Reference dialog box.

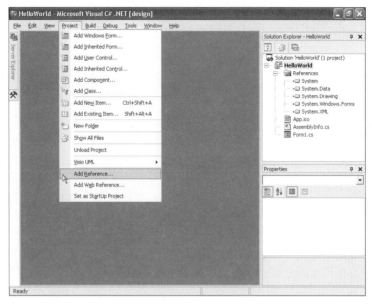

**Figure 3-3**   The Add Reference command is found in the Project menu.

Select "Microsoft Tablet PC API" from the .NET tab, as shown in Figure 3-4.

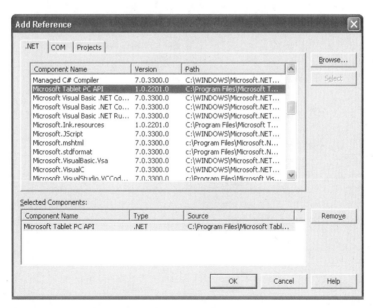

**Figure 3-4**   The Add Reference dialog box is where you add a new reference to your project.

You can see that you have successfully added the reference if the Solution Explorer shows "Microsoft.Ink" as one of the references, shown in Figure 3-5.

**Figure 3-5** A successfully added reference to Microsoft.Ink shows up in the Solution Explorer.

If you're using Ink controls, you may want to add them to the Toolbox for easy drag-and-drop into application forms. To add the Ink controls to the Toolbox, right click the Toolbox and select Customize Toolbox, as shown in Figure 3-6.

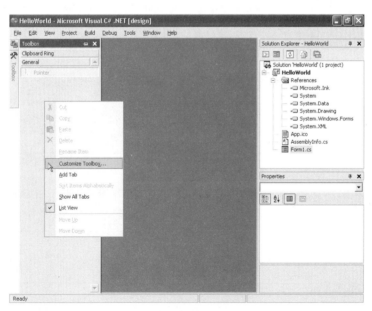

**Figure 3-6** The Customize Toolbox link can be found by right clicking on the Toolbox.

From the Customize Toolbox dialog box's .NET Framework Components tab, select and check both InkEdit and InkPicture, as shown in Figure 3-7. The Ink controls will now be available in the General tab of the Toolbox, as shown in Figure 3-8.

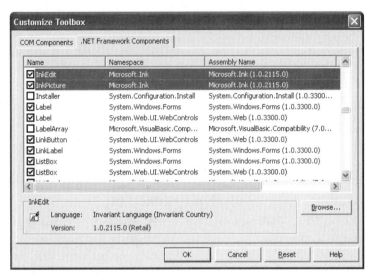

**Figure 3-7**   Adding new components to the Toolbox using the Customize Toolbox dialog box.

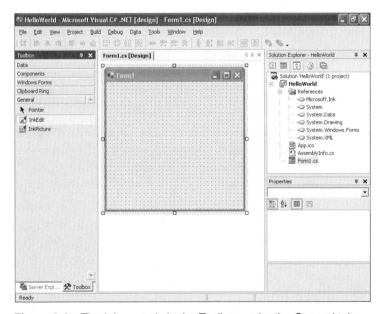

**Figure 3-8**   The Ink controls in the Toolbox under the General tab.

# Anatomy of the Tablet PC Platform SDK

Following are the location and names of some important files installed as part of a standard installation of the SDK.

> **Note** A full installation of the SDK copies more than 160 files! The list below highlights the files of interest and reflects a small subset of what is actually installed.

- **Microsoft.Ink (\Windows\Assembly\GAC)** This is the heart of the managed API. Almost the entire managed API is implemented within this assembly, which is the focal point of the Tablet PC Platform SDK. It is stored in the Global Assembly Cache (GAC) because many applications will share its functionality.

- **InkObj.dll (\Program Files\Common Files\Microsoft Shared\Ink)** This file includes most of the core ink services used internally by the platform. In addition, it includes the COM automation APIs and type libraries.

- **TPCSDK10.chm (\Windows\Help)** This is the SDK's help documentation in HTML Help format. You will find a convenient shortcut to this in the Microsoft Tablet PC Platform SDK entry of your Start menu.

- **MSInkAut.h (\Program Files\Microsoft Tablet PC Platform SDK\Include)** The main COM automation API header is available here to include in your C++ projects. Alternatively, you can import InkObj.dll to access the same type information.

- **\Program Files\Microsoft Tablet PC Platform SDK\Samples** All SDK samples are included in subdirectories of the Samples directory. There are nearly 20 samples, ranging from "Advanced Recognition" to "TPC Info." Some samples come in multiple languages, in which case code for each language is put into its own directory.

- **\Program Files\Microsoft Tablet PC Platform SDK\Bin** The compiled executables from the SDK samples are installed in the Bin directory (if you choose to install the sample binaries).

- **InkEd.dll (\Windows\System32)** The InkEdit control is implemented in this dynamic-link library (DLL).

- **Wisptis.exe (\Windows\System32)**   This executable runs as a system service that provides pen-data collection for other components of the SDK. When a component needs to interact with the pen (for example, to collect ink or to detect gestures), this executable is spawned as a service to communicate directly with the input device. On a Tablet PC, Wisptis.exe interacts with the digitizer, whereas on a desktop it interacts with the mouse as well. The executable's name is an acronym that references an outdated internal name for the team that developed it (Windows Ink Services Platform Tablet Input Subsystem).

# Overview of the Managed API

You've now been introduced to the various components that constitute the Tablet PC Platform SDK. You've also successfully set up the SDK in your development environment. It's high time for some code! The following code listing shows the Tablet Input API, Ink Data Management API, and Ink Recognition API interacting together in one application. The bulk of the code sets up the necessary UI—very little code is required to demonstrate the application's simple use of the managed API.

The application creates a window with an area that permits inking. When the "Recognize" button is pressed, ink is recognized into text at the bottom of the dialog. The next three chapters describe in detail the parts of the managed API used in this application. The code below is available on the companion CD as HelloManagedAPI. If you try the code directly from the installed samples, simply open its solution file (HelloManagedAPI.sln), compile, and run. Alternatively, if you'd like to get a better feel for the code by entering it directly, create a new project and add the following code as its own C# file into the project. Then you'll be able to compile and run the code you've entered.

**HelloManagedAPI.cs**

```
/////////////////////////////////////////////////////////////////////
// HelloManagedAPI.cs
//
// (c) 2002 Microsoft Press, by Philip Su
//
// This program demonstrates basic usage of the managed API
/////////////////////////////////////////////////////////////////////
using System;
using System.Drawing;
using System.Windows.Forms;
using Microsoft.Ink;
```

*(continued)*

**HelloManagedAPI.cs** *(continued)*

```csharp
public class HelloManagedAPI : Form
{
    private Panel          m_pnlInput;     // The inking surface
    private Button         m_btnReco;      // Recognize button
    private Label          m_labelReco;    // Recognition text
    private InkCollector   m_inkCollector; // Ink collector object

    static void Main()
    {
        Application.Run(new HelloManagedAPI());
    }

    public HelloManagedAPI()
    {
        SuspendLayout();

            // Create and place all of our controls
        m_pnlInput = new Panel();
        m_pnlInput.BorderStyle = BorderStyle.Fixed3D;
        m_pnlInput.Location = new Point(8, 8);
        m_pnlInput.Size = new Size(352, 192);

        m_btnReco = new Button();
        m_btnReco.Location = new Point(8, 204);
        m_btnReco.Size = new Size(100, 24);
        m_btnReco.Text = "Recognize";
        m_btnReco.Click += new EventHandler(BtnRecoClick);

        m_labelReco = new Label();
        m_labelReco.Location = new Point(120, 204);
        m_labelReco.Size = new Size(230, 24);
        m_labelReco.Text = "(press Recognize to interpret ink)";

            // Configure the form itself
        AutoScaleBaseSize = new Size(5, 13);
        ClientSize = new Size(368, 236);
        Controls.AddRange(new Control[] { m_pnlInput,
                                          m_btnReco,
                                          m_labelReco });
        FormBorderStyle = FormBorderStyle.FixedDialog;
        MaximizeBox = false;
        Text = "HelloManagedAPI";

        ResumeLayout(false);
```

```
            // Create a new InkCollector using m_pnlInput
            // for the collection area and turn on ink
            // collection.
        m_inkCollector = new InkCollector(m_pnlInput.Handle);
        m_inkCollector.Enabled = true;
    }


        // Handle the tap of the Recognize button
    private void BtnRecoClick(object sender, EventArgs e)
    {
        Strokes strokes = m_inkCollector.Ink.Strokes;

            // When no recognizers are installed, such as on a
            // non-Tablet PC computer, recognition attempts will
            // throw an exception.
        try
        {
                // Recognize the strokes from the ink collector's
                // ink object by using the ToString() method
            m_labelReco.Text = "Recognized text: \"" +
                            strokes.ToString() + "\"";
        }
        catch (Exception)
        {
            m_labelReco.Text = "No recognizers installed!";
        }
    }
}
```

The *HelloManagedAPI* class derives from Form to provide the application's main UI. In its construction, we create and size a few controls. More importantly, at the end of the constructor we create and enable an *InkCollector* object, which is one of the objects that capture digital ink in the managed API. The only other thing we do is respond to a tap on the Recognize button by converting all the strokes of the collected ink into a string. Don't worry if you don't quite understand all that's going on yet—HelloManagedAPI is here only to introduce you to some managed API fundamentals. You'll get a chance to explore the managed API in much greater depth in coming chapters.

## All That You Can't Leave Behind

Let's step back a second to take a high-level view of the managed API and its role alongside the rest of the SDK. In this section, we'll begin by discussing the design goals of the API as well as the features that are (and are not) meant to be addressed by it. Then we present the chief components and objects of the managed API and the interrelationships among them. Finally we dive into a brief survey of the distinctions between the core managed API and the Ink controls, which will help you decide which to use based on your needs.

The managed API is *the* essential component of the Tablet PC Platform SDK. All other components of the SDK are either variations or simplifications of the managed API and its capabilities. For instance, the COM automation API is simply a variation of the managed API, rigged to be automation compatible so that it can be used from both native C++ and Visual Basic 6. Similarly, the Ink controls are subsets of the managed API, packaged as controls to make them even easier to use.

You will see the influence of the managed API pervading all other components of the SDK because it is the fundamental way by which Tablet PC technologies are exposed. Various methods and properties will sound familiar even when using the Ink controls or the COM automation API because they have been shaped by the managed API design.

A solid understanding of the managed API is thus indispensable when using the SDK. This section presents the foundations of the managed API that will be useful to all Tablet PC developers, whether you end up using the Ink controls, the COM automation API, or the managed API itself.

## Design Goals of the API

The managed API was designed with several key goals in mind. In designing any API, there are always trade-offs to be made that favor some imagined usage scenarios over others. As with all first-version APIs, only time (and candid feedback from alert readers such as you!) will tell how closely the imagined usage scenarios match real needs.

That said, several of the design goals behind the managed API follow. Keep in mind that these are merely goals, and that the jury is still out on whether they have indeed been achieved!

- **Ease of use**   One of the key motivators behind the SDK being grounded in the managed API (as opposed to, say, the COM automation API) is its ease of use. There are certainly more developers that understand C++/COM and Visual Basic/automation than there are Microsoft .NET developers (at least at the time of writing this book!). However, Microsoft as a whole has bet very heavily on .NET as the future of Windows development. In similar style, the Tablet PC Platform SDK features the managed API as its core technology. Both C# and Visual Basic .NET are easier to use than traditional COM, as almost any developer who has tried both will attest.

- **Flexibility**   It is impossible, particularly in designing the first version of an API, to foresee all the uses to which developers will put an API. Recognizing this, the API has been developed in a way that permits a bit of flexibility in what can be done with it. There are numerous ways in which the API enables you to control its assortment of features. However, it is likely that you will find certain aspects of the API not flexible enough, especially if your usage scenarios differ greatly from those that the API's designers imagined. This book will endeavor to provide you with knowledge of how to work around some of these limitations.

- **Performance**   As always, there are many difficult trade-offs that can be made in the arena of performance. Designers of the managed API definitely sought to optimize some scenarios in favor of others. Perhaps the most important performance goal that drove the API's development is that digital ink should be as close to physical ink as possible in both its capture and its appearance. API performance characteristics and their implications are discussed in detail in Chapter 9.

## The Prime Directive

The goal of the SDK in general, and of the managed API in particular, can be summarized in two words: digital ink. Enabling digital ink and its many scenarios is the primary driver behind the managed API's design. One of the key differentiators between the Tablet PC and the tablet-like devices that came before it is that the Tablet PC experience is focused around the intelligent use of digital ink. Other devices and their respective SDKs have largely aimed at supporting pens as a means of text entry. However, the Tablet PC is all about digital ink. When someone mentions the Tablet PC Platform SDK or the managed API, you should think digital ink.

## What's Covered by the Managed API

There are many aspects of Tablet PCs and the Tablet PC way of life that could have been addressed by the managed API. The managed API distills from all these possibilities three main categories of Tablet PC features, all related to digital ink. In logical order, these are

- **Capture**   Digital ink must be captured before it can be stored or put to other use. Features related to the capture and concurrent display of ink are conceptually bundled together as the Tablet Input API, which works with hardware drivers to collect digital ink and gestures. It dynamically renders ink as it's drawn by the user, supports basic access to pen buttons and pen tips, and provides notification of pen events.

- **Manipulation** Once digital ink has been captured, you may wish to do a variety of things with it. Common ink manipulation features supporting the structure, appearance, and storage of ink are grouped in the Ink Data Management API. This API handles ink strokes and their properties (for example, width, shape, and color), and loads, saves, and renders ink.

- **Interpretation** Digital ink also has an important semantic significance. When a user writes on the Tablet PC, it is often useful to know what was written so that the underlying intended text or gesture can be used as well. Algorithms that interpret digital ink are contained in the Ink Recognition API, which accepts biases when making the interpretation, based on suggestions by the application.

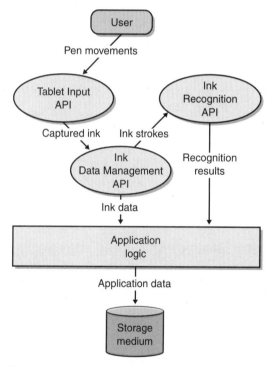

**Figure 3-9** Data flow between the Tablet Input API, Ink Data Management API, and Ink Recognition API. It is possible to omit either (or both) the Tablet Input API or the Ink Recognition API from a particular application.

## What's Not Covered by the Managed API

An equally important consideration when using the managed API is the set of features that are *not* supported. Although you may take the omission of some of these features for granted, others may surprise you. Several features explicitly not addressed by the managed API are

- **Hardware features**   Does this Tablet PC have special buttons on the side meant to perform Tablet-specific functions? What type of pen and screen technology is being used? Is the pen in its holster? Does this Tablet have a built-in keyboard? None of these questions is addressed by the managed API, which gives very little access to hardware-specific information.

- **Document model**   Collections of ink invariably have semantic structure or meaning. For instance, maybe your application is Super-Doodle, in which case the digital ink is most likely a series of small drawings. Or perhaps you're developing PowerJot, in which the user writes words and sentences. The managed API does not support (or alternatively, enforce) a particular document model. Although the API supports recognition of ink as text, there isn't much in the API that facilitates the development of semantically structured documents. Depending on your expectations, this may be a boon or an unpleasant surprise.

> **Note**   Semantically structured hierarchical document models are prevalent in the SDK world. For instance, Microsoft Word's object model supports manipulations of pages, paragraphs, and lines (all semantic or hierarchical constructs) in addition to just supporting characters. Similarly, the Document Object Model (DOM) from HTML and XML imposes a specific hierarchical structure to its documents. In contrast, the Tablet PC Platform SDK managed API provides only a flat view of digital ink, in which you have ink strokes with no semantic relationships with one another.

- **Ink storage and organization**   The managed API does not enforce the method by which digital ink is to be stored. You may choose to store ink data within the existing file format of your application on disk or in any other inventive place you devise. What the

API provides is the ability to save ink to and restore ink from a binary stream. In similar fashion, the API does not provide an automatic way to organize or search ink that has been captured and stored.

- **Non-ink data types**   This is probably obvious but bears calling out explicitly. There are no provisions for the handling or storage of non-ink objects natively by the managed API, although it does allow simple association of arbitrary data with ink. So if your application's document requires support for other data types (for instance, text or images), you'll have to handle that yourself. This restriction does not apply to the Ink controls, which do indeed support text or images in a limited manner.

- **Ink user interface**   Although the SDK documentation makes many suggestions about the proper design of ink-based user interfaces, the managed API often does not directly support the suggested designs. This poses a particular predicament for developers. In the upcoming chapters, we have tried to address as many of these suggestions as possible so that the effects of these omissions are minimized. Here are two of the ink user interface elements missing from the API:

  - ❏ **Selection feedback and heuristics**   There is no support for the recommended selection feedback of both the area being selected and the selected ink. An example of the desired feedback is shown in Figure 3-10. If you want to render the recommended selection feedback, you'll have to implement your own way of manually achieving the same effect. Fortunately, your trusty authors have detailed how this can be done via samples in the next two chapters.

  - ❏ **Correcting misrecognition**   If your application supports recognition of ink into text, you may also want to provide a way for the user to correct the text when it's misrecognized. The Tablet Input Panel and Windows Journal provide the recommended way of doing this by means of a little green widget. This widget, shaped like an inverted "L", appears when you hover the cursor over text in the Tablet Input Panel. Tapping the widget reveals a droplist containing alternative interpretations of recognized ink. The managed API, however, does not provide a way for you to programmatically display the correction widget in your own application.

**Figure 3-10**   The suggested selection feedback includes a dotted trail to indicate the user's path of selection, as well as glowing ink to show what's been selected.

## Managed API Object Survey

Now that you understand the design of the managed API and the basic grouping of its features, you're ready to survey in more detail the objects that are part of the managed API. Figure 3-11 shows where various objects in the managed API are conceptually grouped. Some objects are used in more than one group, so they are represented as straddling the groups in which they are used. The managed API contains many more objects than are shown in the figure, which shows only the key objects belonging to each group.

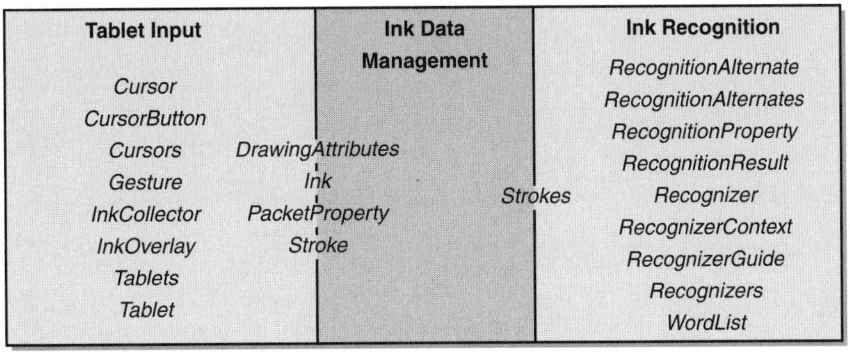

| Tablet Input | Ink Data Management | Ink Recognition |
|---|---|---|
| Cursor | | RecognitionAlternate |
| CursorButton | | RecognitionAlternates |
| Cursors | DrawingAttributes | RecognitionProperty |
| Gesture | Ink | RecognitionResult |
| InkCollector | PacketProperty | Strokes · Recognizer |
| InkOverlay | Stroke | RecognizerContext |
| Tablets | | RecognizerGuide |
| Tablet | | Recognizers |
| | | WordList |

**Figure 3-11**   Objects in the managed API grouped into the main categories in which they are used.

In the following sections we'll introduce the most frequently used objects from the Tablet Input, Ink Data Management, and Ink Recognition APIs.

### Tablet Input API

The *InkCollector* and *InkOverlay* objects, as key components of the Tablet Input API, facilitate the capture and live rendering of digital ink as it is entered by the user. They do this by communicating directly with the hardware input drivers and abstracting hardware-generated activity into various events. The application responds to these events by prescribing a course of action to be taken, whether it be rendering a newly captured point, responding to a user's pen gesture, or even ignoring the event. A typical (and greatly simplified) Tablet Input API usage timeline is shown in Figure 3-12.

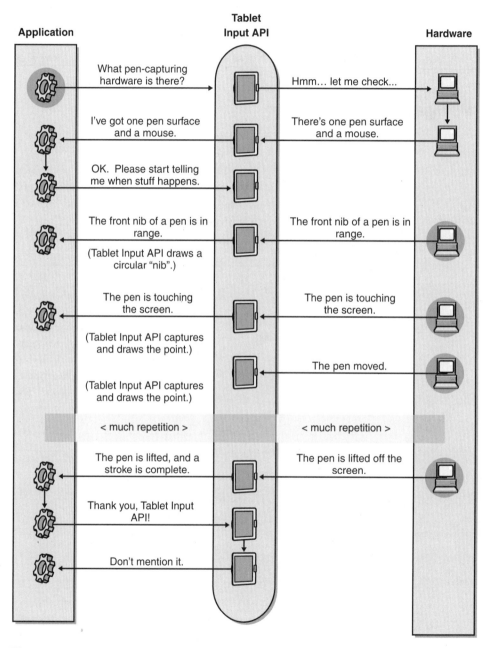

**Figure 3-12**    A sample timeline of an interaction with the Tablet Input API

Objects in the Tablet Input API fall into two domains: hardware-related objects and ink-capturing objects. Chapter 5 discusses these objects and their events in depth, but for now we'll just introduce them in Table 3-1 and Table 3-2 so you get a feel for what's available.

**Table 3-1   Hardware-Related Objects in the Tablet Input API**

| Object | Description |
| --- | --- |
| *Tablet* | The naming of this object is a somewhat confusing and unfortunate holdover from calling pen-sensitive digitizer pads "tablets." The *Tablet* object represents a two-dimensional hardware input device, such as a mouse, a touch pad, a digitizer tablet, or the pen-sensitive screen on a Tablet PC. You can query a *Tablet* object to determine the characteristics and capabilities of the hardware it represents. |
| *Tablets* | A collection of *Tablet* objects. Because a *Tablet* object represents a hardware input device, a system can easily have multiple *Tablet* objects, each representing a different device. In addition to supporting enumeration, the *Tablets* collection also lets you determine which capabilities are supported by all devices on the system. |
| *Cursor* | This is another easily misunderstood name in the API. The *Cursor* object represents the conceptual tip of a pen, not the arrow that moves around the screen as you move your mouse. To add to the blurring of terminologies, mice and other input devices also have *Cursor* objects representing them. The *Cursor* object represents their locus of interaction. Remember—the *Cursor* object is *not* the visual representation of a pen's tip on screen! |
| *Cursors* | A collection of *Cursor* objects. Some pens may have multiple *Cursor* objects associated with them (like the nib and eraser ends of a pen). Because mice and other input devices also have *Cursor* representatives, a computer can easily have three or more *Cursor* objects. |

**Table 3-2   Ink-Capturing Objects in the Tablet Input API**

| Object | Description |
| --- | --- |
| InkCollector | The fundamental object used to collect and render ink as it is being entered by the user. *InkCollector* fires events to your application as they happen and also packages *Cursor* movements into ink strokes for you. You can tell it what events and what sorts of data you're interested in receiving, as well as whether you want it to paint ongoing ink strokes as they are collected. |
| *InkOverlay* | A superset of *InkCollector* that adds selecting and erasing of the ink that's been captured. For many applications, *InkOverlay* will be the object of choice to use because its implementation of selection-related features is a real time-saver. |

Given the objects listed in Table 3-1, we can imagine what you'd do with the Tablet Input API. You might start by investigating the *Tablets* object to determine what hardware capabilities are available. You'd then create an *InkOverlay* or *InkCollector*, asking it to capture the user's ink strokes while simultaneously rendering them on screen. As the *InkOverlay* or *InkCollector* sends you more events, you might vary its behavior depending on the *Cursor* being used (for instance, perhaps you've decided that the front end of the pen will write ink while the back end will erase). These examples are typical of how an application would use the Tablet Input API.

## Ink Data Management API

Informally referred to as the Ink API, the Ink Data Management API provides access to the bulk of ink-related activities supported by the Tablet PC Platform. This API assists in such essential actions as changing ink strokes and their properties, merging and splitting strokes, rendering ink, and persisting ink. Surprisingly, there are relatively few objects that belong to this core portion of the managed API. However, don't let their numbers fool you—the few objects in the Ink Data Management API are loaded with features!

Several objects belonging to this API are listed in Table 3-3. Note that some of the objects listed may also be used as part of the Tablet Input API or the Ink Recognition API, but the Ink Data Management API is considered to be their home.

**Table 3-3  Several Objects from the Ink Data Management API**

| Object | Description |
| --- | --- |
| *Ink* | The mother of all ink-related activity, the *Ink* object is the one indispensable part of any Tablet PC programmer's arsenal. All digital ink lives within *Ink* objects, which support a myriad of methods to add and remove ink strokes to and from them. In addition, a key function of *Ink* objects is to support several hit detection methodologies to determine whether ink has been hit. Finally, *Ink* objects can save and load themselves from both binary streams and the clipboard. |
| *Stroke* | The *Stroke* object provides access to a single ink stroke within an Ink object. One of its primary uses is to obtain detailed point-level data about a particular ink stroke, such as its length or pressure. It also supports a small subset of behaviors normally available on an *Ink* object. |

**Table 3-3   Several Objects from the Ink Data Management API**   *(continued)*

| Object | Description |
|---|---|
| *Strokes* | A collection of *Stroke* objects that implement an eclectic subset of the functionality available through the *Ink* object. One thing to remember when working with a *Strokes* object is that it is only a collection of references to ink strokes contained within some *Ink* object. As a consequence, the object's strokes don't have a life of their own independent of the *Ink* object to which they belong. |
| *DrawingAttributes* | Each *Stroke* object allows for the setting of its *DrawingAttributes*, which determines the visual appearance of the ink stroke when drawn on screen. Major characteristics of interest include *Color*, *Transparency*, *Width*, and *Antialiased*, but there are many other tweaks that can be made to the appearance of *Stroke* objects. |

Although much of the API is fairly straightforward, there are several important pitfalls to avoid when using Ink and Stroke objects. Much more will be said about the Ink Data Management API in Chapter 6.

# Ink Recognition API

The final pillar of the managed API is the Ink Recognition API, which encapsulates technology originating from Microsoft's ink recognition team. The fundamental purpose of the Ink Recognition API is to suggest possible textual interpretations of written digital ink. Keeping in line with the managed API's flat view of ink, the Ink Recognition API does not provide interpretations regarding the semantic structure of ink, such as whether a set of ink is a drawing or whether a group of ink appears to be a paragraph. Instead, its only function is to suggest what words the writer might have intended when given some ink.

## Stay On Target...Stay On Target...

The Ink Recognition API is unique in that language-specific recognition engines are provided for use in different countries. This creates a situation in which it's hard to discuss the accuracy of the Ink Recognition API in general. Instead, it's only meaningful to discuss the accuracy of any particular language's recognizer exposed via the Ink Recognition API.

Compared with other existing technologies, the Tablet PC Platform's English recognizer is fairly accurate when analyzing cursive English.

There are quite a few objects that belong in the Ink Recognition API. Those most often used are described in Table 3-4.

**Table 3-4  The Most Frequently Used Objects in the Ink Recognition API**

| Object | Description |
| --- | --- |
| *Recognizer* | The *Recognizer* object represents a particular recognition engine installed on the user's machine. Recognition engines may support one or more languages and may also vary in the features they support. |
| *RecognizerContext* | *RecognizerContext* objects are the usual means by which you interact with recognition engines to perform ink recognition. An instance of this object is created each time you want ink to be recognized, and any hints about the likely content of the ink are set to give the recognizer its context. When all available information has been given to the *RecognizerContext*, a call to its *Recognize* method performs the recognition. |
| *RecognitionResult* | Results from performing recognition are returned in this object. Its primary use is to provide the text that was recognized as well as possible alternative interpretations of the ink. |

# Ink Control Comparison with Managed API

Now that you understand the design goals of the API as well as what it does and does not provide, you may be wondering whether one of the Ink controls might be suitable for your application. Fear not—help is on the way in the form of a stress-free flowchart tailored to aid your decision making (Figure 3-13). The controls are discussed in more detail in Chapter 8, but for now their basic features are contrasted with the managed API in Table 3-5.

A key point when deciding whether to use the managed API or the Ink controls is that the decision is not truly either/or. The Ink controls are usable from managed code and indeed expose portions of the managed API. So in a sense the question is really whether an Ink control supplies all the features and flexibility that you need. If not, the managed API usually offers a more direct way to implement your design.

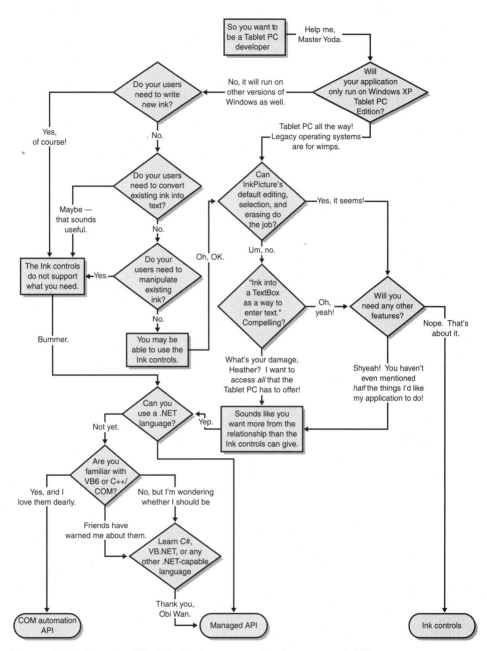

**Figure 3-13**   The simplified choice between using the managed API or the Ink controls is depicted by a set of boxes and arrows.

**Table 3-5**   **Differences Between Controls and the Managed API**

| Function | Managed API | InkEdit Control | InkPicture Control |
|---|---|---|---|
| Captures ink | ✓ | ✓* | ✓* |
| Recognizes ink | ✓ | ✓* | |
| Allows editing of ink appearance | ✓ | ✓* | ✓* |
| Natively supports erasing | ✓ | | ✓* |
| Accepts input from arbitrary window | ✓ | | |
| Character-based text editing | | ✓ | |
| Automatic conversion of ink to text | | ✓ | |
| Maps gestures to text (space, return, backspace) | | ✓ | |
| Scales ink to match text font height | | ✓ | |
| Handles images | | | ✓ |

\* Available only when running on Windows XP Tablet PC Edition.

For most features involving digital ink, you'll find that the managed API provides the power and flexibility required to build applications for the Tablet PC. However, as shown in Figure 3-13 and Table 3-5, the Ink controls may be ideal if your needs match well with the particular usage scenarios they were designed to address. The Ink controls will be covered in more depth in Chapter 7.

# Welcome to the Great Adventure

You've bought a Tablet PC and a digitizer pad for easy desktop development. You've been using Visual Studio .NET and are familiar with C#, Visual Basic .NET, or C++/COM. You've bought this book and installed the Tablet PC Platform SDK. You've even built and run some of the SDK sample applications to verify your installation. How much more ready could you be?

The real excitement begins in the next chapters. Armed with the SDK, this book, and your cleverness, you'll conquer the world of pen-based and ink-based computing with ease. Together, we'll explore the tips, avoid the pitfalls, and develop the software that will define the Tablet PC revolution!

# 4

# Tablet PC Platform SDK: Tablet Input

The previous chapter illustrated how the Tablet PC platform is divided into three logical pieces: tablet input, ink data management, and ink recognition. This chapter will take a close look at the tablet input piece of the platform from an architectural as well as a programmatic standpoint.

We'll begin by learning about how physical pen strokes become useful input to both tablet-aware and tablet-unaware applications. Then we'll see how to use the Tablet PC Platform SDK to enumerate, introspect, and—most important—capture input from tablet devices. At the end of the chapter, some best practice methods to help yield the best Tablet PC user experience will be discussed.

## Sample Applications

Various sample applications with source code are provided to demonstrate the practical application of concepts as they are presented. Each application was designed to focus only on what's necessary to illustrate relevant material—other aspects of the applications were intentionally kept minimal for clarity's sake. Considerable effort has been put into testing the applications and making sure that they follow correct usage of the Tablet PC Platform SDK, though in the spirit of software design it's always possible for a bug to creep in. You certainly don't have to be prepared to call the fire department if you copy and paste code from this book into your own application, but please don't call "Mr. T's House of SmackDown!" if an unexpected "feature" crops up during a demo of your app to your boss.

# Capturing Input from the Pen

Before we cover how to write applications that receive pen input from the tablet digitizer, let's take a look at the software that enables us to harness the power of the pen.

> **Note**    This section can be considered optional reading because one doesn't really need to know the internals of tablet input to get inking in an application. You can therefore skip ahead to the section titled "Platform SDK Support for Tablet Input" if you're not interested in how things work, though we do hope you stick around here because we think it's interesting stuff.

The Tablet PC's tablet input subsystem refers to the logical pieces of software that transfer and transform the data generated from a tablet digitizer into the input an application can make use of. Exactly what kind of input is it that an application can make use of? Chapter 2 gives us a good idea of the experience we want to provide for a Tablet PC user, so let's see whether we can come up with some requirements here that might help us better understand the functions of the input subsystem.

## Requirement #1—Mouse Emulation

As you know by now, all tablet-unaware Microsoft Windows XP–compatible applications are fully supported under Windows XP Tablet PC Edition—the pen behaves like a mouse in these cases. It also happens that mouse input is valuable to tablet-aware applications—standard Windows behaviors, controls, and the like are already driven by the mouse, so it's convenient to be able to leverage this functionality for the pen. And of course, it's likely that a physical mouse device will be used to drive the application because many Tablet PCs will have integrated mouse hardware such as a touch pad or mini-trackball.

> **Note**    We predict that someday all mouse input handling in Windows will also become tablet input–enabled. This will pave the way for pen-specific behaviors in all areas of the Windows user interface.

Because most applications rely heavily on mouse input, our first requirement of the input subsystem is that it be able to map pen input to mouse input—a process we'll refer to as *mouse emulation*. Both left-mouse and right-mouse buttons should be supported for compatibility.

## Requirement #2—Digital Ink

Tablet-enabled applications often accept user input in the form of digital ink, which can be added to a document or recognized into a command. Capturing ink from the pen is one of the most important aspects of realizing an electronic paper paradigm. As such, digital ink must mirror physical ink as closely as possible to provide the most natural and unobtrusive end-user experience. From a user's perspective, ink should "just work" on a Tablet PC and be practically indistinguishable in behavior from physical ink. We can therefore impose the following sub-requirements on a system that's used to capture digital ink:

- **Performance**   Ink should appear to be flowing directly out of the tip of the pen in real time and never lagging behind. This requires that the time between sampling the position of the pen and rendering ink on screen be imperceptible to an average user.

- **Accuracy**   Ink should follow the exact path of the pen as the pen moves. This requires that the frequency and resolution at which data is captured should result in the digital ink appearing to be smooth in shape to an average user. And as you'll see later, using data captured at higher frequency and resolution also helps improve handwriting and gesture recognition results.

- **Robust data capture**   Ink should reflect as much of the physical handling that the pen is subjected to as possible. This requires that not only the pen position be sampled, but that support for sampling of pen tip pressure, the angle between the pen and tablet surface, the rotation of the pen body, and the like should also be provided.

In the initial version of the Tablet PC Platform, normal pressure is the only property besides $X$ and $Y$ position that the rendering of ink can reflect. However, future versions of the Tablet PC Platform will likely take more properties into account.

It is entirely possible for you to custom draw ink if you wish to have more properties taken into account, as we'll learn in Chapter 5. In the majority of cases, we think $x$, $y$, and pressure yield incredible results.

# Requirement #3—Pen-Based Actions

Pen-specific actions like press-and-hold, using the top-of-pen eraser, and pressing pen buttons can become powerful means to streamline the user model of a tablet-aware application. In addition, employing pen input for means other than digital ink is useful because pen-specific properties can enhance existing user interface behaviors. For example, pen rotation could be used to rotate a selection while it's being dragged, or pen pressure could be used to determine how large an erasing area should be used for an eraser tool. Distinguishing between the user tapping the pen and the user dragging it is therefore important functionality.

> **Note** Pen-specific actions should not be confused with ink-based gestures such as scratchout, up arrow, and "curlique". Pen actions—which are formally known as *system gestures*—don't use ink and don't define any application behavior. They are on a par with mouse actions such as click and drag.

Although the tablet hardware's device driver can easily report top-of-pen use (called *pen inversion*) and pen button presses, detecting press-and-hold and associated actions such as tap and drag is a nontrivial algorithm that arguably falls outside the driver's scope; this algorithm is best centralized so that any tablet device can use it.

## Summing Up the Requirements

We have now specified that the input system must be able to transform raw pen movement into mouse input (supporting left-mouse and right-mouse button emulation), provide realistic digital ink, and detect higher-level pen-based actions (press-and-hold, pen inversion, pen button presses, and tap versus drag). The Tablet PC Platform's tablet input subsystem (which we'll start referring to as "the TIS" for brevity) provides all this and more.

# Anatomy of the Tablet PC's Tablet Input Subsystem

An architectural view of the TIS is outlined in Figures 4-1 and 4-2. There are two main configurations under which the subsystem runs: the first is with Windows XP Tablet PC Edition, and the second is with a Windows 2000–based or Windows XP–based operating system with the Tablet PC runtime libraries installed.

We'll be focusing primarily on the subsystem as it runs on Windows XP Tablet PC Edition because it's a superset of the Tablet PC runtime. But don't worry; any differences between the two configurations will be pointed out as they arise.

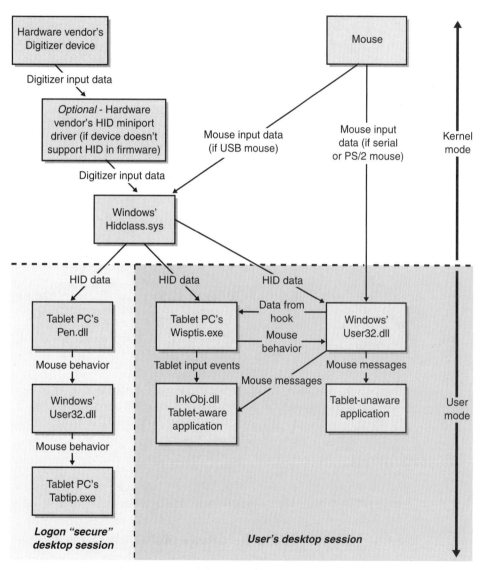

**Figure 4-1**   The Tablet PC tablet input subsystem architecture, shown running on Windows XP Tablet PC Edition

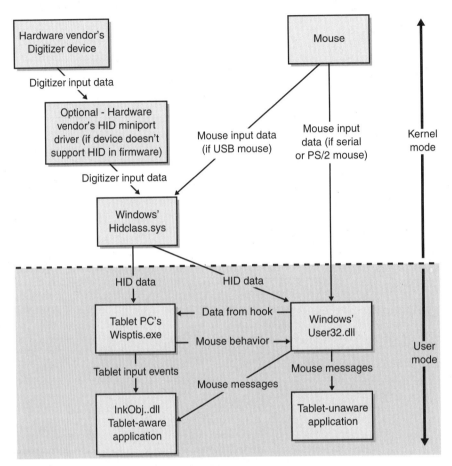

**Figure 4-2**   The Tablet PC tablet input subsystem architecture, shown running as the Tablet PC runtime libraries on a Windows-based operating system

## Tablet Hardware

In Chapter 1, the essence of a Tablet PC was identified as a portable PC combined with a digitizer integrated with the screen, driven by Windows XP Tablet PC Edition. A digitizer (sometimes ambiguously referred to as just a *tablet*) in the Tablet PC Platform's view is a device that provides user input to a computer via a pointer on a flat rectangular surface. The device is able to sample the *X* and *Y* position of the pointer at regular time intervals and determine whether the pointer is *active*—typically, this means whether the pointer is touching the tablet's surface. In most cases, the pointer is a pen stylus, although the Tablet PC Platform also recognizes a mouse as a tablet device. Indeed, a mouse is an example of a tablet device—it reports *X* and *Y* position as well as whether the pointer is active.

> **Note**    Placing the pointer tip on the digitizer surface is called making the pointer *active*. A synonym for active is *down*.

## Chock-full of HID-y Goodness

Before the days of Tablet PC, a low-level standard already existed that directly facilitated getting input from a tablet device. Known as HID (short for Human Interface Device), the specification was initially developed to standardize communication to USB hardware such as keyboards, mice, joysticks, tablets, and just about any other device we can use to generate input for using a computer. The tablet input subsystem exclusively leverages HID devices for tablet input, and as such, the digitizers on Tablet PCs (even ones integrated with the video display) are either USB-based and HID-compliant via firmware or come supplied with a miniport driver emulating a HID interface.

> **Note**    At the time of this writing, the full HID specification can be found at the USB Implementers Forum Web site, at *http://www.usb.org/ developers/hidpage.html*, under the heading "Device Class Definition for Human Interface Devices (HID)."

### WinTab

Some alert readers may be aware of another standard tablet input API called WinTab (*http://www.pointing.com/WINTAB.HTM*). It was discovered during the development of the TIS that using WinTab would prove problematic—WinTab's API design puts all responsibility for functional conformance on the shoulders of the driver's implementers (third parties). Some already released WinTab drivers' behavior deviated slightly from the spec, so it became difficult or impossible for the TIS to support WinTab in a generic way. Contrast this with the HID model in which the device or device driver has to specify only supported functionality (named *usages*) and Windows takes care of the API nuances. It was therefore decided that HID devices were the better way to go.

The HID driver, like most other Windows XP drivers, runs at the kernel level, constantly acquiring data from the tablet device and packaging it into HID format if it needs to. This allows the TIS to read input data from the device in a generic fashion.

## The Center of the TIS Universe: Wisptis.exe

Arguably the most interesting piece in both Figures 4-1 and 4-2 is a process called Wisptis.exe because it's pretty much the heart and soul of the TIS. It acts like a hub between the HID driver of tablet hardware and applications, and it turns out to be responsible for realizing most of the requirements of the input system we defined earlier in the chapter. The Wisptis process performs the retrieval of input from the tablet devices, mouse emulation, detection of pen-based actions, and the dispatching of events to tablet-aware applications.

---

### Why Wisptis.exe?

Wisptis.exe refers to "WISP TIS." WISP (Windows Ink Services for Pen) was the former name for the Tablet PC Platform, and TIS—well, hopefully at this point in the chapter you know what that means.

---

> **Note**    Multiple tablet devices may be installed and used at the same time, a feature fully supported by the TIS. This is actually quite a common occurrence because, as we now know, the mouse is considered a tablet device, so if your Tablet PC has an integrated touchpad or is ever docked in a desktop scenario, or if you've attached an external tablet to your desktop machine, from the TIS perspective there will be at least two tablet devices installed.

### Getting Input from the Driver

Input is received from the digitizer via the HID driver and from the mouse via a low-level mouse hook. Data received from the digitizer is used for performing mouse emulation and detecting pen-based actions.

It's interesting to note that even though the mouse is viewed as a tablet device and a USB mouse uses a HID driver to communicate with Windows, the

TIS does *not* get mouse data from the HID driver. Why? There are a couple of reasons. First, the mouse might not be USB-based (serial and PS/2 mice are still common) and a generic solution to reading mouse input is desirable; second, User32.dll opens the mouse driver exclusively, making it impossible for the TIS to get at the mouse directly. That's why the TIS gets the mouse input data from User32.dll via a low-level hook.

You might be thinking that a cleaner architectural model would be to integrate tablet support directly into User32.dll, and we'd tend to agree with you. However, a design goal of the TIS (and a practical one at that) was to merely augment the existing OS as much as possible, rather than "invade" it with new code. Additionally, we'll soon see that User32's existing message-based input architecture doesn't lend itself too well to tablet input.

## Performing Mouse Emulation

The mouse cursor is controlled by the pen through one of two sets of mappings. The first set is used when the press-and-hold option (see Chapter 2) is disabled. Table 4-1 lists which pen actions will result in what mouse actions.

**Table 4-1   A Simple Mapping of Pen Actions to Mouse Actions to Perform Mouse Emulation**

| User Pen Action | Resulting Mouse Action |
| --- | --- |
| In-air pen movement | Mouse movement with no buttons pressed, typically matching the pen tip location but using a hover filter |
| Pen touches digitizer with no barrel buttons pressed | Mouse left button pressed |
| Pen touches digitizer with barrel button pressed | Mouse right button pressed |
| Pen moves across digitizer's surface | Mouse movement with left or right button pressed, depends on which mouse button was determined to be pressed upon pen's contact with digitizer; movement matches pen tip location exactly |
| Pen lifted from digitizer | Mouse left or right button released, depends on which mouse button was determined to be pressed upon pen's contact with digitizer |

This works pretty well in practice, with one small exception. Getting Tool-Tips to pop up can be pretty tough because the mouse cursor has to be completely still when hovering over, say, a toolbar button. Most people have a slight sway to the pen when they try to hold it still, so getting the mouse cursor to be motionless will typically require too much effort. Thus, a requirement for a *hover filter* is imposed, whose purpose is to ignore small changes in pen movement while the pen is in the air. Chapter 2 covers the hovering problem in more detail.

The second set of mappings is used when the press-and-hold option is enabled; observe that Table 4-2 is a little more complex than Table 4-1.

**Table 4-2    The Mapping of Higher-Level Pen Actions to Mouse Actions to Perform Mouse Emulation when Press-and-Hold Is Active**

| Pen Action | Mouse Action |
| --- | --- |
| In-air pen movement | Mouse movement with no buttons pressed, typically matching the pen tip location but using a hover filter |
| Pen taps the digitizer | Mouse left button pressed, mouse left button released |
| Pen held down on the digitizer within press-and-hold time window and then pen lifted | Mouse right button pressed, mouse right button released |
| Pen held down on the digitizer and pen starts to move | Mouse left button pressed |
| Pen held down on the digitizer within press-and-hold time window and pen starts to move | Mouse right button pressed |
| Pen held down on the digitizer beyond press-and-hold time-out | Mouse left button pressed |
| Pen moves across digitizer's surface while held down | Mouse movement with left or right button pressed, depends on which mouse button was determined to be pressed upon pen's contact with digitizer; movement matches pen tip location exactly |
| Pen lifted from digitizer | Mouse left or right button released, depends on which mouse button was determined to be pressed upon pen's contact with digitizer |

Notice how we need to trigger mouse actions on pen actions such as press-and-hold, tap, and drag. This is because when the pen initially touches the digitizer, the fact that press-and-hold is enabled means we don't yet know whether the user wants to perform a left button or a right button operation. You might think that the left mouse button can always get pressed on pen down, and when a press-and-hold occurs the left button would get released immediately, followed by a right button down, but that won't work well at all. Consider the following example: using everyone's favorite accessory, Notepad, select some text and right click it with the mouse. Notice how the selection stays intact and a context menu appears. If we use the "pen touching the digitizer always causes a left button down" method, whenever the user performs a press-and-hold it will cause a mouse left click followed by a right button down. Try doing those actions with the selection in Notepad. You'll see that the selection gets dismissed on the left click, and the right click displays the context menu with different items enabled—definitely not desirable behavior.

Detecting press-and-hold, tap versus drag, and hover filtering brings us to the next bit of functionality Wisptis.exe provides: detection of pen-based actions.

## Detecting Pen-Based Actions

One of the things that makes a Tablet PC so appealing is its emphasis on *natural computing*—that is, taking human physiology into account for its input model. It's more natural for most people to use a pen than a mouse, as was discussed in Chapter 2.

Contrasting the pen with the mouse brings up an interesting difference: pens tend to be much "noisier" with their data. That's not really the correct term, as it implies low accuracy of data capture, but what's being referred to is how a pen generates much more subtle variance in movement than a mouse does because of the human factor. A mouse is normally at rest and gets interrupted from that state when we move it, whereas a pen that's held is at the mercy of our central nervous system's accuracy. To improve the Tablet PC user experience, therefore, it's a good idea for certain pen input to be filtered a little.

> **Note**    Consider this author's observation: the difficulty of making ToolTips appear is exponentially proportional to the amount of caffeine ingested.

Figure 4-3 is a state diagram of how the detection of pen-based actions occurs. The boxes represent events that should be both mapped to mouse input and sent to tablet-aware applications.

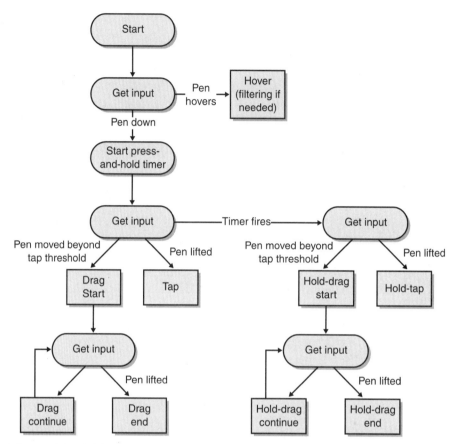

**Figure 4-3** A high-level state diagram illustrating how pen-based actions are detected

The precise algorithms for determining pen hovering and tap versus drag won't be covered here because they're a little out of this book's scope.

## Dispatching Events

It's not helpful if Wisptis.exe can determine all sorts of useful pen and mouse input but can't tell anybody about it. Luckily for us, the last key function Wisptis.exe performs is client notification of input events for both mouse and tablet input.

Mouse input is easy enough to send to applications because User32.dll provides a convenient function named *SendInput* to automate mouse action. Tablet input, on the other hand, needs a more efficient mechanism because there's typically so much data to send. Remember that in order to have great ink, the frequency of data sampling must be high and pen handling such as pressure and tilt should be captured if possible. Both of these variables raise the required data throughput of tablet input data across processes substantially. The Windows mouse message architecture would not be able to efficiently handle the data throughput requirements of tablet input because of both the high amount of data per message and its sampling frequency. Realistically behaving ink needs to be responsive and accurate; therefore, another mechanism must be used.

Wisptis.exe communicates tablet input events to a tablet-aware application using RPC (remote procedure) calls and a shared-memory queue. A DLL running in the app's process space, InkObj.dll, receives notifications from Wisptis.exe that events are occurring, reads them from the shared-memory queue, and dispatches them to the appropriate handler in the tablet-aware app. Figure 4-4 illustrates the communication of data between Wisptis.exe and a tablet-aware application.

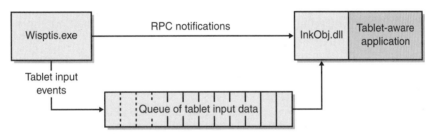

**Figure 4-4**   Wisptis.exe communicates tablet input data to a tablet-aware application through a queue to avoid losing any data.

Although tablet-unaware applications receive mouse events, it's interesting to note that tablet-aware applications receive *both* mouse events and tablet input events. The reason for this is simple: backward compatibility. Many existing Windows technologies rely only on mouse messages—OLE drag and drop, windowless controls, and even setting the mouse cursor properly all require mouse input. We'll cover some interesting side effects of receiving two sets of events later in the chapter.

## Making Sense of It All

Wisptis.exe sure does a lot of stuff, doesn't it? To help illustrate what's going on, the following pseudocode highlights the main functionality of Wisptis.exe.

```
// WISPTIS.EXE Pseudocode
while (true)
{
    foreach (tablet in globalTabletList)
    {
        // First, get raw pen input (down, move, up)
```

*(continued)*

```
input = GetInputDataFromHID(tablet);
if (no input retrieved)
    continue;

// See if the input is for a tablet-aware app. If
// it is, dispatch it to the app's instance of InkObj.dll.
app = GetTargetedApplication(input);
if (app is tablet-aware)
    DispatchInputEventToQueue(app, input);

// Now see if a higher-level action can be detected
penAction = GetPenBasedAction(input, pressAndHoldMode);
if (no penAction detected yet)
    continue;

// See if action is for a tablet-aware app. If
// it is, dispatch it to the app's instance of InkObj.dll.
if (app is tablet-aware)
    DispatchInputEventToQueue(app, penAction);

// Map pen action to mouse action. User32.dll will do
// the "hard stuff" as far as targeting windows, posting
// messages to queues, etc.
mouseAction = MapPenActionToMouseAction(penAction);
DispatchMouseEvents(mouseAction);
    }
}
```

In essence, the data that is retrieved from the HID driver is used to determine whether the targeted application is tablet aware. If the application is tablet aware, the data is dispatched to it. The data is then processed by some code to detect pen-based actions, and if an action is detected the pen action is then dispatched to the targeted tablet-aware application, if there is one. Finally, the corresponding mouse behavior is performed.

## Winlogon Desktop Support

*The following applies only to Windows XP Tablet PC Edition.* Notice how the diagram in Figure 4-1 is divided into left and right portions—this logical division represents the *Winlogon "secure" desktop* and the *Application desktop*. The Winlogon desktop is the one you see at the Windows XP login screen; it operates at a high security level. When the Winlogon desktop is active (for example, the user is logging in or is unlocking his or her machine), the Tablet PC Input Panel (TIP) can be used to enter credentials. Because the Wisptis.exe process executes only in a user's session, mouse emulation is then needed to be able to use the

TIP. A small DLL file, named Tpgwlnot.dll, executes in the Winlogon.exe process and performs that mouse emulation, though only with basic functionality—no pen-based actions are detected. Tpgwlnot.dll also launches Wisptis.exe when a user first logs on and restarts it if needed (for example, Wisptis.exe terminates because the user ends the process or an exception occurs).

## What About Ink?

So far, everything we've covered in the Tablet PC's TIS has met the requirements of the input system we defined, except for one thing: real-time ink! Some of the pieces are there—such as good data capture and throughput—but rendering and storing the strokes in memory aren't. The Tablet PC Platform supports this, though not as part of the TIS. Instead, that functionality lies in the domain of ink data management, mostly the subject of the next two chapters.

Now that we conceptually understand what the tablet input subsystem does, let's actually use it to do something, shall we? It's time to write some code!

# Platform SDK Support for Tablet Input

There are two key classes in the Tablet PC managed API that facilitate tablet input—the *InkCollector* class and the *InkOverlay* class. You may also recall that the Tablet PC Platform SDK provides some controls that perform tablet input as well; they will be the subject of Chapter 8. For the time being, we'll focus on tablet input at the class level.

## Getting Ink from a Tablet

Real-time inking is arguably the most desirable functionality in a Tablet PC application. After all, that's one of the key differentiators between a Tablet PC and a traditional PC, and it turns out to be one of the most nontrivial to implement. The designers of the Tablet PC Platform realize this, and they have turned a non-trivial task into a trivial one by packaging real-time inking functionality into the *InkCollector* and *InkOverlay* classes.

### Say Hello to the *InkCollector*

We'll start off by looking at *InkCollector*—a class whose primary purpose is to provide real-time ink input to an application. *InkCollector* objects use a Windows Forms–based window as an *ink canvas*—a rectangular region in which pen input will be captured. This window is commonly referred to as the *InkCollector*'s *host window*.

The *InkCollector* class can provide an application with useful events such as system gesture detection and ink gesture recognition if desired. It also remembers the ink that the user has drawn, so repaints of the host window preserve any ink that was previously drawn. The bonus here is that the *InkCollector* class is extremely easy to use, as you'll see in this first sample application.

> **Note**    Recall that only Windows XP Tablet PC Edition ships "out of the box" with ink recognition capability.

## Sample Application: "HelloInkCollector"

Let's dive right into learning about using *InkCollector* by looking at some code. This sample shows the most straightforward use of the *InkCollector* class in an application: a form is created and an *InkCollector* instance is attached to the window. Digital ink can then be drawn on the form, as shown in Figure 4-5, using the tablet hardware installed in the system, including the mouse.

**Figure 4-5**    Greetings from the HelloInkCollector sample application

Perhaps what's most surprising about the HelloInkCollector application is that the key functionality is only two lines of code! Check it out:

### HelloInkCollector.cs

```
///////////////////////////////////////////////////////////////////
//
// HelloInkCollector.cs
//
// (c) 2002 Microsoft Press
// by Rob Jarrett
//
// This program demonstrates the simplest usage of the InkCollector
// class.
//
///////////////////////////////////////////////////////////////////

using System;
using System.Drawing;
using System.Windows.Forms;
using Microsoft.Ink;

public class frmMain : Form
{
    private InkCollector inkCollector;

    // Entry point of the program
    [STAThread]
    static void Main()
    {
        Application.Run(new frmMain());
    }

    public frmMain()
    {
        // Set up the form which will be the host window for an
        // InkCollector instance
        ClientSize = new Size(400, 250);
        Text = "HelloInkCollector";

        // Create a new InkCollector, using the form for the host
        // window
        inkCollector = new InkCollector(Handle);

        // We're now set to go, so turn on ink collection
        inkCollector.Enabled = true;
    }
}
```

You'll notice how the Visual Studio .NET forms designer was not used to create the user interface for the application—this was done purposefully. All the sample applications are like this, for two reasons: it simplifies things for those who wish to manually type in the code, and it keeps the code succinct (hopefully) in its meaning.

After creating a form, the HelloInkCollector application includes the form's handle property in the *InkCollector* constructor—this tells *InkCollector* we want the form to be the host window:

```
// Create a new InkCollector, using the form for the host
// window
inkCollector = new InkCollector(Handle);
```

Once the *InkCollector* object has been created, inking functionality can be activated by setting the *Enabled* property to *true*.

```
// We're now set to go, so turn on ink collection
inkCollector.Enabled = true;
```

At this point, the user is free to ink on the form using any installed tablet device. When the form is invalidated the ink will repaint automatically, and if you try to draw ink off the edge of the form, the ink will be clipped to the form's boundaries. Not bad for a couple of lines of code!

> **Note** The HelloInkCollector sample uses an entire form's client area for the ink canvas. If a smaller area in the form is desired, there are three ways to accomplish this: the first method is to use a child window on the form as the host window (which is what the rest of the samples in this chapter do), the second method is to specify to *InkCollector* an input rectangle within the host window via the *SetWindowInputRectangle* API, and the third is to set the *InkCollector's* Margin X and Margin Y properties.

Now that we have a basic application that provides inking functionality up and running, let's see how easy it is to get some editing functionality running.

## When Ink Is Not Enough

The *InkCollector* class is great at providing real-time ink, but oftentimes you'll want to give your users the ability to select, manipulate, and erase the ink they've drawn. *InkCollector* doesn't have any support for this, but it's definitely possible to augment *InkCollector* and write all that functionality yourself. However, that would be a rather time-consuming task, and quite a wasteful one—

especially if only standard ink interaction behavior was desired! Tablet PC developers everywhere would be reinventing the wheel, which isn't exactly an indicator of a great software platform. Fortunately, the Tablet PC Platform SDK provides a class named *InkOverlay* that implements common ink-interaction behaviors—it supports selecting, moving, resizing, and erasing ink, as well as all the real-time inking capability that *InkCollector* has.

> **Note**   *InkOverlay* is a proper superset of the *InkCollector*—an instance of *InkCollector* can be replaced by an instance of *InkOverlay* and it will always function identically.

## The Ink Controls: InkPicture and InkEdit

In addition to the *InkCollector* and *InkOverlay* classes, the Tablet PC Platform provides two controls that are capable of accepting input: InkPicture and InkEdit. They are both Windows Forms controls and are designed to make forms-based ink capture easier. We'll discuss them in detail in Chapter 8.

*InkOverlay* has a property named *EditingMode* that indicates the input behavior (or input *mode*) that should be currently active. The property is of the type *InkOverlayEditingMode*. Table 4-3 lists its members and the resulting behaviors.

**Table 4-3   The Members of *InkOverlayEditingMode* and Their Meanings**

| Member | Editing Behavior |
| --- | --- |
| *Ink* | Real-time inking mode—ink is drawn wherever the pen touches in the input area. *InkOverlay* will act just like *InkCollector*. |
| *Select* | Selection mode—tapping or lassoing ink selects it, and tapping on white space dismisses the selection. The selection can be moved or resized. |
| *Delete* | Eraser mode—ink is erased whenever encountered by the pen. The erase granularity is either at the stroke level or the point level, determined by *InkOverlay*'s *EraseMode* property. |

## Sample Application: HelloInkOverlay

Demonstrating most of the extra functionality that *InkOverlay* has over *Ink-Collector* is quite easy. This next sample application is similar to HelloInkCollector except it uses a panel control as the host window, adds a ComboBox to change the *EditingMode*, and adds a push button to change ink color. You could also use a panel as the host window and include the ability to change ink color in HelloInkCollector because inking functionality is identical between *InkCollector* and *InkOverlay*. For the first sample to be as brief as possible we opted not to include them. Figure 4-6 shows what HelloInkOverlay looks like in action.

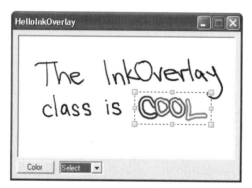

**Figure 4-6**   The *InkOverlay* class provides everything *InkCollector* does and also has selection and erasing abilities.

### HelloInkOverlay.cs

```
///////////////////////////////////////////////////////////////////////
//
// HelloInkOverlay.cs
//
// (c) 2002 Microsoft Press
// by Rob Jarrett
//
// This program demonstrates basic usage of the InkOverlay class.
//
///////////////////////////////////////////////////////////////////////

using System;
using System.Drawing;
using System.Reflection;
using System.Windows.Forms;
using Microsoft.Ink;

public class frmMain : Form
```

```
{
    private Panel      pnlInput;
    private Button     btnColor;
    private ComboBox   cbxEditMode;
    private InkOverlay inkOverlay;

    // Entry point of the program
    [STAThread]
    static void Main()
    {
        Application.Run(new frmMain());
    }

    // Main form setup
    public frmMain()
    {
        SuspendLayout();

        // Create and place all of our controls
        pnlInput = new Panel();
        pnlInput.BackColor = Color.White;
        pnlInput.BorderStyle = BorderStyle.Fixed3D;
        pnlInput.Location = new Point(8, 8);
        pnlInput.Size = new Size(352, 192);

        btnColor = new Button();
        btnColor.Location = new Point(8, 204);
        btnColor.Size = new Size(60, 20);
        btnColor.Text = "Color";
        btnColor.Click += new System.EventHandler(btnColor_Click);

        cbxEditMode = new ComboBox();
        cbxEditMode.DropDownStyle = ComboBoxStyle.DropDownList;
        cbxEditMode.Location = new Point(76, 204);
        cbxEditMode.Size = new Size(72, 20);
        cbxEditMode.SelectedIndexChanged +=
            new System.EventHandler(cbxEditMode_SelIndexChg);

        // Configure the form itself
        ClientSize = new Size(368, 236);
        Controls.AddRange(new Control[] { pnlInput,
                                          btnColor,
                                          cbxEditMode});
        FormBorderStyle = FormBorderStyle.FixedDialog;
        MaximizeBox = false;
        Text = "HelloInkOverlay";

        ResumeLayout(false);
```

*(continued)*

**HelloInkOverlay.cs** *(continued)*

```csharp
        // Fill up the editing mode combobox
        foreach (InkOverlayEditingMode m in
            InkOverlayEditingMode.GetValues(
            typeof(InkOverlayEditingMode)))
        {
            cbxEditMode.Items.Add(m);
        }

        // Create a new InkOverlay, using pnlInput for the
        // collection area
        inkOverlay = new InkOverlay(pnlInput.Handle);

        // Set eraser mode to be point-level rather than stroke-level
        //inkOverlay.EraserMode = InkOverlayEraserMode.PointErase;
        //inkOverlay.EraserWidth = 200;

        // Select the current editing mode in the combobox
        cbxEditMode.SelectedItem = inkOverlay.EditingMode;

        // We're now set to go, so turn on tablet input
        inkOverlay.Enabled = true;
    }

    // Handle the click of the color button
    private void btnColor_Click(object sender, System.EventArgs e)
    {
        // Create and display the common color dialog, using the
        // current ink color as its initial selection
        ColorDialog dlgColor = new ColorDialog();
        dlgColor.Color = inkOverlay.DefaultDrawingAttributes.Color;
        if (dlgColor.ShowDialog(this) == DialogResult.OK)
        {
            // Set the current ink color to the selection chosen in
            // the dialog
            inkOverlay.DefaultDrawingAttributes.Color = dlgColor.Color;
        }
    }

    // Handle the selection change of the editing mode combobox
    private void cbxEditMode_SelIndexChg(object sender,
        System.EventArgs e)
    {
        // Set the current editing mode to the selection chosen
        // in the combobox
        inkOverlay.EditingMode =
            (InkOverlayEditingMode)cbxEditMode.SelectedItem;
    }
}
```

That's a fair bit longer of a listing than HelloInkCollector, isn't it? There isn't much more Tablet Input API usage, though—you'll notice that most of the extra code deals with the child controls on the form. Let's take a closer look at the interesting parts of the sample.

After creating the child controls, placing them on the form, and filling up the ComboBox using C#'s awesome reflective abilities, an *InkOverlay* object is created, specifying the panel control as the host window:

```
// Create a new InkOverlay, using pnlInput for the
// collection area
inkOverlay = new InkOverlay(pnlInput.Handle);
```

That's a bit different from using the entire form as the host window, but *InkCollector* and *InkOverlay* can handle this situation nicely (pardon the pun). Ink will be clipped to the edge of the control, and the user won't be able to start inking outside the control's boundaries. By using the 3-D border effect and white background on the panel control we get a nice visual representation of where the user can and cannot ink.

Next the selection in the ComboBox is updated using the *EditingMode* property of *InkOverlay*, and then tablet input is enabled.

```
// Select the current editing mode in the combobox
cbxEditMode.SelectedItem = inkOverlay.EditingMode;

// We're now set to go, so turn on tablet input
inkOverlay.Enabled = true;
```

This code snippet changes the color of the ink using the common color dialog:

```
// Handle the click of the color button
private void btnColor_Click(object sender, System.EventArgs e)
{
    // Create and display the common color dialog, using the
    // current ink color as its initial selection
    ColorDialog dlgColor = new ColorDialog();
    dlgColor.Color = inkOverlay.DefaultDrawingAttributes.Color;
    if (dlgColor.ShowDialog(this) == DialogResult.OK)
    {
        // Set the current ink color to the selection chosen in
        // the dialog
        inkOverlay.DefaultDrawingAttributes.Color = dlgColor.Color;
    }
}
```

*InkCollector* and *InkOverlay* objects keep a set of ink rendering properties around named *default drawing attributes*. These are characteristics such as color, thickness, and pen tip style that are encapsulated by a class named *DrawingAttributes*. *InkCollector* uses a property of type *DrawingAttributes* to maintain the default drawing attributes, named *DefaultDrawingAttributes*.

Subsequent strokes created in the *InkCollector* will take on the new color set from the dialog. More detailed coverage of drawing attributes and ink rendering will be covered in the next chapter.

Lastly, when the *EditingMode* ComboBox selection is changed, the editing mode of the *InkOverlay* instance is updated.

```
// Handle the selection change of the editing mode combobox
private void cbxEditMode_SelIndexChg(object sender,
    System.EventArgs e)
{
    // Set the current editing mode to the selection chosen
    // in the combobox
    inkOverlay.EditingMode =
        (InkOverlayEditingMode)cbxEditMode.SelectedItem;
}
```

When you run the HelloInkOverlay application, it will quickly become apparent just how much functionality *InkOverlay* has. You can draw ink, select the ink, move it, resize it, and erase it—all from a small program.

## Changing the Eraser Mode

The *Delete* mode can be either stroke-based or point-based, referring to the granularity of ink that is removed when the stroke is touched. Stroke-based erasure will delete the entire stroke when it's hit, and point-based erasure chops out ink from a stroke when it's hit (much like a real eraser does). The property *EraserMode* in the *InkOverlay* class indicates which form of erasing should be performed. It is of type *InkOverlayEraserMode*, which is an enumeration with two members: *StrokeErase* and *PointErase*. The default value of the *EraserMode* property is *InkOverlayEraserMode.StrokeErase*. Point-based erase has an eraser size—essentially the amount of ink to erase from within a stroke—that is specified by the *EraserWidth* property on an *InkOverlay* object.

Try uncommenting the code just after the *InkOverlay* object is created to play around with the point-level erase functionality:

```
// Create a new InkOverlay, using pnlInput for the
// collection area
inkOverlay = new InkOverlay(pnlInput.Handle);

// Set eraser mode to be point-level rather than stroke-level
inkOverlay.EraserMode = InkOverlayEraserMode.PointErase;
inkOverlay.EraserWidth = 200;
```

The eraser width is specified in 100ths of a millimeter, otherwise known as *HIMETRIC units*—the coordinate measurement used for all ink in the Tablet PC Platform.

## The *InkControl* Class in the *BuildingTabletApps* Library

Included on the CD-ROM of this book is the *BuildingTabletApps* library, containing numerous helper classes and functions you are free to leverage in your own applications. The functionality of HelloInkOverlay is encapsulated in the *InkControl* class, used in upcoming chapters' sample applications to provide a "quick and dirty" editing UI, avoiding the replication of HelloInkOverlay's code in every case.

## *InkOverlay*'s Attach Mode

Another advantage the *InkOverlay* class has over *InkCollector* is the ability to attach to the host window in two ways. By default, *InkCollector* and *InkOverlay* objects will use the actual host window as the canvas to collect and draw ink on. Depending on the behavior of the host window, though, it is possible for redraw problems to occur.

For example, a host window might draw on itself when an event other than paint occurs, which could result in ink being obscured until the next paint event occurs. Another example is if a control is specified as the host window when the host window belongs to another process (perhaps an OCX is used that is implemented in a separate .exe). In this case, ink collection will fail because the *InkCollector* and *InkOverlay* require the host window to belong to the same process as they do.

To solve these problems, the *InkOverlay* class can use a window of its own to collect and render ink. Setting the *AttachMode* property of an *InkOverlay* to *InkOverlayAttachMode.InFront* results in a transparent window being used instead of the host window. The default value of the *AttachMode* property is *InkOverlayAttachMode.Behind*, the other value in the *InkOverlayAttachMode* enumeration.

The *InkOverlay* class is a great way for your application to get common ink behavior. However, it can't fully provide the ink experience that the Tablet PC can in an application like Windows Journal. A brief summary of the functionality that the *InkOverlay* class *doesn't* provide you is listed here:

- Using the top-of-pen as an eraser

- Press-and-hold (or right-click and right-drag) in ink mode to modelessly switch to select mode

- An insert/remove space mode

■ Showing selection feedback in real time (for instance, as the lasso is being drawn, ink becomes selected or deselected immediately as it is enclosed or excluded by the lasso)

■ Using a scratchout gesture to delete strokes

Luckily, that's a pretty short list. And these deficiencies are addressed by sample applications in this book. The first two items are covered in this chapter; the next two are covered in the next chapter, and the last is covered in Chapter 7.

> **Note**   It's not really fair to do a full-out feature comparison of *InkOverlay* and Windows Journal because Journal was written as an end-to-end application. However, there is a quantifiable set of features that defines an inking experience, and it's that set that is being used to compare the two pieces of software.

> **Note**   If the *InkOverlay* class is a superset of *InkCollector* with commonly used functionality, you might ask why *InkCollector* even exists. That's a good question! The most reasonable answer we can come up with is this: *InkCollector* is useful if you want to customize tablet input behavior and when little or none of *InkOverlay's* functionality is desired—that makes a cleaner basis to start from. Otherwise, you might as well always use *InkOverlay* and get its extra functionality for free.

Now that we've seen the surface of tablet input functionality that the Tablet PC Platform provides, let's move on to studying tablet input events of *InkCollector* and *InkOverlay*. To keep things simple, we'll return to using *InkCollector* as the subject for tablet input capture; later on the extra events *InkOverlay* has will be discussed.

## *InkCollector* Events

The default behavior of *InkCollector* and *InkOverlay* is cool—but what if you wanted to extend or alter that behavior, or perform certain custom actions for your own application's needs? For example, you might want your application to

- Be notified whenever an ink stroke is drawn so that the stroke can be serialized and sent over a network connection to another machine, perhaps as part of a collaborative whiteboard application.

- Be notified when a press-and-hold system gesture occurs so that an object can be selected.

- Prevent inking entirely but still receive "raw" tablet input events so that direct-manipulation editing operations can be performed.

> **Note**   Applying the term *raw* to tablet input refers to the simplest form of events that occur when a pen interacts with a digitizer: hover, pen down, pen move, and pen up.

*InkCollector* and *InkOverlay* expose an extensive set of event notifications that can be used to trigger other functionality or alter default behavior. These events can be grouped into various categories of notifications to better understand their purpose.

### Ink Stroke Events

This first class of events occurs as a result of digital ink being created. An ink stroke can cause either the *Stroke* event or *Gesture* event to fire when it's created—by default, *InkCollector* and *InkOverlay* do not try to recognize strokes as gestures, so the *Stroke* event always is fired when a stroke is created. *InkCollector* and *InkOverlay* have a property named *CollectionMode* (of type *CollectionMode*) that indicates how gesture recognition should take place—collect ink only and not recognize gestures (the default value of *InkOnly*), collect ink and recognize ink as gestures if possible (*InkAndGesture*), or recognize ink as gestures only (*GestureOnly*). The *Stroke* and *Gesture* events are shown in Table 4-4.

**Table 4-4 *Stroke* and *Gesture* Events**

| Event Name | Event Arguments Class | Description |
|---|---|---|
| *Stroke* | *InkCollectorStrokeEventArgs* | An ink stroke was just created. |
| *Gesture* | *InkCollectorGestureEventArgs* | An ink stroke was just created and was recognized as a gesture. |

When either the *Stroke* or *Gesture* event fires, the corresponding *Event-Args*-based object has a property named *Cancel* that allows the ink stroke to be thrown away or added to the *InkCollector* or *InkOverlay*'s *Ink* object. By default, the *Stroke* event has this property set to *false* (to mean always save the stroke unless code in the event handler says otherwise), as does the *Gesture* event (to mean always throw the stroke away and fire the *stroke* event unless code in the event handler says otherwise).

## Pen Movement Events

The next category of events occurs as a result of discrete physical actions with the cursor. A *cursor* in the Tablet PC Platform sense simply refers to a pen or a mouse. Take a look at the pen movement events in Table 4-5. You can see how the names of these events map easily to their descriptions.

**Table 4-5 The Pen Movement Events**

| Event Name | Event Arguments Class | Description |
|---|---|---|
| *CursorInRange* | *InkCollectorCursorInRangeEventArgs* | The cursor has come within proximity of the digitizer device or hovered into the ink canvas's space. |
| *NewInAirPackets* | *InkCollectorNewInAirPacketsEventArgs* | An update of the cursor state when it is hovering. |
| *CursorButtonDown* | *InkCollectorCursorButtonDownEventArgs* | A button on the cursor has been pressed. |
| *CursorDown* | *InkCollectorCursorDownEventArgs* | The cursor tip has touched the surface of the digitizer. |
| *NewPackets* | *InkCollectorNewPacketsEventArgs* | An update of the cursor state when it is on the digitizer's surface. |
| *SystemGesture* | *InkCollectorSystemGestureEventArgs* | A system gesture (pen-based action) has occurred. |

**Table 4-5**   **The Pen Movement Events**   *(continued)*

| Event Name | Event Arguments Class | Description |
|---|---|---|
| *CursorButtonUp* | *InkCollectorCursorButtonUpEventArgs* | A button on the cursor has been released. |
| *CursorOutOfRange* | *InkCollectorCursorOutOfRangeEventArgs* | The cursor has left the proximity of the digitizer or hovered out of the ink canvas's space. |

The *CursorInRange* and *CursorOutOfRange* events indicate the cursor is coming in or out of physical range with the ink canvas area—this can mean either horizontally (within the x and y plane) or vertically (if the tablet hardware supports this). The *CursorDown*, *CursorButtonDown*, and *CursorButtonUp* events refer to the cursor tip going down or pen buttons being pressed or released.

The *NewPackets* and *NewInAirPackets* events signal that the current cursor state has been updated. They will be further discussed later in this chapter.

The *SystemGesture* event is one of the most useful events in this list because it refers to the fact that a system gesture (referred to as a pen-based action earlier in the chapter) has been recognized. The *InkCollectorSystemGestureEventArgs* object given to the event handler specifies which system gesture was recognized through its *Id* property—a value in the *SystemGesture* enumeration. System gestures are useful when implementing your own editing behaviors.

> **Note**   Members of the *SystemGesture* enumeration include *Tap*, *Drag*, *RightTap*, *RightDrag*, and *DoubleTap*.

## Mouse Trigger Events

Mouse events are typically sent alongside tablet input events. The mouse trigger events of the *InkCollector* class, described in Table 4-6, are used to prevent those mouse events from being fired.

**Table 4-6**  **Mouse Trigger Events**

| Event Name | Event Arguments Class | Description |
|---|---|---|
| *DoubleClick* | *System.ComponentModel.CancelEventArgs* | A DoubleClick event is about to be fired. |
| *MouseDown* | *CancelMouseEventArgs* | A MouseDown event is about to be fired. |
| *MouseMove* | *CancelMouseEventArgs* | A MouseMove event is about to be fired. |
| *MouseUp* | *CancelMouseEventArgs* | A MouseUp event is about to be fired. |
| *MouseWheel* | *CancelMouseEventArgs* | A MouseWheel event is about to be fired. |

Each event's *EventArg*-based parameter has a *Cancel* property that is initially set to *false*. If the event handler sets the value to *true*, the corresponding mouse event will not fire.

## Tablet Hardware Events

The class of events pertaining to tablet hardware occurs when a tablet device is either added or removed from the system. These events are listed in Table 4-7.

**Table 4-7**  **Tablet Hardware Events**

| Event Name | Event Arguments Class | Description |
|---|---|---|
| *TabletAdded* | *InkCollectorTabletAddedEventArgs* | A new digitizer device has been added to the system. |
| *TabletRemoved* | *InkCollectorTabletRemovedEventArgs* | A digitizer device has been removed. |

**Note**  The *InkCollectorTabletRemovedEventArgs* class's property *TabletId* is the index into the *Tablets* collection of the *Tablet* object being removed. The *Tablets* collection is introduced in the upcoming section, "Getting Introspective."

## Rendering Events (*InkOverlay* Only)

The *InkOverlay* class provides two events related to rendering—the *Painting* event, which indicates that the *InkOverlay* object is about to draw itself, and the *Painted* event, which indicates that drawing is complete. This is shown in Table 4-8.

**Table 4-8   *InkOverlay* Rendering Events**

| Event Name | Event Arguments Class | Description |
| --- | --- | --- |
| *Painting* | *InkOverlayPaintingEventArgs* | The *InkOverlay* is about to paint itself. |
| *Painted* | *System.Windows.Forms.PaintEventArgs* | The *InkOverlay* is finished painting itself. |

The *Painting* event proves useful if you'd ever want to alter any properties of the *Graphic* object being drawn to, adjust the clipping rectangle, or cancel rendering from happening altogether. The *Painted* event allows you to augment the rendering of the *InkOverlay* with any drawing of your own—for example, when implementing some tagging functionality an application would draw its tag icons in an event handler for the *Painted* event.

## Ink Editing Events (*InkOverlay* Only)

The events in this ink editing category, described in Table 4-9, are fairly interesting because they can be used to somewhat alter the *InkOverlay*'s behavior.

**Table 4-9   Ink Editing Events**

| Event Name | Event Arguments Class | Description |
| --- | --- | --- |
| *SelectionChanging* | *InkOverlaySelectionChangingEventArgs* | The selection is about to change. |
| *SelectionChanged* | *System.EventArgs* | The selection has changed. |
| *SelectionMoving* | *InkOverlaySelectionMovingEventArgs* | The selection is in the process of moving. |
| *SelectionMoved* | *InkOverlaySelectionMovedEventArgs* | The selection has been moved. |
| *SelectionResizing* | *InkOverlaySelectionResizingEventArgs* | The selection is in the process of being resized. |
| *SelectionResized* | *InkOverlaySelectionResizedEventArgs* | The selection has been resized. |
| *StrokesDeleting* | *InkOverlayStrokesDeletingEventArgs* | One or more strokes is about to be deleted. |
| *StrokesDeleted* | *System.EventArgs* | One or more strokes has been deleted. |

The events with the suffix "ing" permit their impending behavior to be changed (or even canceled) by setting relevant data in the *EventArgs*-based object given to an event handler. *SelectionChanging* event's *EventArgs* object makes available for inspection and modification the collection of strokes that is to become selected, *SelectionMoving* makes available for inspection and modification the rectangle of the in-progress move location, *SelectionResizing* makes available for inspection and modification the rectangle of the in-progress resize amount, and *StrokesDeleting* makes available for inspection and modification the collection of strokes to be deleted.

Exposing data such as this enables an application to implement functionality such as read-only ink, unselectable ink, or even remotely automated user interface interaction.

## Sample Application: InputWatcher

After all this talking about events, it would be great to get a better idea of exactly what *InkCollector* events get fired, when, and in what order. This next sample application lets you see just that—the events from an *InkCollector* object are monitored. The sample allows you to turn on those events you want to see logged, and when events fire their results are logged to a window. You can also change the collection mode of the *InkCollector* to observe the effect it has. The application is shown in Figure 4-7.

**Figure 4-7** InputWatcher logs events from *InkCollector* to an output window.

The source for this sample is quite lengthy, but you might find it's well worth playing around with it in Visual Studio .NET to get a better feel for the various properties on the *EventArgs*-based objects. So here is the source listing in its entirety:

**InputWatcher.cs**

```
///////////////////////////////////////////////////////////////////
//
// InputWatcher.cs
//
// (c) 2002 Microsoft Press
// by Rob Jarrett
//
// This program demonstrates how and when events are dispatched for
// the InkCollector class.
//
///////////////////////////////////////////////////////////////////

using System;
using System.ComponentModel;
using System.Drawing;
using System.Windows.Forms;
using Microsoft.Ink;

public class frmMain : Form
{
    private Panel           pnlInput;
    private ComboBox        cbxMode;
    private CheckedListBox  clbEvents;
    private ListBox         lbOutput;
    private Button          btnClear;
    private InkCollector    inkCollector;

    // Entry point of the program
    [STAThread]
    static void Main()
    {
        Application.Run(new frmMain());
    }

    // Main form setup
    public frmMain()
    {
        SuspendLayout();

        // Create and place all of our controls
        pnlInput = new Panel();
        pnlInput.BorderStyle = BorderStyle.Fixed3D;
        pnlInput.Location = new Point(8, 8);
        pnlInput.Size = new Size(240, 192);

        btnClear = new Button();
```

*(continued)*

**InputWatcher.cs**   *(continued)*

```
        btnClear.Size = new Size(40, 23);
        btnClear.Text = "Clear";
        btnClear.Click += new System.EventHandler(btnClear_Click);

        pnlInput.SuspendLayout();
        pnlInput.Controls.AddRange(new Control[] {btnClear});
        pnlInput.ResumeLayout(false);

        cbxMode = new ComboBox();
        cbxMode.DropDownStyle = ComboBoxStyle.DropDownList;
        cbxMode.Location = new Point(256, 8);
        cbxMode.Size = new Size(144, 21);
        cbxMode.SelectedIndexChanged +=
            new System.EventHandler(cbxMode_SelIndexChg);

        clbEvents = new CheckedListBox();
        clbEvents.CheckOnClick = true;
        clbEvents.Location = new Point(256, 40);
        clbEvents.Size = new Size(144, 154);
        clbEvents.ThreeDCheckBoxes = true;
        clbEvents.ItemCheck +=
            new ItemCheckEventHandler(clbEvents_ItemCheck);

        lbOutput = new ListBox();
        lbOutput.Location = new Point(8, 208);
        lbOutput.ScrollAlwaysVisible = true;
        lbOutput.Size = new Size(392, 94);
        lbOutput.Sorted = false;

        // Configure the form itself
        ClientSize = new Size(408, 310);
        Controls.AddRange(new Control[] { pnlInput,
                                          cbxMode,
                                          clbEvents,
                                          lbOutput});
        FormBorderStyle = FormBorderStyle.FixedDialog;
        MaximizeBox = false;
        Text = "InputWatcher";

        ResumeLayout(false);

        // Fill up the collection mode ComboBox
        foreach (CollectionMode c in
            CollectionMode.GetValues(typeof(CollectionMode)))
        {
            cbxMode.Items.Add(c);
        }
```

```
        // Fill up the events ListBox
        clbEvents.Items.Add("CursorButtonDown");
        clbEvents.Items.Add("CursorButtonUp");
        clbEvents.Items.Add("CursorDown");
        clbEvents.Items.Add("CursorInRange");
        clbEvents.Items.Add("CursorOutOfRange");
        clbEvents.Items.Add("DoubleClick");
        clbEvents.Items.Add("Gesture");
        clbEvents.Items.Add("MouseDown");
        clbEvents.Items.Add("MouseMove");
        clbEvents.Items.Add("MouseUp");
        clbEvents.Items.Add("MouseWheel");
        clbEvents.Items.Add("NewInAirPackets");
        clbEvents.Items.Add("NewPackets");
        clbEvents.Items.Add("Stroke");
        clbEvents.Items.Add("SystemGesture");
        clbEvents.Items.Add("TabletAdded");
        clbEvents.Items.Add("TabletRemoved");

        // Create a new InkCollector, using pnlInput for the
        // collection area
        inkCollector = new InkCollector(pnlInput.Handle);

        // Set the selection in the collection mode ComboBox to
        // the current collection mode in inkCollector
        cbxMode.SelectedItem = inkCollector.CollectionMode;

        // We're now set to go, so turn on tablet input
        inkCollector.Enabled = true;
    }

// Events checked-ListBox item checked handler
private void clbEvents_ItemCheck(object sender,
    ItemCheckEventArgs e)
{
    if (e.NewValue == CheckState.Checked)
    {
        // Add the desired event handler to inkCollector
        switch (e.Index)
        {
            case 0:
                inkCollector.CursorButtonDown +=
                    new InkCollectorCursorButtonDownEventHandler(
                    inkCollector_CursorButtonDown);
                break;

            case 1:
```

*(continued)*

**InputWatcher.cs**    *(continued)*

```
            inkCollector.CursorButtonUp +=
                new InkCollectorCursorButtonUpEventHandler(
                inkCollector_CursorButtonUp);
            break;

        case 2:
            inkCollector.CursorDown +=
                new InkCollectorCursorDownEventHandler(
                inkCollector_CursorDown);
            break;

        case 3:
            inkCollector.CursorInRange +=
                new InkCollectorCursorInRangeEventHandler(
                inkCollector_CursorInRange);
            break;

        case 4:
            inkCollector.CursorOutOfRange +=
                new InkCollectorCursorOutOfRangeEventHandler(
                inkCollector_CursorOutOfRange);
            break;

        case 5:
            inkCollector.DoubleClick +=
                new InkCollectorDoubleClickEventHandler(
                inkCollector_DoubleClick);
            break;

        case 6:
            inkCollector.Gesture +=
                new InkCollectorGestureEventHandler(
                inkCollector_Gesture);
            break;

        case 7:
            inkCollector.MouseDown +=
                new InkCollectorMouseDownEventHandler(
                inkCollector_MouseDown);
            break;

        case 8:
            inkCollector.MouseMove +=
                new InkCollectorMouseMoveEventHandler(
                inkCollector_MouseMove);
            break;

        case 9:
```

```
        inkCollector.MouseUp +=
            new InkCollectorMouseUpEventHandler(
            inkCollector_MouseUp);
        break;

case 10:
        inkCollector.MouseWheel +=
            new InkCollectorMouseWheelEventHandler(
            inkCollector_MouseWheel);
        break;

case 11:
        inkCollector.NewInAirPackets +=
            new InkCollectorNewInAirPacketsEventHandler(
            inkCollector_NewInAirPackets);
        break;

case 12:
        inkCollector.NewPackets +=
            new InkCollectorNewPacketsEventHandler(
            inkCollector_NewPackets);
        break;

case 13:
        inkCollector.Stroke +=
            new InkCollectorStrokeEventHandler(
            inkCollector_Stroke);
        break;

case 14:
        inkCollector.SystemGesture +=
            new InkCollectorSystemGestureEventHandler(
            inkCollector_SystemGesture);
        break;

case 15:
        inkCollector.TabletAdded +=
            new InkCollectorTabletAddedEventHandler(
            inkCollector_TabletAdded);
        break;

case 16:
        inkCollector.TabletRemoved +=
            new InkCollectorTabletRemovedEventHandler(
            inkCollector_TabletRemoved);
        break;
}
```

*(continued)*

**InputWatcher.cs** *(continued)*

```
        }
        else
        {
            // Remove the desired event handler from inkCollector
            switch (e.Index)
            {
                case 0:
                    inkCollector.CursorButtonDown -=
                        new InkCollectorCursorButtonDownEventHandler(
                        inkCollector_CursorButtonDown);
                    break;

                case 1:
                    inkCollector.CursorButtonUp -=
                        new InkCollectorCursorButtonUpEventHandler(
                        inkCollector_CursorButtonUp);
                    break;

                case 2:
                    inkCollector.CursorDown -=
                        new InkCollectorCursorDownEventHandler(
                        inkCollector_CursorDown);
                    break;

                case 3:
                    inkCollector.CursorInRange -=
                        new InkCollectorCursorInRangeEventHandler(
                        inkCollector_CursorInRange);
                    break;

                case 4:
                    inkCollector.CursorOutOfRange -=
                        new InkCollectorCursorOutOfRangeEventHandler(
                        inkCollector_CursorOutOfRange);
                    break;

                case 5:
                    inkCollector.DoubleClick -=
                        new InkCollectorDoubleClickEventHandler(
                        inkCollector_DoubleClick);
                    break;

                case 6:
                    inkCollector.Gesture -=
                        new InkCollectorGestureEventHandler(
                        inkCollector_Gesture);
                    break;
```

```
case 7:
    inkCollector.MouseDown -=
        new InkCollectorMouseDownEventHandler(
        inkCollector_MouseDown);
    break;

case 8:
    inkCollector.MouseMove -=
        new InkCollectorMouseMoveEventHandler(
        inkCollector_MouseMove);
    break;

case 9:
    inkCollector.MouseUp -=
        new InkCollectorMouseUpEventHandler(
        inkCollector_MouseUp);
    break;

case 10:
    inkCollector.MouseWheel -=
        new InkCollectorMouseWheelEventHandler(
        inkCollector_MouseWheel);
    break;

case 11:
    inkCollector.NewInAirPackets -=
        new InkCollectorNewInAirPacketsEventHandler(
        inkCollector_NewInAirPackets);
    break;

case 12:
    inkCollector.NewPackets -=
        new InkCollectorNewPacketsEventHandler(
        inkCollector_NewPackets);
    break;

case 13:
    inkCollector.Stroke -=
        new InkCollectorStrokeEventHandler(
        inkCollector_Stroke);
    break;

case 14:
    inkCollector.SystemGesture -=
        new InkCollectorSystemGestureEventHandler(
```

*(continued)*

**InputWatcher.cs**   *(continued)*

```
                    inkCollector_SystemGesture);
                break;

            case 15:
                inkCollector.TabletAdded -=
                    new InkCollectorTabletAddedEventHandler(
                    inkCollector_TabletAdded);
                break;

            case 16:
                inkCollector.TabletRemoved -=
                    new InkCollectorTabletRemovedEventHandler(
                    inkCollector_TabletRemoved);
                break;
        }
    }
}

// Collection mode ComboBox selection changed handler
private void cbxMode_SelIndexChg(object sender,
    System.EventArgs e)
{
    // Turn off ink collection since we're changing collection mode
    inkCollector.Enabled = false;

    // Set the new mode
    inkCollector.CollectionMode =
        (CollectionMode)cbxMode.SelectedItem;

    // Set up the gestures we're interested in recognizing
    if ((inkCollector.CollectionMode ==
        CollectionMode.InkAndGesture) ||
        (inkCollector.CollectionMode ==
        CollectionMode.GestureOnly))
    {
        inkCollector.SetGestureStatus(
            ApplicationGesture.AllGestures, true);
    }
    else
    {
        inkCollector.SetGestureStatus(
            ApplicationGesture.AllGestures, false);
    }

    // We're done, so turn ink collection back on
    inkCollector.Enabled = true;
}
```

```
// Clear Button clicked handler
private void btnClear_Click(object sender, System.EventArgs e)
{
    // Clear out all strokes
    inkCollector.Ink.DeleteStrokes();
    pnlInput.Invalidate();

    // Clear output window
    lbOutput.Items.Clear();
}

// Log a string to the output window
private void LogToOutput(string strLog)
{
    lbOutput.Items.Add(strLog);
    lbOutput.TopIndex = lbOutput.Items.Count - 1;
}

// Various tablet input event handlers - each logs its relevant
// EventArgs values
private void inkCollector_CursorButtonDown(object sender,
    InkCollectorCursorButtonDownEventArgs e)
{
    LogToOutput(String.Format(
        "CursorButtonDown CursorId={0} BtnName={1} BtnId={2}",
        e.Cursor.Id, e.Button.Name, e.Button.Id));
}

private void inkCollector_CursorButtonUp(object sender,
    InkCollectorCursorButtonUpEventArgs e)
{
    LogToOutput(String.Format(
        "CursorButtonUp CursorId={0} BtnName={1} BtnId={2}",
        e.Cursor.Id, e.Button.Name, e.Button.Id));
}

private void inkCollector_CursorDown(object sender,
    InkCollectorCursorDownEventArgs e)
{
    LogToOutput(String.Format(
        "CursorDown CursorId={0} CursorName={1}",
        e.Cursor.Id, e.Cursor.Name));
}

private void inkCollector_CursorInRange(object sender,
    InkCollectorCursorInRangeEventArgs e)
{
```

*(continued)*

**InputWatcher.cs**  *(continued)*

```
        LogToOutput(String.Format(
            "CursorInRange CursorId={0} Inverted={1} NewCursor={2}",
            e.Cursor.Id, e.Cursor.Inverted, e.NewCursor));
    }

    private void inkCollector_CursorOutOfRange(object sender,
        InkCollectorCursorOutOfRangeEventArgs e)
    {
        LogToOutput(String.Format(
            "CursorOutOfRange CursorId={0}", e.Cursor.Id));
    }

    private void inkCollector_DoubleClick(object sender,
        CancelEventArgs e)
    {
        LogToOutput(String.Format("DoubleClick"));
    }

    private void inkCollector_Gesture(object sender,
        InkCollectorGestureEventArgs e)
    {
        LogToOutput(String.Format(
            "Gesture CursorId={0} Gesture={1} Confidence={2}",
            e.Cursor.Id, e.Gestures[0].Id, e.Gestures[0].Confidence));
    }

    private void inkCollector_MouseDown(object sender,
        CancelMouseEventArgs e)
    {
        LogToOutput(String.Format("MouseDown"));
    }

    private void inkCollector_MouseMove(object sender,
        CancelMouseEventArgs e)
    {
        LogToOutput(String.Format("MouseMove"));
    }

    private void inkCollector_MouseUp(object sender,
        CancelMouseEventArgs e)
    {
        LogToOutput(String.Format("MouseUp"));
    }

    private void inkCollector_MouseWheel(object sender,
        CancelMouseEventArgs e)
    {
        LogToOutput(String.Format("MouseWheel"));
```

```
    }

    private void inkCollector_NewInAirPackets(object sender,
        InkCollectorNewInAirPacketsEventArgs e)
    {
        LogToOutput(String.Format(
            "NewInAirPackets CursorId={0} PacketCount={1}",
            e.Cursor.Id, e.PacketCount));
    }

    private void inkCollector_NewPackets(object sender,
        InkCollectorNewPacketsEventArgs e)
    {
        LogToOutput(String.Format(
            "NewPackets CursorId={0} PacketCount={1}",
            e.Cursor.Id, e.PacketCount));
    }

    private void inkCollector_Stroke(object sender,
        InkCollectorStrokeEventArgs e)
    {
        LogToOutput(String.Format(
            "Stroke CursorId={0} Id={1}", e.Cursor.Id, e.Stroke.Id));
    }

    private void inkCollector_SystemGesture(object sender,
        InkCollectorSystemGestureEventArgs e)
    {
        LogToOutput(String.Format(
            "SystemGesture CursorId={0} Id={1} EventLocation=({2},{3})",
            e.Cursor.Id, e.Id, e.Point.X, e.Point.Y));
    }

    private void inkCollector_TabletAdded(object sender,
        InkCollectorTabletAddedEventArgs e)
    {
        LogToOutput(String.Format(
            "TabletAdded TabletName={0}", e.Tablet.Name));
    }

    private void inkCollector_TabletRemoved(object sender,
        InkCollectorTabletRemovedEventArgs e)
    {
        LogToOutput(String.Format(
            "TabletRemoved TabletId={0}", e.TabletId));
    }
}
```

Whew, that *is* a really long listing! But don't worry, it's not as complex as it appears. Unfortunately, there's a lot of bloat that occurs because we are unable to generically add and remove delegates to the *InkCollector*, and also because we can't generically process events received.

The InputWatcher application starts off in a similar fashion to what we've already seen. The main form creates its child controls: a panel to be used as an *InkCollector*'s host window, a button to clear out any ink in the *InkCollector* and any output in the log window, a ComboBox to specify collection mode, a checked ListBox for choosing events to log, and a ListBox used for crude output logging. The user interface elements are then initialized with relevant data, and an *InkCollector* instance is created using the panel as the host window.

Things start to get interesting in the *clbEvents_ItemCheck* event handler, which adds or removes *InkCollector* event handlers from the *InkCollector* object depending on the CheckBox state of the ListBox item. Each handler is responsible for logging interesting properties of the event to the output window.

The *cbxMode_SelIndexChg* event handler deals with the selection changing in the ComboBox that specifies collection mode. Note that the *InkCollector* is disabled when the collection mode is changed and then re-enabled afterward:

```
// Turn off ink collection since we're changing collection mode
inkCollector.Enabled = false;

// Set the new mode
inkCollector.CollectionMode =
    (CollectionMode)cbxMode.SelectedItem;

// Set up the gestures we're interested in recognizing
if ((inkCollector.CollectionMode ==
    CollectionMode.InkAndGesture) ||
    (inkCollector.CollectionMode ==
    CollectionMode.GestureOnly))
{
    inkCollector.SetGestureStatus(
        ApplicationGesture.AllGestures, true);
}
else
{
    inkCollector.SetGestureStatus(
        ApplicationGesture.AllGestures, false);
}

// We're done, so turn ink collection back on
inkCollector.Enabled = true;
```

Some of the *InkCollector*'s properties and methods require tablet input to be shut off in order for them to be used—a safeguard to prevent simultaneous user input and programmatic usage.

The purpose of the *SetGestureStatus* calls in the preceding code is to provide the gesture recognizer component with the list of gestures we're interested in recognizing. This can improve recognition performance and accuracy, which will be discussed in Chapter 7. By default, the gesture recognizer won't try to recognize any gestures; it will merely return *ApplicationGesture.NoGesture* in the *InkCollectorGestureEventArgs* object's *Gestures* array. To get some recognition results, when a collection mode in which gesture recognition can occur is set, we'll ask for every gesture to be recognized for simplicity.

The last piece of code we'll look at in this sample is the *btnClear_Click* event handler. This method removes all strokes from the *InkCollector* with the following code:

```
// Clear out all strokes
inkCollector.Ink.DeleteStrokes();
pnlInput.Invalidate();
```

The *Ink* object attached to the *InkCollector* provides a method named *DeleteStrokes* we can use to remove all the strokes from it. Once the strokes are removed, we need to refresh the host window to reflect the absence of ink in the *Ink* object.

## Analyzing the Events

After running InputWatcher and doing some inking on the ink canvas, you'll quickly notice that the log window shows no output. That's because all the events are turned off when the application starts up—try turning on the *Stroke* and *Gesture* events and drawing some ink. Notice how in *InkOnly* collection mode only *Stroke* events occur. If you have a gesture recognizer installed, set the collection mode to *InkAndGesture* and write some text (for instance, your name). You might see some *Gesture* events firing as well as *Stroke* events, meaning that the gesture recognizer thinks one or more of the strokes you wrote looks like a known gesture. If the collection mode is set to *GestureOnly*, you'll notice that only *Gesture* events will fire—this means that every stroke is being recognized as a gesture, although perhaps an unknown one. Additionally, multiple strokes can form a gesture such as a double circle.

Let's take a look at some sequences of events for common actions, so try this: turn on every single event type and draw a stroke across the ink canvas. Whoa! The output window is deluged with loads of events, mostly of the types *MouseMove, NewInAirPackets,* and *NewPackets.* This actually does make sense because those events represent an update to the current state of the cursor, when it's either on the digitizer's surface or hovering over it. More information on what exactly "the current state of the cursor" means will be discussed in the upcoming section, "Specifying the Tablet Data to Capture—Packet Properties."

To reduce the quantity of events logged to the output window, turn off the *MouseDown*, *MouseMove*, *MouseUp*, and *NewInAirPackets* events and tap the Clear button. Now draw a stroke again—this time the output won't be quite as overwhelming. You should see something similar to the following:

```
CursorButtonDown CursorId=8 BtnName=tip BtnId={GUID value}
CursorDown CursorId=8 CursorName=Pressure Stylus
NewPackets CursorId=8 PacketCount=1
NewPackets CursorId=8 PacketCount=13
NewPackets CursorId=8 PacketCount=5
SystemGesture CursorId=8 EventName=Drag EventLocation=(1391,1797)
NewPackets CursorId=8 PacketCount=11
NewPackets CursorId=8 PacketCount=2
NewPackets CursorId=8 PacketCount=1
NewPackets CursorId=8 PacketCount=2
...lots of NewPackets...
Stroke CursorId=8 Id=2
CursorButtonUp CursorId=8 BtnName=tip BtnId={GUID value}
```

The installed tablet devices each have at least one cursor that is used to perform input. To distinguish between various cursors, they are assigned a unique ID, known as the *CursorId*. Each cursor also has one or more cursor buttons, where a cursor button can be either a tip on a stylus or a physical button on a cursor.

The preceding events show that when the pen touches the digitizer surface, a *CursorButtonDown* event is fired and immediately followed by a *CursorDown* event. Remember that a cursor button can be a tip of a pen, so the tip being touched to the digitizer surface is considered the button being pressed down— hence the *CursorButtonDown* event being fired. The *CursorDown* event refers to the fact that a tip or the primary button on the cursor has been pressed down, signaling the start of an ink stroke.

The various *NewPackets* events following the *CursorDown* mean the cursor's input state is updated—that is, the cursor's location and possibly other data such as pressure amount and tilt has been sampled and packaged into one or more packets and then sent to the *InkCollector* instance. These events are received throughout the duration of the cursor being pressed down.

The *SystemGesture* event indicates that a *Drag* system gesture was detected, though in your case it could be *Tap*, *RightDrag*, or *RightTap*, depending on how the stroke was drawn. Notice how the system gesture event didn't fire immediately after *CursorDown* because Wisptis.exe needs to compute whether a tap or a drag is occurring, as we found out earlier in the chapter. The other *NewPackets* events following *SystemGesture* indicate how data is continuously being sampled for the cursor and sent to the *InkCollector* object.

Finally a *Stroke* event is fired, indicating that a new stroke has been created, and a *CursorButtonUp* event is fired, meaning that the cursor has been lifted or its primary button has been released.

> **Tip**    The *CursorButtonDown* and *CursorButtonUp* events always book-end each other, as does *CursorDown* with *Stroke* or *Gesture*.

Now try hovering the pen over the input area and clicking the barrel button if it has one. You should see something similar to this output:

```
CursorButtonDown CursorId=8 BtnName=barrel BtnId={GUID value}
CursorButtonUp CursorId=8 BtnName=barrel BtnId={GUID value}
```

The cursor ID is the same as before, but this time the button name and perhaps the GUID value are different, implying that a different button was detected.

If your pen has an eraser tip, try inverting the pen over the input area and then turning it back over to the writing end—observe:

```
CursorInRange CursorId=9 Inverted=True NewCursor=True
CursorOutOfRange CursorId=9
CursorInRange CursorId=8 Inverted=False NewCursor=False
CursorOutOfRange CursorId=8
```

The *NewCursor* property of the *InkCollectorCursorInRangeEventArgs* class discloses whether the *InkCollector* instance has seen that cursor over the *InkCollector's* lifetime. That information can be useful for your application to initialize some data structures to handle unique properties of the cursor, or even to trigger some user interface prompting the user to set some initial properties for the cursor (for instance, ink color and ink vs. eraser functionality). The collection of cursors encountered by the *InkCollector* is provided by the cursor's property of the *InkCollector* class. The preceding example also shows how the eraser tip is considered a different cursor from the ink tip because it has a different cursor ID and *NewCursor* equals *true*. Note also how the *Inverted* property equals *true*—we'll use that information later when we implement top-of-pen erase functionality. When the pen is righted again, we see that the cursor ID is the original value it was before the eraser tip was used—and we also know the ink tip is being used because the *Inverted* property equals *false*, and the *InkCollector* has seen the cursor before.

## Mouse Message Synchronization

Events from the *InkCollector* travel a different path through the Windows OS than mouse messages do. *InkCollector* events come from Wisptis.exe, dispatched to a tablet-aware application by RPC. Mouse events are triggered by Wisptis.exe, but come from User32.dll and are dispatched to an application through the application's message queue. Both processes (Wisptis.exe and the application receiving the event) are naturally executing asynchronously to one another. Because of this, you cannot rely on the ordering of *InkCollector* events *in conjunction with* mouse events. It's perfectly OK to rely on the ordering of just *InkCollector* events and/or just mouse events, *but not both together.*

## *InkOverlay* Events

The additional events that the *InkOverlay* class fires, that is, *Painting, Painted, SelectionChanging, SelectionChanged, SelectionMoving, Selection-Moved, SelectionResizing, SelectionResized, StrokesDeleting,* and *StrokesDeleted,* weren't included in the already long sample for brevity, and for the fact that they are straightforward in their behavior. Hence, it's left as an exercise for the reader to add the *InkOverlay* events to InputWatcher and observe when they fire.

What you'll see in the modified InputWatcher application is that the events suffixed with "ing" always precede their corresponding counterpart suffixed with "ed". For example, *SelectionChanging* will always fire before *Selection-Changed,* and *SelectionMoving* will always fire before *SelectionMoved.*

## Specifying the Tablet Data to Capture—Packet Properties

Now it's time to take a closer look at the data received by the *NewPackets* and *NewInAirPackets* events. What exactly is a packet, and what information is in one? To explain this, we'll take another quick dive under the covers of the TIS to see what's going on.

Recall that in addition to the location of the cursor, tablet digitizer hardware may provide other data such as pen pressure, tilt angle, and rotation angle to Wisptis.exe via the HID driver. This data can be used to render ink in a more expressive and realistic manner, and/or provide extended user input capabilities as discussed earlier. The various properties available from a digitizer are known as packet properties, referring to how data is communicated from the HID driver to Wisptis.exe in the form of packets—chunks of data with a format known to both the driver and Wisptis.exe. Packet properties are communicated from Wisptis.exe to a tablet-aware application, though it is the application's responsibility to tell Wisptis.exe which properties it wants to receive.

> **Tip**   The availability of various packet properties is totally dependent on the hardware manufacturer (and software driver if applicable) of the tablet device. The sample application DeviceWalker found later in this chapter is able to display exactly which properties are supported by your installed hardware.

The *InkCollector* class exposes packet properties via its *DesiredPacketDescription* property. A packet description is defined to be simply a list of packet properties. As such, the *DesiredPacketDescription* property is an array of zero or more *System.Guids*—valid values of which are found as static members in the *Microsoft.Ink.PacketProperty* class. A few of the properties and their descriptions are given in Table 4-10.

**Table 4-10   A Partial Listing of *PacketProperty* Members and Their Descriptions**

| *PacketProperty* Member Name | Description |
| --- | --- |
| *X* | The *X* coordinate of the pointer's location |
| *Y* | The *Y* coordinate of the pointer's location |
| *NormalPressure* | The pressure measurement of the pointer |
| *PacketStatus* | Private Wisptis data |
| *RollRotation* | The rotation angle about the long axis of the pointer |
| *PitchRotation* | The rotation angle about the normal vector to the digitizer surface of the pointer |

Figure 4-8 shows how packets relate to packet properties, packet property values, and the packet description.

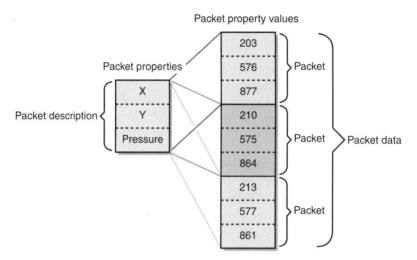

**Figure 4-8**   The relationship of packets, packet properties, packet property values, and packet description

*InkCollector* always ensures that *X, Y*, and *PacketStatus* are in the packet description it provides to Wisptis.exe, even if *DesiredPacketDescription* is null or doesn't contain those values. In fact, if the *X, Y*, or *PacketStatus* packet property is present in the desired packet description of an *InkCollector* object, that property is ignored. Those packet properties are always prepended by *InkCollector* to the packet description when it's specified to Wisptis.exe to make sure that the location and cursor button state of the pointer is always captured.

If the tablet digitizer you're using supports pressure information, you'll notice that ink drawn in HelloInkCollector will vary in width according to how much pressure was applied. This is because by default the *DesiredPacketDescription* property of an *InkCollector* object is an array containing the *X, Y*, and *NormalPressure* packet properties. Figure 4-9 shows what pressurized ink looks like—cool!

If your tablet hardware does support pressure sensitivity, try adding the following line of code in HelloInkCollector just after the *InkCollector* object is created:

```
// We'll ask the InkCollector to not receive any pressure data
// from the devices
inkCollector.DesiredPacketDescription = new Guid [] {
    PacketProperty.X, PacketProperty.Y };
```

When you compile and run the application, you'll notice that ink thickness will not change with the amount of pressure used as strokes are drawn.

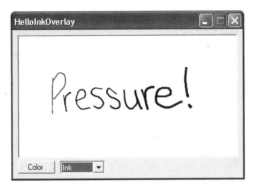

**Figure 4-9**   The result of pressure support in the HelloInkCollector application

---

# Requesting Packet Properties

If an *InkCollector* object's desired packet description contains packet properties that aren't supported by an installed tablet device, that's OK—they're properties that are *desired*, not required. The *InkCollector* won't yield any data from that tablet for those properties, and it will work fine. To prove this point, notice how ink can be drawn with the mouse in the HelloInkCollector application when the *DesiredPacketProperties* contain *PacketProperty.NormalPressure*—the ink just won't have any pressure data.

---

We'll see how to determine the list of packet properties that are supported by a tablet device in the next sample application.

The *NewPackets* and *NewInAirPackets* events notify an application that a set of packet property values was received—*NewPackets* indicates the packets were received when the cursor was down, and *NewInAirPackets* indicates the packets were received when the cursor was hovering. They are two separate events instead of one because not all the *EventArgs* data overlaps between them.

### Sample Application: *PacketPropertyWatcher*
To illustrate using packet property values, this sample application will list all supported packet properties for the default tablet device, allow the selection of any number of them, and display the corresponding values as the pointer is used with an instance of *InkCollector*.

> **Tip**    Because the Tablet PC Platform supports multiple tablet devices being installed, a default tablet exists to identify which tablet device should be used as the primary one.

If the only tablet device you have installed is a mouse, or if the default tablet device installed is rather meager in capability, chances are that there won't be any packet properties available besides *X* and *Y* coordinates and *PacketStatus*. In this case, this sample application might not clearly demonstrate much functionality, but it is hopefully still useful for reference.

Figure 4-10 shows what the sample looks like in action.

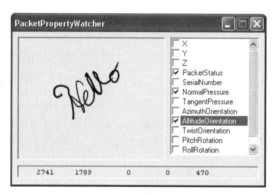

**Figure 4-10**   The PacketPropertyWatcher sample application displaying the values of desired packet property types from the default tablet.

Now let's take a look at the source code to PacketPropertyWatcher:

**PacketPropertyWatcher.cs**

```
/////////////////////////////////////////////////////////////////
//
// PacketPropertyWatcher.cs
//
// (c) 2002 Microsoft Press
// by Rob Jarrett
//
// This program allows the user to choose packet properties to
// collect and then displays their values in real time.
//
/////////////////////////////////////////////////////////////////

using System;
```

```
using System.Collections;
using System.Drawing;
using System.Reflection;
using System.Text;
using System.Windows.Forms;
using Microsoft.Ink;

public class frmMain : Form
{
    private Panel          pnlInput;
    private CheckedListBox clbPacketProps;
    private TextBox        txtOutput;
    private InkCollector   inkCollector;

    // Entry point of the program
    [STAThread]
    static void Main()
    {
        Application.Run(new frmMain());
    }

    // Main form setup
    public frmMain()
    {
        SuspendLayout();

        // Create and place all of our controls
        pnlInput = new Panel();
        pnlInput.BorderStyle = BorderStyle.Fixed3D;
        pnlInput.Location = new Point(8, 8);
        pnlInput.Size = new Size(240, 192);

        clbPacketProps = new CheckedListBox();
        clbPacketProps.CheckOnClick = true;
        clbPacketProps.Location = new Point(256, 8);
        clbPacketProps.Size = new Size(144, 192);
        clbPacketProps.ThreeDCheckBoxes = true;
        clbPacketProps.ItemCheck += new ItemCheckEventHandler(
            clbPacketProps_ItemCheck);

        txtOutput = new TextBox();
        txtOutput.Font = new Font(FontFamily.GenericMonospace, 8.0f);
        txtOutput.Location = new Point(8, 208);
        txtOutput.ReadOnly = true;
        txtOutput.Size = new Size(392, 24);
        txtOutput.WordWrap = false;
```

*(continued)*

**PacketPropertyWatcher.cs**   *(continued)*

```csharp
        // Configure the form itself
        ClientSize = new Size(408, 238);
        Controls.AddRange(new Control[] { pnlInput,
                                          clbPacketProps,
                                          txtOutput});
        FormBorderStyle = FormBorderStyle.FixedDialog;
        MaximizeBox = false;
        Text = "PacketPropertyWatcher";

        ResumeLayout(false);

        // Create an InkCollector object
        inkCollector = new InkCollector(pnlInput.Handle);

        // For simplicity, we're only going to have InkCollector
        // use the default tablet since multiple tablets will
        // probably have different sets of supported packet
        // properties - that would make the code/UI more complex
        // and obsfucate what's we're trying to illustrate.
        Tablet t = (new Tablets()).DefaultTablet;
        inkCollector.SetSingleTabletIntegratedMode(t);

        // Fill up ListBox with supported packet properties
        foreach (FieldInfo f in
            typeof(PacketProperty).GetFields())
        {
            // We're only interested in static public members of
            // the class.
            if (f.IsStatic && f.IsPublic)
            {
                Guid g = (Guid)f.GetValue(f);
                if (t.IsPacketPropertySupported(g))
                {
                    clbPacketProps.Items.Add(f.Name);
                }
            }
        }

        // Hook up event handlers to inkCollector
        inkCollector.NewInAirPackets +=
            new InkCollectorNewInAirPacketsEventHandler(
            inkCollector_NewInAirPackets);
        inkCollector.NewPackets +=
            new InkCollectorNewPacketsEventHandler(
            inkCollector_NewPackets);

        // We're now set to go, so turn on ink collection
```

```
        inkCollector.Enabled = true;
}


// InkCollector stroke event handler
private void clbPacketProps_ItemCheck(object sender,
    ItemCheckEventArgs e)
{
    // Get the Guid value of the item being (un)checked
    string n = clbPacketProps.Items[e.Index] as string;
    Guid g = new Guid();
    foreach (FieldInfo f in
        typeof(PacketProperty).GetFields())
    {
        // We're only interested in static public members
        // of the class.
        if (f.IsStatic && f.IsPublic)
        {
            if (f.Name == n)
            {
                // Found it!
                g = (Guid)f.GetValue(f);
                break;
            }
        }
    }

    // Wait until any current input is finished
    while (inkCollector.CollectingInk) {}

    // Turn off ink collection so we can alter the desired
    // packet description
    inkCollector.Enabled = false;

    if (e.NewValue == CheckState.Checked)
    {
        // Add the new packet property to the desired packet
        // properties
        ArrayList propList = new ArrayList(
            inkCollector.DesiredPacketDescription);
        propList.Add(g);
        inkCollector.DesiredPacketDescription =
            (Guid[])propList.ToArray(typeof(Guid));
    }
    else
    {
        // Remove the packet property from the desired
        // packet properties
```

*(continued)*

**PacketPropertyWatcher.cs**  *(continued)*

```csharp
            ArrayList propList = new ArrayList(
                inkCollector.DesiredPacketDescription);
            propList.Remove(g);
            inkCollector.DesiredPacketDescription =
                (Guid[])propList.ToArray(typeof(Guid));
        }


        // We're done, so turn ink collection back on
        inkCollector.Enabled = true;
    }


    // InkCollector new in-air packets event handler
    private void inkCollector_NewInAirPackets(object sender,
        InkCollectorNewInAirPacketsEventArgs e)
    {
        // Update the output window with the packet data
        UpdateOutput(e.PacketCount, e.PacketData);
    }


    // InkCollector new packets event handler
    private void inkCollector_NewPackets(object sender,
        InkCollectorNewPacketsEventArgs e)
    {
        // Update the output window with the packet data
        UpdateOutput(e.PacketCount, e.PacketData);
    }


    // Updates the UI with new packet values
    private void UpdateOutput(int cPktCount, int [] packetData)
    {
        // This shouldn't ever occur, but let's be safe to avoid a
        // divide-by-zero exception
        if (cPktCount == 0)
        {
            return;
        }


        // Compute the length of one packet
        int nPktLen = packetData.GetLength(0) / cPktCount;

        // Compute the starting index of the last packet
        int nOffset = nPktLen * (cPktCount-1);

        // Get all of the packet property values
        StringBuilder builder = new StringBuilder();
        for (int n = 0; n < nPktLen; n++)
        {
```

```
        builder.AppendFormat("{0,8} ",
            packetData[nOffset+n].ToString());
    }


    // Update the EditBox's text
    txtOutput.Text = builder.ToString();
    }
}
```

The main form of the application starts off as usual by creating its child controls: a Panel to be used as an *InkCollector* host window, a CheckedListBox to list all the supported packet properties, and an EditBox to act as a crude UI for displaying the packet property values.

After an *InkCollector* instance is created using *pnlInput* as the host window, it is followed by some rather curious-looking code:

```
Tablet t = (new Tablets()).DefaultTablet;
inkCollector.SetSingleTabletIntegratedMode(t);
```

Recall that by default an *InkCollector* instance receives tablet input from all installed tablet devices. Different tablet devices can (and usually do) have different sets of supported packet properties, so to keep the user interface of this application as simple as possible we'll just deal with the default tablet. Any other installed tablet device could be used, but the default one is typically the most capable. We tell the *InkCollector* which tablet device to accept input from by calling *InkCollector*'s *SetSingleTabletIntegratedMode* method.

---

## Single vs. Multiple Tablet Mode

Most tablet-aware applications will want all installed tablet devices used for input. However, if that's not desirable for whatever reason, the *Ink-Collector* class supports excluding the mouse from input as well as listening to a single tablet device. *InkCollector* constructor overloads or the methods *SetAllTabletsMode* and *SetSingleTabletIntegratedMode* are used, respectively.

The term "integrated" indicates how input on the digitizer device should be mapped to the screen. It loosely refers to the physical relationship of the tablet device to the screen display, though it doesn't enforce that relationship: external tablets are nonintegrated with the display, and tablets layered over the display are integrated. In the integrated case, digitizer input should be mapped to the entire screen area so that the mouse cursor will follow the pen. In the nonintegrated case, digitizer input is mapped to the *InkCollector* object's host window dimensions to typically allow greater precision.

Version 1 of the Tablet PC Platform supports only integrated mapping; sometime in the future, nonintegrated mapping may be added.

---

The *Tablets* class encapsulates the collection of installed tablet devices in the system—its elements are *Tablet* objects. By simply creating an instance of *Tablets*, the collection is automatically filled and can then be used—or as the preceding code shows, its *DefaultTablet* property can be queried. We'll learn more about the *Tablets* and *Tablet* classes toward the end of the chapter in the section "Getting Introspective."

Next the PacketPropertyWatcher application uses the reflective abilities of C# and the .NET Framework to fill up the CheckedListBox with the packet properties supported by the default tablet device. The *Tablet* class method *IsPacketPropertySupported(Guid g)* determines whether a given tablet device supports a given packet property. As the various packet property GUIDs are iterated over, adding only the supported ones to the CheckedListBox is done as follows:

```
Guid g = (Guid)f.GetValue(f);
if (t.IsPacketPropertySupported(g))
{
    clbPacketProps.Items.Add(f.Name);
}
```

The event handlers to the *InkCollector* events *NewPackets* and *NewInAir-Packets* are added, and the *InkCollector* is enabled so that tablet input can begin.

When an item is checked or unchecked in the CheckedListBox, the *clbPacketProps_ItemCheck* event handler adds or removes the corresponding packet property from the *InkCollector*'s *DesiredPacketDescription*. The first part of the function computes the GUID of the packet property because items in the CheckedListBox are stored as strings, and the second part does the adding or removing:

```
// Wait until any current input is finished
while (inkCollector.CollectingInk) {}

// Turn off ink collection so we can alter the desired
// packet description
inkCollector.Enabled = false;

if (e.NewValue == CheckState.Checked)
{
    // Add the new packet property to the desired packet
    // properties
    ArrayList propList = new ArrayList(
        inkCollector.DesiredPacketDescription);
    propList.Add(g);
    inkCollector.DesiredPacketDescription =
```

```
            (Guid[])propList.ToArray(typeof(Guid));
}
else
{
    // Remove the packet property from the desired
    // packet properties
    ArrayList propList = new ArrayList(
        inkCollector.DesiredPacketDescription);
    propList.Remove(g);
    inkCollector.DesiredPacketDescription =
        (Guid[])propList.ToArray(typeof(Guid));
}

// We're done, so turn ink collection back on
inkCollector.Enabled = true;
```

You might be wondering what's going on with that first *while* statement. Well, it turns out that to change the *DesiredPacketDescription* property of an *InkCollector* it must be in the disabled state. When changing the enabled state of an *InkCollector* object, no current ink collection can be occurring or else an exception will be thrown. *InkCollector*'s property *CollectingInk* is polled to cause the program flow to temporarily halt if any in-progress inking is occurring. You might now be thinking that in order for the checked ListBox's *itemChecked* event to fire, the *InkCollector* couldn't be in the middle of inking because the pointer was used to select the item, right? Yes, physically that's what might have happened, but recall the asynchronous execution of Windows messages and tablet input, and how either form of event could occur in any order. If the user is quick enough, he or she could stop inking and immediately choose an item in the ListBox, causing a Windows message to fire indicating an item has been checked or unchecked in the ListBox. This would cause *InkCollector*'s *Enabled* property to be set to *false*, but in the meantime it's possible that the *InkCollector* is *still processing tablet input* from the ink stroke. That would cause the *Enabled* property to throw an exception—an undesirable behavior.

The simple rule here is this: whenever you're going to disable an *InkCollector* object, make sure you wait until any inking is completed to avoid any problems.

Once the *InkCollector* is disabled, the desired packet description is modified to either add or remove the chosen packet property GUID from it. Then the *InkCollector* is re-enabled so that tablet input can resume.

The *inkCollector_NewInAirPackets* and *inkCollector_NewPackets* event handlers call the *UpdateOutput* method to get the packet data displayed in the output window. Packets arrive as an array of integers along with the count of the number of packets contained in the array. Because multiple packets can arrive in one event, *UpdateOutput* displays only the data in the last packet—there's no use in trying to display the others as they'd just quickly flicker by in the output window. You can see how this is handled in the following code:

```
// Compute the length of one packet
int nPktLen = packetData.GetLength(0) / cPktCount;

// Compute the starting index of the last packet
int nOffset = nPktLen * (cPktCount-1);

// Get all of the packet property values
StringBuilder builder = new StringBuilder();
for (int n = 0; n < nPktLen; n++)
{
    builder.AppendFormat("{0,8} ",
        packetData[nOffset+n].ToString());
}

// Update the edit box's text
txtOutput.Text = builder.ToString();
```

The method first computes the length of one packet in the array, easily accomplished by dividing the number of packets into the total array length. An offset to the last packet in the array is computed, and then a for-loop concatenates each packet value to a string. The resulting string is then displayed in the output window.

If we wanted to actually make sense of the various members in the packet, we'd need the packet description for the tablet device. This is easily obtained in a *NewPackets* event handler because a *Stroke* object is available in the *EventArgs* that has a specific *PacketDescription* property. For a *NewInAirPackets* event handler, the packet description would have to be manually computed, and this is accomplished by obtaining the *DesiredPacketDescription* from the *InkCollector*, seeing if each GUID in the packet description is supported by the tablet device using the method *Tablet.IsPacketPropertySupported*, and then constructing an array of supported properties, always prepending the GUIDs for *X* and *Y*.

Notice that in the PacketPropertyWatcher application if you turn off the *X* and *Y* properties their values will still be displayed in the output window, proving that those properties are always collected.

## Ink Coordinates

You may have noticed that the *X* and *Y* values in the packet may seem rather large in magnitude—too big to be screen pixels. Recall that tablet input not only needs to be captured quickly, but its resolution must be significantly high enough to give a great inking experience and yield high recognition accuracy.

The *X* and *Y* values in a packet are in ink coordinate space—otherwise known as HIMETRIC units. We'll learn more about them in the next chapter, along with how to convert *X* and *Y* values into screen pixels (for example, to implement your own editing behavior or a custom ink type, perhaps).

## Extending InkOverlay Behaviors

The functionality in the *InkOverlay* is cool, and it provides us with some pretty complex functionality for free. As we saw earlier, though, if you contrast *InkOverlay* to the inking experience Windows Journal yields, you'll see that some functionality is missing. That functionality is what your application's users may request once they begin using a Tablet PC with your application. Recall the list of missing functionality we enumerated earlier:

- Using the top-of-pen as an eraser

- Press-and-hold (or right-click and right-drag) in ink mode to modelessly switch to select mode

- An insert/remove space mode

- Showing selection feedback in real time (for example, as the lasso is being drawn, ink becomes selected or deselected immediately as it is enclosed or excluded by the lasso)

- Using a scratchout gesture to delete strokes

This section addresses the first two items listed: lack of top-of-pen erase and modeless switching to select mode. The samples here illustrate possible solutions to rolling your own functionality into these areas.

## Sample Application: TopOfPenErase

Top-of-pen erase is an extremely handy shortcut to access ink erasing functionality, not to mention an easy one to understand. The *InkOverlay* class provides an explicit editing mode for erasing ink (EditingMode == DeleteMode), and we saw earlier that eraser tip usage of a pen is detected through the *Cursor* class's property *Inverted*. If we can put these two pieces of functionality together, it seems that we're most of the way there in implementing top-of-pen erase.

The task at hand here then is to switch an *InkOverlay* into *DeleteMode* when the cursor becomes inverted and switch back to the previous mode when the pen returns to being right side up. Sounds easy enough, doesn't it? Let's enhance the HelloInkOverlay sample presented earlier so that it provides top-of-pen erasing:

**TopOfPenErase.cs**

```
/////////////////////////////////////////////////////////////////////
//
// TopOfPenErase.cs
//
// (c) 2002 Microsoft Press
// by Rob Jarrett
//
// This program demonstrates usage of the InkOverlay class and how
// to respond to system gestures in order to implement top-of-pen
// erase functionality.
//
/////////////////////////////////////////////////////////////////////

using System;
using System.Drawing;
using System.Reflection;
using System.Windows.Forms;
using Microsoft.Ink;

public class frmMain : Form
{
    private Panel                    pnlInput;
    private Button                   btnColor;
    private ComboBox                 cbxEditMode;
    private InkOverlay               inkOverlay;
    private InkOverlayEditingMode    modeSaved;

    // Entry point of the program
    [STAThread]
    static void Main()
    {
        Application.Run(new frmMain());
    }

    // Main form setup
    public frmMain()
    {
        SuspendLayout();
```

```
// Create and place all of our controls
pnlInput = new Panel();
pnlInput.BorderStyle = BorderStyle.Fixed3D;
pnlInput.Location = new Point(8, 8);
pnlInput.Size = new Size(352, 192);

btnColor = new Button();
btnColor.Location = new Point(8, 204);
btnColor.Size = new Size(60, 20);
btnColor.Text = "Color";
btnColor.Click += new System.EventHandler(btnColor_Click);

cbxEditMode = new ComboBox();
cbxEditMode.DropDownStyle = ComboBoxStyle.DropDownList;
cbxEditMode.Location = new Point(76, 204);
cbxEditMode.Size = new Size(72, 20);
cbxEditMode.SelectedIndexChanged +=
    new System.EventHandler(cbxEditMode_SelIndexChg);

// Configure the form itself
ClientSize = new Size(368, 232);
Controls.AddRange(new Control[] { pnlInput,
                                  btnColor,
                                  cbxEditMode});
FormBorderStyle = FormBorderStyle.FixedDialog;
MaximizeBox = false;
Text = "TopOfPenErase";

ResumeLayout(false);

// Fill up the editing mode combobox
foreach (InkOverlayEditingMode m in
    InkOverlayEditingMode.GetValues(
    typeof(InkOverlayEditingMode)))
{
    cbxEditMode.Items.Add(m);
}

// Create a new InkOverlay, using pnlInput for the collection
// area
inkOverlay = new InkOverlay(pnlInput.Handle);

// Select the current editing mode in the combobox
cbxEditMode.SelectedItem = inkOverlay.EditingMode;
```

*(continued)*

**TopOfPenErase.cs** *(continued)*

```
        // Install handler for cursor in range so we can detect when
        // the eraser tip or ink tip is used.
        inkOverlay.CursorInRange +=
            new InkCollectorCursorInRangeEventHandler(
            inkOverlay_CursorInRange);

        // Initialize the saved editing mode value
        modeSaved = inkOverlay.EditingMode;

        // We're now set to go, so turn on tablet input
        inkOverlay.Enabled = true;
    }

    // Handle the click of the color button
    private void btnColor_Click(object sender, System.EventArgs e)
    {
        // Create and display the common color dialog, using the
        // current ink color as its initial selection
        ColorDialog dlgColor = new ColorDialog();
        dlgColor.Color = inkOverlay.DefaultDrawingAttributes.Color;
        if (dlgColor.ShowDialog(this) == DialogResult.OK)
        {
            // Set the current ink color to the selection chosen in
            // the dialog
            inkOverlay.DefaultDrawingAttributes.Color = dlgColor.Color;
        }
    }

    // Handle the selection change of the editing mode combobox
    private void cbxEditMode_SelIndexChg(object sender,
        System.EventArgs e)
    {
        // Set the current editing mode to the selection chosen in the
        // combobox
        inkOverlay.EditingMode =
            (InkOverlayEditingMode)cbxEditMode.SelectedItem;

        // Save current editing mode in case it gets restored later
        modeSaved = inkOverlay.EditingMode;
    }

    // Handle cursor in range events from inkOverlay
    private void inkOverlay_CursorInRange(object sender,
        InkCollectorCursorInRangeEventArgs e)
    {
        if (e.Cursor.Inverted)
```

```
        {
            // Eraser tip is being used, so switch to delete mode if
            // we need to

            if (inkOverlay.EditingMode != InkOverlayEditingMode.Delete)
            {
                // Save current editing mode so we can restore it later
                modeSaved = inkOverlay.EditingMode;

                // Switch to delete mode
                inkOverlay.EditingMode = InkOverlayEditingMode.Delete;
            }
        }
        else
        {
            // Ink tip is being used, so restore previous mode if we
            // need to

            if (inkOverlay.EditingMode == InkOverlayEditingMode.Delete &&
                modeSaved != InkOverlayEditingMode.Delete)
            {
                // Restore the previous editing mode
                inkOverlay.EditingMode = modeSaved;
            }
        }
    }
}
```

The example differs only slightly from the original—a member variable *modeSaved* and an event handler for *CursorInRange* are added. The *inkOverlay_CursorInRange* event handler switches to *DeleteMode* when the pen is inverted and reverts to the previous mode when it is righted again. The *modeSaved* member stores the current *InkOverlayEditingMode* before the switch to *DeleteMode* occurs so that we know which mode to return to when the ink tip gets detected.

Notice how the *modeSaved* member is also updated in *cbxEditMode_SelIndexChg*. This is done to avoid a bug—the accidental reverting to *modeSaved*'s value if the *CursorInRange* event fires when the eraser tip isn't used (for instance, the cursor goes outside the input area and then returns). To see the problem, try this: comment out the line that updates the value and run the application. Switch to select mode, move the pen outside the input area and then back into it—you'll see that ink mode gets switched to instead of select mode.

# Sample Application: ModelessSwitch

Explicit mode switching, particularly between inking and editing, is cumbersome, inefficient, and annoying. Using right-tap and right-drag (via press-and-hold, a pen barrel button, or the right mouse button) to access selection and editing behavior is convenient, not to mention powerful.

This next sample application shows an implementation of modeless switching between ink and input modes via right-tap and right-drag. In Chapter 6, at which point we'll better understand rendering and hit-testing ink, we'll utilize some homemade lasso selection capability (with real-time selection feedback!) so that we can complete this application's functionality.

The application is based on the HelloInkCollector sample with one initial change—an *InkOverlay* is used instead of an *InkCollector* to get selection functionality.

**ModelessSwitch.cs**

```
//////////////////////////////////////////////////////////////////////
//
// ModelessSwitch.cs
//
// (c) 2002 Microsoft Press
// by Rob Jarrett
//
// This program demonstrates the basis for how to do an editing mode
// switch in a modeless fashion using the InkOverlay class.
//
//////////////////////////////////////////////////////////////////////

using System;
using System.Drawing;
using System.Windows.Forms;
using Microsoft.Ink;

public class frmMain : Form
{
    private InkOverlay inkOverlay;

    private Stroke  strkCurr = null;
    private Stroke  strkCancel = null;

    // Entry point of the program
    [STAThread]
    static void Main()
    {
        Application.Run(new frmMain());
    }
```

```csharp
// Main form setup
public frmMain()
{
    // Set up the form which will be the host window for an
    // InkCollector instance
    ClientSize = new Size(472, 240);
    Text = "ModelessSwitch";

    // Create a new InkOverlay, using the form for the collection
    // area
    inkOverlay = new InkOverlay(this.Handle);

    // Set up event handlers for inkOverlay
    inkOverlay.CursorDown +=
        new InkCollectorCursorDownEventHandler(
        inkOverlay_CursorDown);
    inkOverlay.Stroke +=
        new InkCollectorStrokeEventHandler(
        inkOverlay_Stroke);
    inkOverlay.SystemGesture +=
        new InkCollectorSystemGestureEventHandler(
        inkOverlay_SystemGesture);

    // We're now set to go, so turn on tablet input
    inkOverlay.Enabled = true;
}

// Handle a cursor down event from inkOverlay
private void inkOverlay_CursorDown(object sender,
    InkCollectorCursorDownEventArgs e)
{
    // Remember the current stroke being created
    strkCurr = e.Stroke;
}

// Handle a stroke event from inkOverlay
private void inkOverlay_Stroke(object sender,
    InkCollectorStrokeEventArgs e)
{
    // Throw away the stroke if a right tap or right drag was
    // detected during it's creation
    if (strkCancel != null && (e.Stroke.Id == strkCancel.Id))
    {
        e.Cancel = true;
        strkCancel = null;

        // Turn dynamic stroke rendering back on
```

*(continued)*

**ModelessSwitch.cs**   *(continued)*

```
            inkOverlay.DynamicRendering = true;
        }


        // Reset current stroke value for the next stroke created
        strkCurr = null;
    }

    // Handle a system gesture event from inkOverlay
    private void inkOverlay_SystemGesture(object sender,
        InkCollectorSystemGestureEventArgs e)
    {
        if (e.Id == SystemGesture.RightTap)
        {
            // Right tap means throw out the stroke, and show a context
            // menu
            strkCancel = strkCurr;
            Invalidate();

            //LATER: hit test the item at e.Point and select it
        }
        else if (e.Id == SystemGesture.RightDrag)
        {
            // Right drag means throw out the stroke, and start up the
            // selection lasso
            strkCancel = strkCurr;
            // Turn off dynamic rendering and set the in-progress ink
            // stroke to be invisible - that way when we invalidate the
            // form no ink will be drawn for the stroke
            inkOverlay.DynamicRendering = false;
            strkCancel.DrawingAttributes.Transparency = 255;
            Invalidate();

            //LATER: start up selection lasso, showing realitme
            // feedback of ink selection
        }
    }
}
```

You can see there's a fair amount of logic over and above HelloInkCollector to support modeless switching. Let's take a look at what this extra code does.

The implicit mode switch to select mode is triggered by a right-tap or right-drag, which the *SystemGesture* event will notify us of. When either system gesture fires, we want to throw away the ink stroke that was created; otherwise, ugly ink blobs will be added into our *Ink* object.

The system gestures *RightTap* and *RightDrag* are responded to in the *InkOverlay_SystemGesture* event handler. In the *RightTap* case, a reference to the stroke is saved so that it can be later thrown away in the imminent *Stroke* event (by setting *Cancel* to *true* in the *InkCollectorStrokeEventArgs*). For *Right-Drag*, not only is a reference to the stroke saved for later disposal, but also dynamic ink rendering is turned off so that the ink stroke doesn't continue to be drawn. Also, the stroke is made completely invisible by having its drawing attributes' *Transparency* property set to 255 (the maximum value). These both give the user the visual impression that the stroke disappears during creation.

# Getting Introspective

Sitting alone in front of a crackling fire, sipping a glass of cabernet, listening to William Shatner's rendition of "Mr. Tambourine Man"… life, the universe—what does it all *mean*? OK, that's actually not what's being referred to here. Rather, we're going to talk about how your tablet-aware application might find it useful to know more about the hardware environment it's running in—perhaps find out how many tablet devices are installed, what their capabilities are, and so on.

This section covers the Platform SDK support to introspect the system, in order to garner all the information you'd ever need about the installed tablet devices.

## Tablets Collection

We briefly saw earlier that the *Tablets* class encapsulates the collection of installed tablet devices in the system. The collection's elements are *Tablet* objects, representing a single installed tablet device. You obtain an instance of *Tablets* simply by allocating it—Tablet PC Platform will automatically fill in the contents.

Besides having the normal collection properties and methods, the Tablets class also has a *DefaultTablet* property that identifies the primary tablet device installed in the system.

## Tablet Class

Tablet devices installed in the system have various attributes, such as a name, a coordinate system, a list of all the packet properties it can report, and other capabilities such as being able to uniquely identify pens.

The *Tablet* class encapsulates the properties of an installed tablet device. Let's take a look at each of these properties in Table 4-11:

**Table 4-11   The Properties of the *Tablet* Class**

| Property Name | Type | Description |
|---|---|---|
| *HardwareCapabilities* | *TabletHardwareCapabilities* | A bitfield of various device capabilities, defined in the *TabletHardwareCapabilities* enumeration |
| *MaximumInputRectangle* | *System.Drawing.Rectangle* | The coordinate space of the entire surface of the tablet device |
| *Name* | *String* | A human-readable form of the tablet's name |
| *PlugAndPlayId* | *String* | The device name reported to the system by the device |

The *HardwareCapabilities* property is a bitfield of values found in the *TabletHardwareCapabilities* enumeration. The various capabilities of tablet hardware that the Tablet PC Platform currently enumerates are as listed in Table 4-12:

**Table 4-12   The Members of the *TabletHardwareCapabilities* Enumeration**

| Hardware Capability | Description |
|---|---|
| *CursorMustTouch* | The pen must be touching the surface for its position to be sampled. |
| *CursorsHavePhysicalIds* | The tablet is able to distinguish between pens used with the device. |
| *HardProximity* | The pen's position can be reported while it's in the air but in close proximity to the device. |
| *Integrated* | The tablet is integrated with the display. |

The *Tablet* class's *IsPacketPropertySupported* method is a useful function that tells you whether the tablet supports or provides a given packet property type. We saw use of this function earlier in the PacketPropertyWatcher sample so that the ListBox could be filled up only with packet properties that the default tablet supported.

The *GetPropertyMetrics* method returns an instance of *TabletPropertyMetrics* given a packet property GUID. *TabletPropertyMetrics* is used to provide the units, resolution, and minimum and maximum values of a packet property type. This is useful information if you ever want to parse packet data beyond just $X$ and $Y$ values—for example, if you wanted pen pressure or rotation to perform some special behavior, the *TabletPropertyMetrics* of the packet property should be used so that you know how to interpret those packet data values.

## Sample Application: DeviceWalker

This final sample application displays all installed tablet devices, their capabilities, and supported packet properties, as shown in Figure 4-11.

**Figure 4-11**   The DeviceWalker sample application shows the capabilities of all the tablet devices installed in the system.

### DeviceWalker.cs

```
/////////////////////////////////////////////////////////////////////
//
// DeviceWalker.cs
//
// (c) 2002 Microsoft Press
// by Rob Jarrett
//
// This program demonstrates introspection of installed Tablet
// devices.
//
/////////////////////////////////////////////////////////////////////

using System;
using System.Drawing;
using System.Reflection;
using System.Windows.Forms;
using Microsoft.Ink;

public class frmMain : Form
{
    private Label        lblTablets;
```

*(continued)*

**DeviceWalker.cs** *(continued)*

```
private Label        lblLine1;
private ComboBox     cbTablets;
private Label        lblExtraInfo;
private Label        lblHardwareCaps;
private Label        lblLine2;
private ListView     lvHardwareCaps;
private Label        lblPacketProps;
private Label        lblLine3;
private ListView     lvPacketProps;
private Button       btnClose;

// Entry point of the program
[STAThread]
static void Main()
{
    Application.Run(new frmMain());
}

// Main form setup
public frmMain()
{
    SuspendLayout();

    // Create and place all of our controls
    lblTablets = new Label();
    lblTablets.Location = new Point(8, 8);
    lblTablets.Size = new Size(128, 16);
    lblTablets.Text = "Installed tablet devices:";

    lblLine1 = new Label();
    lblLine1.BorderStyle = BorderStyle.Fixed3D;
    lblLine1.Location = new Point(136, 16);
    lblLine1.Size = new Size(144, 2);

    cbTablets = new ComboBox();
    cbTablets.DropDownStyle = ComboBoxStyle.DropDownList;
    cbTablets.Location = new Point(16, 32);
    cbTablets.Size = new Size(264, 21);
    cbTablets.SelectedIndexChanged +=
        new System.EventHandler(cbTablets_SelIndexChg);

    lblExtraInfo = new Label();
    lblExtraInfo.Location = new Point(16, 56);
    lblExtraInfo.Size = new Size(264, 16);

    lblHardwareCaps = new Label();
    lblHardwareCaps.Location = new Point(8, 80);
    lblHardwareCaps.Size = new Size(120, 16);
```

```
lblHardwareCaps.Text = "Hardware capabilities:";

lblLine2 = new Label();
lblLine2.BorderStyle = BorderStyle.Fixed3D;
lblLine2.Location = new Point(128, 88);
lblLine2.Size = new Size(152, 3);

lvHardwareCaps = new ListView();
lvHardwareCaps.FullRowSelect = true;
lvHardwareCaps.Location = new Point(16, 104);
lvHardwareCaps.MultiSelect = false;
lvHardwareCaps.Size = new Size(264, 80);
lvHardwareCaps.View = View.Details;

lblPacketProps = new Label();
lblPacketProps.Location = new Point(8, 200);
lblPacketProps.Size = new Size(96, 16);
lblPacketProps.Text = "Packet properties:";

lblLine3 = new Label();
lblLine3.BorderStyle = BorderStyle.Fixed3D;
lblLine3.Location = new Point(104, 208);
lblLine3.Size = new Size(176, 3);

lvPacketProps = new ListView();
lvPacketProps.FullRowSelect = true;
lvPacketProps.Location = new Point(16, 224);
lvPacketProps.MultiSelect = false;
lvPacketProps.Size = new Size(264, 97);
lvPacketProps.View = View.Details;

btnClose = new Button();
btnClose.DialogResult = DialogResult.OK;
btnClose.Location = new Point(208, 328);
btnClose.Text = "Close";
btnClose.Click +=
    new System.EventHandler(btnClose_Click);

// Configure the form itself
AcceptButton = btnClose;
CancelButton = btnClose;
ClientSize = new Size(292, 360);
Controls.AddRange(new Control[] { lblTablets,
                                  lblLine1,
                                  cbTablets,
                                  lblExtraInfo,
                                  lblHardwareCaps,
                                  lblLine2,
```

*(continued)*

**DeviceWalker.cs**   *(continued)*

```
                                        lvHardwareCaps,
                                        lblPacketProps,
                                        lblLine3,
                                        lvPacketProps,
                                        btnClose });
        FormBorderStyle = FormBorderStyle.FixedDialog;
        MaximizeBox = false;
        Text = "DeviceWalker";

        ResumeLayout(false);

        // Fill the combobox with the currently installed tablet
        // devices
        Tablets tablets = new Tablets();
        foreach (Tablet t in tablets)
        {
            cbTablets.Items.Add(t);
        }

        // Trigger a UI update to fill in the rest of the properties
        cbTablets.SelectedIndex = 0;
    }

    // Tablet device combobox selection changed handler
    private void cbTablets_SelIndexChg(object sender,
        System.EventArgs e)
    {
        // Turn off listview invalidatation for performance
        lvHardwareCaps.BeginUpdate();
        lvPacketProps.BeginUpdate();

        // Remove all items from the listviews
        lvHardwareCaps.Clear();
        lvPacketProps.Clear();

        // Set up their columns
        lvHardwareCaps.Columns.Add("Capability", 150,
            HorizontalAlignment.Left);
        lvHardwareCaps.Columns.Add("Possessed", 100,
            HorizontalAlignment.Left);
        lvPacketProps.Columns.Add("Property", 100,
            HorizontalAlignment.Left);
        lvPacketProps.Columns.Add("Supported", 150,
            HorizontalAlignment.Left);

        // Get the tablet device to introspect
        Tablet t = cbTablets.SelectedItem as Tablet;
        if (t != null)
```

```csharp
{
    // Fill in "extra" info about the tablet
    lblExtraInfo.Text = String.Format(
        "PnP ID: {0}  InputRect: ({1},{2},{3},{4})",
        t.PlugAndPlayId,
        t.MaximumInputRectangle.Left,
        t.MaximumInputRectangle.Top,
        t.MaximumInputRectangle.Bottom,
        t.MaximumInputRectangle.Right);

    // Fill in hardware capabilities by walking through each
    // value in the TabletHardwareCapabilities enum and seeing
    // if the device supports it
    foreach (TabletHardwareCapabilities c in
        TabletHardwareCapabilities.GetValues(
        typeof(TabletHardwareCapabilities)))
    {
        ListViewItem item = new ListViewItem();
        item.Text = c.ToString();
        if ((t.HardwareCapabilities & c) == c)
        {
            item.SubItems.Add("Yes");
        }
        else
        {
            item.SubItems.Add("No");
        }
        lvHardwareCaps.Items.Add(item);
    }

    // Fill in packet properties by walking through each value
    // in the PacketProperty class and seeing if the device
    // supports it
    foreach (FieldInfo f in
        typeof(PacketProperty).GetFields())
    {
        // We're only interested in static public members of
        // the class
        if (f.IsStatic && f.IsPublic)
        {
            ListViewItem item = new ListViewItem();
            item.Text = f.Name;

            Guid g = (Guid)f.GetValue(f);
            if (t.IsPacketPropertySupported(g))
            {
                TabletPropertyMetrics tm =
                    t.GetPropertyMetrics(g);
```

*(continued)*

**DeviceWalker.cs**   *(continued)*

```
                        item.SubItems.Add(
                            String.Format(
                            "Yes: ({0}-{1} {2})",
                            tm.Minimum.ToString(),
                            tm.Maximum.ToString(),
                            tm.Units.ToString())));
                    }
                    else
                    {
                        item.SubItems.Add("No");
                    }
                    lvPacketProps.Items.Add(item);
                }
            }
        }

        // Turn on listview invalidation now that we're done
        lvHardwareCaps.EndUpdate();
        lvPacketProps.EndUpdate();
    }

    // Close Button clicked handler
    private void btnClose_Click(object sender, System.EventArgs e)
    {
        Application.Exit();
    }
}
```

The *cbTablets_SelIndexChg* method does the lion's share of the work in this application—it fills in the UI with the hardware capabilities and supported packet properties of the currently selected tablet device. Again we take advantage of C#'s reflection abilities to enumerate various members of enumerations and classes.

## Common Properties on *InkCollector* and *InkOverlay*

In an effort to bring together all that we've learned thus far, we've put together a mini-review of the *InkCollector* and *InkOverlay* classes by listing the commonly used properties, methods, and events in them. Tables 4-13 and 4-14 aren't meant to be an exhaustive reference, merely an effort to summarize the information that has been covered in the chapter.

### Table 4-13   *InkCollector* and *InkOverlay* Mini-Reference

| Property | Type | Description | Input Can Be Enabled |
|---|---|---|---|
| *AutoRedraw* | *Bool* (read-write) | Whether to redraw currently captured ink when the host window gets invalidated | Read: Yes Write: Yes |
| *CollectingInk* | *Bool* (read-only) | Reports if the *InkCollector* is currently collecting an ink stroke | Read: Yes |
| *CollectionMode* | *CollectionMode* (read-write) | Whether the *InkCollector* should recognize ink gestures | Read: Yes Write: No |
| *DefaultDrawingAttributes* | *DrawingAttributes* (read-write) | Specifies the drawing attributes to be used when creating new ink strokes | Read: Yes Write: Yes |
| *DesiredPacketDescription* | *Guid[]* (read-write) | Specifies which tablet input properties to collect | Read: Yes Write: No |
| *DynamicRendering* | *Bool* (read-write) | Whether in-progress ink strokes should be drawn | Read: Yes Write: Yes |
| *Enabled* | *Bool* (read-write) | Turns tablet input data capture on and off | Read: Yes Write: N/A |
| *Handle* | *IntPtr32* (read-write) | The *InkCollector*'s host window's handle | Read: Yes Write: No |
| *Ink* | *Ink* (read-write) | The object used to store collected ink strokes | Read: Yes Write: No |

### Table 4-14   *InkOverlay* Mini-Reference

| Property | Type | Description | Input Can Be Enabled |
|---|---|---|---|
| *EditingMode* | *InkOverlayEditingMode* (read-write) | The current editing mode used for interaction | Read: Yes Write: Yes |
| *EraserMode* | *InkOverlayEraserMode* (read-write) | The type of erasing used when in DeleteMode | Read: Yes Write: Yes |
| *EraserWidth* | *int* (read-write) | The eraser width and height for point-level erase | Read: Yes Write: Yes |

# Best Practices for *InkCollector* and *InkOverlay*

Now that you're armed with a boatload of knowledge about tablet input, it's worth covering a few points of interest in properly using certain facilities. To sum up the core philosophy behind getting the most out of tablet input, "conservation is key."

Let's look at some things you should keep in mind when using either the *InkCollector* or *InkOverlay* classes.

### *NewPackets* and *NewInAirPackets* Events

Remember that tablet events occur a lot more frequently than mouse events do. Performance is crucial when you use the *NewPackets* and *NewInAirPackets* event handlers because they're called so often. Ink performance can suffer dramatically if too much time is taken executing code in them—so if you can, don't even use those handlers in your application. You might be able to use the mouse events instead.

If you do need to use *NewPackets* and *NewInAirPackets*, the code in the handlers should be efficient; try to avoid potentially slow operations such as rendering or network access.

### Choosing Desired Packet Properties

Packet property types are cool, but try to be conservative when requesting them. Recall that Wisptis.exe packs the property values into packets that are sent to a tablet-aware application via a packet queue. Because each packet property adds an integer value to each packet, requesting many packet properties can cause the packet size to be large. This can slow down the communication between Wisptis.exe and your application, resulting in poor inking performance.

### Gesture Recognition

A similar philosophy to packet properties should be taken with gesture recognition. Gestures can take a long time to recognize, so the set of gestures your application uses should be kept to a minimum. This is not to say gestures are bad because they're definitely not! It's just that executing code that recognizes gestures your application isn't interested in will only slow down getting the results of gestures your application *is* interested in. Therefore, use the *Ink-Collector*'s *SetGestureStatus* method to specify only the gestures you're interested in being recognized.

### Mouse Events

Recall that mouse events occur asynchronously to tablet input events. This can have a negative effect on user interface behavior if you're not careful. If your application changes the user interface state as a result of a tablet event (for example, showing a context menu, bringing up a dialog, or hiding a form), the corresponding mouse event may occur either before or after that user interface change. That may cause some strange behavior that can be tough to debug.

Consider this example—in the *SystemGesture* event handler, an application chooses to show a context menu as the result of a *RightTap*. Sometimes the menu will randomly immediately disappear, not allowing the user to choose any item in it. What's happening? The mouse events that Wisptis.exe is generating are getting processed *after* the tablet input event is, and that causes User32.dll to think that the user has clicked the right-mouse button, causing the menu to be dismissed. Yuck!

The general rule of thumb here is: perform user interface changes only for those mouse events that have an effect in mouse event handlers.

## Summary

This chapter covered a lot of material—hopefully everything you'd ever want to know about tablet input.

We started off looking at the requirements and the architecture of the tablet input subsystem in Windows XP Tablet PC Edition and under a Windows-based OS running Tablet PC runtime libraries. We were then introduced to the *Ink-Collector* and *InkOverlay* classes and how they facilitate any occurring tablet input. We learned about the capabilities of *InkCollector* and *InkOverlay* and how to leverage them in a hands-on sense through various sample applications. And finally we presented some real-world knowledge from folks who have used the stuff.

Now that you know all about collecting ink, the next two chapters will show you how to manipulate it in all sorts of fun ways.

# 5

# Tablet PC Platform SDK: Ink Data Management, Part I

The last chapter covered how to enable your application to collect digital ink—a rather fundamental requirement to be met by an ink-enabled application. We explained in Chapter 2 that one of the key philosophies behind Tablet PC application design is "ink as a first-class citizen," so it follows that the ability to interact with, manipulate, and persist ink data is also of great importance. Whether it's simply changing the color of ink to green or performing custom real-time lasso selection, you'll more than likely find a need to use the Ink Data Management API in your application. Fortunately, the Tablet PC Platform team has done a great job of providing powerful, easy-to-use, and flexible APIs for us! We have little doubt you'll find that the material covered here and in the next chapter is some of the most fun to work with out of the entire Tablet PC Platform SDK.

This first chapter on ink data management begins by discussing the constructs used in ink data management along with their ownership and lifetimes. The functionality of creating, managing, and destroying ink is then presented, followed by the rendering of ink. By the end of the chapter, we will have covered the Tablet PC Platform APIs that are used to create and delete ink strokes, manage collections of strokes, and draw ink in different styles. Sample applications are presented throughout this chapter to illustrate the concepts discussed.

So how about we "think in ink," and get going!

# *Ink* and *Stroke* Objects

We know that digital ink is captured in the form of *Stroke* objects that are obtained through user input occurring on *InkCollector* and *InkOverlay* objects. *Stroke* objects are the fundamental building blocks of an ink document, with each object representing a stroke of digital ink. Because *Stroke* objects are essentially a collection of packets, where each packet contains an $x,y$ location and optionally other packet properties such as pen pressure, it follows that a *Stroke* is really just a fancy polyline.

A *Stroke* object is contained by an instance of the *Ink* class. The *Ink* class is the outermost entry point into the Ink Data API, and it is analogous to a document class—the root of an ownership hierarchy for ink data. *Ink* objects define a scope in which multiple *Stroke* objects can exist. An *Ink* object owns zero or more *Stroke* objects, and a *Stroke* can be contained by exactly one *Ink* object—therefore, an *Ink* object owns a collection of *Stroke* objects. Although a *Stroke* may be transferred between different *Ink* objects, it cannot exist without an *Ink* object as its owner.

> **Note** Recall that *InkCollector* and *InkOverlay* each have a property on them called *Ink*. That's an instance of the *Ink* class that is being described here. An *InkCollector* or *InkOverlay* object creates the *Stroke* objects in the ownership scope of the *Ink* object currently set with that property.

The *Ink* class typically exposes its *Stroke* objects through a collection class called *Strokes*. A *Strokes* collection indeed lives up to its name—it is a collection of *Stroke* objects, with some extra capabilities we'll find out about later. The *Ink* class has a read-only property named *Strokes* whose purpose is to return an instance of a *Strokes* collection containing the current list of *Stroke* objects owned by the *Ink* object.

---

### *Stroke* Objects vs. *Strokes*

You might have noticed that in the last couple of paragraphs I've referred to a plurality of *Stroke* objects explicitly as *Stroke objects* and not simply *Strokes*, specifically to avoid confusion with the *Strokes* collection. Although it may be a little more cumbersome to read, hopefully it will keep things clear.

---

The *Strokes* collection is actually a collection of *references* to *Stroke* objects—adding or removing *Stroke* objects to or from a *Strokes* collection has no effect on the *Stroke* objects' lifetimes or on their containment. The lifetime of a *Stroke* object is only tied to its owning *Ink* object, and the containment of a *Stroke* object is only changed by an *Ink* object—hence, it's possible for a *Strokes* collection to refer to a *Stroke* object that has been destructed. Don't fear, though, as the Ink Data Management API takes this into account and deals with it nicely, as we'll soon see.

To reiterate the point we just made: a *Strokes* collection plays no role in the ownership or lifetime of *Stroke* objects; it only references them. To further explain this, consider the following code snippet:

```
// An attempt to remove all Stroke objects from an Ink object
inkOverlay.Ink.Strokes.Clear();
```

This code has no observable effect. The *Strokes* collection returned from the *Ink* object's property *Strokes* is actually a copy of the current list of *Stroke* objects it owns, and the *Strokes* collection only references, not owns, *Stroke* objects anyway, so removing *Stroke* objects from the collection will have no effect on whether they are destroyed. Similarly, adding *Stroke* objects to a *Strokes* collection does not imply that their owning *Ink* objects will be changed.

A *Strokes* collection is created by an *Ink* object and can refer only to *Stroke* objects owned by that same *Ink* object. It is impossible for a *Strokes* collection to refer to *Stroke* objects contained in different *Ink* objects, and if an attempt is made to do so an exception will be thrown. It is perfectly allowable (and common) for multiple *Strokes* collections to be created from one *Ink* object, each referring to zero or more *Stroke* objects owned by the *Ink* object.

## Introduction to the *Ink*, *Stroke*, and *Strokes* Classes

Figure 5-1 shows the relationship between *Ink*, *Stroke*, and *Strokes* objects using the HelloInkOverlay sample from Chapter 4. In a nutshell, an *Ink* object is a container for *Stroke* objects, and a *Strokes* collection references *Stroke* objects. This is one of the most fundamental and important concepts to understand about the Ink Data Management API.

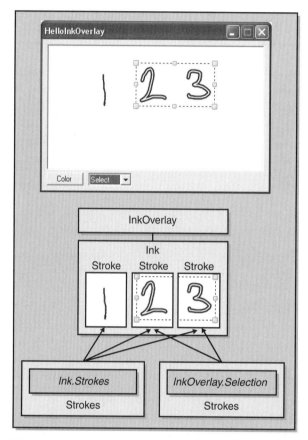

**Figure 5-1**   A diagram of the relationship between *Ink*, *Stroke*, and *Strokes* objects.

### The *Ink* Class

An instance of the *Ink* class is automatically created when an *InkCollector* or *InkOverlay* object is created, and it is made accessible through the *Ink* property. An *Ink* object can also be created explicitly via the C# *new* operator, and there are a couple of Ink Data Management APIs that return new *Ink* objects. Once it has been created, an *Ink* object requires no special setup for use.

All *Ink* objects and *Stroke* objects use the HIMETRIC coordinate system. A HIMETRIC unit represents 0.01mm, where the measurement is derived from the screen's current dpi. The coordinate space is the usual Microsoft Windows–style fourth quadrant in which the origin (0,0) represents the upper-left corner of the space and positive $x$ and $y$ coordinates imply locations to the right and down, respectively. The *Stroke* objects contained in an *Ink* object all share the coordinate space, so each *Stroke* object's packet's $x$, $y$ values are based from a common (0,0) origin.

The *Ink* class provides a number of functions that operate on *Strokes* collections and *Stroke* objects, performing such operations as creation and destruction, transformations, and persistence. As already discussed, the class most notably defines a read-only property called *Strokes* that returns a snapshot of the current collection of *Stroke* objects it contains.

## The *Stroke* Class

*Stroke* objects are a series of packets comprised of $(x, y)$ coordinates and optionally some other packet properties, defined at the time of the *Stroke*'s creation. One stroke represents exactly one continuous stroke of ink—it cannot have multiple start and end points in it.

Each *Stroke* object is assigned a unique ID within the scope of its owning *Ink* object. The ID is an integer that is assigned by the *Ink* object at the time of the *Stroke*'s creation or addition to the *Ink* object, and it remains constant for the *Stroke*'s lifetime—even when the *Stroke* object is modified. If the *Stroke* is later transferred to another *Ink* object, the ID will be changed because the uniqueness of a *Stroke*'s ID is only guaranteed within the scope of its owning *Ink* object. The ID of a *Stroke* object is obtained via the *Stroke* class's *Id* property and is of type *int*.

*Stroke* objects also possess the read-only property *Deleted*, indicating if the *Stroke* object exists anymore. Exists anymore? Huh? Let's find out what that means by first learning a little about how *Strokes* collections work.

## The *Strokes* Class

As has already been mentioned, a *Strokes* collection is a collection of references to *Stroke* objects. *Strokes* collections provide a useful way to deal with multiple *Stroke* objects, first by acting as an aggregation of *Stroke* objects, and second by defining common operations on groups of *Stroke* objects, such as transformation and visual style formatting.

A *Strokes* collection is really just an encapsulation of an array of stroke IDs. When it needs to dereference one of its elements, a *Strokes* collection queries the owning *Ink* object for the *Stroke* object with the ID found in the element being dereferenced.

If a *Strokes* collection references a *Stroke* object that has been destroyed by the owning *Ink* object, the reference will still remain in the *Strokes* collection and will still yield a *Stroke* object when dereferenced. However, no operations can be executed on that stroke, and only two of its properties will be readable: *Id* and *Deleted*. An attempt to call a method or query any other properties on that *Stroke* object will cause an exception to occur. This is why the *Deleted* property was noted previously; a *Strokes* collection will always yield *Stroke* objects, though they may not necessarily be usable. Given a *Strokes* collection whose contents are not under your full control, it's always a good idea to check the *Deleted* property of *Stroke* objects once they're dereferenced before performing any operations on them.

*Strokes* collections are commonly found by querying the *Ink* class's *Strokes* property (which we've learned always returns a copy of the current collection) and the *InkOverlay* class's *Selection* property (which returns a copy of the current collection of selected *Stroke* objects).

### Sample Application—StrokeIdViewer

To best illustrate the behavior of stroke ID values, we'll jump right into the StrokeIdViewer sample application, shown in Figure 5-2. Its purpose is to present an *InkOverlay*-based UI and draw each *Stroke* object's corresponding stroke ID at the start point of the *Stroke*. Then, as strokes are created, deleted, moved, resized, and so forth, we can observe the stroke ID values.

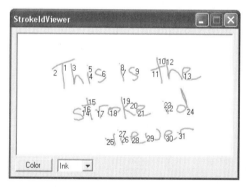

**Figure 5-2**   The StrokeIdViewer sample application.

The first block of code presented shows the implementation of the *DrawStrokeIds* method found in the *RendererEx* class, which is part of the BuildingTabletApps utility library. There are in fact two overloads of the *DrawStrokeIds* method, defined as:

```
public static void DrawStrokeIds(Graphics g, Font font, Ink ink)
public static void DrawStrokeIds(Renderer renderer, Graphics g,
                                 Font font, Strokes strks)
```

These static functions render each *Stroke* object's stroke ID value to the *Graphics* object *g* using the *Font font*. The *Stroke* objects are obtained from the *Ink* object *ink* or referenced by the *Strokes* collection *strokes*. The meaning of the *Renderer* object *renderer* will be covered later in the chapter, but for now it's sufficient to say that it's used to convert ink coordinates into screen pixels.

```
namespace MSPress.BuildingTabletApps
{
    public class RendererEx
    {
        // Draw the stroke IDs in the top-left corner of each stroke's
        // bounding rectangle for an Ink object
        public static void DrawStrokeIds(Graphics g, Font font, Ink ink)
        {
            DrawStrokeIds(new Renderer(), g, font, ink.Strokes);
        }

        // Draw the stroke IDs for a Strokes collection
        public static void DrawStrokeIds(
            Renderer renderer, Graphics g, Font font, Strokes strokes)
        {
            // Iterate through every stroke referenced by the collection
            foreach (Stroke s in strokes)
            {
                // Make sure each stroke has not been deleted
                if (!s.Deleted)
                {
                    // Draw the stroke's ID at its starting point
                    string str = s.Id.ToString();
                    Point pt = s.GetPoint(0);
                    renderer.InkSpaceToPixel(g, ref pt);
                    g.DrawString(
                        str, font, Brushes.White, pt.X-1, pt.Y-1);
                    g.DrawString(
                        str, font, Brushes.White, pt.X+1, pt.Y+1);
                    g.DrawString(
                        str, font, Brushes.Black, pt.X, pt.Y);
                }
            }
        }
    }
}
```

Notice that the implementation of *DrawStrokeIds* that accepts *Ink* as a parameter calls the other overload of *DrawStrokeIds*, passing the *ink* parameter's *Strokes* property and creating a new instance of the *Renderer* class—thus the real meat of the functionality in this application is this code:

```
// Iterate through every stroke referenced by the collection
foreach (Stroke s in strokes)
{
    // Make sure each stroke has not been deleted
    if (!s.Deleted)
    {
        // Draw the stroke's ID at its starting point
        string str = s.Id.ToString();
        Point pt = s.GetPoint(0);
        renderer.InkSpaceToPixel(g, ref pt);
        g.DrawString(str, font, Brushes.White, pt.X-1, pt.Y-1);
        g.DrawString(str, font, Brushes.White, pt.X+1, pt.Y+1);
        g.DrawString(str, font, Brushes.Black, pt.X, pt.Y);
    }
}
```

Because the *Strokes* collection class implements the *IEnumerator* interface defined by the Microsoft .NET Framework, *Strokes* collections can be used with the *foreach* statement. The preceding snippet iterates over all *Stroke* objects referenced by the collection, and for every *Stroke* object obtained the function checks to see whether the *Stroke* is usable by looking at its *Deleted* property. Recall that *Stroke* objects are always returned when dereferencing from a *Strokes* collection, even if the *Stroke* doesn't exist anymore in the owning *Ink* object.

Upon determining whether the *Stroke* object is usable, the function obtains the *Stroke* object's ID via the *Id* property. The function then gets the starting point of the *Stroke* object (defined to be the zero point in the stroke), and because that value is in HIMETRIC units it must be converted to pixels using the *Renderer* class's *InkSpaceToPixel* method so the ID can be drawn to the *graphics* object. The stroke ID is then drawn—it is actually rendered three times to help with readability of the value. If the ID is drawn over the top of any black strokes, it likely would not be readable; therefore, a white space is created around the value by rendering it in white and slightly offset from the final real rendering of the value in black.

Now let's take a look at the actual sample program listing that leverages the *DrawStrokeIds* method:

## StrokeIdViewer.cs

```
///////////////////////////////////////////////////////////////////
//
// StrokeIdViewer.cs
//
// (c) 2002 Microsoft Press
// by Rob Jarrett
//
// This program demonstrates the behavior of Stroke IDs. An
// InkOverlaySharp control is created and as strokes are added,
// removed, and modified, their IDs are drawn to show their
// behavior.
//
///////////////////////////////////////////////////////////////////

using System;
using System.Drawing;
using System.Windows.Forms;
using Microsoft.Ink;
using MSPress.BuildingTabletApps;

public class frmMain : Form
{
    private InkControl          inkCtl;
    private StrokesEventHandler evtInkAdded;
    private StrokesEventHandler evtInkDeleted;

    // Entry point of the program
    [STAThread]
    static void Main()
    {
        Application.Run(new frmMain());
    }

    // Main form setup
    public frmMain()
    {
        SuspendLayout();

        // Create and place all of our controls
        inkCtl = new InkControl();
        inkCtl.Location = new Point(8, 8);
        inkCtl.Size = new Size(352, 216);

        // Configure the form itself
        ClientSize = new Size(368, 232);
```

*(continued)*

**StrokeIdViewer.cs** *(continued)*

```csharp
        Controls.AddRange(new Control[] { inkCtl });
        FormBorderStyle = FormBorderStyle.FixedDialog;
        MaximizeBox = false;
        Text = "StrokeIdViewer";

        ResumeLayout(false);

        // Hook up to the InkOverlay's event handlers
        inkCtl.InkOverlay.Painted +=
            new InkOverlayPaintedEventHandler(inkCtl_Painted);
        inkCtl.InkOverlay.Ink.InkAdded +=
            new StrokesEventHandler(inkCtl_InkAdded);
        inkCtl.InkOverlay.Ink.InkDeleted +=
            new StrokesEventHandler(inkCtl_InkDeleted);

        // Create event handlers so we can be called back on the correct
        // thread
        evtInkAdded = new StrokesEventHandler(inkCtl_InkAdded_Apt);
        evtInkDeleted = new StrokesEventHandler(inkCtl_InkDeleted_Apt);

        // Set the ink color to something other than black so it's
        // easier to see the stroke ID values
        inkCtl.InkOverlay.DefaultDrawingAttributes.Color =
            Color.DarkOrange;

        // We're now set to go, so turn on tablet input
        inkCtl.InkOverlay.Enabled = true;
    }

    // Handle the InkOverlay having been painted
    private void inkCtl_Painted(object sender, PaintEventArgs e)
    {
        RendererEx.DrawStrokeIds(
            e.Graphics, Font, inkCtl.InkOverlay.Ink);
    }

    // Handle ink having been added
    private void inkCtl_InkAdded(object sender, StrokesEventArgs e)
    {
        // Make sure the event fires on the correct thread
        this.Invoke(evtInkAdded, new object[] { sender, e });
    }
    private void inkCtl_InkAdded_Apt(object sender, StrokesEventArgs e)
    {
        inkCtl.InkInputPanel.Invalidate();
    }
```

```
// Handle ink having been deleted
private void inkCtl_InkDeleted(object sender, StrokesEventArgs e)
{
    // Make sure the event fires on the correct thread
    this.Invoke(evtInkDeleted, new object[] { sender, e });
}
private void inkCtl_InkDeleted_Apt(object sender, StrokesEventArgs e)
{
    inkCtl.InkInputPanel.Invalidate();
}
}
```

The sample application begins its execution by creating an instance of the *InkControl* class that was first mentioned in Chapter 4. The *InkControl* class is a control based on the HelloInkOverlay sample. The *InkControl*'s *Ink-Overlay* then has a *Paint* event handler installed, which when triggered will call *RendererEx.DrawStrokeIds*, resulting in the stroke IDs being drawn. Next, two more event handlers are installed, this time on the *InkOverlay*'s *Ink* property:

```
inkCtl.InkOverlay.Ink.InkAdded +=
    new StrokesEventHandler(inkCtl_InkAdded);
inkCtl.InkOverlay.Ink.InkDeleted +=
    new StrokesEventHandler(inkCtl_InkDeleted);
```

The *InkAdded* and *InkDeleted* events are triggered when an *Ink* object has *Stroke* objects created and deleted from it as a result of either tablet input or programmatic means. The implementations of the *StrokesEventHandler* event handlers merely cause a full redraw to occur on *pnlInput*, resulting in the latest stroke ID values to be displayed.

Notice that the implementations of both the *InkAdded* and *InkDeleted* events actually trigger another event handler using the .NET Framework's *Control.Invoke* method. This is because the *InkAdded* and *InkDeleted* events can be fired on a thread other than the application's main thread of execution. To avoid any multithreading problems, the application ensures that only Windows Forms data access occurs on the main thread.

## Analysis of Stroke ID Behavior

When you first start the StrokeIdViewer application, try drawing a stroke using the mouse or pen. You'll see that once you complete the stroke, a stroke ID of 1 should appear at the stroke's starting point. Now try drawing another stroke and observe it is assigned a stroke ID of 2. Draw yet another stroke and it should be assigned a stroke ID of 3. Notice the pattern—the stroke ID increments by 1 for every stroke drawn.

Now, switch to Select mode and select a stroke by either tapping or lassoing. Once you have a selection, drag it around the input area. Observe that the stroke IDs remain constant. Try resizing the selection, and again notice the stroke ID values don't change.

When you switch back to Ink mode and draw another stroke, the assigned stroke ID value isn't what you might expect. If the last stroke ID assigned before you switched to select mode was 3, you would think that the next stroke drawn would be assigned a stroke ID of 4 in keeping with the pattern we have observed. Instead, an ID of 8 gets assigned (your value might be different, but it won't be 4). What happened to the IDs in between? Well, each pen action you just performed in select mode was assigned an ID, even though no ink was drawn. So if the ink stroke you just created was assigned an ID of 8, switch back to select mode and tap the pen or click the mouse. Then switch to ink mode and draw an ink stroke—the ID assigned should be 10 because ID 9 was assigned to the tap or click you just performed.

Finally we'll take a look at erase mode. Switch into Delete mode and make sure that StrokeErase is chosen. Now, try erasing a stroke or two, and observe that the other stroke IDs don't change. Any pen or mouse operation in this mode will increment the stroke ID as in select mode; you can easily confirm this by switching to ink mode, drawing a stroke, and observing its stroke ID.

Now choose PointErase and swipe the eraser through some ink. Notice that as you erase ink, the number of stroke IDs increases because the point-level erasing is splitting strokes into two separate pieces. The first half of the stroke is preserved from the original stroke, but the second half is created from scratch and this results in a new (and therefore larger valued than the first half) stroke ID being assigned.

> **Note**    All pen actions actually result in a *Stroke* object being created and the *InkCollectorStrokeEventHandler* event being fired. In *Select* and *Delete* modes, the *InkOverlay* will automatically set the *InkCollectorStrokeEventArgs Cancel* property to *true*, resulting in no residual ink strokes left in the *Ink* object.

## Using *Strokes* Collections

Apart from being obtained from the *Ink* class's *Strokes* property and *InkOverlay*'s *Selection* property, *Strokes* collections can also be explicitly created from an *Ink* object. The *Ink* class's *CreateStrokes* method serves this purpose, and it has two overloads:

```
Strokes CreateStrokes();
Strokes CreateStrokes(int[] ids);
```

The first variant of the method constructs an empty *Strokes* collection, and the second variant constructs a *Strokes* collection filled with the set of *Stroke* object references as determined by the array of stroke IDs passed in via the *ids* parameter. If a stroke ID is encountered that doesn't exist in the ink object (for example, if the *Stroke* object has been deleted or it hasn't been created yet), *CreateStrokes* will throw an exception.

### Collection Functionality

The *Strokes* collection provides all common list operations, such as adding and removing *Stroke* object references. The *Strokes* collection's list functionality is presented in Table 5-1.

**Table 5-1  The List Management Methods and Properties of the *Strokes* Class**

| Method or Property Name | Description |
| --- | --- |
| *void Add(Stroke s)*<br>*void Add(Strokes strokes)* | Appends a reference to a *Stroke* object or appends references to the *Stroke* objects in a *Strokes* collection to the end of the collection |
| *void Clear()* | Removes all *Stroke* object references from the collection |
| *bool Contains(Stroke s)* | Determines if a reference to the given *Stroke* object is present in the collection |
| *int Count* | Returns the number of elements in the collection |
| *int IndexOf(Stroke s)* | Returns the index of the reference to the given *Stroke* object in the collection |
| *Ink Ink* | Returns the Ink object whose *Stroke* objects the *Strokes* collection can hold references to |
| *operator[]* | Returns the *Stroke* object referenced at the specified index |
| *void Remove(Stroke s)*<br>*void Remove(Strokes strokes)* | Removes the reference to the *Stroke* object or removes references to the *Stroke* objects in a *Strokes* collection |
| *void RemoveAt(int index)* | Removes the references of the *Stroke* object found at the specified index |

### Receiving Notification of Stroke Addition or Removal

Much like the *Ink* class provides event notification of strokes being added or deleted from an *Ink* object via *InkAdded* and *InkDeleted*, the *Strokes* collection class provides the *StrokesAdded* and *StrokesRemoved* events that are fired when *Stroke* object references are added or removed from the collection. Similar to *InkAdded* and *InkDeleted* events, the *StrokesAdded* and *StrokesRemoved* events can be fired on a thread other than the main thread of execution—be aware of this when implementing their event handlers. The *StrokesAdded* and

*StrokesRemoved* events, like *InkAdded* and *InkDeleted*, also use *Stroke-EventHandler*-based event handlers.

## Sample Application—InkSelector

This next sample application illustrates the usage of *Strokes* collections by implementing common menu operations on an *InkOverlay*'s selection. The sample provides menu items to select all ink currently in the *InkOverlay*'s *Ink* object, select the next stroke after the current selection in the *Ink* object, toggle the selection state of the strokes, and deselect all strokes.

**InkSelector.cs**

```
/////////////////////////////////////////////////////////////////////
//
// InkSelector.cs
//
// (c) 2002 Microsoft Press
// by Rob Jarrett
//
// This program demonstrates working with the Strokes collection by
// showing various operations on the selection.
//
/////////////////////////////////////////////////////////////////////

using System;
using System.Drawing;
using System.Windows.Forms;
using Microsoft.Ink;
using MSPress.BuildingTabletApps;

public class frmMain : Form
{
    private InkControl  inkCtl;
    private MenuItem    miSelectAll;
    private MenuItem    miSelectNext;
    private MenuItem    miSelectToggle;
    private MenuItem    miSelectNone;

    // Entry point of the program
    [STAThread]
    static void Main()
    {
        Application.Run(new frmMain());
    }

    // Main form setup
    public frmMain()
    {
        SuspendLayout();
```

```
// Create the main menu
Menu = new MainMenu();

MenuItem miFile = new MenuItem("&File");
Menu.MenuItems.Add(miFile);

MenuItem miExit = new MenuItem("E&xit");
miExit.Click += new EventHandler(miExit_Click);
Menu.MenuItems[0].MenuItems.Add(miExit);

MenuItem miEdit = new MenuItem("&Edit");
miEdit.Popup += new EventHandler(miEdit_Popup);
Menu.MenuItems.Add(miEdit);

miSelectAll = new MenuItem("Select &All");
miSelectAll.Click += new EventHandler(miSelectAll_Click);
Menu.MenuItems[1].MenuItems.Add(miSelectAll);

miSelectNext = new MenuItem("Select &Next");
miSelectNext.Click += new EventHandler(miSelectNext_Click);
Menu.MenuItems[1].MenuItems.Add(miSelectNext);

miSelectToggle = new MenuItem("&Toggle Selection");
miSelectToggle.Click += new EventHandler(miSelectToggle_Click);
Menu.MenuItems[1].MenuItems.Add(miSelectToggle);

miSelectNone = new MenuItem("&Deselect All");
miSelectNone.Click += new EventHandler(miSelectNone_Click);
Menu.MenuItems[1].MenuItems.Add(miSelectNone);

// Create and place all of our controls
inkCtl = new InkControl();
inkCtl.Location = new Point(8, 8);
inkCtl.Size = new Size(352, 220);

// Configure the form itself
ClientSize = new Size(368, 236);
Controls.AddRange(new Control[] { inkCtl });
FormBorderStyle = FormBorderStyle.FixedDialog;
MaximizeBox = false;
Text = "InkSelector";

ResumeLayout(false);

// We're now set to go, so turn on tablet input
inkCtl.InkOverlay.Enabled = true;
}
```

*(continued)*

**InkSelector.cs** *(continued)*

```csharp
// Handle the "Exit" menu item being clicked
private void miExit_Click(object sender, EventArgs e)
{
    Application.Exit();
}

// Handle the "Edit" submenu popping up
private void miEdit_Popup(object sender, EventArgs e)
{
    bool fSelectMode = (inkCtl.InkOverlay.EditingMode ==
        InkOverlayEditingMode.Select);

    // Enable or disable the various menu items
    miSelectAll.Enabled = fSelectMode &&
        (inkCtl.InkOverlay.Ink.Strokes.Count > 0);
    miSelectNext.Enabled = fSelectMode &&
        (inkCtl.InkOverlay.Selection.Count > 0);
    miSelectToggle.Enabled = fSelectMode &&
        (inkCtl.InkOverlay.Ink.Strokes.Count > 0);
    miSelectNone.Enabled = fSelectMode &&
        (inkCtl.InkOverlay.Selection.Count > 0);
}

// Handle the "Select All" menu item being clicked
private void miSelectAll_Click(object sender, EventArgs e)
{
    // Set the selection strokes collection to be all strokes
    inkCtl.InkOverlay.Selection =
        inkCtl.InkOverlay.Ink.Strokes;
}

// Handle the "Select Next" menu item being clicked
private void miSelectNext_Click(object sender, EventArgs e)
{
    // Find the index of the last stroke in the selection
    int nIndex = inkCtl.InkOverlay.Ink.Strokes.IndexOf(
        inkCtl.InkOverlay.Selection[0]);

    // Increment the index's value, and wrap around to 0 if it goes
    // beyond the end of the number of strokes in the ink object
    nIndex++;
    if (nIndex >= inkCtl.InkOverlay.Ink.Strokes.Count)
    {
        nIndex = 0;
    }
```

```
    // Set the selection to be the stroke located at the new index
    inkCtl.InkOverlay.Selection =
        inkCtl.InkOverlay.Ink.CreateStrokes(new int [] {
        inkCtl.InkOverlay.Ink.Strokes[nIndex].Id });
}

// Handle the "Toggle Selection" menu item being clicked
private void miSelectToggle_Click(object sender, EventArgs e)
{
    // Add the strokes which are not in the selection to a new
    // strokes collection
    Strokes strks = inkCtl.InkOverlay.Ink.CreateStrokes();
    foreach (Stroke s in inkCtl.InkOverlay.Ink.Strokes)
    {
        if (!inkCtl.InkOverlay.Selection.Contains(s))
        {
            strks.Add(s);
        }
    }

    // Set the selection to the new strokes collection
    inkCtl.InkOverlay.Selection = strks;
}

// Handle the "Deselect All" menu item being clicked
private void miSelectNone_Click(object sender, EventArgs e)
{
    // Set the selection strokes collection to an empty collection
    inkCtl.InkOverlay.Selection =
        inkCtl.InkOverlay.Ink.CreateStrokes();
}
}
```

Again, this sample makes use of the *InkControl* class found in the BuildingTabletApps library. A rather straightforward initialization in *frmMain()* results in the main menu being constructed along with menu item handlers, and an *InkControl* being created. The interesting part of the application comes in the implementation of the various menu item handlers.

To manipulate the selection, the *Strokes* collection of *InkOverlay's Strokes* property is reassigned to a different *Strokes* collection altogether. Consider the code to perform a "select all" operation:

```
// Set the selection strokes collection to be all strokes
inkCtl.InkOverlay.Selection = inkCtl.InkOverlay.Ink.Strokes;
```

The *Selection* property is assigned the *Strokes* collection that references all the *Stroke* objects contained in the *Ink* object. That seems easy enough, doesn't it?

The implementation of the "select next" operation is a bit more complex, however. The purpose of this operation is to shift the selection to the next item in the document using some logical order. In our case, we'll define the next item to be the next *Stroke* object ordered in the *Ink* object's collection of strokes:

```
// Find the index of the last stroke in the selection
int nIndex = inkCtl.InkOverlay.Ink.Strokes.IndexOf(
    inkCtl.InkOverlay.Selection[0]);

// Increment the index's value, and wrap around to 0 if it goes
// beyond the end of the number of strokes in the ink object
nIndex++;
if (nIndex >= inkCtl.InkOverlay.Ink.Strokes.Count)
{
    nIndex = 0;
}

// Set the selection to be the stroke located at the new index
inkCtl.InkOverlay.Selection =
    inkCtl.InkOverlay.Ink.CreateStrokes(new int [] {
    inkCtl.InkOverlay.Ink.Strokes[nIndex].Id });
```

The code first computes the index of the selected stroke in the collection of all *Stroke* objects contained in the *Ink* object via the *Strokes* class's *IndexOf* method. If multiple *Stroke* objects are selected (and hence multiple items are in the *Strokes* collection), the first one, the zeroth element, is used.

Next the index of the selected stroke is incremented and wrapped around to 0 if it exceeds the upper limit of allowable indexes in the *Strokes* collection. Finally the selection is altered by assigning a new *Strokes* collection to the *Selection* property of *InkOverlay*. The *Strokes* collection that's used is created via the *Ink* class's *CreateStrokes* method, passing in the stroke ID of the next logical *Stroke* object as the sole element of an array of IDs.

You might think that instead of reassigning the *Selection* property to a new *Strokes* collection, the existing *Strokes* collection used for *Selection* simply could be manipulated as thus:

```
// Set the selection to be the stroke located at the new index
inkCtl.InkOverlay.Selection.Clear();
inkCtl.InkOverlay.Selection.Add(
    inkCtl.InkOverlay.Ink.Strokes[nIndex]);
```

That method won't work, however—recall that *InkOverlay*'s *Selection* property returns a copy of the current *Strokes* collection used, the same way *Ink*'s *Strokes* property does.

Toggling the selection state of ink objects becomes easy work using the *Strokes* collection's methods. To toggle the selected ink strokes, we want to select only those strokes that are not currently found in the selection:

```
// Add the strokes which are not in the selection to a new
// strokes collection
Strokes strks = inkCtl.InkOverlay.Ink.CreateStrokes();
foreach (Stroke s in inkCtl.InkOverlay.Ink.Strokes)
{
    if (!inkCtl.InkOverlay.Selection.Contains(s))
    {
        strks.Add(s);
    }
}

// Set the selection to the new strokes collection
inkCtl.InkOverlay.Selection = strks;
```

The code first creates an empty Strokes collection. Next, every *Stroke* object contained by the *Ink* object is checked to see if it is found in the current selection. Those *Stroke* objects that are not found in the current selection are added to the *Strokes* collection that was just created. Finally, the selection is changed to be those strokes that were not part of the original selection.

An alternative (and simpler!) method can actually be used to accomplish "toggle selection":

```
// Shorter way of toggling the selection
Strokes strks = inkCtl.InkOverlay.Ink.Strokes;
strks.Remove(inkCtl.InkOverlay.Selection);
inkCtl.InkOverlay.Selection = strks;
```

This method takes advantage of the *Strokes* collection's *Remove* method. The entire collection of *Stroke* objects contained by the *Ink* object has the current selection set removed from it, and the resulting *Strokes* collection is assigned to the selection. Pretty neat, huh? We decided to include the first longer method because it was a little more illustrative, but the second method is probably preferable because it requires less code and is less complex.

Lastly, the "deselect all" operation is a straightforward one to implement:

```
// Set the selection strokes collection to an empty collection
inkCtl.InkOverlay.Selection =
    inkCtl.InkOverlay.Ink.CreateStrokes();
```

The *Selection* property is assigned an empty *Strokes* collection, very similar in principle to the preceding "select all" implementation.

## Creation, Deletion, and Ownership of *Stroke* Objects

Instances of the *InkCollector* and *InkOverlay* classes create *Stroke* objects as a result of tablet input, but oftentimes it is desirable to copy, delete, remove, or construct new *Stroke* objects contained within an *Ink* object through programmatic means. This section covers the methods found in the Ink Data Management API that provide that functionality.

Table 5-2 lists the methods found in the *Ink* class that result in *Stroke* objects being either added to or removed from an *Ink* object.

**Table 5-2   Object Creation and Deletion Functions of the *Ink* Class**

| Method Name | Description |
| --- | --- |
| *void AddStrokesAtRectangle(Strokes strokes, Rectangle rect)* | Copies the *Stroke* objects referenced by a *Strokes* collection into the *Ink* object at a specified location |
| *Ink Clone()* | Copies the entire contents of the *Ink* object and returns a new *Ink* object instance |
| *Stroke CreateStroke(Point[] pts)* | Creates a new *Stroke* object using an (*x,y*) coordinate array |
| *void DeleteStroke(Stroke s)* | Destroys a *Stroke* object |
| *void DeleteStrokes(Strokes strokes)* | Destroys all *Stroke* objects referenced by a *Strokes* collection |
| *Ink ExtractStrokes()* <br> *Ink ExtractStrokes(Strokes strokes)* <br> *Ink ExtractStrokes(Strokes strokes, ExtractFlags f)* <br> *Ink ExtractStrokes(Rectangle r)* <br> *Ink ExtractStrokes(Rectangle r, ExtractFlags f)* | Removes or copies *Stroke* objects from an *Ink* object, returning them in a new instance of *Ink* |

## Adding Ink

*AddStrokesAtRectangle* is a useful method for adding existing strokes into an *Ink* object. The owning *Ink* object of the source *Strokes* collection does not have to be the same as the destination, though it can be. The *Rectangle* parameter passed to the method defines the bounding box that the *Stroke* objects referenced by the *Strokes* collection will be fit into. Like most coordinate parameters to Ink Data Management API functions, it is in HIMETRIC units.

Unfortunately, the *AddStrokesAtRectangle* method of the *Ink* class does not return a *Strokes* collection referencing the newly added ink. However if this functionality is needed, the BuildingTabletApps utility library supplies an identical method *InkEx.AddStrokesAtRectangle* which does.

The *CreateStroke* method constructs a new *Stroke* object out of a series of points given in ink space coordinates. The newly created stroke is returned by the method so that it can be further manipulated if desired.

> **Note**    Astute readers might notice that *Stroke* objects are actually
> made up of packets that may have other data besides *x* and *y* informa-
> tion. Unfortunately, the *CreateStroke* method allows *Stroke* objects to
> be created only from *x* and *y* data—it is impossible to use the Ink Data
> Management API to programmatically generate *Stroke* objects with
> packet properties other than *x* and *y*.

The *Clone* method does exactly what its name purports—it generates an
exact copy of the *Ink* object that the method is called on.

## Deleting Ink

The *DeleteStroke* and *DeleteStrokes* methods both do exactly the same thing:
they destroy *Stroke* objects. The only difference between them is the way the
*Stroke* objects to be deleted are specified—*DeleteStroke* takes a *Stroke* object
as a parameter, and *DeleteStrokes* takes a *Strokes* collection as a parameter. I
mentioned earlier it is possible for a *Strokes* collection to contain a reference to a
*Stroke* object that has been destroyed. The *Stroke* object that results from the dereference will be unusable but its *Deleted* and *Id* properties can be read (*Deleted*
will equal *true*, *Id* will equal the expected stroke ID); any other property or
method usage causes an exception. And let me reiterate that good programming
practice is to check the *Deleted* property of *Stroke* objects when dereferencing
from a *Strokes* collection if code other than your own maintains the collection.

*ExtractStrokes* is a method that copies or moves *Stroke* objects into a
new *Ink* object. There are five variations of this function that can be put into
three groups:

```
Ink ExtractStrokes()
```

This version of *ExtractStrokes* will remove all the *Stroke* objects from an *Ink*
object, add them into a newly created *Ink* object, and return the new *Ink* object.
There will be no ink left in the *Ink* object that has *ExtractStrokes* called on it.

The next two versions of *ExtractStrokes* will remove the *Stroke* objects from
an *Ink* object as identified by either a *Strokes* collection or a rectangle, add them
into a newly created *Ink* object, and return the new *Ink* object. The rectangle,
specified in ink coordinates, will clip out the *Stroke* objects, hopping them
into segments if needed.

```
Ink ExtractStrokes(Strokes strokes)
Ink ExtractStrokes(Rectangle r)
```

These last two versions of *ExtractStrokes* allow you to specify whether the
*Stroke* objects are removed or copied from the *Ink* object via the *ExtractFlags*

parameter, whose values are listed in Table 5-3. The use of the *Strokes* collection and *Rectangle* parameters are the same as for the previous versions.

```
Ink ExtractStrokes(Strokes strokes, ExtractFlags f)
Ink ExtractStrokes(Rectangle r, ExtractFlags f)
```

**Table 5-3   The *ExtractFlags* Enumeration Used by the *Ink* Class's *ExtractStrokes* Method**

| ExtractFlags Values | Description |
| --- | --- |
| *CopyFromOriginal* | Preserve strokes in the source ink object |
| *RemoveFromOriginal* | Remove the strokes from the source ink object |
| *Default* | Use the default value, which is *RemoveFromOriginal* |

You might be wondering why *ExtractStrokes* doesn't just return a *Strokes* collection from the method rather than a whole *Ink* object. The answer is this: a *Stroke* object cannot live outside an *Ink* object, and because the *ExtractStrokes* method removes *Stroke* objects from their owning *Ink* object, the *Stroke* objects no longer have an owning *Ink* object—thus a new *Ink* object *must* be created as a place for the extracted *Stroke* objects to live.

### Receiving Notification of Ink Addition and Deletion

As mentioned earlier, the *Ink* class provides two events that allow notification of *Stroke* objects being added and deleted: *InkAdded* and *InkDeleted*, respectively.

## Implementing a Live *Strokes* Collection

We know that the *Ink* class's *Strokes* property returns a copy of a *Strokes* collection. However, if we hold onto that *Strokes* collection and *Stroke* objects are then added or removed on the *Ink* object, the *Strokes* collection we're holding a reference to will not be accurately reflecting the state of the *Ink* object anymore. Under most circumstances that's OK; we would just get the *Strokes* collection generated over again by querying the *Strokes* property. But if for some reason we wanted to keep a reference to a *Strokes* collection and not have the reference be updated, by using the *InkAdded* and *InkDeleted* handlers we can implement a *live Strokes* collection that always reflects the *Stroke* objects contained in an *Ink* object. When a *Stroke* object is added to the *Ink* object we simply add a reference to it in the *Strokes* collection, and similarly when a *Stroke* object is deleted from the *Ink* object we remove its reference from the *Strokes* collection.

### Sample Application—InkCopy

The InkCopy sample application demonstrates some of the functionality we've just been talking about. Two *InkControl* objects are displayed on a form and each can have ink drawn, selected, moved, resized, and deleted. The illustrative functionality comes from menu items that allow copying the entire contents of the top *InkControl* to the bottom one, copying or moving the top *InkControl*'s current selection to the bottom one, and deleting the top *InkControl*'s current selection completely.

**InkCopy.cs**

```
///////////////////////////////////////////////////////////////////////
//
// InkCopy.cs
//
// (c) 2002 Microsoft Press
// by Rob Jarrett
//
// This program demonstrates how to copy, delete, and move Stroke
// objects between two Ink objects.
//
///////////////////////////////////////////////////////////////////////

using System;
using System.Drawing;
using System.Windows.Forms;
using Microsoft.Ink;
using MSPress.BuildingTabletApps;

public class frmMain : Form
{
    private InkControl  inkCtl1;
    private InkControl  inkCtl2;
    private MenuItem    miCopy;
    private MenuItem    miMove;
    private MenuItem    miDelete;

    // Entry point of the program
    [STAThread]
    static void Main()
    {
        Application.Run(new frmMain());
    }

    // Main form setup
    public frmMain()
    {
        SuspendLayout();
```

*(continued)*

**InkCopy.cs** *(continued)*

```
// Create the main menu
Menu = new MainMenu();

MenuItem miFile = new MenuItem("&File");
Menu.MenuItems.Add(miFile);

MenuItem miExit = new MenuItem("E&xit");
miExit.Click += new EventHandler(miExit_Click);
Menu.MenuItems[0].MenuItems.Add(miExit);

MenuItem miEdit = new MenuItem("&Edit");
miEdit.Popup += new EventHandler(miEdit_Popup);
Menu.MenuItems.Add(miEdit);

MenuItem miDuplicate = new MenuItem("D&uplicate All");
miDuplicate.Click += new EventHandler(miDuplicate_Click);
Menu.MenuItems[1].MenuItems.Add(miDuplicate);

Menu.MenuItems[1].MenuItems.Add(new MenuItem("-"));

miCopy = new MenuItem("&Copy");
miCopy.Click += new EventHandler(miCopy_Click);
Menu.MenuItems[1].MenuItems.Add(miCopy);

miMove = new MenuItem("&Move");
miMove.Click += new EventHandler(miMove_Click);
Menu.MenuItems[1].MenuItems.Add(miMove);

miDelete = new MenuItem("&Delete");
miDelete.Click += new EventHandler(miDelete_Click);
Menu.MenuItems[1].MenuItems.Add(miDelete);

// Create and place all of our controls
inkCtl1 = new InkControl();
inkCtl1.Location = new Point(8, 8);
inkCtl1.Size = new Size(352, 216);

inkCtl2 = new InkControl();
inkCtl2.Location = new Point(8, 232);
inkCtl2.Size = new Size(352, 216);

// Configure the form itself
ClientSize = new Size(368, 456);
Controls.AddRange(new Control[] { inkCtl1,
                                  inkCtl2});
FormBorderStyle = FormBorderStyle.FixedDialog;
MaximizeBox = false;
Text = "InkCopy";
```

```csharp
        ResumeLayout(false);

        // We're now set to go, so turn on tablet input
        inkCtl1.InkOverlay.Enabled = true;
        inkCtl2.InkOverlay.Enabled = true;
    }

    // Handle the "Exit" menu item being clicked
    private void miExit_Click(object sender, EventArgs e)
    {
        Application.Exit();
    }

    // Handle the "Edit" submenu popping up
    private void miEdit_Popup(object sender, EventArgs e)
    {
        // Only enable the Copy, Move, and Delete menu items if there
        // is a current selection
        bool fSelection = (inkCtl1.InkOverlay.EditingMode ==
            InkOverlayEditingMode.Select) &&
            (inkCtl1.InkOverlay.Selection.Count > 0);

        miCopy.Enabled = fSelection;
        miMove.Enabled = fSelection;
        miDelete.Enabled = fSelection;
    }

    // Handle the "Duplicate" menu item being clicked
    private void miDuplicate_Click(object sender, EventArgs e)
    {
        // Turn off input in inkCtl2 since we're going to assign a new
        // Ink object to it
        inkCtl2.InkOverlay.Enabled = false;

        // Copy over the entire ink object from inkCtl1 to inkCtl2
        inkCtl2.InkOverlay.Ink = inkCtl1.InkOverlay.Ink.Clone();

        // Turn tablet input back on for inkCtl2
        inkCtl2.InkOverlay.Enabled = true;

        // Draw the new ink in inkCtl2
        inkCtl2.InkInputPanel.Invalidate();
    }

    // Handle the "Copy" menu item being clicked
    private void miCopy_Click(object sender, EventArgs e)
```

*(continued)*

**InkCopy.cs** *(continued)*

```
{
    // Copy over the selection from inkCtl1 to inkCtl2
    Strokes strokes = inkCtl1.InkOverlay.Selection;
    inkCtl2.InkOverlay.Ink.AddStrokesAtRectangle(
        strokes, strokes.GetBoundingBox());

    // Draw the new ink in inkCtl2
    inkCtl2.InkInputPanel.Invalidate();
}

// Handle the "Move" menu item being clicked
private void miMove_Click(object sender, EventArgs e)
{
    // Copy over the selection from inkCtl1 to inkCtl2
    Strokes strokes = inkCtl1.InkOverlay.Selection;
    inkCtl2.InkOverlay.Ink.AddStrokesAtRectangle(
        strokes, strokes.GetBoundingBox());

    // Delete the selection from inkCtl1
    inkCtl1.InkOverlay.Ink.DeleteStrokes(strokes);

    // Clear the selection in inkCtl1
    inkCtl1.InkOverlay.Selection =
        inkCtl1.InkOverlay.Ink.CreateStrokes();

    // Redraw the ink in both inkCtl1 and inkCtl2
    inkCtl1.InkInputPanel.Invalidate();
    inkCtl2.InkInputPanel.Invalidate();
}

// Handle the "Delete" menu item being clicked
private void miDelete_Click(object sender, EventArgs e)
{
    // Delete the selection from inkCtl1
    Strokes strokes = inkCtl1.InkOverlay.Selection;
    inkCtl1.InkOverlay.Ink.DeleteStrokes(strokes);

    // Clear the selection in inkCtl1
    inkCtl1.InkOverlay.Selection =
        inkCtl1.InkOverlay.Ink.CreateStrokes();

    // Redraw the ink in inkCtl1
    inkCtl1.InkInputPanel.Invalidate();
}
}
```

The application creates its main menu, hooks up event handlers to the menu items, and then creates the two *InkControl* controls. *inkCtl1* is the top InkControl and *inkCtl2* is the bottom one. As with the InkSelector sample, the code we're most interested in lies within the menu item handlers.

The "duplicate all" menu item results in the entire *Ink* object in *inkCtl1*'s *InkOverlay* being copied to *inkCtl2*'s *InkOverlay*. This is accomplished by using the *Ink* class's *Clone* method and assigning the results to the *Ink* property of *inkCtl2*'s *InkOverlay*:

```
// Turn off input in inkCtl2 since we're going to assign a new
// Ink object to it
inkCtl2.InkOverlay.Enabled = false;

// Copy over the entire ink object from inkCtl1 to inkCtl2
inkCtl2.InkOverlay.Ink = inkCtl1.InkOverlay.Ink.Clone();

// Turn tablet input back on for inkCtl2
inkCtl2.InkOverlay.Enabled = true;
```

Besides the use of *Clone*, something to note here is that an *InkOverlay* instance must disable tablet input to have its *Ink* property value changed; hence the "bookending" of setting the *inkCtl2.InkOverlay.Enabled* property.

The "copy" menu item utilizes the *AddStrokesAtRectangle* method to take the currently selected *Stroke* objects in *inkCtl1*'s *InkOverlay* and copy them into *inkCtl2*'s *InkOverlay*:

```
// Copy over the selection from inkCtl1 to inkCtl2
Strokes strokes = inkCtl1.InkOverlay.Selection;
inkCtl2.InkOverlay.Ink.AddStrokesAtRectangle(
    strokes, strokes.GetBoundingBox());
```

Notice that the second argument to *AddStrokesAtRectangle* is something we haven't learned about yet—*GetBoundingBox*. That function computes the smallest rectangle that fully encloses all the *Stroke* objects referenced by the *Strokes* collection. We'll learn more about that function in the next chapter. The result of the *AddStrokesAtRectangle* method is that the *Stroke* objects are copied into the *Ink* object found in the *InkOverlay*. Also note that because the *Ink* object's value in *inkCtl2*'s *InkOverlay* isn't changing we don't need to disable and re-enable tablet input in the *InkOverlay* object.

The menu item "move" is the same as "copy" except it also deletes the selected *Stroke* objects from *inkCtl1*'s *InkOverlay*:

```
// Copy over the selection from inkCtl1 to inkCtl2
Strokes strokes = inkCtl1.InkOverlay.Selection;
inkCtl2.InkOverlay.Ink.AddStrokesAtRectangle(
    strokes, strokes.GetBoundingBox());
```

*(continued)*

```
// Delete the selection from inkCtl1
inkCtl1.InkOverlay.Ink.DeleteStrokes(strokes);

// Clear the selection in inkCtl1
inkCtl1.InkOverlay.Selection =
    inkCtl1.InkOverlay.Ink.CreateStrokes();
```

Once the selected *Stroke* objects have been copied over to *inkCtl2*'s *Ink-Overlay*, the *DeleteStrokes* method is used to destroy the selected *Stroke* objects in *inkCtl1*'s *InkOverlay*. Once deleted, the current selection in the *InkOverlay* is reset because otherwise the *Strokes* collection returned via the *Selection* property will reference deleted *Stroke* objects.

The "delete" functionality is almost the same as "move"—it skips the step of copying the selected *Stroke* objects into *inkCtl2*'s *InkOverlay* but otherwise performs the same operations. It deletes the currently selected *Stroke* objects and then resets the current selection.

## Sample Application—InkFactory

This next sample application, InkFactory, shown in Figure 5-3, demonstrates how to programmatically create *Stroke* objects. It allows the user the choice of a circle or a square created in an InkControl via the application's main menu.

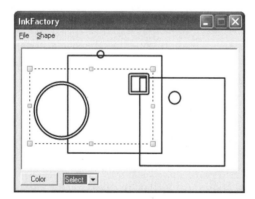

**Figure 5-3**   The InkFactory sample application in action.

**InkFactory.cs**
```
///////////////////////////////////////////////////////////////////////
//
// InkFactory.cs
//
// (c) 2002 Microsoft Press
// by Rob Jarrett
//
```

```
// This program demonstrates how to create new strokes
// programmatically.
//
/////////////////////////////////////////////////////////////////////

using System;
using System.Drawing;
using System.Windows.Forms;
using Microsoft.Ink;
using MSPress.BuildingTabletApps;

public class frmMain : Form
{
    private InkControl  inkCtl;

    // Entry point of the program
    [STAThread]
    static void Main()
    {
        Application.Run(new frmMain());
    }

    // Main form setup
    public frmMain()
    {
        SuspendLayout();

        // Create the main menu
        Menu = new MainMenu();

        MenuItem miFile = new MenuItem("&File");
        Menu.MenuItems.Add(miFile);

        MenuItem miExit = new MenuItem("E&xit");
        miExit.Click += new EventHandler(miExit_Click);
        Menu.MenuItems[0].MenuItems.Add(miExit);

        MenuItem miShape = new MenuItem("&Shape");
        Menu.MenuItems.Add(miShape);

        MenuItem miCircle = new MenuItem("&Circle");
        miCircle.Click += new EventHandler(miCircle_Click);
        Menu.MenuItems[1].MenuItems.Add(miCircle);

        MenuItem miSquare = new MenuItem("&Square");
        miSquare.Click += new EventHandler(miSquare_Click);
        Menu.MenuItems[1].MenuItems.Add(miSquare);
```

*(continued)*

**InkFactory.cs** *(continued)*

```csharp
        // Create and place all of our controls
        inkCtl = new InkControl();
        inkCtl.Location = new Point(8, 8);
        inkCtl.Size = new Size(352, 216);

        // Configure the form itself
        ClientSize = new Size(368, 232);
        Controls.AddRange(new Control[] { inkCtl });
        FormBorderStyle = FormBorderStyle.FixedDialog;
        MaximizeBox = false;
        Text = "InkFactory";

        ResumeLayout(false);

        // We're now set to go, so turn on tablet input
        inkCtl.InkOverlay.Enabled = true;
    }

    // Handle the "Exit" menu item being clicked
    private void miExit_Click(object sender, EventArgs e)
    {
        Application.Exit();
    }

    // Handle the "Circle" menu item being clicked
    private void miCircle_Click(object sender, EventArgs e)
    {
        // Get the size of the input area in ink coordinates
        Rectangle rcBounds = new Rectangle(
            new Point(0,0), inkCtl.InkInputPanel.ClientSize);
        Graphics g = inkCtl.InkInputPanel.CreateGraphics();
        RendererEx.PixelToInkSpace(
            inkCtl.InkOverlay.Renderer, g, ref rcBounds);
        g.Dispose();

        // Compute a random size and location for the circle
        Random r = new Random((int)DateTime.Now.Ticks);
        int nRadius = r.Next(1, rcBounds.Height/2);
        int X = r.Next(nRadius, rcBounds.Width - nRadius);
        int Y = r.Next(nRadius, rcBounds.Height - nRadius);

        // Compute the points of the circle
        Point[] pts = new Point[101];
        double fRadian = 2f*Math.PI;
        for (int i = 0; i < 100; i++)
        {
            pts[i].X = X + (int)(nRadius * Math.Cos(fRadian * i/100f));
            pts[i].Y = Y + (int)(nRadius * Math.Sin(fRadian * i/100f));
```

```
    }
    // "Connect" the endpoint with the start point — note it doesn't
    // really get connected (strokes cannot be closed polygons), but
    // rather the endpoint is a copy of the start point
    pts[100].X = pts[0].X;
    pts[100].Y = pts[0].Y;

    // Create the new stroke using the points
    Stroke stroke = inkCtl.InkOverlay.Ink.CreateStroke(pts);

    // Give it the current drawing attributes of inkCtl1
    stroke.DrawingAttributes =
        inkCtl.InkOverlay.DefaultDrawingAttributes;

    // Draw the new ink stroke
    inkCtl.InkInputPanel.Invalidate();
}

// Handle the "Square" menu item being clicked
private void miSquare_Click(object sender, EventArgs e)
{
    // Get the size of the input area in ink coordinates
    Rectangle rcBounds = new Rectangle(
        new Point(0,0), inkCtl.InkInputPanel.ClientSize);
    Graphics g = inkCtl.InkInputPanel.CreateGraphics();
    RendererEx.PixelToInkSpace(
        inkCtl.InkOverlay.Renderer, g, ref rcBounds);
    g.Dispose();

    // Compute a random size and location for the square
    Random r = new Random((int)DateTime.Now.Ticks);
    int nSizeLength = r.Next(1, rcBounds.Height);
    int X = r.Next(0, rcBounds.Width - nSizeLength);
    int Y = r.Next(0, rcBounds.Height - nSizeLength);

    // Compute the points of the square
    Point[] pts = new Point[101];
    for (int i = 0; i < 25; i++)
    {
        pts[i].X = X + (int)(nSizeLength * i / 25f);
        pts[i].Y = Y;
        pts[i+25].X = X + nSizeLength;
        pts[i+25].Y = Y + (int)(nSizeLength * i / 25f);
        pts[i+50].X = X + (nSizeLength - (pts[i].X - X));
        pts[i+50].Y = Y + nSizeLength;
        pts[i+75].X = X;
        pts[i+75].Y = Y + (nSizeLength - (pts[i+25].Y - Y));
    }
```

*(continued)*

**InkFactory.cs** *(continued)*

```
        // "Connect" the endpoint with the start point — note it doesn't
        // really get connected (strokes cannot be closed polygons), but
        // rather the endpoint is a copy of the start point
        pts[100].X = pts[0].X;
        pts[100].Y = pts[0].Y;

        // Create the new stroke using the points
        Stroke stroke = inkCtl.InkOverlay.Ink.CreateStroke(pts);

        // Give it the current drawing attributes of inkCtl1
        stroke.DrawingAttributes =
            inkCtl.InkOverlay.DefaultDrawingAttributes;

        // Draw the new ink stroke
        inkCtl.InkInputPanel.Invalidate();
    }
}
```

The real guts of this application are found in the menu handlers, as they were in the last couple of samples. Let's take a look at the code snippet to create a circle (the code to create a square is the same, except for the algorithm used to compute the points):

```
// Get the size of the input area in ink coordinates
Rectangle rcBounds = new Rectangle(
    new Point(0,0), inkCtl.InkInputPanel.ClientSize);
Graphics g = inkCtl.InkInputPanel.CreateGraphics();
RendererEx.PixelToInkSpace(
    inkCtl.InkOverlay.Renderer, g, ref rcBounds);
g.Dispose();

// Compute a random size and location for the circle
Random r = new Random((int)DateTime.Now.Ticks);
int nRadius = r.Next(1, rcBounds.Height/2);
int X = r.Next(nRadius, rcBounds.Width — nRadius);
int Y = r.Next(nRadius, rcBounds.Height — nRadius);

// Compute the points of the circle
Point[] pts = new Point[101];
double fRadian = 2f*Math.PI;
for (int i = 0; i < 100; i++)
{
    pts[i].X = X + (int)(nRadius * Math.Cos(fRadian * i/100f));
    pts[i].Y = Y + (int)(nRadius * Math.Sin(fRadian * i/100f));
}
// "Connect" the endpoint with the start point — note it doesn't
// really get connected (strokes cannot be closed polygons), but
// rather the endpoint is a copy of the start point
```

```
pts[100].X = pts[0].X;
pts[100].Y = pts[0].Y;

// Create the new stroke using the points
Stroke stroke = inkCtl.InkOverlay.Ink.CreateStroke(pts);

// Give it the current drawing attributes of inkCtl1
stroke.DrawingAttributes =
    inkCtl.InkOverlay.DefaultDrawingAttributes;
```

The *Ink* class's *CreateStroke* method is the key enabler of this sample's functionality. As described earlier, this method constructs a *Stroke* object given an array of points that are specified in ink coordinates (HIMETRIC units). Most of the functionality in the code snippet is to compute the array of points that are passed into *CreateStroke*.

The first section of code figures out how big the input area is in ink coordinates, also known as *ink space*. A method in the BuildingTabletApps utility library named *RendererEx.PixelToInkSpace* is utilized that converts a rectangle of screen pixels into ink coordinates. It will be discussed in further detail in the next section.

Next, the circle's radius and location are determined by randomly picking some numbers, ensuring the circle won't be created outside the input area. An array of 101 points is allocated to hold all the points making up the circle, and the values are then filled in. Lastly the circle shape is closed by setting the 101st point to be equal to the first. The polyline for the stroke doesn't actually get closed—it's just a polyline whose start and end points perfectly overlap.

---

## Polylines vs. Curves

The Tablet PC Platform implements ink strokes as polylines—that is, as a set of discrete $(x,y)$ values that connect. This is largely a result of the method by which ink strokes are captured—tablet digitizers are only capable of providing an $(x,y)$ location of the stylus at a regular sampling interval. Because physical ink by nature is curved, the points in an electronic ink stroke should be sufficiently close together to give the illusion of curvature, and/or Bézier curve fitting should be employed. We'll learn more about curve fitting in the next section.

---

Once the point array has been computed, the *Stroke* object is created via the *CreateStrokes* method. The style of the ink stroke (its color, width, and so forth) is set to the current style used by *inkCtl*'s *InkOverlay*, so the stroke is displayed in all its glory.

And speaking of ink style, it's time to move on to the next section, which is all about rendering ink.

# Rendering Digital Ink

If you take a look through the full list of properties and methods for the *Ink* and *Stroke* classes, you'll notice that any functions for drawing ink strokes are conspicuously missing. The Tablet PC Platform in fact provides a lot of functionality to do this—so much so that it is encapsulated into its own class, called *Renderer*.

## *Renderer* Class

The primary purpose of the *Renderer* class is to draw ink into a viewport and maintain a transformation on the ink space. A *viewport* can be thought of as an opening to a drawing surface such as the screen, a printer, or a bitmap. The transformation on the ink space is used to achieve zooming, sizing, scrolling, and rotation effects without having to modify the (*x,y*) data of the *Stroke* objects themselves.

An instance of the *Renderer* class is able to draw individual *Stroke* objects or the *Stroke* objects referenced by a *Strokes* collection. In addition, ink formatting style attributes such as color and width can be nondestructively overridden; that is, the ink data won't be modified as a result of drawing it in an arbitrary style.

In its simplest use, a *Renderer* object will draw ink to the screen using a 1:1 mapping from HIMETRIC units to pixels. More complex use may mean multiple *Renderer* objects are maintained, with each drawing to a separate view in the application and perhaps providing robust zooming and scrolling behaviors.

Figure 5-4 illustrates the role that a *Renderer* object performs to draw ink and transform ink coordinates. To draw a *Stroke* object to the viewport, a *Renderer* object obtains the ink coordinates from the *Stroke* object, transforms them, converts them into pixels, and finally renders that data on the viewport. Note that the use of pixels here doesn't necessarily correspond to pixels on your monitor—they are whatever unit the *Graphics* object or graphics device context (HDC) being drawn to is set to use. Whenever an application interacts with a *Renderer* object, ink coordinates are always specified and returned in their transformed version.

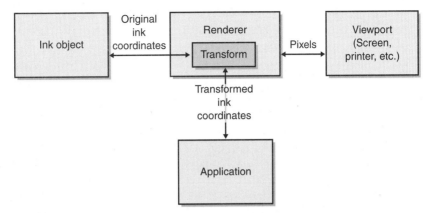

**Figure 5-4**  How a *Renderer* object draws ink strokes to a viewport.

## Creating and Maintaining *Renderer* Objects

The *InkCollector* and *InkOverlay* classes each reference a *Renderer* object, much like they do an *Ink* object. When an *InkCollector* or *InkOverlay* is instantiated, so is a *Renderer*, accessible via the *Renderer* property. This *Renderer* object is used for the drawing of *Stroke* objects on the window that the *InkCollector* or *InkOverlay* is attached to. It can also be used to draw to any *Graphics* object or device context.

Renderer objects can be created with the C# *new* operator, and they can be used either temporarily or kept around indefinitely. The lifetime or use of *Renderer* objects aren't tied to *Ink* or to any other type, and they can be used to draw ink from different *Ink* objects.

## Drawing Ink

The *Renderer* class supports drawing ink to either a *Graphics* object or a device context with the *Draw* method. It comes in a variety of overloads, which are listed here:

```
void Draw(Graphics g, Stroke s)
void Draw(Graphics g, Stroke s, DrawingAttributes da)
void Draw(Graphics g, Strokes strokes)
void Draw(IntPtr hdc, Stroke s)
void Draw(IntPtr hdc, Stroke s, DrawingAttributes da)
void Draw(IntPtr hdc, Strokes strokes)
```

There are really three main flavors of the method: drawing a single stroke, drawing a single stroke while overriding its formatting, and drawing multiple strokes. Versions for each case can draw to either a *Graphics* object or a Windows GDI device context (HDC).

The location on the *Graphics* device or HDC where the *Stroke* objects are drawn is not explicitly supplied in the function because *Stroke* objects have their position as part of their data. The HIMETRIC ink coordinates of the *Stroke* objects' (*x,y*) values are converted into pixels by using the *Graphics* object's or HDC's dpi setting by the *Renderer* object.

## Sample Application—InkLayers

The InkLayers sample application shows an implementation of virtual layers of ink—it's kind of like having a stack of transparencies that ink can be drawn on, and each transparency can be shown or hidden. The application uses a single *Ink* object to hold all the ink, and one *Strokes* collection is maintained for each layer. The input panel's paint handler selectively draws the *Stroke* objects for each layer that is visible, using the *InkOverlay*'s instance of a *Renderer*.

**InkLayers.cs**

```csharp
//////////////////////////////////////////////////////////////////////
//
// InkLayers.cs
//
// (c) 2002 Microsoft Press
// by Rob Jarrett
//
// This program demonstrates usage of the Strokes and Renderer
// classes by showing how layers of ink can be implemented.
//
//////////////////////////////////////////////////////////////////////

using System;
using System.Collections;
using System.Drawing;
using System.Windows.Forms;
using Microsoft.Ink;
using MSPress.BuildingTabletApps;

public class frmMain : Form
{
    // Data structure for an ink layer
    private class Layer
    {
        public Strokes  Strokes;
        public bool     bVisible;
    }

    // Total number of layers we'll allow
    private const int       nNumLayers = 3;

    // Layer management
    private ArrayList       arrLayers;
    private int             nCurrLayer;
```

```
// User interface
private InkInputPanel   pnlInput;
private ComboBox        cbxLayer;
private CheckBox        cbVisible;
private InkOverlay      inkOverlay;

// Entry point of the program
[STAThread]
static void Main()
{
    Application.Run(new frmMain());
}

// Main form setup
public frmMain()
{
    SuspendLayout();

    // Create and place all of our controls
    pnlInput = new InkInputPanel();
    pnlInput.BackColor = Color.White;
    pnlInput.BorderStyle = BorderStyle.Fixed3D;
    pnlInput.Location = new Point(8, 8);
    pnlInput.Size = new Size(352, 192);

    cbxLayer = new ComboBox();
    cbxLayer.DropDownStyle = ComboBoxStyle.DropDownList;
    cbxLayer.Location = new Point(8, 204);
    cbxLayer.Size = new Size(72, 24);
    cbxLayer.SelectedIndexChanged +=
        new EventHandler(cbxLayer_SelIndexChg);

    cbVisible = new CheckBox();
    cbVisible.Location = new Point(88, 204);
    cbVisible.Size = new Size(80, 20);
    cbVisible.Text = "Visible";
    cbVisible.Click += new EventHandler(cbVisible_Click);

    // Configure the form itself
    ClientSize = new Size(368, 236);
    Controls.AddRange(new Control[] { pnlInput,
                                      cbxLayer,
                                      cbVisible});
    FormBorderStyle = FormBorderStyle.FixedDialog;
    MaximizeBox = false;
    Text = "InkLayers";

    ResumeLayout(false);
```

*(continued)*

**InkLayers.cs** *(continued)*

```csharp
        // Fill up the layers combobox
        for (int i = 0; i < nNumLayers; i++)
        {
            cbxLayer.Items.Add("Layer " + (i+1).ToString());
        }

        // Create a new InkOverlay, using pnlInput for the collection
        // area
        inkOverlay = new InkOverlay(pnlInput.Handle);

        // Turn off auto-redraw since we'll be drawing the ink in our
        // paint handler
        inkOverlay.AutoRedraw = false;

        // Add the paint handler so we can conditionally draw ink layers
        pnlInput.Paint += new PaintEventHandler(pnlInput_Paint);

        // Create all of the Layers objects
        arrLayers = new ArrayList();
        for (int i = 0; i < nNumLayers; i++)
        {
            Layer layer = new Layer();
            layer.Strokes = inkOverlay.Ink.CreateStrokes();
            layer.bVisible = true;
            arrLayers.Add(layer);
        }

        // Select the current layer in the combobox .
        nCurrLayer = 0;
        cbxLayer.SelectedIndex = nCurrLayer;

        // Listen for new strokes so they can be added to the current
        // layer
        inkOverlay.Stroke +=
            new InkCollectorStrokeEventHandler(inkOverlay_Stroke);

        // We're now set to go, so turn on tablet input
        inkOverlay.Enabled = true;
    }

    // Handle the selection changed of the layers combobox
    private void cbxLayer_SelIndexChg(object sender, EventArgs e)
    {
        // Set the selection strokes collection to be all strokes
        nCurrLayer = cbxLayer.SelectedIndex;
        Layer layer = arrLayers[nCurrLayer] as Layer;
        cbVisible.Checked = layer.bVisible;
    }
```

```csharp
// Handle the click of the visible checkbox
private void cbVisible_Click(object sender, EventArgs e)
{
    Layer layer = arrLayers[nCurrLayer] as Layer;
    layer.bVisible = cbVisible.Checked;
    pnlInput.Invalidate();
}

// Handle the input panel's painting
private void pnlInput_Paint(object sender, PaintEventArgs e)
{
    // Paint all the visible layers
    for (int i = 0; i < nNumLayers; i++)
    {
        Layer layer = arrLayers[i] as Layer;
        if (layer.bVisible)
        {
            inkOverlay.Renderer.Draw(e.Graphics, layer.Strokes);
        }
    }
}

// Handle the new stroke of the InkOverlay
private void inkOverlay_Stroke(object sender,
    InkCollectorStrokeEventArgs e)
{
    // Add the new stroke to the current layer
    Layer layer = arrLayers[nCurrLayer] as Layer;
    layer.Strokes.Add(e.Stroke);

    // Show the layer if it's currently invisible
    if (!layer.bVisible)
    {
        layer.bVisible = true;
        cbVisible.Checked = true;
        pnlInput.Invalidate();
    }
}
}
```

The sample defines a simple data type for a layer of ink—a class that owns a *Strokes* collection along with a flag indicating the visible state of the layer. During initialization, the application creates an *InkOverlay* and a simple UI to select a layer and turn it on and off using a ComboBox and CheckBox, respectively. An array of *Layer* objects is also created, used to track the data and state of the layers.

Because the application itself will be painting the *Stroke* objects contained by the *InkOverlay*'s *Ink* object, the *AutoRedraw* property of the *InkOverlay* is set to false. A paint event handler for the *pnlInput* window is then installed that performs the custom painting operation.

When a *Stroke* object is created, it's added to the currently active *Layer* object's *Strokes* collection. The ComboBox containing the list of layers is used to determine which *Layer* object is current. As the visible CheckBox is checked and unchecked, the current *Layer* object's visible state is toggled, and the input panel is invalidated to cause a repaint.

The painting operation that performs the selective rendering is implemented like so:

```
// Paint all the visible layers
for (int i = 0; i < nNumLayers; i++)
{
    Layer layer = arrLayers[i] as Layer;
    if (layer.bVisible)
    {
        inkOverlay.Renderer.Draw(e.Graphics, layer.Strokes);
    }
}
```

Each *Layer* object is iterated over, and if its visibility state indicates the *Layer* object is visible, the *Layer*'s *Strokes* collection is rendered in its entirety to the *Graphics* object passed into the *Paint* handler. *Layer* objects that are not visible are skipped, and hence no ink will be rendered for them.

## Converting Between Ink Space and Pixels

Often you'll find the need to convert from ink space to pixels, or vice versa. This need particularly comes into play when writing code that allows interaction with ink, as we'll see in the upcoming sample application.

The *Renderer* class provides two methods, *InkSpaceToPixel* and *PixelToInkSpace*, that allow for the conversion to occur. Each has four variants, enabling the conversion of a single point or an array of points, using either a *Graphics* object or an HDC to obtain the pixel dpi.

```
// The various overloads of InkSpaceToPixel
void InkSpaceToPixel(Graphics g, ref Point pt)
void InkSpaceToPixel(Graphics g, ref Point[] pts)
void InkSpaceToPixel(IntPtr hdc, ref Point pt)
void InkSpaceToPixel(IntPtr hdc, ref Point[] pts)

// The various overloads of PixelToInkSpace
void PixelToInkSpace(Graphics g, ref Point pt)
void PixelToInkSpace(Graphics g, ref Point[] pts)
void PixelToInkSpace(IntPtr hdc, ref Point pt)
void PixelToInkSpace(IntPtr hdc, ref Point[] pts)
```

Additionally, the BuildingTabletApps helper library (included on the Book's CD) contains versions of *InkSpaceToPixel* and *PixelToInkSpace* that operate on a *Rect* structure, found in the *RendererEX* class.

### *Renderer* Transforms—Scrolling and Zooming

You've now seen how the *Renderer* class can draw *Stroke* objects. Earlier it was mentioned how a renderer can maintain a transformation on ink coordinates; this ability is very useful to facilitate functionality such as zooming, resizing, and scrolling ink.

The *Renderer* class actually maintains two transformations, known as the *view transformation* and *object transformation*. They are two-dimensional transformation matrices, and they can be stored and retrieved using the *Matrix* class. The difference between the two transformations is quite subtle and has to do with how stroke thickness is treated—the view transformation will scale stroke thickness, whereas the object transformation will not. The two transformations otherwise can serve the same purpose. The object transformation is applied before the view transformation when transforming stroke point data.

Common use of a *Renderer*'s transformation capability will be with the view transformation; this is because when scaling is applied, the typically desired result is for ink strokes to appear to move closer or farther away—their thickness changes proportionately with their size. If scaling is applied via the object transformation, however, ink strokes will appear to grow or shrink in size—their thickness will not change. An object transformation is typically used to alter the size of the ink strokes drawn with the *Renderer* without altering the actual stroke data, for example, to have ink stretch to fit inside an input area.

## Big Ink vs. Little Ink

Up to this point we have used a single instance of the *Ink* class as the container for all the ink strokes in a document. This model is informally known as *Big Ink* because all the document's ink strokes are contained by one *Ink* object. However, some applications might want to use multiple *Ink* objects in a document; for example, each annotation or even each word could be represented by one *Ink* object. This model is known as the *Little Ink* model because multiple *Ink* objects are used to contain the ink strokes. Each *Ink* object is little in comparison to all the ink data in the document. Further discussion of the pros and cons of Big Ink vs. Little Ink is in Chapter 9.

The *Renderer* class provides the functions shown in Table 5-4 to obtain and alter the transformations.

**Table 5-4    The *Renderer* Class's Methods to Work With the Object and View Transformations**

| Method Name | Description |
|---|---|
| *void Move(float offsetX, offsetY)* | Offsets the current view transformation by offset *x* and offset *y* amounts, specified in ink coordinates |
| *void Rotate(float degrees)*<br>*void Rotate(float degrees, Point point)* | Rotates the view transformation by degrees amount, either about the origin (0,0) or the point specified |
| *void Scale(float scaleX, scaleY)*<br>*void Scale(float scaleX, scaleY, bool applyOnPenWidth)* | Scales the view transformation by scale *x* and scale *y*, or if `applyOnPenWidth=false` then scales the object transformation by scale *x* and scale *y* |
| *void GetObjectTransform(ref Matrix m)* | Returns the transformation matrix of the object transform |
| *void GetViewTransform(ref Matrix m)* | Returns the transformation matrix of the view transform |
| *void SetObjectTransform(Matrix m)* | Sets the transformation matrix of the object transform |
| *void SetViewTransform(Matrix m)* | Sets the transformation matrix of the view transform |

The *Move*, *Rotate*, and *Scale* methods make easy work of adjusting the view transformation matrix; alternatively you could get, adjust, and set the *Matrix* object explicitly with the *GetViewTransform* and *SetViewTransform* methods. Note that an overload of the *Scale* method can also adjust the object transformation matrix if its *applyOnPenWidth* parameter is *false*—*Move* and *Rotate* don't have overloads with this parameter because their results don't affect ink thickness.

## Sample Application—InkMagnify

The InkMagnify sample application, shown in Figure 5-5, implements zooming and scrolling functionality. An *InkControl* object and a *Panel* control are created on a form, with the *Panel* mirroring the ink in the *InkControl* as it's created, deleted, moved, and resized. The mirrored ink displayed in the panel can be scrolled by dragging within the panel, and it can be magnified by tapping two Zoom buttons on the form.

**Figure 5-5**   The InkMagnify application implements zooming and scrolling.

### InkMagnify.cs

```
/////////////////////////////////////////////////////////////////////
//
// InkMagnify.cs
//
// (c) 2002 Microsoft Press
// by Rob Jarrett
//
// This program demonstrates how to render ink at a different
// magnifications, as well as scroll it around via a "pan" mode.
//
/////////////////////////////////////////////////////////////////////

using System;
using System.Drawing;
using System.Drawing.Drawing2D;
using System.Windows.Forms;
using Microsoft.Ink;
using MSPress.BuildingTabletApps;

public class frmMain : Form
{
    private InkControl            inkCtl;
    private InkInputPanel         pnlViewer;
    private Button                btnZoomIn;
    private Button                btnZoomOut;
    private Renderer              rndrMagnified;
    private StrokesEventHandler   evtInkAdded;
```

*(continued)*

**InkMagnify.cs** *(continued)*

```csharp
    private StrokesEventHandler evtInkDeleted;
    private Point              ptStart;
    private bool               fPanning = false;

    // Entry point of the program
    [STAThread]
    static void Main()
    {
        Application.Run(new frmMain());
    }

    // Main form setup
    public frmMain()
    {
        SuspendLayout();

        // Create and place all of our controls
        inkCtl = new InkControl();
        inkCtl.Location = new Point(8, 8);
        inkCtl.Size = new Size(352, 216);

        pnlViewer = new InkInputPanel();
        pnlViewer.BackColor = Color.White;
        pnlViewer.BorderStyle = BorderStyle.Fixed3D;
        pnlViewer.Cursor = System.Windows.Forms.Cursors.SizeAll;
        pnlViewer.Location = new Point(8, 228);
        pnlViewer.Size = new Size(352, 192);
        pnlViewer.MouseDown +=
            new MouseEventHandler(pnlViewer_MouseDown);
        pnlViewer.MouseMove +=
            new MouseEventHandler(pnlViewer_MouseMove);
        pnlViewer.MouseUp +=
            new MouseEventHandler(pnlViewer_MouseUp);
        pnlViewer.Paint += new PaintEventHandler(pnlViewer_Paint);

        btnZoomIn = new Button();
        btnZoomIn.Location = new Point(8, 428);
        btnZoomIn.Size = new Size(60, 20);
        btnZoomIn.Text = "Zoom in";
        btnZoomIn.Click += new EventHandler(btnZoomIn_Click);

        btnZoomOut = new Button();
        btnZoomOut.Location = new Point(76, 428);
        btnZoomOut.Size = new Size(60, 20);
        btnZoomOut.Text = "Zoom out";
        btnZoomOut.Click += new EventHandler(btnZoomOut_Click);
```

```
    // Configure the form itself
    ClientSize = new Size(368, 456);
    Controls.AddRange(new Control[] { inkCtl,
                                      pnlViewer,
                                      btnZoomIn,
                                      btnZoomOut});
    FormBorderStyle = FormBorderStyle.FixedDialog;
    MaximizeBox = false;
    Text = "InkMagnify";

    ResumeLayout(false);

    // Create a new Renderer to draw the ink in the viewer panel
    rndrMagnified = new Renderer();

    // Hook up to various stroke modification events so the viewer
    // display can be updated
    inkCtl.InkOverlay.SelectionMoved +=
        new InkOverlaySelectionMovedEventHandler(inkCtl_Moved);
    inkCtl.InkOverlay.SelectionResized +=
        new InkOverlaySelectionResizedEventHandler(inkCtl_Resized);
    inkCtl.InkOverlay.Ink.InkAdded +=
        new StrokesEventHandler(inkCtl_InkAdded);
    inkCtl.InkOverlay.Ink.InkDeleted +=
        new StrokesEventHandler(inkCtl_InkDeleted);

    // Create event handlers so we can be called back on the correct
    // thread
    evtInkAdded = new StrokesEventHandler(inkCtl_InkAdded_Apt);
    evtInkDeleted = new StrokesEventHandler(inkCtl_InkDeleted_Apt);

    // We're now set to go, so turn on tablet input
    inkCtl.InkOverlay.Enabled = true;
}

// Handles the mouse button going down/pen touching the surface in
// the magnified view — starts the panning operation
private void pnlViewer_MouseDown(object sender, MouseEventArgs e)
{
    if (e.Button == MouseButtons.Left)
    {
        Graphics g = pnlViewer.CreateGraphics();

        // Store the start point of this mouse drag in ink coords
        ptStart = new Point(e.X, e.Y);
        rndrMagnified.PixelToInkSpace(g, ref ptStart);
```

*(continued)*

**InkMagnify.cs** *(continued)*

```
                g.Dispose();

                fPanning = true;
        }
    }


    // Handles the mouse/pen moving in the magnifyied view - continues
    // the panning operation if one is occurring
    private void pnlViewer_MouseMove(object sender, MouseEventArgs e)
    {
        if ((e.Button == MouseButtons.Left) && fPanning)
        {
            Graphics g = pnlViewer.CreateGraphics();

            // Offset the viewer by the position of the pen in relation
            // to its starting point
            Point ptCurr = new Point(e.X, e.Y);
            rndrMagnified.PixelToInkSpace(g, ref ptCurr);
            rndrMagnified.Move((ptCurr.X - ptStart.X),
                               (ptCurr.Y - ptStart.Y));

            g.Dispose();

            // Update the viewer display
            pnlViewer.Invalidate();
        }
    }


    // Handles the mouse button being released/pen being lifted in the
    // magnified view - ends the panning operation if one is occurring
    private void pnlViewer_MouseUp(object sender, MouseEventArgs e)
    {
        if ((e.Button == MouseButtons.Left) && fPanning)
        {
            fPanning = false;
        }
    }

    // Helper function for zooming
    private void ZoomByFactor(float fFactor)
    {
        Graphics g = pnlViewer.CreateGraphics();

        // Reset the current view to (0,0)
        Point ptOldOrg = new Point(0,0);
        rndrMagnified.PixelToInkSpace(g, ref ptOldOrg);
        rndrMagnified.Move(ptOldOrg.X / fFactor, ptOldOrg.Y / fFactor);
```

```csharp
    // Compute the center point
    Point ptOldCenter = new Point(
        pnlViewer.ClientSize.Width/2,
        pnlViewer.ClientSize.Height/2);
    rndrMagnified.PixelToInkSpace(g, ref ptOldCenter);

    // Scale the view transformation
    rndrMagnified.Scale(fFactor, fFactor);

    // Compute the new center point
    Point ptNewCenter = new Point(
        pnlViewer.ClientSize.Width/2,
        pnlViewer.ClientSize.Height/2);
    rndrMagnified.PixelToInkSpace(g, ref ptNewCenter);

    // Offset the current view to the initial center point
    rndrMagnified.Move(
        (-(ptOldOrg.X + ptOldCenter.X - ptNewCenter.X) * fFactor),
        (-(ptOldOrg.Y + ptOldCenter.Y - ptNewCenter.Y) * fFactor));

    g.Dispose();

    // Update the viewer display
    pnlViewer.Invalidate();
}

// Handles zooming out
private void btnZoomIn_Click(object sender, EventArgs e)
{
    // Increase magnification by 25%
    ZoomByFactor(1.25f);
}

// Handles zooming in
private void btnZoomOut_Click(object sender, EventArgs e)
{
    // Decrease magnification by 20%
    ZoomByFactor(0.8f);
}

// Handler for the selection getting moved
private void inkCtl_Moved(object sender,
    InkOverlaySelectionMovedEventArgs e)
{
    // Update the viewer display
    pnlViewer.Invalidate();
}
```

*(continued)*

**InkMagnify.cs** *(continued)*

```csharp
// Handler for the selection getting resized
private void inkCtl_Resized(object sender,
    InkOverlaySelectionResizedEventArgs e)
{
    // Update the viewer display
    pnlViewer.Invalidate();
}


// Handler for ink getting added
private void inkCtl_InkAdded(object sender, StrokesEventArgs e)
{
    // Make sure the event fires on the correct thread
    this.Invoke(evtInkAdded, new object[] { sender, e });
}
private void inkCtl_InkAdded_Apt(object sender, StrokesEventArgs e)
{
    // Update the viewer display
    pnlViewer.Invalidate();
}


// Handler for ink getting deleted
private void inkCtl_InkDeleted(object sender, StrokesEventArgs e)
{
    // Make sure the event fires on the correct thread
    this.Invoke(evtInkDeleted, new object[] { sender, e });
}
private void inkCtl_InkDeleted_Apt(object sender, StrokesEventArgs e)
{
    // Update the viewer display
    pnlViewer.Invalidate();
}


// Handler for painting the viewer panel
private void pnlViewer_Paint(object sender, PaintEventArgs e)
{
    // Draw the Ink object using the viewer's Renderer object
    rndrMagnified.Draw(e.Graphics, inkCtl.InkOverlay.Ink.Strokes);
}
}
```

The application creates InkControl and InkInputPanel controls used for the input area and ink viewer, respectively. The *InkInputPanel* class found in the BuildingTabletApps utility library is a simple derivative of the Panel control; it gets rid of flickering during painting by employing .NET Framework support for double buffering. Because the InkInputPanel will be mirroring the ink strokes found in the InkControl's *InkOverlay*, a *Paint* event handler is installed.

Event handlers for *MouseDown*, *MouseMove*, and *MouseUp* events are also installed to facilitate drag scrolling otherwise known as "panning".

The renderer object *rndrMagnified* maintains the current view transformation for the InkInputPanel viewer and is used for painting the ink strokes. Event handlers for various ink stroke manipulation events are used to trigger repainting the InkInputPanel viewer, and again take notice that the *InkAdded* and *InkDeleted* events are triggered on the main thread of the application's execution to avoid multithreading problems.

The *MouseDown* event for *pnlInput* initiates scrolling. The location of the mouse button press is converted into ink coordinates, used later in the *MouseMove* event:

```
if (e.Button == MouseButtons.Left)
{
    Graphics g = pnlViewer.CreateGraphics();

    // Store the start point of this mouse drag in ink coords
    ptStart = new Point(e.X, e.Y);
    rndrMagnified.PixelToInkSpace(g, ref ptStart);

    g.Dispose();

    fPanning = true;
}
```

A *Graphics* object is temporarily created to allow the conversion from pixels to ink space. The *fPanning* member simply tracks whether a panning operation is taking place.

The *MouseMove* handler for *pnlInput* performs the scrolling operation by offsetting the view transformation by the difference between the button down point and the current point:

```
if ((e.Button == MouseButtons.Left) && fPanning)
{
    Graphics g = pnlViewer.CreateGraphics();

    // Offset the viewer by the position of the pen in relation
    // to its starting point
    Point ptCurr = new Point(e.X, e.Y);
    rndrMagnified.PixelToInkSpace(g, ref ptCurr);
    rndrMagnified.Move((ptCurr.X - ptStart.X),
                       (ptCurr.Y - ptStart.Y));

    g.Dispose();

    // Update the viewer display
    pnlViewer.Invalidate();
}
```

Recall that the units for *Renderer*'s *Move* method are ink coordinates (HIMETRIC). Once the transformation has been applied, the *pnlInput* control is invalidated to trigger a repaint.

Zooming is performed by the helper function *ZoomByFactor* that scales the view transformation by a desired amount, preserving the current center point to give the effect of moving inward:

```
private void ZoomByFactor(float fFactor)
{
    Graphics g = pnlViewer.CreateGraphics();

    // Reset the current view to (0,0)
    Point ptOldOrg = new Point(0,0);
    rndrMagnified.PixelToInkSpace(g, ref ptOldOrg);
    rndrMagnified.Move(ptOldOrg.X / fFactor, ptOldOrg.Y / fFactor);

    // Compute the center point
    Point ptOldCenter = new Point(
        pnlViewer.ClientSize.Width/2,
        pnlViewer.ClientSize.Height/2);
    rndrMagnified.PixelToInkSpace(g, ref ptOldCenter);

    // Scale the view transformation
    rndrMagnified.Scale(fFactor, fFactor);

    // Compute the new center point
    Point ptNewCenter = new Point(
        pnlViewer.ClientSize.Width/2,
        pnlViewer.ClientSize.Height/2);
    rndrMagnified.PixelToInkSpace(g, ref ptNewCenter);

    // Offset the current view to the initial center point
    rndrMagnified.Move(
        (-(ptOldOrg.X + ptOldCenter.X - ptNewCenter.X) * fFactor),
        (-(ptOldOrg.Y + ptOldCenter.Y - ptNewCenter.Y) * fFactor));

    g.Dispose();

    // Update the viewer display
    pnlViewer.Invalidate();
}
```

The key operation in this method is *rndrMagnified.Scale*, which adjusts the *Renderer*'s scaling amount (hence, the zoom effect). The translations done with *rndrMagnified.Move* preserve the center point of the view. Similar to the panning case in *MouseMove*, *pnlInput* is invalidated to trigger a repaint once the transformation has been updated. If you like, try using the other overload of the *Scale* method to see the effect of setting the object transform by passing *false* as the value to the *applyOnPenWidth* parameter.

The Tablet PC Platform SDK also contains a sample application demonstrating scrolling and zooming, called InkZoom. It takes on a more traditional UI of having scrollbars control scrolling and a ComboBox specify the zoom level.

## Adding Style—The *DrawingAttributes* Class

Now that you know how to draw ink to the screen or other graphics device, let's take a look at the various properties that define the ink's visual characteristics. The *DrawingAttributes* class encapsulates the formatting information that defines the style electronic ink is rendered with.

The Windows Journal utility found in Windows XP Tablet PC Edition provides a number of predefined pen types for writing and highlighting. This is because the purpose or context of ink drawn on a page isn't always consistent. The style of ink can be categorized by its usage, and it can take on many different forms. A few of the common ones are listed here:

- **Writing ink**   Typically black or blue in color, thin, circular pen tip, and primarily used for note taking and diagramming

- **Markup ink**   Often brighter in color, such as red or green, thicker than writing ink, and mostly used to annotate documents

- **Highlighter ink**   Usually yellow, pink, or light green, very thick with a rectangular tip, transparent in appearance, and often used to highlight text or writing

The *DrawingAttributes* class encapsulates the properties used to render ink to a device. This class's full list of properties is found in Table 5-5 along with a brief description of each.

**Table 5-5  Properties of the *DrawingAttributes* Class**

| Property Name | Type | Description |
|---|---|---|
| *AntiAliased* | *bool* | Turns antialiasing on (*true*) and off (*false*). |
| *Color* | *Color* | The color used to draw the ink. |
| *FitToCurve* | *bool* | Whether ink is rendered as a series of straight lines (*false*) or Bézier curves (*true*). |
| *Height* | *float* | The height of the ink specified in ink coordinates when using the rectangle pen tip. |

*(continued)*

**Table 5-5**  **Properties of the *DrawingAttributes* Class**  *(continued)*

| Property Name | Type | Description |
|---|---|---|
| *IgnorePressure* | *bool* | Whether to avoid varying the thickness of ink with pressure data (true) or not (false). |
| *PenTip* | *PenTip* | The style of tip used to draw ink: *PenTip.Ball* or *PenTip.Rectangle*. |
| *RasterOperation* | *RasterOperation* | The raster operation (ROP) used when drawing ink. The most common value is *RasterOperation.CopyPen* though highlighter ink uses *RasterOperation.MaskPen*. |
| *Transparency* | *Byte* | The transparency amount of the ink, where 0 = opaque and 255 = invisible. |
| *Width* | *Float* | The thickness of the ink when using the ball pen tip, or the width of the ink specified in ink coordinates when using the rectangle pen tip. |

Let's take a look at some of these properties in greater detail.

## Antialiased

*Jaggies* occur when the pixels used to render graphics are not of high enough resolution to make angled or curved edges appear smooth to the human eye. Antialiasing is a remedy for this problem—it takes advantage of how humans perceive contrast by making edge pixels translucent. The translucency is proportional to how much the rendered pixel is contained within the logical edge of an image. Algorithms to compute antialiasing aside, all we really care about here is that antialiasing ink is visually more pleasing to most users.

You will almost always want to use antialiasing when rendering your ink, as it is a dramatic step toward realism. Future versions of the Tablet PC Platform will include ClearInk, a technique borrowing from ClearType in which subpixel rendering is employed, offering even more dramatic results in perceived smoothness.

## *FitToCurve* Property

The *FitToCurve* property specifies whether curve fitting (also known as *smoothing* or *Bézier fitting*) is employed.

As we know, *Stroke* objects are stored as a series of (*x,y*) data, perhaps along with some other packet properties. In essence, a stroke is a polyline. By definition a polyline is a sequence of lines, and by definition a line is straight. This can cause ink to look very polygonal (and artificial) if the (*x,y*) points are spaced far enough apart, perhaps as a result of high-velocity inking. A solution to this problem is to calculate a series of curves that intersect the points of the ink stroke, to better approximate the path of the pen when the stroke was initially drawn. This process is known as *curve fitting*; Figure 5-6 illustrates how it is performed.

## High-Velocity Inking

Don't ink and drive.

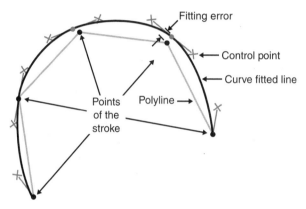

**Figure 5-6**   Curve fitting smooths out the straight edges of polyline-based strokes.

Like antialiasing, curve fitting does a great job of making digital ink appear more realistic—therefore, you'll typically want to take advantage of this feature by setting the property to *true*.

**Note**   If a stroke that is in the process of being created with the pen has its *DrawingAttributes*'s *FitToCurve* property set to *true*, curve fitting will not be applied unless the stroke is explicitly redrawn. This is done on purpose. Because of the inexact fitting of Bézier points during curve fitting, a stroke would appear to wiggle around slightly while it is being drawn if curve fitting were constantly applied. Therefore, it is best practice to wait until the stroke has been completed before setting the *FitToCurve* property, and invalidate the area occupied by the stroke so it is redrawn.

### IgnorePressure Property

In the last chapter we saw that if a tablet device used to collect ink supports the *NormalPressure* packet property, and that property is listed in the *DesiredPacketDescription* attribute of the *InkCollector* or *InkOverlay* used to collect ink, the collected *Stroke* objects can be rendered with varying thickness, corresponding to the pressure value.

The *IgnorePressure* property specifies whether the *NormalPressure* packet property of an ink stroke will be used to vary ink thickness. If an ink stroke doesn't contain any *NormalPressure* data, altering the value of this property will have no effect.

### PenTip Attribute

The *PenTip* attribute is used to indicate the shape of the pen used to draw ink to the device—Values are *PenTip.Ball* and *PenTip.Rectangle.*

When using the *PenTip.Rectangle* tip, both of the *DrawingAttributes'* *Width* and *Height* properties are used to specify size. In contrast, the *PenTip.Ball* tip style only uses the *Width* property—the *Height* property is ignored—because a purely circular pen tip was implemented, in keeping with a physical ballpoint pen. Both properties' values are specified in ink space coordinates.

### RasterOperation Property

The *RasterOperation* property allows specification of the manner in which the pixels of the ink stroke are combined with the destination drawing surface. This is known as the *ROP code* in its short form, and it harkens back to the Graphical Device Interface (GDI) library for its origins. The Win32 Platform SDK documentation has lots of information about ROP codes, so we suggest looking them up via the *SetROP2* function—you'll be glad you did.

There are two ROP codes that are particularly useful when drawing *Stroke* objects: *RasterOperation.CopyPen* and *RasterOperation.MaskPen.* The former is the default value, resulting in ink being drawn on top of the destination surface. The latter is used typically with highlighter ink, taking away color from the destination surface. This is used so that highlighter ink doesn't obscure any ink that may be underneath it (for instance, we don't want black ink turned yellow).

### Using the DrawingAttributes Property

In the last chapter we were briefly introduced to the *DefaultDrawingAttributes* property of the *InkCollector* and *InkOverlay* classes, which denotes the set of drawing attributes to be used on future ink stroke creation. Once an *InkCollector* or *InkOverlay* object is created, the *DefaultDrawingAttributes* property can be immediately modified or even set to another *DrawingAttributes* instance entirely.

> **Note**    The rendering code in the Tablet PC Platform primarily utilizes the GDI+ library for drawing functionality—specifically, it is used for antialiasing and transparency effects. Transparency is a great effect for ink as it can add an extra dimension of visual realism. Unfortunately, the GDI+ library doesn't support ROP codes, so when a ROP code other than *RasterOperation.CopyPen* is desired, ye olde GDI library is enlisted to help. This results in the loss of GDI+ effects such as antialiasing and transparency! Please keep this in mind when using ROP codes in a *DrawingAttributes* object.

The *DefaultDrawingAttributes* property applies to any new ink strokes that are created from the *InkCollector* or *InkOverlay* instance. Also, if the digitizer hardware supports distinguishing between pens, it is possible to have *DrawingAttributes* associated on a per-cursor basis. Setting the *Cursor* class's *DrawingAttributes* property overrides the current *DefaultDrawingAttributes* of an *InkCollector* or *InkOverlay*.

Setting the cursors class's *DrawingAttributes* property to null indicates the cursor will use the *InkCollector*'s or *InkOverlay*'s *DefaultDrawingAttribute*.

After a *Stroke* object has been created, it may be useful to change the *DrawingAttributes* used to render it—for example, a "format ink" dialog may be desirable to include in an application to allow a user to change ink color, thickness, and so forth, or perhaps if the stroke was generated programmatically then some initial *DrawingAttributes* may be desirable to set. The *Stroke* class's *DrawingAttributes* property exposes the drawing attributes used to render the *Stroke* object. When modifying the drawing attributes of a *Stroke*, they are reflected the next time the *Stroke* object is drawn via a *Renderer* object.

The drawing attributes on multiple *Stroke* objects can be set using the *Strokes* collection class's *ModifyDrawingAttributes* method. The method takes a *DrawingAttributes* instance as the sole argument, which is then assigned to the *DrawingAttributes* property of the referenced *Stroke* objects.

The *Stroke* class's *DrawingAttributes* property and the *Strokes* collection class's *ModifyDrawingAttributes* method both permanently alter the drawing attributes of *Stroke* objects. However, sometimes it is useful to temporarily override the drawing attributes without modifying the ink data, for example, when highlighting ink as the result of a search operation, or using high-contrast colors to support accessibility. As we saw earlier in the chapter, the *Renderer* class contains an override of the *Draw* method to perform this task:

```
void Draw(Graphics g, Stroke s, DrawingAttributes da)
```

The drawing attributes are used only to render the ink stroke and do not alter the *Stroke* settings in any way.

## Sample Application—InkFormatter

This last sample in the chapter, shown in Figure 5-7, allows us to play around with the various settings of *DrawingAttributes*. The application uses an InkControl to collect and edit ink, but its Color button is replaced by a Format button that's used to present a dialog in which the various *DrawingAttributes* properties can be changed. The sample takes advantage of a class we'll add to the BuildingTabletApps utility library called *FormatInkDlg* that implements a UI to edit all the properties in a *DrawingAttributes* object.

**Figure 5-7** The InkFormatter application provides a UI to edit all the *DrawingAttributes* class's properties.

---

**FormatInkDlg.cs**

```
/////////////////////////////////////////////////////////////////////////////
//
// FormatInkDlg.cs
//
// (c) 2002 Microsoft Press
// by Rob Jarrett
//
```

```csharp
// This class implements a dialog which provides editing of a
// DrawingAttributes object.
//
/////////////////////////////////////////////////////////////////////

using System;
using System.Collections;
using System.Drawing;
using System.Reflection;
using System.Windows.Forms;
using Microsoft.Ink;

namespace MSPress.BuildingTabletApps
{
    public class FormatInkDlg : Form
    {
        private DrawingAttributes    attrsData;
        private Button               btnColor;
        private ComboBox             cbxThickness;
        private CheckBox             cbAntialiased;
        private CheckBox             cbFitToCurve;
        private CheckBox             cbIgnorePressure;
        private ComboBox             cbxTipStyle;
        private ComboBox             cbxROP;
        private ComboBox             cbxTransparency;
        private Button               btnOK;
        private Button               btnCancel;

        // Dialog setup
        public FormatInkDlg()
        {
            SuspendLayout();

            // Create and place all of our controls
            Label lblColor = new Label();
            lblColor.Location = new Point(8, 8);
            lblColor.Size = new Size(96, 20);
            lblColor.Text = "Color:";
            lblColor.TextAlign = ContentAlignment.MiddleRight;

            btnColor = new Button();
            btnColor.Location = new Point(104, 8);
            btnColor.Size = new Size(45, 20);
            btnColor.Text = "";
            btnColor.Click += new System.EventHandler(btnColor_Click);
```

*(continued)*

**FormatInkDlg.cs** *(continued)*

```
        Label lblThickness = new Label();
        lblThickness.Location = new Point(8, 36);
        lblThickness.Size = new Size(96, 20);
        lblThickness.Text = "Thickness:";
        lblThickness.TextAlign = ContentAlignment.MiddleRight;

        cbxThickness = new ComboBox();
        cbxThickness.Location = new Point(104, 36);
        cbxThickness.Size = new Size(45, 20);
        cbxThickness.DropDownStyle = ComboBoxStyle.DropDownList;
        cbxThickness.SelectedIndexChanged +=
            new System.EventHandler(cbxThickness_SelIndexChg);

        Label lblTipStyle = new Label();
        lblTipStyle.Location = new Point(8, 64);
        lblTipStyle.Size = new Size(96, 20);
        lblTipStyle.Text = "Tip style:";
        lblTipStyle.TextAlign = ContentAlignment.MiddleRight;

        cbxTipStyle = new ComboBox();
        cbxTipStyle.DropDownStyle = ComboBoxStyle.DropDownList;
        cbxTipStyle.Location = new Point(104, 64);
        cbxTipStyle.Size = new Size(90, 20);
        cbxTipStyle.SelectedIndexChanged +=
            new System.EventHandler(cbxTipStyle_SelIndexChg);

        cbAntialiased = new CheckBox();
        cbAntialiased.CheckAlign = ContentAlignment.MiddleRight;
        cbAntialiased.Location = new Point(8, 92);
        cbAntialiased.Size = new Size(108, 16);
        cbAntialiased.Text = "Antialiased:";
        cbAntialiased.TextAlign = ContentAlignment.MiddleRight;
        cbAntialiased.CheckStateChanged += new System.EventHandler(
            cbAntialiased_CheckStateChanged);

        cbFitToCurve = new CheckBox();
        cbFitToCurve.CheckAlign = ContentAlignment.MiddleRight;
        cbFitToCurve.Location = new Point(8, 116);
        cbFitToCurve.Size = new Size(108, 16);
        cbFitToCurve.Text = "Fit to curve:";
        cbFitToCurve.TextAlign = ContentAlignment.MiddleRight;
        cbFitToCurve.CheckStateChanged +=
            new System.EventHandler(cbFitToCurve_CheckStateChanged);

        cbIgnorePressure = new CheckBox();
        cbIgnorePressure.CheckAlign = ContentAlignment.MiddleRight;
        cbIgnorePressure.Location = new Point(8, 140);
```

```
cbIgnorePressure.Size = new Size(108, 16);
cbIgnorePressure.Text = "Ignore pressure:";
cbIgnorePressure.TextAlign = ContentAlignment.MiddleRight;
cbIgnorePressure.CheckStateChanged +=
    new System.EventHandler(
    cbIgnorePressure_CheckStateChanged);

Label lblROP = new Label();
lblROP.Location = new Point(8, 164);
lblROP.Size = new Size(96, 20);
lblROP.Text = "ROP code:";
lblROP.TextAlign = ContentAlignment.MiddleRight;

cbxROP = new ComboBox();
cbxROP.DropDownStyle = ComboBoxStyle.DropDownList;
cbxROP.Location = new Point(104, 164);
cbxROP.Size = new Size(90, 20);
cbxROP.SelectedIndexChanged +=
    new System.EventHandler(cbxROP_SelIndexChg);

Label lblTransparency = new Label();
lblTransparency.Location = new Point(8, 192);
lblTransparency.Size = new Size(96, 20);
lblTransparency.Text = "Transparency:";
lblTransparency.TextAlign = ContentAlignment.MiddleRight;

cbxTransparency = new ComboBox();
cbxTransparency.DropDownStyle = ComboBoxStyle.DropDownList;
cbxTransparency.Location = new Point(104, 192);
cbxTransparency.Size = new Size(90, 20);
cbxTransparency.SelectedIndexChanged +=
    new System.EventHandler(cbxTransparency_SelIndexChg);

btnOK = new Button();
btnOK.Location = new Point(64, 226);
btnOK.Size = new Size(60, 20);
btnOK.Text = "OK";
btnOK.Click += new System.EventHandler(btnOK_Click);

btnCancel = new Button();
btnCancel.Location = new Point(132, 226);
btnCancel.Size = new Size(60, 20);
btnCancel.Text = "Cancel";
btnCancel.Click += new System.EventHandler(btnCancel_Click);

// Configure the form itself
AcceptButton = btnOK;
```

*(continued)*

**FormatInkDlg.cs** *(continued)*

```
CancelButton = btnCancel;
ClientSize = new Size(200, 256);
Controls.AddRange(new Control[] { lblColor,
                                  btnColor,
                                  lblThickness,
                                  cbxThickness,
                                  lblTipStyle,
                                  cbxTipStyle,
                                  cbAntialiased,
                                  cbFitToCurve,
                                  cbIgnorePressure,
                                  lblROP,
                                  cbxROP,
                                  lblTransparency,
                                  cbxTransparency,
                                  btnOK,
                                  btnCancel});
FormBorderStyle = FormBorderStyle.FixedDialog;
MinimizeBox = false;
MaximizeBox = false;
Text = "Format Ink";

ResumeLayout(false);

// Fill up the thickness combobox with some values
cbxThickness.Items.Add(1f);
cbxThickness.Items.Add(50f);
cbxThickness.Items.Add(100f);
cbxThickness.Items.Add(150f);
cbxThickness.Items.Add(300f);
cbxThickness.Items.Add(500f);

// Fill up the pen tip combobox with all pen tip values
foreach (PenTip t in PenTip.GetValues(typeof(PenTip)))
{
    cbxTipStyle.Items.Add(t);
}

// Fill up the ROP code combobox with all raster operation
// values
foreach (RasterOperation o in
    RasterOperation.GetValues(typeof(RasterOperation)))
{
    cbxROP.Items.Add(o);
}

// Fill up the transparency combobox with some values
```

```
        cbxTransparency.Items.Add((byte)0);
        cbxTransparency.Items.Add((byte)64);
        cbxTransparency.Items.Add((byte)128);
        cbxTransparency.Items.Add((byte)192);
        cbxTransparency.Items.Add((byte)255);
}

// Allow the dialog data to be externally viewable and settable
public DrawingAttributes DrawingAttributes
{
    get
    {
        return attrsData;
    }
    set
    {
        attrsData = value.Clone();

        // Reflect the values of the DrawingAttributes in the
        // controls

        btnColor.BackColor = attrsData.Color;

        // Add thickness value to the combobox if not there
        if (!cbxThickness.Items.Contains(attrsData.Width))
        {
            int nLoc = 0;
            while (nLoc < cbxThickness.Items.Count &&
                (float)cbxThickness.Items[nLoc] < attrsData.Width)
            {
                nLoc++;
            }

            if (nLoc < cbxThickness.Items.Count)
            {
                cbxThickness.Items.Insert(nLoc, attrsData.Width);
            }
            else
            {
                cbxThickness.Items.Add(attrsData.Width);
            }
        }
        cbxThickness.SelectedItem = attrsData.Width;

        cbxTipStyle.SelectedItem = attrsData.PenTip;

        cbAntialiased.CheckState = attrsData.AntiAliased ?
```

*(continued)*

**FormatInkDlg.cs** *(continued)*

```
                CheckState.Checked : CheckState.Unchecked;

        cbFitToCurve.CheckState = attrsData.FitToCurve ?
            CheckState.Checked : CheckState.Unchecked;

        cbIgnorePressure.CheckState = attrsData.IgnorePressure ?
            CheckState.Checked : CheckState.Unchecked;

        cbxROP.SelectedItem = attrsData.RasterOperation;

        // Add transparenccy value to the combobox if not there
        if (!cbxTransparency.Items.Contains(
            attrsData.Transparency))
        {
            int nLoc = 0;
            while (nLoc < cbxTransparency.Items.Count &&
                (byte)cbxTransparency.Items[nLoc] <
                attrsData.Transparency)
            {
                nLoc++;
            }
            if (nLoc < cbxTransparency.Items.Count)
            {
                cbxTransparency.Items.Insert(nLoc,
                    attrsData.Transparency);
            }
            else
            {
                cbxTransparency.Items.Add(
                    attrsData.Transparency);
            }
        }
        cbxTransparency.SelectedItem = attrsData.Transparency;
    }
}

// Handle the click of the color button
private void btnColor_Click(object sender, System.EventArgs e)
{
    // Display the common color dialog
    ColorDialog dlgColor = new ColorDialog();
    dlgColor.AllowFullOpen = false;
    dlgColor.Color = attrsData.Color;
    if (dlgColor.ShowDialog(this) == DialogResult.OK)
    {
        // Set the current ink color to the selection chosen in
        // the dialog
```

```
                attrsData.Color = dlgColor.Color;
                btnColor.BackColor = attrsData.Color;
            }
        }


        // Handle the selection change of the width combobox
        private void cbxThickness_SelIndexChg(object sender,
            System.EventArgs e)
        {
            attrsData.Width = (float)cbxThickness.SelectedItem;
            attrsData.Height = attrsData.Width;
        }


        // Handle the selection change of the pen tip combobox
        private void cbxTipStyle_SelIndexChg(object sender,
            System.EventArgs e)
        {
            attrsData.PenTip = (PenTip)cbxTipStyle.SelectedItem;
        }


        // Handle the checked state change of the antialiased checkbox
        private void cbAntialiased_CheckStateChanged(object sender,
            System.EventArgs e)
        {
            attrsData.AntiAliased =
                (cbAntialiased.CheckState == CheckState.Checked);
        }


        // Handle the checked state change of the fit to curve checkbox
        private void cbFitToCurve_CheckStateChanged(object sender,
            System.EventArgs e)
        {
            attrsData.FitToCurve =
                (cbFitToCurve.CheckState == CheckState.Checked);
        }


        // Handle the checked state change of the ignore pressure checkbox
        private void cbIgnorePressure_CheckStateChanged(object sender,
            System.EventArgs e)
        {
            attrsData.IgnorePressure =
                (cbIgnorePressure.CheckState == CheckState.Checked);
        }


        // Handle the selection change of the raster operation combobox
        private void cbxROP_SelIndexChg(object sender,
            System.EventArgs e)
```

*(continued)*

**FormatInkDlg.cs** *(continued)*

```
    {
        attrsData.RasterOperation =
            (RasterOperation)cbxROP.SelectedItem;
    }


    // Handle the selection change of the transparency combobox
    private void cbxTransparency_SelIndexChg(object sender,
        System.EventArgs e)
    {
        attrsData.Transparency = (byte)cbxTransparency.SelectedItem;
    }


    // Handle the button click of the OK button
    private void btnOK_Click(object sender, System.EventArgs e)
    {
        DialogResult = DialogResult.OK;
    }


    // Handle the button click of the cancel button
    private void btnCancel_Click(object sender, System.EventArgs e)
    {
        DialogResult = DialogResult.Cancel;
    }
  }
}
```

To accommodate the FormatInkDlg UI, we'll duplicate the *InkControl* class and rename it to *InkControl2*. The format functionality can then be added in place of color choosing. We'll take this approach in an effort to keep the utility library's implementation as illustrative as possible, as opposed to a "nicer" design such as using derivation.

The Format button handler's implementation is fairly similar to the Color button handler of the original InkControl, except the entire *DrawingAttributes* object is used:

```
// Handle the click of the color button
private void btnFormat_Click(object sender, System.EventArgs e)
{
    // Display the common color dialog
    FormatInkDlg dlgFormat = new FormatInkDlg();
    dlgFormat.DrawingAttributes =
        inkOverlay.DefaultDrawingAttributes;
    if (dlgFormat.ShowDialog(this) == DialogResult.OK)
    {
        // Set the current drawing attributes to the values
        // chosen in the dialog
```

```
        inkOverlay.DefaultDrawingAttributes =
            dlgFormat.DrawingAttributes;
    }
}
```

Finally, here is the rather short and simple listing of the application itself. It creates an instance of the *InkControl2* control and enables tablet input. The result of the functionality is courtesy of our new *InkControl2* class.

### InkFormatter.cs

```
/////////////////////////////////////////////////////////////////////
//
// InkFormatter.cs
//
// (c) 2002 Microsoft Press
// by Rob Jarrett
//
// This program demonstrates the various rendering properties of ink.
//
/////////////////////////////////////////////////////////////////////

using System;
using System.Drawing;
using System.Windows.Forms;
using Microsoft.Ink;
using MSPress.BuildingTabletApps;

public class frmMain : Form
{
    private InkControl2 inkCtl;

    // Entry point of the program
    static void Main()
    {
        Application.Run(new frmMain());
    }

    // Main form setup
    public frmMain()
    {
        SuspendLayout();

        // Create and place all of our controls
        inkCtl = new InkControl2();
        inkCtl.Location = new Point(8, 8);
        inkCtl.Size = new Size(352, 216);
```

*(continued)*

**InkFormatter.cs** *(continued)*

```
// Configure the form itself
ClientSize = new Size(368, 232);
Controls.AddRange(new Control[] { inkCtl });
FormBorderStyle = FormBorderStyle.FixedDialog;
MaximizeBox = false;
Text = "InkFormatter";

ResumeLayout(false);

// We're now set to go, so turn on tablet input
inkCtl.InkOverlay.Enabled = true;
}
}
```

Now, let's try running the application and playing around with all the different settings the FormatInkDlg makes available. Table 5-6 lists some common pen styles and their attributes that you might incorporate into your applications.

**Table 5-6   Common Pen Styles and Their Attributes**

| Pen Style | Color | Thickness (Ink Units) | Pen Tip | ROP Code |
|---|---|---|---|---|
| Writing ink | Black, blue | 1–60 | Ball | *CopyPen* |
| Markup pen | Red, dark green | 60–150 | Ball | *CopyPen* |
| Highlighter ink | Yellow, pink, light green | 500–1000 | Rectangle | *MaskPen* |

You, the developer extraordinaire, must implement the saving and restoring of pen style settings. Typically pen style is user-specific data, hence it should be written and read on a per-user basis. It might be nice if a future version of the Tablet PC Platform provided a central repository for pen styles, but for now we'll have to make do on our own.

## Special Rendering Effects

Using the *DrawingAttributes* class to achieve the look of a specific type of ink isn't its only use. Overriding drawing attributes on existing *Stroke* objects can allow for some interesting UI effects, for example, the UI might show ink selection or perhaps flash the object's colors to show that it's the target of some operation.

## Rendering Selection State

The Tablet PC Platform version 1.0 provides no programmatic support for drawing ink in a selected state. There are cases where we might want to maintain our own set of selected strokes or implement our own select mode functionality, which means we'll have to implement drawing of ink in a selected state on our own. Fortunately, manually drawing ink strokes in a selected state is easier than it looks. Figure 5-8 shows an example of manually drawn ink strokes.

**Figure 5-8**   Drawing ink in the halo style to indicate selection.

The algorithm to achieve the selected look is fairly simple:

1. Create a new *DrawingAttributes* instance from the one currently set on the stroke via the *Clone* method

2. Set *IgnorePressure* to *true* to avoid an outline with varying thickness

3. Inflate the stroke's thickness by 4 pixels (use Renderer's *PixelToInkSpace* to compute how many ink units that is)

4. Draw the ink stroke, overriding its *DrawingAttributes* with the new instance—this is the outline of the stroke

5. Restore the original thickness for the new *DrawingAttributes* instance and set the *Color* property to the inking area's background color

6. Draw the ink stroke using the new *DrawingAttributes* instance—this will cut out the center of the ink

The listing below shows a sample implementation of this algorithm:

```
// Compute selection ink thickness
Point ptThickness = new Point(4, 4);
renderer.PixelToInkSpace(graphics, ref ptThickness);

// Copy the DrawingAttributes since we'll be modifying them
DrawingAttributes da = stroke.DrawingAttributes.Clone();
```

*(continued)*

```
// Turn off pressure so thickness draws uniformly
da.IgnorePressure = true;

// Draw the thick outer stroke
da.Width += ptThickness.X;
da.Height += ptThickness.Y;
renderer.Draw(graphics, stroke, da);

// Draw the inner "transparent" stroke
da.Width -= ptThickness.X;
da.Height -= ptThickness.Y;
da.Color = Color.White;
renderer.Draw(graphics, stroke, da);
```

The utility library includes a method named *RendererEx.DrawSelected* to draw a *Stroke* object or *Strokes* collection in a selected state. We'll be making use of that function in the next chapter when we implement our own selection UI.

## Glowing Ink

Let's have a little more fun, and embellish the selected ink appearance by taking advantage of the *DrawingAttributes* property *Transparency*. If we alter the transparency value while adjusting ink thickness, we can make the ink appear to glow.

The code to achieve this is quite similar to the code for drawing selection, except it has a couple more steps involved; Figure 5-9 illustrates how it's done.

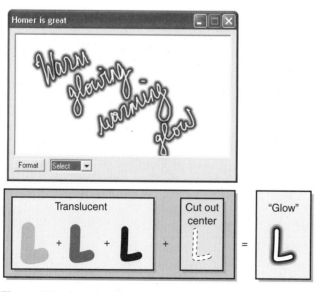

**Figure 5-9**   A method to draw glowing ink.

```
// Compute glowing ink thickness
Point ptThickness = new Point(3, 3);
renderer.PixelToInkSpace(graphics, ref ptThickness);

// Draw the thick outer stroke
da.Width += ptThickness.X*4;
da.Height += ptThickness.Y*4;
da.Transparency = 224;
renderer.Draw(graphics, stroke, da);

da.Width -= ptThickness.X;
da.Height -= ptThickness.Y;
da.Transparency = 192;
renderer.Draw(graphics, stroke, da);

da.Width -= ptThickness.X;
da.Height -= ptThickness.Y;
da.Transparency = 128;
renderer.Draw(graphics, stroke, da);

da.Width -= ptThk.X;
da.Height -= ptThk.Y;
renderer.Draw(graphics, stroke, da);

// Draw the inner "transparent" stroke
da.Transparency = 0;
da.Width -= ptThickness.X;
da.Height -= ptThickness.Y;
da.Color = Color.White;
renderer.Draw(graphics, stroke, da);
```

## Truly Transparent Ink

Both methods to draw ink in a selected state have assumed that the interior hollowed out part of the stroke is a solid color. If the background that the ink was being drawn to was a bitmap with a lot of color variation, or if some other ink was behind the stroke, the hollowed out appearance would not be realized. The proper solution to hollowing out ink is to make the center of the stroke truly transparent. There are at least a couple of methods to do this: the first is to draw the outline of the stroke with a path generated by surrounding the stroke to be selected, and the second is to draw the thick version of the stroke to a bitmap object, manually adjust the interior pixels to be transparent, and draw the bitmap to the screen. We have found that the latter method, while easier to implement, is slower in performance.

## Performance Implications of These Methods

The cost of drawing ink strokes is unfortunately pretty high. This comes primarily from the GDI+ library's performance for basic drawing operations, and the speed at which Bézier curves can be generated for polylines. Antialiasing, curve fitting, and variable thickness from pressure are all quite performance intensive, so they should be used with care. As a big proponent of realistic-looking ink (something we feel is very important to the Tablet PC experience), it's hard for us to say no to those effects because they look so good. Some advice: you might want to offer some UI in your ink-enabled application to turn off some of or all these effects to ultimately leave the choice up to the user. After all, they matter the most!

There is a good performance analysis of rendering operations in Chapter 9.

## Summary

The *Ink* class contains instances of the *Stroke* class. The *Strokes* collection references *Stroke* objects via a unique stroke ID value. *Strokes* collections are just like a .NET Framework collection, that is, references can be added, removed, and searched, all without affecting the lifetime or ownership of *Stroke* objects.

*Stroke* objects are generated as a result of tablet input by the *InkCollector* and *InkOverlay* classes, and they can also be programmatically created with the *CreateStroke* method of the *Ink* class. They can be copied to other *Ink* objects, and they can never live outside the ownership of an *Ink* object.

The *Renderer* class is used to draw ink strokes to a *Graphics* object or Windows device context, and it can apply an arbitrary transformation on the ink. The *DrawingAttributes* class enables the ink to be formatted in a wide variety of ways, and it includes specifying functionality such as antialiasing, curve fitting, and rendering with pressure data.

Now let's turn to the next chapter, which continues our discussion of ink data management.

# 6

# Tablet PC Platform SDK: Ink Data Management, Part II

This chapter explores more of the Tablet PC Platform's Ink Data Management API. In Chapter 5, we learned about the creation, ownership, and rendering of ink data. Now we can use this knowledge to work with the platform's more advanced functionality.

We'll begin the chapter by delving into ink stroke geometry. This includes topics such as computing bounds, intersections, and applying transformations. Then we'll move on to study hit-testing ink strokes, where among other things a solution for performing real-time lasso selection is presented. Next we'll discuss how to split and chop strokes into pieces. Finally, we'll discuss how to persist ink data to and from a stream and from the Microsoft Windows clipboard. In doing so we'll see how to perform an ink data drag and drop operation.

We provide plenty of examples showing how the APIs are used, and in fact much of this chapter is code. As a developer, I find that there's no better way to learn than by seeing firsthand how something is done. Hopefully, you agree. There's a lot to cover, so let's jump right in.

## Stroke Geometry

This (somewhat ambiguously titled) section is devoted to working with ink strokes. Specifically, we'll discuss the aspects that apply to their measurement and shape.

# Computing the Bounding Box of a Stroke

The *bounding box* of ink strokes is the smallest rectangle that completely encloses the ink. Often, it is useful to compute the bounds of this box for an *Ink* object, a *Stroke* object, or a *Strokes* collection. If, for example, one or more attributes of a *Stroke* object's *DrawingAttributes* property are altered, we might want to trigger a redraw for the changes to be reflected; it is much more efficient to invalidate the rectangular area surrounding the ink rather than the entire viewing window. Of course, this notion of determining boundaries begs the following questions, "What is the *edge* of an ink stroke?" "Are the points in a stroke the edge?" "Does the thickness of the ink stroke matter?" "What if curve fitting is turned on, and the curve doesn't quite intersect points on the edge?"

To address these questions, *Ink* objects supply two types of bounding boxes. The first type uses only the ink stroke's polyline points when calculating the bounding box, ignoring the rendered appearance of the ink entirely. This means factors like stroke thickness and curve-fitting are ignored. The second type of bounding box accounts for the rendered appearance of the ink.

## The *GetBoundingBox* Method

The *Ink*, *Strokes*, and *Stroke* classes all contain a *GetBoundingBox* method, which computes the bounding box (or "bounds") of ink strokes. The object type calling the function determines which strokes are included when computing the bounds. For an *Ink* object, the bounds of all its ink strokes are used; for a *Strokes* collection, the *Stroke* objects the collection references are used; and for a *Stroke* object, the *Stroke* object is used.

The *GetBoundingBox* method comes in two overloaded forms, and both return a *Rectangle* structure of the bounds in ink coordinates:

```
Rectangle Ink.GetBoundingBox()
Rectangle Ink.GetBoundingBox(BoundingBoxMode mode)
Rectangle Strokes.GetBoundingBox()
Rectangle Strokes.GetBoundingBox(BoundingBoxMode mode)
Rectangle Stroke.GetBoundingBox()
Rectangle Stroke.GetBoundingBox(BoundingBoxMode mode)
```

The first overload takes no parameters and computes the bounds of the ink according to its drawing attributes (how it looks on the screen). The second overload takes a member from the *BoundingBoxMode* enumeration as a parameter and returns the bounds as described by the values presented in Table 6-1.

**Table 6-1**  *BoundingBoxMode* **Values**

| *BoundingBoxMode* Value | Description |
|---|---|
| *CurveFit* | Bounding box of the stroke taking into account its *DrawingAttributes* property when *FitToCurve* is true |
| *Default* | Bounding box of the stroke taking into account its *DrawingAttributes* property |
| *NoCurveFit* | Bounding box of the stroke taking into account its *DrawingAttributes* property when *FitToCurve* is false |
| *PointsOnly* | Bounding box of the stroke without taking into account its *Drawing-Attributes* property (using only its points) |
| *Union* | Union of the results from *BoundingBoxMode.CurveFit* and *Bounding-BoxMode.NoCurveFit* |

Figure 6-1 defines members in the *BoundingBoxMode* enumeration. Notice that the version of *GetBoundingBox* without parameters gives the same results as calling *GetBoundingBox(BoundingBoxMode.Default)*.

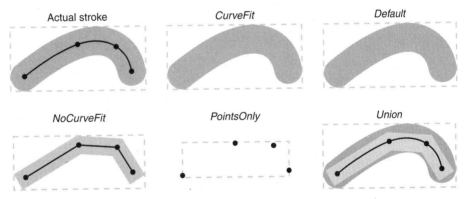

**Figure 6-1**   Types of bounding box modes.

## The *Renderer* Class's *Measure* Method

There is another method for obtaining the bounds of ink strokes in addition to the *GetBoundingBox* method. The *Renderer* class's *Measure* method is able to take into account any view or object transformation in calculating the bounding box:

```
Rectangle Renderer.Measure(Stroke s)
Rectangle Renderer.Measure(Stroke s, DrawingAttributes da)
Rectangle Renderer.Measure(Strokes strokes)
```

Notice that the *Measure* method doesn't use the *BoundingBoxMode* enumeration—the only method it employs is using drawing attributes, obtained either from the *DrawingAttributes* property of the strokes being measured or from those that are explicitly provided. This method takes into account any view or object transforms set in the renderer.

### Code Snippet—*DrawBoundingBoxes*

The following function renders the bounding box of *Stroke* objects contained in an *Ink* object or referenced by a *Strokes* collection. This code can be found in the *RendererEx* class in the BuildingTabletApps helper library.

```
// Draw the bounding rect of each stroke in an Ink object
public static void DrawBoundingBoxes(Graphics g, Ink ink)
{
    DrawBoundingBoxes(g, ink.Strokes,
        new Renderer(), Pens.LightGreen, BoundingBoxMode.Default);
}

// Draw the various bounding rects of each stroke in a strokes
// collection
public static void DrawBoundingBoxes(Graphics g, Strokes strokes,
    Renderer renderer, Pen pen, BoundingBoxMode mode)
{
    foreach (Stroke s in strokes)
    {
        // Make sure each stroke has not been deleted
        if (!s.Deleted)
        {
            Rectangle rcBounds = s.GetBoundingBox(mode);
            RendererEx.InkSpaceToPixel(renderer, g, ref rcBounds);
            g.DrawRectangle(pen, rcBounds);
        }
    }
}
```

The *RendererEx.InkSpaceToPixel* method is a utility function, also found in the BuildingTabletApps library. It does what the *Renderer* class's *InkSpaceToPixel* method does, except it uses a *Rectangle* structure.

## Retrieving the Points of a Stroke

It can sometimes be useful to get at the (X,Y) values that form an ink stroke, for example, to implement custom drawing of ink or for some custom recognition capability. Two kinds of points can be obtained from a *Stroke* object—polyline points and Bézier points.

## Polyline Points

The *Stroke* class natively stores data for ink strokes in a polyline format, which is essentially an array of *Point* structures. The following functions are provided to get and set the polyline points of a *Stroke* object:

```
Point Stroke.GetPoint(int index)
Point[] Stroke.GetPoints()
Point[] Stroke.GetPoints(int index, int count)
int Stroke.SetPoint(int index, Point pt)
int Stroke.SetPoints(Point[] pts)
int Stroke.SetPoints(int index, Point[] pts)
```

The *GetPoint* and *GetPoints* methods are straightforward—they simply return a *Stroke* object's points in ink coordinates. The overload of *GetPoints*, which accepts two parameters, allows for a specified range of points to be queried. The first parameter is the start index into the array of points, and the second is the count of how many points should be returned.

The *SetPoint* method provides a means to adjust one point in a *Stroke* object. The *index* parameter's value must lie within the range of the *Stroke* object's point array, or else an exception will be thrown. The method returns the number of points changed in the ink stroke, that is, 1.

*SetPoints* similarly sets multiple points in a *Stroke* object. An array of points is passed, with an optional starting index, and the total number of points set is returned. This method cannot alter the total number of points making up an ink stroke; therefore, the array of points used should not exceed the range of the *Stroke* object's point array.

> **Note**   Any extra packet property data contained in a *Stroke* object (for example, pressure data) will be left unaltered when either the *SetPoint* or *SetPoints* method is used.

## Bézier Control Points

The *Stroke* class's *BezierPoints* property provides the control points of the Bézier curve that is drawn when its *DrawingAttributes'* *CurveFit* property is true. These control points can then be used to compute the actual (X,Y) points that make up the curved line, or they can be passed along to a Bézier curve drawing function such as the *Graphics* class's *DrawBeziers* method.

Alternatively, the *Stroke* class's *GetFlattenedBezierPoints* method will compute the actual (*X*,*Y*) points that approximate the Bézier curve, optionally accepting an error value specified in ink units as its parameter:

```
Point[] Stroke.GetFlattenedBezierPoints()
Point[] Stroke.GetFlattenedBezierPoints(int fittingError)
```

The array of points returned can then be used in conjunction with a call to *Graphics'* *DrawLines* method to draw an approximation of the Bézier curve. The default value for the *fittingError* parameter is 0. This results in the smoothest line but yields the greatest number of points returned. It could therefore adversely affect the performance of subsequent operations with the line (such as rendering).

## Code Snippet—*DrawPoints* (Draws Bézier or Polyline Points of Ink)

This function, found in the BuildingTabletApps helper library, will render the (*X*,*Y*) points of a *Stroke* object. The type of data used for the points is determined by the custom *StrokePointType* enumeration, whose values are *Polyline*, *Bezier*, and *FlattenedBezier*. Overloads of the *DrawPoints* method are also provided for a *Strokes* collection and an entire *Ink* object.

```
public enum StrokePointType
{
    Polyline,
    Bezier,
    FlattenedBezier
}


// Draw the polyline points each stroke has in an Ink object
public static void DrawPoints(Graphics g, Ink ink)
{
    DrawPoints(g, ink.Strokes, new Renderer(), Brushes.Red,
        StrokePointType.Polyline);
}


// Draw the various kinds of points each stroke has in a
// strokes collection
public static void DrawPoints(Renderer renderer, Graphics g, Strokes strokes,
    Brush brush, StrokePointType type)
{
    foreach (Stroke s in strokes)
    {
        // Make sure each stroke has not been deleted
        if (!s.Deleted)
        {
            DrawPoints(g, s, renderer, brush, type);
```

```
        }
    }
}


// Draw the various kinds of points for a stroke
public static void DrawPoints(Renderer renderer, Graphics g,
    Stroke stroke, Brush brush, StrokePointType type)
{
    // Get the array of points according to the type desired
    Point [] pts = null;
    switch (type)
    {
        case StrokePointType.Bezier:
            pts = stroke.BezierPoints;
            break;

        case StrokePointType.FlattenedBezier:
            pts = stroke.GetFlattenedBezierPoints();
            break;

        case StrokePointType.Polyline:
            pts = stroke.GetPoints();
            break;
    }

    // Render the points if they were retrieved
    if (pts != null)
    {
        renderer.InkSpaceToPixel(g, ref pts);
        foreach (Point pt in pts)
        {
            g.FillEllipse(brush, pt.X-1, pt.Y-1, 4, 4);
        }
    }
}
```

The preceding code is fairly self-explanatory—based on the value of *StrokePointType*, the appropriate property or method of the *Stroke* object is used to retrieve an array of points to draw. The *FillEllipse* method is used to perform the actual rendering of each point.

## Computing Intersections of a Stroke

Computing the intersections of ink strokes can be useful for a number of tasks—performing stroke erasing or recognition, for example. Figure 6-2 shows the three kinds of intersections that the Tablet PC Platform can compute:

- Self-intersection, which occurs when a stroke crosses itself

- Stroke intersection, which occurs when a stroke crosses another stroke

- Rectangle intersection, which occurs when a stroke crosses the bounds of a rectangle

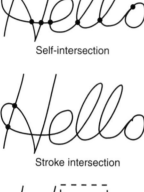

Self-intersection

Stroke intersection

Rectangle intersection

**Figure 6-2**   The three kinds of intersections—self, stroke, and rectangle.

The *Stroke* class's *SelfIntersections* property returns an array of floating-point index values that specify where along the stroke any self-intersections occur. A *floating-point index* is a value that defines an arbitrary position along the length of an ink stroke. You can think of the value in the same way as an integer index value, except that the fractional part of the number represents where between adjacent point indexes the specified point actually is. Figure 6-3 shows an example for a floating-point index value of 2.4; this means that the point defined is 40 percent of the way along the line segment between points at indexes 2 and 3. Similarly, a floating-point index value of 6.8 defines a point that is 80 percent of the way along the line segment between points at indexes 6 and 7.

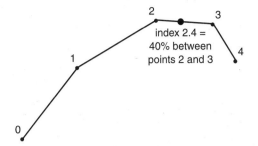

**Figure 6-3**    Partial index values allow for interpolation between points.

The *Stroke* class's *FindIntersections* method computes intersections between *Stroke* objects. This method returns an array of floating-point indexes that define the intersections between the *Stroke* object that is calling the method and the *Stroke* objects that are referenced by the method's *Strokes* collection parameter:

```
float[] FindIntersections(Strokes strokes)
```

This is the only function in the Tablet PC Platform in which the *Stroke* objects referenced by the *Strokes* collection must belong to the same *Ink* object as the *Stroke* object that's calling the method. An exception will be thrown otherwise. If *null* is passed for the *strokes* parameter, the method uses all ink strokes in the *Ink* object.

The *GetRectangleIntersections* method is a little more complex. This method computes the intersections between a rectangle and a *Stroke* object, but instead of returning an array of floating-point indexes it returns an array of *StrokeIntersection* structures. *StrokeIntersection* primarily encapsulates two properties, *BeginIndex* and *EndIndex*, that provide information about how the stroke intersects the rectangle.

The *BeginIndex* property is the floating-point index for where the stroke enters the rectangle, and the *EndIndex* property is the floating-point index for where the stroke leaves the rectangle. A special case occurs when *BeginIndex* equals –1.0, meaning the stroke begins inside the rectangle (there is no entry point), or if *EndIndex* equals –1.0, meaning that the stroke ends inside the rectangle. Figure 6-4 illustrates the various forms that the values of *BeginIndex* and *EndIndex* can take.

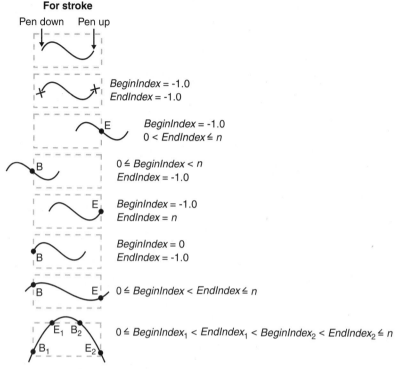

**For stroke**

Pen down    Pen up

$BeginIndex = -1.0$
$EndIndex = -1.0$

$BeginIndex = -1.0$
$0 < EndIndex \leq n$

$0 \leq BeginIndex < n$
$EndIndex = -1.0$

$BeginIndex = -1.0$
$EndIndex = n$

$BeginIndex = 0$
$EndIndex = -1.0$

$0 \leq BeginIndex < EndIndex \leq n$

$0 \leq BeginIndex_1 < EndIndex_1 < BeginIndex_2 < EndIndex_2 \leq n$

**Figure 6-4**   Given an ink stroke of *n* points, these are the possible values of *StrokeIntersection*'s *BeginIndex* and *EndIndex* properties when returned from *GetRectangleIntersections*.

## Code Snippet—*DrawIntersections*

This function in the *RendererEx* class draws all three types of intersections we've just covered—stroke intersections, self-intersections, and rectangle intersections (using the bounding boxes of the other strokes). The custom enum *StrokeIntersection* Type can be provided to *DrawIntersections* to specify the type of intersection to render.

```
public enum StrokeIntersectionType
{
    Self,
    Stroke,
    BoundingBox
}


// Draw the stroke intersections for the strokes in an Ink object
public static void DrawIntersections(Graphics g, Ink ink)
{
    DrawIntersections(g, ink.Strokes, new Renderer(),
```

```
                Pens.DarkRed, StrokeIntersectionType.Stroke);
}


// Draw the various intersections for the strokes in a Strokes
// collection
public static void DrawIntersections(
    Graphics g, Strokes strokes, Renderer renderer,
    Pen pen, StrokeIntersectionType type)
{
    foreach (Stroke s in strokes)
    {
        // Make sure each stroke has not been deleted
        if (!s.Deleted)
        {
            if (type == StrokeIntersectionType.BoundingBox)
            {
                // Draw bounding box intersections
                DrawIntersections(g, s, renderer, pen);
            }
            else
            {
                // Compute either self or stroke intersections
                float[] fResults = null;
                switch (type)
                {
                    case StrokeIntersectionType.Self:
                        fResults = s.SelfIntersections;
                        break;

                    case StrokeIntersectionType.Stroke:
                        fResults = s.FindIntersections(null);
                        break;
                }

                // Draw the intersections (if any)
                if (fResults != null)
                {
                    DrawIntersection(
                        g, s, renderer, fResults, pen);
                }
            }
        }
    }
}

// Helper function to draw intersections between each stroke's
// bounding rect and all other strokes
private static void DrawIntersections(Graphics g,
    Stroke s, Renderer renderer, Pen pen)
```

*(continued)*

```csharp
{
    Rectangle rcBounds = renderer.Measure(s);

    // Generate a strokes collection containing all strokes
    // except the one being used for its bounding rect
    Strokes strksToCheck = s.Ink.CreateStrokes();
    strksToCheck.Add(s.Ink.Strokes);
    strksToCheck.Remove(s);

    foreach (Stroke s2 in strksToCheck)
    {
        if (!s2.Deleted)
        {
            StrokeIntersection[] siResults =
                s2.GetRectangleIntersections(rcBounds);

            ArrayList arrResults = new ArrayList();
            foreach (StrokeIntersection si in siResults)
            {
                if (si.BeginIndex >= 0)
                {
                    arrResults.Add(si.BeginIndex);
                }
                if (si.EndIndex > 0)
                {
                    arrResults.Add(si.EndIndex);
                }
            }

            if (arrResults.Count > 0)
            {
                // Fill up a float array with the intersection
                // indicies
                float[] fResults =
                    (float[])arrResults.ToArray(typeof(float));

                // Use a handy helper to draw the intersections
                DrawIntersection(g, s2, renderer, fResults, pen);
            }
        }
    }
}

// Helper function to draw intersections along a stroke
private static void DrawIntersection(Graphics g,
    Stroke s, Renderer renderer, float[] fIndicies, Pen pen)
{
    foreach (float fIndex in fIndicies)
    {
```

```
// Get the whole-number point of the intersection
int nIndex = (int)fIndex;
Point pt = s.GetPoint(nIndex);

// Compute the fractional point of the intersection if
// possible
if (nIndex < s.GetPoints().Length - 1)
{
    float fFraction = fIndex - nIndex;
    Point pt2 = s.GetPoint(nIndex+1);
    pt.X += (int)Math.Round((pt2.X - pt.X) * fFraction);
    pt.Y += (int)Math.Round((pt2.Y - pt.Y) * fFraction);
}

            renderer.InkSpaceToPixel(g, ref pt);
            g.DrawEllipse(pen, pt.X-3, pt.Y-3, 7, 7);
        }
}
```

For handling self-intersection and stroke intersection cases, the same code path is used because the *SelfIntersections* property and the *GetStrokeIntersections* method return an array of floating-point indexes. For rectangle intersection, the collective values of the *StrokeIntersection* properties *BeginIndex* and *EndIndex* are appended to an ArrayList, which is then converted to a floating-point array to leverage the drawing code used for self-intersections and stroke intersections.

Consider the code to compute the point given a floating-point index value:

```
// Get the whole-number point of the intersection
int nIndex = (int)fIndex;
Point pt = s.GetPoint(nIndex);

// Compute the fractional point of the intersection if
// possible
if (nIndex < s.GetPoints().Length - 1)
{
    float fFraction = fIndex - nIndex;
    Point pt2 = s.GetPoint(nIndex+1);
    pt.X += (int)Math.Round((pt2.X - pt.X) * fFraction);
    pt.Y += (int)Math.Round((pt2.Y - pt.Y) * fFraction);
}
```

The index is separated into two parts: a whole number part and a fractional part. The whole number is used to obtain the two adjacent polyline points for the purpose of interpolation, and the fractional part is used to compute the final point along their corresponding line segment.

## Retrieving and Setting the Packet Data of a Stroke

As we first learned in Chapter 4, there is often more to ink strokes than just ·(*X*,*Y*) data. Packet properties such as pressure and tilt angle can literally add an extra dimension of realism to digital ink. This section explains how to get and set packet property data on *Stroke* objects, which can be handy when custom rendering your own ink type, among other uses.

Every *Stroke* object has its own *PacketDescription* property, which is an array of *PacketProperty* Guid values—the property acts as the template for the layout of packet data. *PacketCount* returns the number of packets making up the stroke, not coincidentally the same value as the length of the array returned by *GetPoints*.

> **Note**   The *PacketSize* property returns the size in bytes of a packet, although this is actually unnecessary information because the length of the *PacketDescription* array multiplied by the size in bytes of an individual packet value gives the same result.

Packet data is retrieved via the *Stroke* class's *GetPacketData* method, which takes on a few forms:

```
int[] Stroke.GetPacketData()
int[] Stroke.GetPacketData(int index)
int[] Stroke.GetPacketData(int index, int count)
```

If no parameters are given, *GetPacketData* will return a *Stroke* object's packet data in one big array of ints. Alternatively, if *GetPacketData* is supplied with an index, a single packet will be returned—or, if both an index and a count are supplied, multiple packets are returned. It is your responsibility to parse the values and interpret the data as the appropriate packet property.

The allowable range and units of packet property values are obtained with the *GetPacketDescriptionPropertyMetrics* method. This function returns a *TabletPropertyMetrics* structure (which we saw in Chapter 4), given a packet property Guid value.

You'll find that working with packet data will often be on the basis of packet property type, making manually parsing through packets a bit of a pain. The *GetPacketValuesByProperty* and *SetPacketValuesByProperty* methods solve this problem:

```
int[] Stroke.GetPacketValuesByProperty(Guid id)
int[] Stroke.GetPacketValuesByProperty(Guid id, int index)
int[] Stroke.GetPacketValuesByProperty(Guid id, int index, int count)
int Stroke.SetPacketValuesByProperty(Guid id, int[] packetValues)
int Stroke.SetPacketValuesByProperty(Guid id, int index, int[] packetValues)
int Stroke.SetPacketValuesByProperty(Guid id, int index, int count, int[] packe
tValues)
```

*GetPacketValuesByProperty* returns the values of a given packet property type in an ink stroke—it can return all values, a single value, or a range of values, depending on the overloaded version used. Similarly, the *SetPacketValuesByProperty* method can set all values, a single value, or a range of values for a packet property type. It returns the number of values that were set as a result of calling the method.

## Code Snippet—*PressureAdjust*
The following snippet of code shows an example of how a *Stroke* object's pressure data can be adjusted using the packet data APIs of the *Stroke* class:

```
// First, check to see if the stroke has PacketProperty.NormalPressure
// data in it
bool fFound = false;
for (int i = 0; i < stroke.PacketDescription.Length; i++)
{
    if (stroke.PacketDescription[i] == PacketProperty.NormalPressure)
    {
        fFound = true;
        break;
    }
}

if (!fFound)
{
    // ERROR: stroke does not contain any pressure information
    return;
}
```

*(continued)*

```
// Get the range of allowable values for pressure
TabletPropertyMetrics tpm =
    stroke.GetPacketDescriptionPropertyMetrics(
    PacketProperty.NormalPressure);

// Figure out how much to increase the pressure by - we'll arbitrarily
// make it 25% of the allowable range
int incAmount = (tpm.Maximum - tpm.Minimum) / 4;

// Get the current pressure values
int[] values =
    stroke.GetPacketValuesByProperty(PacketProperty.NormalPressure);

// Adjust all of the pressure values, clipping at the maximum value
for (int i = 0; i < stroke.PacketCount; i++)
{
    values[i] += incAmount;
    if (values[i] > tpm.Maximum)
    {
        values[i] = tpm.Maximum;
    }
}

// Set the changed values back on the ink stroke
stroke.SetPacketValuesByProperty(
    PacketProperty.NormalPressure, values);
```

## Retrieving the Cusps of a Stroke

A *cusp* in an ink stroke is defined as a point at which the direction of the ink changes in a discontinuous fashion. In other words, a cusp is a point along a stroke where the direction changes quickly—for example, the elbow of a capital *L* or the point of a *v*. Cusps are useful for logically dividing a stroke into segments. They can aid in performing gesture recognition or partial stroke erasing.

The Tablet PC Platform can compute two kinds of cusps: polyline cusps and Bézier cusps. The difference between the two is merely the set of points that are analyzed—polyline cusps are computed from polyline points, and Bézier cusps are computed from Bézier points. Note that for both kinds of cusps, illustrated in Figure 6-5, the first and last point of a stroke are considered to be cusps because the direction of ink is changed in a discontinuous fashion (it starts or stops).

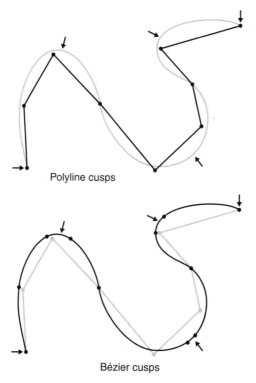

Polyline cusps

Bézier cusps

**Figure 6-5**   The two kinds of cusps—Bézier and polyline.

Both the *Stroke* class's *BezierCusps* and *PolylineCusps* properties return an array of integers that identify the point indexes at which a cusp was determined.

## Code Snippet—*DrawCusps*

This code snippet will render the location of either the polyline or Bézier cusps for an ink stroke:

```
public enum StrokeCuspType
{
    Bezier,
    Polyline
}


// Draw the polyline cusps for the strokes in an Ink object
public static void DrawCusps(Graphics g, Ink ink)
{
    DrawCusps(g, ink.Strokes, new Renderer(),
        Pens.Blue, StrokeCuspType.Polyline);
}
```

*(continued)*

```
// Draw the various cusps for the strokes in a strokes
// collection
public static void DrawCusps(Graphics g, Strokes strokes,
    Renderer renderer, Pen pen, StrokeCuspType type)
{
    foreach (Stroke s in strokes)
    {
        // Make sure each stroke has not been deleted
        if (!s.Deleted)
        {
            DrawCusps(g, s, renderer, pen, type);
        }
    }
}

// Draw the various cusps for a stroke
public static void DrawCusps(Graphics g, Stroke stroke,
    Renderer renderer, Pen pen, StrokeCuspType type)
{
    // Get the cusp indexes and point array according to the
    // type desired
    int [] cusps = null;
    Point [] pts = null;
    switch (type)
    {
        case StrokeCuspType.Bezier:
            cusps = stroke.BezierCusps;
            pts = stroke.BezierPoints;
            break;

        case StrokeCuspType.Polyline:
            cusps = stroke.PolylineCusps;
            pts = stroke.GetPoints();
            break;
    }

    // Render the points if they were retrieved
    if (cusps != null && pts != null)
    {
        foreach (int n in cusps)
        {
            Point pt = pts[n];
            renderer.InkSpaceToPixel(g, ref pt);
            g.DrawEllipse(pen, pt.X-3, pt.Y-3, 7, 7);
        }
    }
}
```

Probably the most important information to note here is that the results obtained from the *PolylineCusps* property apply to the *Stroke* object's polyline points, just as the results from the *BezierCusps* property apply to the Bézier points.

# Putting It Together—the StrokeDataViewer Example

To better understand the stroke geometry data we've been discussing, this next sample application shows the data in visual form. The BuildingTabletApps helper library contains a class, *RendererEx*, whose methods can render the various stroke data and is therefore heavily leveraged by the sample. The code snippets that have been presented here were taken from the *RendererEx* class.

## Sample Application—StrokeDataViewer

Loosely based on the StrokeIdViewer sample application from the last chapter, this sample, shown in Figure 6-6, can show all sorts of information about ink strokes—stroke ID, bounding box, points, intersections, and cusps. The main form's menu lets the user choose the data to view.

**Figure 6-6**  The StrokeDataViewer sample application displays all the stroke data you can handle.

```
StrokeDataViewer.cs
/////////////////////////////////////////////////////////////////////////////
//
// StrokeDataViewer.cs
//
// (c) 2002 Microsoft Press
// by Rob Jarrett
//
```

*(continued)*

**StrokeDataViewer.cs** *(continued)*

```csharp
// This program displays lots of different information for
// Stroke objects. An InkOverlaySharp control is created and the
// user can choose various data attributes from the app's menu
// to be drawn, such as points, bounding box, cusps, and
// intersections. The data is kept up to date as strokes are added,
// removed, and modified.
//
////////////////////////////////////////////////////////////////////

using System;
using System.Drawing;
using System.Windows.Forms;
using Microsoft.Ink;
using MSPress.BuildingTabletApps;

public class frmMain : Form
{
    private InkControl2       inkCtl;

    private MenuItem          miStrokeId;
    private MenuItem          miNoPoints;
    private MenuItem          miPolylinePoints;
    private MenuItem          miBezierPoints;
    private MenuItem          miFlattenedBezierPoints;
    private MenuItem          miNoCusps;
    private MenuItem          miBezierCusps;
    private MenuItem          miPolylineCusps;
    private MenuItem          miNoBoundingBox;
    private MenuItem          miDefaultBoundingBox;
    private MenuItem          miCurveFitBoundingBox;
    private MenuItem          miNoCurveFitBoundingBox;
    private MenuItem          miPointsOnlyBoundingBox;
    private MenuItem          miUnionBoundingBox;
    private MenuItem          miNoIntersections;
    private MenuItem          miSelfIntersections;
    private MenuItem          miStrokeIntersections;
    private MenuItem          miBoundingBoxIntersections;

    private bool              fDrawStrokeId = false;
    private bool              fDrawPoints = false;
    private RendererEx.StrokePointType strokePointType =
                    RendererEx.StrokePointType.Polyline;
    private bool              fDrawCusps = false;
    private RendererEx.StrokeCuspType strokeCuspType =
                    RendererEx.StrokeCuspType.Polyline;
    private bool              fDrawBoundingBox = false;
    private BoundingBoxMode bboxMode = BoundingBoxMode.Default;
```

```csharp
private bool              fDrawIntersections = false;
private RendererEx.StrokeIntersectionType
                     strokeIntersectionType =
                     RendererEx.StrokeIntersectionType.Stroke;

// Entry point of the program
[STAThread]
static void Main()
{
    Application.Run(new frmMain());
}

// Main form setup
public frmMain()
{
    SuspendLayout();

    // Create the main menu
    Menu = new MainMenu();

    MenuItem miFile = new MenuItem("&File");
    Menu.MenuItems.Add(miFile);

    MenuItem miExit = new MenuItem("E&xit");
    miExit.Click += new EventHandler(miExit_Click);
    Menu.MenuItems[0].MenuItems.Add(miExit);

    MenuItem miView = new MenuItem("&View");
    miView.Popup += new EventHandler(miView_Popup);
    Menu.MenuItems.Add(miView);

    miStrokeId = new MenuItem("Stroke Id");
    miStrokeId.Click += new EventHandler(miStrokeId_Click);
    Menu.MenuItems[1].MenuItems.Add(miStrokeId);

    Menu.MenuItems[1].MenuItems.Add(new MenuItem("-"));

    MenuItem miPoints = new MenuItem("Points");
    miPoints.Popup += new EventHandler(miPoints_Popup);
    Menu.MenuItems[1].MenuItems.Add(miPoints);

    miNoPoints = new MenuItem("None");
    miNoPoints.Click += new EventHandler(miNoPoints_Click);
    Menu.MenuItems[1].MenuItems[2].MenuItems.Add(miNoPoints);

    Menu.MenuItems[1].MenuItems[2].MenuItems.Add(new MenuItem("-"));
```

*(continued)*

**StrokeDataViewer.cs** *(continued)*

```csharp
miPolylinePoints = new MenuItem("Polyline");
miPolylinePoints.Click +=
    new EventHandler(miPolylinePoints_Click);
Menu.MenuItems[1].MenuItems[2].MenuItems.Add(miPolylinePoints);

miBezierPoints = new MenuItem("Bezier");
miBezierPoints.Click += new EventHandler(miBezierPoints_Click);
Menu.MenuItems[1].MenuItems[2].MenuItems.Add(miBezierPoints);

miFlattenedBezierPoints = new MenuItem("Flattened Bezier");
miFlattenedBezierPoints.Click +=
    new EventHandler(miFlattenedBezierPoints_Click);
Menu.MenuItems[1].MenuItems[2].MenuItems.Add(
    miFlattenedBezierPoints);

MenuItem miCusps = new MenuItem("Cusps");
miCusps.Popup += new EventHandler(miCusps_Popup);
Menu.MenuItems[1].MenuItems.Add(miCusps);

miNoCusps = new MenuItem("None");
miNoCusps.Click += new EventHandler(miNoCusps_Click);
Menu.MenuItems[1].MenuItems[3].MenuItems.Add(miNoCusps);

Menu.MenuItems[1].MenuItems[3].MenuItems.Add(new MenuItem("-"));

miPolylineCusps = new MenuItem("Polyline");
miPolylineCusps.Click +=
    new EventHandler(miPolylineCusps_Click);
Menu.MenuItems[1].MenuItems[3].MenuItems.Add(miPolylineCusps);

miBezierCusps = new MenuItem("Bezier");
miBezierCusps.Click += new EventHandler(miBezierCusps_Click);
Menu.MenuItems[1].MenuItems[3].MenuItems.Add(miBezierCusps);

MenuItem miBoundingBox = new MenuItem("Bounding Box");
miBoundingBox.Popup += new EventHandler(miBoundingBox_Popup);
Menu.MenuItems[1].MenuItems.Add(miBoundingBox);

miNoBoundingBox = new MenuItem("None");
miNoBoundingBox.Click += new EventHandler(miNoBoundingBox_Click);
Menu.MenuItems[1].MenuItems[4].MenuItems.Add(miNoBoundingBox);

Menu.MenuItems[1].MenuItems[4].MenuItems.Add(new MenuItem("-"));

miDefaultBoundingBox = new MenuItem("Default");
miDefaultBoundingBox.Click +=
    new EventHandler(miDefaultBoundingBox_Click);
```

```
Menu.MenuItems[1].MenuItems[4].MenuItems.Add(
    miDefaultBoundingBox);

miCurveFitBoundingBox = new MenuItem("CurveFit");
miCurveFitBoundingBox.Click +=
    new EventHandler(miCurveFitBoundingBox_Click);
Menu.MenuItems[1].MenuItems[4].MenuItems.Add(
    miCurveFitBoundingBox);

miNoCurveFitBoundingBox = new MenuItem("NoCurveFit");
miNoCurveFitBoundingBox.Click +=
    new EventHandler(miNoCurveFitBoundingBox_Click);
Menu.MenuItems[1].MenuItems[4].MenuItems.Add(
    miNoCurveFitBoundingBox);

miPointsOnlyBoundingBox = new MenuItem("PointsOnly");
miPointsOnlyBoundingBox.Click +=
    new EventHandler(miPointsOnlyBoundingBox_Click);
Menu.MenuItems[1].MenuItems[4].MenuItems.Add(
    miPointsOnlyBoundingBox);

miUnionBoundingBox = new MenuItem("Union");
miUnionBoundingBox.Click +=
    new EventHandler(miUnionBoundingBox_Click);
Menu.MenuItems[1].MenuItems[4].MenuItems.Add(
    miUnionBoundingBox);

MenuItem miIntersections = new MenuItem("Intersections");
miIntersections.Popup +=
    new EventHandler(miIntersections_Popup);
Menu.MenuItems[1].MenuItems.Add(miIntersections);

miNoIntersections = new MenuItem("None");
miNoIntersections.Click +=
    new EventHandler(miNoIntersections_Click);
Menu.MenuItems[1].MenuItems[5].MenuItems.Add(
    miNoIntersections);

Menu.MenuItems[1].MenuItems[5].MenuItems.Add(new MenuItem("-"));

miSelfIntersections = new MenuItem("Self");
miSelfIntersections.Click +=
    new EventHandler(miSelfIntersections_Click);
Menu.MenuItems[1].MenuItems[5].MenuItems.Add(
    miSelfIntersections);

miStrokeIntersections = new MenuItem("Stroke");
```

*(continued)*

**StrokeDataViewer.cs** *(continued)*

```
        miStrokeIntersections.Click +=
            new EventHandler(miStrokeIntersections_Click);
        Menu.MenuItems[1].MenuItems[5].MenuItems.Add(
            miStrokeIntersections);

        miBoundingBoxIntersections = new MenuItem("BoundingBox");
        miBoundingBoxIntersections.Click +=
            new EventHandler(miBoundingBoxIntersections_Click);
        Menu.MenuItems[1].MenuItems[5].MenuItems.Add(
            miBoundingBoxIntersections);

        // Create and place all of our controls
        inkCtl = new InkControl2();
        inkCtl.Location = new Point(8, 8);
        inkCtl.Size = new Size(352, 216);

        // Configure the form itself
        ClientSize = new Size(368, 232);
        Controls.AddRange(new Control[] { inkCtl });
        FormBorderStyle = FormBorderStyle.FixedDialog;
        MaximizeBox = false;
        Text = "StrokeDataViewer";

        ResumeLayout(false);

        // Hook up to the InkOverlay's event handlers
        inkCtl.InkOverlay.Painted +=
            new InkOverlayPaintedEventHandler(inkCtl_Painted);
        inkCtl.InkOverlay.Ink.InkAdded +=
            new StrokesEventHandler(inkCtl_InkAdded);
        inkCtl.InkOverlay.Ink.InkDeleted +=
            new StrokesEventHandler(inkCtl_InkDeleted);

        // Set the ink color to something other than black so it's
        // easier to see the data
        inkCtl.InkOverlay.DefaultDrawingAttributes.Color =
            Color.DarkGray;

        // We're now set to go, so turn on tablet input
        inkCtl.InkOverlay.Enabled = true;
    }

// Handle the "Exit" menu item being clicked
private void miExit_Click(object sender, EventArgs e)
{
    Application.Exit();
}
```

```
// Handle the "View" submenu popping up
private void miView_Popup(object sender, EventArgs e)
{
    miStrokeId.Checked = fDrawStrokeId;
}


// Handle the "Stroke Id" menu being clicked
private void miStrokeId_Click(object sender, EventArgs e)
{
    fDrawStrokeId = !fDrawStrokeId;
    inkCtl.InkInputPanel.Invalidate();
}


// Handle the "Points" submenu popping up
private void miPoints_Popup(object sender, EventArgs e)
{
    miNoPoints.Checked = !fDrawPoints;
    miPolylinePoints.Checked = fDrawPoints &&
        strokePointType ==
        RendererEx.StrokePointType.Polyline;
    miBezierPoints.Checked = fDrawPoints &&
        strokePointType ==
        RendererEx.StrokePointType.Bezier;
    miFlattenedBezierPoints.Checked = fDrawPoints &&
        strokePointType ==
        RendererEx.StrokePointType.FlattenedBezier;
}


// Handle the "NoPoints" menu item being clicked
private void miNoPoints_Click(object sender, EventArgs e)
{
    fDrawPoints = false;
    inkCtl.InkInputPanel.Invalidate();
}


// Handle the "Polyline" menu item being clicked
private void miPolylinePoints_Click(object sender, EventArgs e)
{
    fDrawPoints = true;
    strokePointType = RendererEx.StrokePointType.Polyline;
    inkCtl.InkInputPanel.Invalidate();
}


// Handle the "Bezier" menu item being clicked
private void miBezierPoints_Click(object sender, EventArgs e)
```

*(continued)*

**StrokeDataViewer.cs** *(continued)*

```csharp
{
    fDrawPoints = true;
    strokePointType = RendererEx.StrokePointType.Bezier;
    inkCtl.InkInputPanel.Invalidate();
}


// Handle the "FlattenedBezier" menu item being clicked
private void miFlattenedBezierPoints_Click(
    object sender, EventArgs e)
{
    fDrawPoints = true;
    strokePointType =
        RendererEx.StrokePointType.FlattenedBezier;
    inkCtl.InkInputPanel.Invalidate();
}


// Handle the "Cusps" submenu popping up
private void miCusps_Popup(object sender, EventArgs e)
{
    miNoCusps.Checked = !fDrawCusps;
    miPolylineCusps.Checked = fDrawCusps &&
        strokeCuspType == RendererEx.StrokeCuspType.Polyline;
    miBezierCusps.Checked = fDrawCusps &&
        strokeCuspType == RendererEx.StrokeCuspType.Bezier;
}


// Handle the "None" menu item being clicked
private void miNoCusps_Click(object sender, EventArgs e)
{
    fDrawCusps = false;
    inkCtl.InkInputPanel.Invalidate();
}


// Handle the "Polyline" menu item being clicked
private void miPolylineCusps_Click(object sender, EventArgs e)
{
    fDrawCusps = true;
    strokeCuspType = RendererEx.StrokeCuspType.Polyline;
    inkCtl.InkInputPanel.Invalidate();
}


// Handle the "Bezier" menu item being clicked
private void miBezierCusps_Click(object sender, EventArgs e)
{
    fDrawCusps = true;
    strokeCuspType = RendererEx.StrokeCuspType.Bezier;
```

```
        inkCtl.InkInputPanel.Invalidate();
}


// Handle the "Bounding Box" submenu popping up
private void miBoundingBox_Popup(object sender, EventArgs e)
{
    miNoBoundingBox.Checked = !fDrawBoundingBox;
    miDefaultBoundingBox.Checked = fDrawBoundingBox &&
        bboxMode == BoundingBoxMode.Default;
    miCurveFitBoundingBox.Checked = fDrawBoundingBox &&
        bboxMode == BoundingBoxMode.CurveFit;
    miNoCurveFitBoundingBox.Checked = fDrawBoundingBox &&
        bboxMode == BoundingBoxMode.NoCurveFit;
    miPointsOnlyBoundingBox.Checked = fDrawBoundingBox &&
        bboxMode == BoundingBoxMode.PointsOnly;
    miUnionBoundingBox.Checked = fDrawBoundingBox &&
        bboxMode == BoundingBoxMode.Union;
}


// Handle the "None" menu item being clicked
private void miNoBoundingBox_Click(object sender, EventArgs e)
{
    fDrawBoundingBox = false;
    inkCtl.InkInputPanel.Invalidate();
}


// Handle the "Default" menu item being clicked
private void miDefaultBoundingBox_Click(object sender, EventArgs e)
{
    fDrawBoundingBox = true;
    bboxMode = BoundingBoxMode.Default;
    inkCtl.InkInputPanel.Invalidate();
}


// Handle the "CurveFit" menu item being clicked
private void miCurveFitBoundingBox_Click(object sender, EventArgs e)
{
    fDrawBoundingBox = true;
    bboxMode = BoundingBoxMode.CurveFit;
    inkCtl.InkInputPanel.Invalidate();
}


// Handle the "NoCurveFit" menu item being clicked
private void miNoCurveFitBoundingBox_Click(
    object sender, EventArgs e)
{
```

*(continued)*

**StrokeDataViewer.cs** *(continued)*

```
        fDrawBoundingBox = true;
        bboxMode = BoundingBoxMode.NoCurveFit;
        inkCtl.InkInputPanel.Invalidate();
    }

    // Handle the "PointsOnly" menu item being clicked
    private void miPointsOnlyBoundingBox_Click(
        object sender, EventArgs e)
    {
        fDrawBoundingBox = true;
        bboxMode = BoundingBoxMode.PointsOnly;
        inkCtl.InkInputPanel.Invalidate();
    }

    // Handle the "Union" menu item being clicked
    private void miUnionBoundingBox_Click(object sender, EventArgs e)
    {
        fDrawBoundingBox = true;
        bboxMode = BoundingBoxMode.Union;
        inkCtl.InkInputPanel.Invalidate();
    }

    // Handle the "Intersections" submenu popping up
    private void miIntersections_Popup(object sender, EventArgs e)
    {
        miNoIntersections.Checked = !fDrawIntersections;
        miSelfIntersections.Checked = fDrawIntersections &&
            strokeIntersectionType ==
            RendererEx.StrokeIntersectionType.Self;
        miStrokeIntersections.Checked = fDrawIntersections &&
            strokeIntersectionType ==
            RendererEx.StrokeIntersectionType.Stroke;
        miBoundingBoxIntersections.Checked = fDrawIntersections &&
            strokeIntersectionType ==
            RendererEx.StrokeIntersectionType.BoundingBox;
    }

    // Handle the "None" menu item being clicked
    private void miNoIntersections_Click(object sender, EventArgs e)
    {
        fDrawIntersections = false;
        inkCtl.InkInputPanel.Invalidate();
    }

    // Handle the "Self" menu item being clicked
    private void miSelfIntersections_Click(object sender, EventArgs e)
    {
```

```
    fDrawIntersections = true;
    strokeIntersectionType =
        RendererEx.StrokeIntersectionType.Self;
    inkCtl.InkInputPanel.Invalidate();
}

// Handle the "Stroke" menu item being clicked
private void miStrokeIntersections_Click(object sender, EventArgs e)
{
    fDrawIntersections = true;
    strokeIntersectionType =
        RendererEx.StrokeIntersectionType.Stroke;
    inkCtl.InkInputPanel.Invalidate();
}

// Handle the "BoundingBox" menu item being clicked
private void miBoundingBoxIntersections_Click(
    object sender, EventArgs e)
{
    fDrawIntersections = true;
    strokeIntersectionType =
        RendererEx.StrokeIntersectionType.BoundingBox;
    inkCtl.InkInputPanel.Invalidate();
}

// Handle the InkOverlay having been painted
private void inkCtl_Painted(object sender, PaintEventArgs e)
{
    // Draw stroke IDs if needed
    if (fDrawStrokeId)
    {
        RendererEx.DrawStrokeIds(
            e.Graphics, Font, inkCtl.InkOverlay.Ink);
    }

    // Draw the stroke points if needed
    if (fDrawPoints)
    {
        RendererEx.DrawPoints(e.Graphics,
            inkCtl.InkOverlay.Ink.Strokes,
            inkCtl.InkOverlay.Renderer,
            Brushes.Red, strokePointType);
    }

    // Draw the stroke cusps if needed
    if (fDrawCusps)
```

*(continued)*

**StrokeDataViewer.cs** *(continued)*

```
        {
            RendererEx.DrawCusps(e.Graphics,
                inkCtl.InkOverlay.Renderer,
                inkCtl.InkOverlay.Ink.Strokes,
                Pens.Blue, strokeCuspType);
        }

        // Draw the stroke bounding box if needed
        if (fDrawBoundingBox)
        {
            RendererEx.DrawBoundingBoxes(e.Graphics,
                inkCtl.InkOverlay.Renderer,
                inkCtl.InkOverlay.Ink.Strokes,
                Pens.LightGreen, bboxMode);
        }

        // Draw the stroke intersections if needed
        if (fDrawIntersections)
        {
            RendererEx.DrawIntersections(e.Graphics,
                inkCtl.InkOverlay.Renderer,
                inkCtl.InkOverlay.Ink.Strokes,
                Pens.DarkRed, strokeIntersectionType);
        }
    }

    // Handle ink having been added
    private void inkCtl_InkAdded(object sender, StrokesEventArgs e)
    {
        inkCtl.InkInputPanel.Invalidate();
    }

    // Handle ink having been deleted
    private void inkCtl_InkDeleted(object sender, StrokesEventArgs e)
    {
        inkCtl.InkInputPanel.Invalidate();
    }
}
```

Wow, that's quite the long listing! Fortunately, most of the code in this sample deals with all the pop-up menu items used to choose from among the different options. The key piece of code we're most interested in is the *inkCtl_Painted* event handler:

```
// Handle the InkOverlay having been painted
private void inkCtl_Painted(object sender, PaintEventArgs e)
{
```

```
// Draw stroke IDs if needed
if (fDrawStrokeId)
{
    RendererEx.DrawStrokeIds(
        e.Graphics, Font, inkCtl.InkOverlay.Ink);
}

// Draw the stroke points if needed
if (fDrawPoints)
{
    RendererEx.DrawPoints(e.Graphics,
        inkCtl.InkOverlay.Renderer,
        inkCtl.InkOverlay.Ink.Strokes,
        Brushes.Red, strokePointType);
}

// Draw the stroke cusps if needed
if (fDrawCusps)
{
    RendererEx.DrawCusps(inkCtl.InkOverlay.Renderer.
            e.Graphics, inkCtl.InkOverlay.Ink.Strokes,
            Pens.Blue, strokeCuspType);
}

// Draw the stroke bounding box if needed
if (fDrawBoundingBox)
{
    RendererEx.DrawBoundingBoxes(inkCtl.InkOverlay.Renderer,
            e.Graphics, inkCtl.InkOverlay.Ink.Strokes,
            Pens.LightGreen, bboxMode);
}

// Draw the stroke intersections if needed
if (fDrawIntersections)
{
    RendererEx.DrawIntersections(inkCtl.InkOverlay.Renderer,
        e.Graphics, inkCtl.InkOverlay.Ink.Strokes,
        Pens.DarkRed, strokeIntersectionType);
    }
}
```

Depending on the stroke data chosen to be viewed, different methods in the StrokeDataViewer example are called to display data for every stroke in *inkCtl*'s *Ink* object. An improvement to this sample that you may find useful is to display the stroke data only for the current selection in *inkCtl*'s *InkOverlay*. All that is required to achieve this is to replace *inkCtl.InkOverlay.Ink.Strokes* with *inkCtl.InkOverlay.Selection*.

# Transforming Strokes

In the last chapter, we saw how the *Renderer* class supports view and object transforms that help with functions such as scrolling and zooming. The transforms that a *Renderer* uses don't modify stroke data, and they are applied to all *Stroke* objects contained in an *Ink* object. Sometimes, though, we'll want to apply transforms on a per-stroke basis and retain the result—for example, to accomplish resizing or moving ink strokes. It's perfectly valid to modify the actual (*X,Y*) points of a *Stroke* object to apply a transformation, but the Tablet PC Platform provides a much more elegant mechanism: each ink stroke owns a transformation matrix.

A *Stroke* object's transformation matrix is automatically applied to any ink coordinates and measurements going into or coming out of its properties and methods. Both the *Strokes* and *Stroke* classes supply the following methods to modify the transformation matrix:

```
void Move(float offsetX, float offsetY)
void Rotate(float degrees, Point ptAbout)
void Scale(float scaleX, float scaleY)
void ScaleToRectangle(Rectangle rectangle)
void Shear(float shearX, float shearY)
void Transform(Matrix m)
void Transform(Matrix m, bool applyOnPenWidth)
```

You'll probably notice that these are all similar to the methods found in the *Renderer* class, and they accomplish pretty much the same thing when it comes to modifying the transformation matrix of a *Stroke* object. With the exception of the *Transform* method, they behave in an additive manner, meaning that any changes to the transformation are performed on the current transformation matrix.

The *Transform* method allows for the direct setting of the desired transformation matrix, optionally applying the matrix's changes to the stroke's width. This is akin to the reason the *Renderer* class has separate view and object transforms—sometimes you might want transformation applied to ink width, but sometimes not. Presumably to save memory, the *Stroke* class contains only one transform and uses a flag to indicate the transform type.

It should be made clear that when altering the transformation matrix of an ink stroke, its (*X,Y*) point data (or any other packet data, for that matter) will remain unchanged. Only the matrix values are ever altered, thereby avoiding any loss of precision in the *Stroke* object's point data. Resetting the transformation matrix to the identity matrix restores the ink stroke to its original created size and orientation.

## Sample Application—StrokeWarper

This next sample application provides the user with the ability to rotate, resize, translate, and shear ink strokes. You first select some ink to perform a transformation on and then choose the desired transformation function from the application's main menu.

### StrokeWarper.cs

```
//////////////////////////////////////////////////////////////////
//
// StrokeWarper.cs
//
// (c) 2002 Microsoft Press
// by Rob Jarrett
//
// This program demonstrates how to apply various transformations
// on ink strokes.
//
//////////////////////////////////////////////////////////////////

using System;
using System.Drawing;
using System.Windows.Forms;
using Microsoft.Ink;
using MSPress.BuildingTabletApps;

public class frmMain : Form
{
    private InkControl2 inkCtl;
    private MenuItem    miTranslate;
    private MenuItem    miScale;
    private MenuItem    miRotate;
    private MenuItem    miShear;

    // Entry point of the program
    [STAThread]
    static void Main()
    {
        Application.Run(new frmMain());
    }

    // Main form setup
    public frmMain()
    {
        SuspendLayout();

        // Create the main menu
        Menu = new MainMenu();
```

*(continued)*

**StrokeWarper.cs** *(continued)*

```csharp
        MenuItem miFile = new MenuItem("&File");
        Menu.MenuItems.Add(miFile);

        MenuItem miExit = new MenuItem("E&xit");
        miExit.Click += new EventHandler(miExit_Click);
        Menu.MenuItems[0].MenuItems.Add(miExit);

        MenuItem miTransform = new MenuItem("&Transform");
        miTransform.Popup += new EventHandler(miTransform_Popup);
        Menu.MenuItems.Add(miTransform);

        miTranslate = new MenuItem("&Translate");
        miTranslate.Click += new EventHandler(miTranslate_Click);
        Menu.MenuItems[1].MenuItems.Add(miTranslate);

        miScale = new MenuItem("&Scale");
        miScale.Click += new EventHandler(miScale_Click);
        Menu.MenuItems[1].MenuItems.Add(miScale);

        miRotate = new MenuItem("&Rotate");
        miRotate.Click += new EventHandler(miRotate_Click);
        Menu.MenuItems[1].MenuItems.Add(miRotate);

        miShear = new MenuItem("S&hear");
        miShear.Click += new EventHandler(miShear_Click);
        Menu.MenuItems[1].MenuItems.Add(miShear);

        // Create and place all of our controls
        inkCtl = new InkControl2();
        inkCtl.Location = new Point(8, 8);
        inkCtl.Size = new Size(352, 216);

        // Configure the form itself
        ClientSize = new Size(368, 232);
        Controls.AddRange(new Control[] { inkCtl });
        FormBorderStyle = FormBorderStyle.FixedDialog;
        MaximizeBox = false;
        Text = "StrokeWarper";

        ResumeLayout(false);

        // We're now set to go, so turn on tablet input
        inkCtl.InkOverlay.Enabled = true;
    }

    // Handle the "Exit" menu item being clicked
    private void miExit_Click(object sender, EventArgs e)
    {
        Application.Exit();
```

```
}

// Handle the "Transform" submenu popping up
private void miTransform_Popup(object sender, EventArgs e)
{
    // Only enable the Translate, Scale, Rotate, and Shear menu
    // items if there is a current selection
    bool fSelection = (inkCtl.InkOverlay.EditingMode ==
        InkOverlayEditingMode.Select) &&
        (inkCtl.InkOverlay.Selection.Count > 0);

    miTranslate.Enabled = fSelection;
    miScale.Enabled = fSelection;
    miRotate.Enabled = fSelection;
    miShear.Enabled = fSelection;
}

// Handle the "Translate" menu item being clicked
private void miTranslate_Click(object sender, EventArgs e)
{
    // Move the current selection 200 ink units in the X and Y
    // direction
    Strokes strokes = inkCtl.InkOverlay.Selection;
    strokes.Move(200, 200);

    // "Refresh" the selection bounds by first clearing it then
    // resetting it
    inkCtl.InkOverlay.Selection =
        inkCtl.InkOverlay.Ink.CreateStrokes();
    inkCtl.InkOverlay.Selection = strokes;

    // Draw the transformed ink
    inkCtl.InkInputPanel.Invalidate();
}

// Handle the "Scale" menu item being clicked
private void miScale_Click(object sender, EventArgs e)
{
    // Scale the current selection 115% along the X axis and 90%
    // along the Y axis. We'll preserve its location by first
    // translating the selection to (0,0), performing the scale,
    // and then translating back to its original location.
    Strokes strokes = inkCtl.InkOverlay.Selection;
    Rectangle rcBounds = strokes.GetBoundingBox();
    strokes.Move(-rcBounds.X, -rcBounds.Y);
    strokes.Scale(1.15f, 0.9f);
    strokes.Move(rcBounds.X, rcBounds.Y);

    // "Refresh" the selection bounds by first clearing it then
```

*(continued)*

**StrokeWarper.cs** *(continued)*

```csharp
        // resetting it
        inkCtl.InkOverlay.Selection =
            inkCtl.InkOverlay.Ink.CreateStrokes();
        inkCtl.InkOverlay.Selection = strokes;

        // Draw the transformed ink
        inkCtl.InkInputPanel.Invalidate();
    }

    // Handle the "Rotate" menu item being clicked
    private void miRotate_Click(object sender, EventArgs e)
    {
        // Rotate the current selection 10 degrees about its center
        // point
        Strokes strokes = inkCtl.InkOverlay.Selection;
        Rectangle rcBounds =
            inkCtl.InkOverlay.Selection.GetBoundingBox();
        Point ptCenter = new Point(rcBounds.X + rcBounds.Width/2,
            rcBounds.Y + rcBounds.Height/2);
        strokes.Rotate(10, ptCenter);

        // "Refresh" the selection bounds by first clearing it then
        // resetting it
        inkCtl.InkOverlay.Selection =
            inkCtl.InkOverlay.Ink.CreateStrokes();
        inkCtl.InkOverlay.Selection = strokes;

        // Draw the transformed ink
        inkCtl.InkInputPanel.Invalidate();
    }

    // Handle the "Shear" menu item being clicked
    private void miShear_Click(object sender, EventArgs e)
    {
        // Shear the current selection 1.1 along the Y axis. We'll
        // preserve its location by first translating the selection to
        // (0,0), performing the scale, and then translating back to
        // its original location.
        Strokes strokes = inkCtl.InkOverlay.Selection;
        Rectangle rcBounds = strokes.GetBoundingBox();
        strokes.Move(-rcBounds.X, -rcBounds.Y);
        strokes.Shear(0f, 1.1f);
        strokes.Move(rcBounds.X, rcBounds.Y);

        // "Refresh" the selection bounds by first clearing it then
        // resetting it
        inkCtl.InkOverlay.Selection =
            inkCtl.InkOverlay.Ink.CreateStrokes();
        inkCtl.InkOverlay.Selection = strokes;
```

```
        // Draw the transformed ink
        inkCtl.InkInputPanel.Invalidate();
    }
}
```

The handlers for the menu items that perform the transformation matrix alternation all have a similar structure: they apply the transform adjustment and then reset the current selection.

```
// "Refresh" the selection bounds by first clearing it then
// resetting it
inkCtl.InkOverlay.Selection =
    inkCtl.InkOverlay.Ink.CreateStrokes();
inkCtl.InkOverlay.Selection = strokes;
```

You may be wondering why the current selection gets reset. It's because the *InkOverlay* doesn't know when the bounds of the *Stroke* objects referenced by its selection *Strokes* collection have changed. If we didn't reset the selection, the resize handles and selection bounds would be unaffected by any transformation. This might cause ink to flow outside the selection bounds' edge or the selection bounds to be too large. By clearing and restoring the selection, we cause the *InkOverlay* to recompute the proper positioning and dimensions of the UI.

# Targeting and Hit-Testing Ink Strokes

In Chapter 2, we learned the importance of making it easy to select ink and manipulate it directly with the pen. Using the pen or mouse to target ink strokes to perform selection or another operation, such as erasing, is known as *hit-testing*.

Just as certain factors of human physiology must be taken into account when detecting tapping vs. dragging with the pen, we must also consider similar factors in the determination of whether ink has been targeted. The specific considerations depend on the kind of hit-testing being performed, so let's take a look at the various forms of hit-testing that apply to ink.

## Different Types of Hit-Testing

A user can perform three main types of targeting, resulting in three types of hit-testing that the Tablet PC Platform supports: point-based, rectangle-based, and lasso-based.

### Point-Based

Point-based hit-testing typically occurs when a user taps the pen stylus on the inking surface, and it is most often used to target objects. Ink strokes can often be quite thin, which makes it difficult for a user to consistently tap exactly within the ink of a stroke. We can alleviate this problem by introducing a *hit radius*, or circular area surrounding the tap point, that an ink stroke merely has to intersect for the point to be considered targeted.

## Rectangle-Based

Rectangle-based hit-testing is useful for functions such as a selection tool or an insert/remove space tool. The size of the rectangle is often dynamically specified by the user dragging the pen on the ink surface, and this can result in the targeted ink being different from what the user intended.

The solution is to slightly relax the criteria used to compute whether a stroke is targeted by the rectangle. Instead of requiring an entire stroke to be contained by the rectangle, we can say that *n* percent of the ink making up a stroke must lie within the rectangle. We'll discuss this further very shortly.

## Lasso-Based

Similar in use to rectangle-based hit-testing, lasso-based hit-testing is useful for a selection tool. Ink strokes that are enclosed by the polyline comprising the lasso are considered targeted. Usability studies showed that exactly enclosing ink strokes with a lasso required significant effort on the user's part; fortunately, lasso-based hit-testing criteria can be relaxed with the same method used by rectangle-based hit-testing criteria. If only a certain percentage of ink lies within the lasso, we can consider it targeted.

## Percentage-Based Enclosure

What exactly does *n* percent of ink being enclosed by a rectangle or lasso really mean, anyway? Is it the ratio of the length of ink contained within the rectangle or lasso to the total length of the stroke? Or maybe the ratio of the viewable area of ink contained to the total viewable area? Interestingly, the answer that usability studies and the Tablet PC teams found was essentially, "It doesn't matter as much as you might think."

The reason for this is quite simple: percentage-based enclosure is meant to combat the imprecise control that humans exhibit when using a pen to target objects. Because humans are mostly correct in their targeting, a percentage-based enclosure algorithm needs to worry about only most of the ink being enclosed by the rectangle or lasso polygon. This makes the idea of *n* percentage enclosure somewhat overkill given the problem being solved; my assertion is therefore that as long as an *n* percentage algorithm is "kind of" correct, users will be happy.

With that said, the algorithm used by the Tablet PC Platform to compute percentage enclosure for both rectangle and lasso polygons is quite accurate. It is actually a hybrid of the length of ink method mentioned earlier. An ink stroke is divided into a number of points, and if *n* percent of those points lie within the rectangle or lasso polygon, the ink is considered enclosed. Figure 6-7 shows a visual explanation of this algorithm.

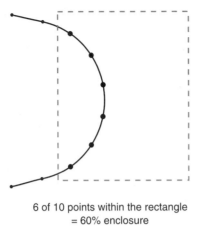

6 of 10 points within the rectangle
= 60% enclosure

**Figure 6-7**   How percentage-based enclosure is actually calculated (not that it really matters).

## Hit-Testing Performance

Percentage-based enclosure is incredibly useful and considerably improves the user experience of targeting ink. As with most very cool things in software, though, there are performance implications to consider. Using enclosure hit-testing functionality is computationally intensive, and the performance can be affected by the following factors:

- **The number of *Stroke* objects contained by an *Ink* object**   The more ink strokes there are, the longer the computation will take.

- **The number of packets in a *Stroke* object**   The more packets there are, the longer the computation will take.

- **The enclosure percentage value**   The computation will take longer if the value is other than 100 (this applies only to rectangle-based hit-testing).

- **The number of points in a lasso polygon**   The more points there are, the longer the computation will take.

Don't get me wrong—provided the end user sees a benefit, I heartily recommend using percentage-based enclosure hit-testing. This is just a heads up to the factors you might want to try to minimize to yield an even better targeting experience.

## Hit-Testing Functions

Hit-testing functionality for ink strokes in an *Ink* object is achieved with these methods:

```
Strokes Ink.HitTest(Point point, float radius)
Strokes Ink.HitTest(Rectangle rectangle, float percentage)
Strokes Ink.HitTest(Point[] points, float percentage)
Strokes Ink.HitTest(Point[] points, float percentage, out Point[] arrLassoPts)
```

The stroke objects that meet the target criteria are returned in a *Strokes* collection as the method's return value. The first three flavors of the *HitTest* method listed above perform point-based, rectangle-based, and lasso-based hit-testing, respectively. They are distinguished by the type of their first parameter: a point, a rectangle, and an array of points (a polygon). Notice that the point-based version of *HitTest* accepts a *radius* parameter (provided in ink space units) and the rectangle and lasso versions accept a *percentage* parameter.

The last version of the *HitTest* method performs lasso-based hit-testing, but it has a rather curious *out* parameter named *arrLassoPts*. Because the lasso polygon is specified as an array of arbitrarily valued points, the polygon can self-intersect. This is an entirely likely scenario, as users often will create all sorts of odd shapes when using a lasso selection tool. One or more self-intersections in a polygon make the user's intent ambiguous, so the *arrLassoPts* parameter returned is the array of points that was used in the actual hit-test computation. It can be handy for displaying the lasso polyline after the fact so the user is clear on what exactly happened to cause the result of the operation.

> **Note** In version 1 of the Tablet PC Platform, if the polygon specified for a lasso-based hit-test has one or more self-intersections, the first proper polygon encountered will be used for the computation. This should not be assumed to always be the case because other algorithms may be employed in the future.

The *Stroke* class also has one handy hit-testing function that simply says whether a *Stroke* object is within the radius of a point:

```
bool Stroke.HitTest(Point point, float radius)
```

The value returned indicates whether the ink stroke was hit—true if it was, and false if it was not.

## Computing the Nearest Point

A variant of hit-testing functionality is the computation of the closest *Stroke* or *point* along a *Stroke* to a target point:

```
Stroke Ink.NearestPoint(Point point)
Stroke Ink.NearestPoint(Point point, out float indexOnStroke)
Stroke Ink.NearestPoint(Point point, out float indexOnStroke, out float distance)
```

These methods return the *Stroke* object, if any, that is closest to the point specified. Optional out-parameters are the floating-point index of the point along the *Stroke* object that is closest and that point's distance away from the input point.

The *Stroke* class also has its own versions of the *NearestPoint* method:

```
float Stroke.NearestPoint(Point point)
float Stroke.NearestPoint(Point point, out float distance)
```

The methods return the floating-point index of the closest point and optionally that point's distance away from the input point.

## Sample Application—InsertRemoveSpace

The InsertRemoveSpace sample application shows an implementation of the insert/remove space mode that can be found in the Windows Journal utility. Dragging the pen up or down a page of ink causes space to be inserted or removed, resulting in the ink below the pen-down location being moved up or down. Usability testing showed that without any tolerance implemented, users had difficulty reliably targeting the ink they wanted to be affected by the operation. That led to using rectangle-based percentage hit-testing when determining the ink strokes to move as a result of the operation.

**InsertRemoveSpace.cs**

```
/////////////////////////////////////////////////////////////////////
//
// InsertRemoveSpace.cs
//
// (c) 2002 Microsoft Press
// by Rob Jarrett
//
// This program demonstrates an implementation of the "Insert/
// Remove Space" mode in Windows Journal.
//
/////////////////////////////////////////////////////////////////////

using System;
using System.Drawing;
```

*(continued)*

**InsertRemoveSpace.cs** *(continued)*

```csharp
using System.Windows.Forms;
using Microsoft.Ink;
using MSPress.BuildingTabletApps;

public class frmMain : Form
{
    private InkInputPanel    pnlInput;
    private Button           btnFormat;
    private CheckBox         cbSpaceMode;
    private InkCollector     inkCollector;
    private Point            ptStart;
    private Point            ptPrev;
    private Strokes          strksToMove;

    // Entry point of the program
    [STAThread]
    static void Main()
    {
        Application.Run(new frmMain());
    }

    // Main form setup
    public frmMain()
    {
        SuspendLayout();

        // Create and place all of our controls
        pnlInput = new InkInputPanel();
        pnlInput.BackColor = Color.White;
        pnlInput.BorderStyle = BorderStyle.Fixed3D;
        pnlInput.Location = new Point(8, 8);
        pnlInput.Size = new Size(352, 192);

        btnFormat = new Button();
        btnFormat.Location = new Point(8, 204);
        btnFormat.Size = new Size(50, 20);
        btnFormat.Text = "Format";
        btnFormat.Click += new System.EventHandler(btnFormat_Click);

        cbSpaceMode = new CheckBox();
        cbSpaceMode.Location = new Point(66, 204);
        cbSpaceMode.Size = new Size(172, 20);
        cbSpaceMode.Text = "Insert/Remove Space mode";
        cbSpaceMode.Click += new System.EventHandler(cbSpaceMode_Click);

        // Configure the form itself
        ClientSize = new Size(368, 236);
```

```csharp
    Controls.AddRange(new Control[] { pnlInput,
                                      btnFormat,
                                      cbSpaceMode});
    FormBorderStyle = FormBorderStyle.FixedDialog;
    MaximizeBox = false;
    Text = "InsertRemoveSpace";

    ResumeLayout(false);

    // Hook up to mouse events to perform custom mode behaviors
    pnlInput.MouseDown += new MouseEventHandler(pnlInput_MouseDown);
    pnlInput.MouseMove += new MouseEventHandler(pnlInput_MouseMove);
    pnlInput.MouseUp += new MouseEventHandler(pnlInput_MouseUp);
    pnlInput.Paint += new PaintEventHandler(pnlInput_Paint);

    // Create a new InkCollector, using pnlInput for the collection
    // area
    inkCollector = new InkCollector(pnlInput.Handle);
    inkCollector.AutoRedraw = false;

    // Start out in ink mode
    inkCollector.CollectionMode = CollectionMode.InkOnly;
    cbSpaceMode.Checked = false;

    // We're set to go, so enable tablet input
    inkCollector.Enabled = true;
}

// Handle the click of the format button
private void btnFormat_Click(object sender, EventArgs e)
{
    FormatInkDlg dlgFormat = new FormatInkDlg();
    dlgFormat.DrawingAttributes =
        inkCollector.DefaultDrawingAttributes;
    if (dlgFormat.ShowDialog(this) == DialogResult.OK)
    {
        inkCollector.DefaultDrawingAttributes =
            dlgFormat.DrawingAttributes;
    }
}

// Handle the click of the Insert/Remove Space checkbox
private void cbSpaceMode_Click(object sender, EventArgs e)
{
    // Turn inking on or off
    inkCollector.Enabled = !cbSpaceMode.Checked;
```

*(continued)*

**InsertRemoveSpace.cs** *(continued)*

```csharp
        // Update the cursor shown
        if (inkCollector.Enabled)
        {
            pnlInput.Cursor = System.Windows.Forms.Cursors.Default;
        }
        else
        {
            pnlInput.Cursor = System.Windows.Forms.Cursors.HSplit;
        }
    }

    // Handle mouse down in the input panel
    private void pnlInput_MouseDown(object sender, MouseEventArgs e)
    {
        if (!inkCollector.Enabled)
        {
            ptStart = ptPrev = new Point(e.X, e.Y);

            // Compute the rectangle to use to hit-test the ink below
            // the mouse-down point - this is done by enumerating all
            // ink strokes and merging all of their rects together.
            // Then, the top of the rect is set to equal the mouse-down
            // point.
            Rectangle rcHitArea = new Rectangle();
            foreach (Stroke s in inkCollector.Ink.Strokes)
            {
                Rectangle rcBounds = inkCollector.Renderer.Measure(s);
                if (rcHitArea.IsEmpty)
                {
                    rcHitArea = rcBounds;
                }
                else
                {
                    rcHitArea = Rectangle.Union(rcHitArea, rcBounds);
                }
            }

            // Convert the mouse-down point into ink coordinates
            Point ptTop = new Point(0, e.Y);
            Graphics g = pnlInput.CreateGraphics();
            inkCollector.Renderer.PixelToInkSpace(g, ref ptTop);
            g.Dispose();

            // Set the top of the hit area to be the mouse-down point
            int nBottom = rcHitArea.Bottom;
            rcHitArea.Y = ptTop.Y;
            rcHitArea.Height = nBottom - rcHitArea.Y;
```

```
            if (rcHitArea.Height > 0)
            {
                // Perform the initial hit-test to determine the
                // candidates to move
                strksToMove = inkCollector.Ink.HitTest(rcHitArea, 70);

                if (strksToMove.Count > 0)
                {
                    // Reflect which strokes are candidates to move
                    pnlInput.Invalidate();
                }
                else
                {
                    strksToMove = null;
                }
            }
        }
    }

// Handle mouse move in the input panel
private void pnlInput_MouseMove(object sender, MouseEventArgs e)
{
    if (!inkCollector.Enabled)
    {
        if (e.Button == MouseButtons.Left)
        {
            // Erase the previous tracking rectangle
            Rectangle rcTrack =
                new Rectangle(0, ptStart.Y,
                    pnlInput.ClientSize.Width,
                    ptPrev.Y - ptStart.Y);
            Rectangle rcDraw = rcTrack;
            rcDraw.Location =
                pnlInput.PointToScreen(rcDraw.Location);
            ControlPaint.DrawReversibleFrame(
                rcDraw, BackColor, FrameStyle.Dashed);

            // Update rectangle with new mouse location,
            // constraining to the input panel's bounds
            rcTrack.Height = e.Y - ptStart.Y;
            if (rcTrack.Y + rcTrack.Height >
                pnlInput.ClientSize.Height)
            {
                rcTrack.Height =
                    pnlInput.ClientSize.Height - rcTrack.Y;
            }
```

*(continued)*

**InsertRemoveSpace.cs**  *(continued)*

```
                else if (rcTrack.Y + rcTrack.Height < 0)
                {
                    rcTrack.Height = -rcTrack.Y;
                }

                // Draw the new tracking rectangle
                rcDraw = rcTrack;
                rcDraw.Location =
                    pnlInput.PointToScreen(rcDraw.Location);
                ControlPaint.DrawReversibleFrame(
                    rcDraw, BackColor, FrameStyle.Dashed);

                ptPrev = new Point(e.X, rcTrack.Bottom);
            }
        }
    }

    // Handle mouse up in the input panel
    private void pnlInput_MouseUp(object sender, MouseEventArgs e)
    {
        if (!inkCollector.Enabled)
        {
            // Erase the previous tracking rectangle
            Rectangle rcTrack = new Rectangle(0, ptStart.Y,
                pnlInput.ClientSize.Width, ptPrev.Y - ptStart.Y);
            Rectangle rcDraw = rcTrack;
            rcDraw.Location = pnlInput.PointToScreen(rcDraw.Location);
            ControlPaint.DrawReversibleFrame(
                rcDraw, BackColor, FrameStyle.Dashed);

            if (strksToMove != null && strksToMove.Count > 0)
            {
                // Compute the distance to move the strokes by
                Point ptTop = ptStart;
                Point ptEnd = new Point(e.X, e.Y);
                Graphics g = pnlInput.CreateGraphics();
                inkCollector.Renderer.PixelToInkSpace(g, ref ptTop);
                inkCollector.Renderer.PixelToInkSpace(g, ref ptEnd);
                g.Dispose();

                // Perform the actual move operation
                strksToMove.Move(0, ptEnd.Y - ptTop.Y);
                strksToMove = null;

                // Show the result of the move
                pnlInput.Invalidate();
            }
```

```
        }
    }

    // Handle painting in the input panel
    private void pnlInput_Paint(object sender, PaintEventArgs e)
    {
        if (strksToMove == null || strksToMove.Count == 0)
        {
            // Draw all the strokes normally since no move tracking
            // operation is going on
            inkCollector.Renderer.Draw(
                e.Graphics, inkCollector.Ink.Strokes);
        }
        else
        {
            // Space tracking going on; show the candidates to be moved
            // by making them transparent
            foreach (Stroke s in inkCollector.Ink.Strokes)
            {
                if (strksToMove.Contains(s))
                {
                    // Draw the stroke partially transparent since it
                    // is a candidate to be moved
                    DrawingAttributes da = s.DrawingAttributes.Clone();
                    da.Transparency = 192;
                    inkCollector.Renderer.Draw(e.Graphics, s, da);
                }
                else
                {
                    // Draw the stroke normally
                    inkCollector.Renderer.Draw(e.Graphics, s);
                }
            }
        }
    }
}
```

The application doesn't use either the *InkControl* or *InkControl2* class because it implements a custom input mode—both of those classes only provide *InkOverlay*'s editing mode functionality and hence cannot be modified. To reduce flicker, an InkInputPanel is used in conjunction with the manual rendering of ink strokes in the panel's *Paint* event.

The *MouseDown* event handler sets up the UI that reflects the amount of space to insert or remove. It then targets the ink strokes to move by computing the bounding box of all the ink strokes in the InkCollector, setting the resulting rectangle's top edge to the *y*-component of the pen-down/mouse-down location, and then calling *Ink.HitTest* with the rectangle:

```
// Perform the initial hit-test to determine the
// candidates to move
strksToMove = inkCollector.Ink.HitTest(rcHitArea, 70);
```

The input panel is then invalidated so the contents of the *strksToMove* collection can be rendered with a transparent style, showing the user the strokes that will be affected when the pen is lifted. The *MouseMove* event handler performs the actual animation for the UI by utilizing the *ControlPaint.DrawReversibleFrame* method.

Finally the *MouseUp* event handler terminates the space amount UI and performs the actual insert or remove space operation using the *Strokes* class's *Move* method:

```
// Perform the actual move operation
strksToMove.Move(0, ptEnd.Y - ptTop.Y);
```

Once the space has been inserted or removed, the *strksToMove* collection is emptied and the input area is invalidated so the results of the operation are drawn.

## Sample Application—RealtimeLasso

Let's jump into another sample application to take a further look at the TabletPC Platform's hit-testing functionality. This sample implements lasso percentage-based selection, updating results in real time with selection feedback similar to Windows Journal. It also supports implicit mode switching out of ink mode with a right-tap or right-drag system gesture and provides point-based selection using the tap and right-tap system events.

The first code listing presented is that of a class found in the BuildingTabletApps helper library named *LassoUI*. This class implements the evenly spaced lasso ink dots that are drawn as a user performs a lasso operation. You may think that the way to implement this effect is to utilize a GDI+ pen style of a circle followed by a space, or something similar. However, this approach has a couple of drawbacks. The first is that we would have to draw the lasso ink in its entirety every single time a point was added to the lasso polyline. That means the longer the lasso ink gets, the longer it will take to render, and we'll see shortly that we already have enough performance issues to deal with. The other drawback is related to an optimization. Recall that I stated earlier that the number of points in a lasso polyline directly affects its performance. The number of points can be minimized if only the points resulting in a dot being drawn are added rather than all points used to trace the lasso's path. That takes some reasonable computation, as we'll soon see—and if GDI+ polyline drawing with a pen-style is used to render lasso dots, we can't even be certain that the set of points we'd compute will equal the dot positions.

The approach taken with the *LassoUI* class is that it computes the location of the dots itself and adds points to the lasso polyline when needed. The number of points used in the polyline is therefore automatically minimized.

## LassoUI.cs

```csharp
/////////////////////////////////////////////////////////////////////
//
// LassoUI.cs
//
// (c) 2002 Microsoft Press
// by Rob Jarrett
//
// This class implements drawing of the lasso selection tool.
//
/////////////////////////////////////////////////////////////////////

using System;
using System.Collections;
using System.Drawing;
using System.Windows.Forms;

namespace MSPress.BuildingTabletApps
{
    public class LassoUI
    {
        private int          nDotSpacing = 7;
        private int          nDotSize = 4;
        private Brush         brDotColor = Brushes.Orange;

        private ArrayList     arrPts;
        private Point         ptLast;
        private Rectangle     rcBounds;

        public LassoUI()
        {
            arrPts = new ArrayList();
            ptLast = new Point(0, 0);
            rcBounds = new Rectangle(0, 0, 0, 0);
        }

        // Start up a lasso
        public void Start(Graphics g, Point ptStart)
        {
            arrPts = new ArrayList();
            arrPts.Add(ptStart);
            ptLast = ptStart;
            rcBounds = new Rectangle(ptStart, new Size(0, 0));

            // Draw the first dot of the lasso
```

*(continued)*

**LassoUI.cs**  *(continued)*

```csharp
        DrawLassoDot(g, ptStart);
}

// Continue creating a lasso
public bool Continue(Graphics g, Point ptNew)
{
    // Compute how far the new point is from the last drawn dot
    int a = (ptNew.X - ptLast.X);
    int b = (ptNew.Y - ptLast.Y);
    double c = Math.Sqrt(a * a + b * b);

    // Is that distance less than the dot spacing? If so, we
    // can throw away this point
    if (c < (double)nDotSpacing)
        return false;

    // Compute how many dots will need to be drawn
    int nSegments = (int)(c / nDotSpacing);

    // Compute new rise and run values "snapped" to dot spacing
    double ap = a * ((nSegments*nDotSpacing) / c);
    double bp = b * ((nSegments*nDotSpacing) / c);

    // Draw lasso dots until the new endpoint is reached
    Point ptCurr = new Point(ptLast.X, ptLast.Y);
    for (int i = 1; i <= nSegments; i++)
    {
        double ratio = (double)i / nSegments;
        ptCurr = new Point(
            ptLast.X + (int)Math.Round(ap * ratio),
            ptLast.Y + (int)Math.Round(bp * ratio));

        DrawLassoDot(g, ptCurr);
    }

    // Update the lasso's bounding rectangle
    if (ptCurr.X < rcBounds.X)
    {
        rcBounds.Width += rcBounds.X - ptCurr.X;
        rcBounds.X = ptCurr.X;
    }
    else if (ptCurr.X > rcBounds.Right)
    {
        rcBounds.Width = ptCurr.X - rcBounds.X;
    }
    if (ptCurr.Y < rcBounds.Y)
```

```
    {
        rcBounds.Height += rcBounds.Y - ptCurr.Y;
        rcBounds.Y = ptCurr.Y;
    }
    else if (ptCurr.Y > rcBounds.Bottom)
    {
        rcBounds.Height = ptCurr.Y - rcBounds.Y;
    }


    // Add the endpoint to the polyline
    arrPts.Add(ptCurr);
    ptLast = ptCurr;

    return true;
}


// Draw the entire lasso in one shot
public void Render(Graphics g)
{
    Render(g, new Rectangle());
}


// Draw the entire lasso in one shot, using a clipping area to
// improve performance
public void Render(Graphics g, Rectangle rcClip)
{
    if (arrPts.Count > 0)
    {
        // Draw the first point
        Point ptPrev = (Point)arrPts[0];
        DrawLassoDot(g, ptPrev);

        foreach (Point ptNext in arrPts)
        {
            // Compute how far the new point is from the last
            // drawn dot
            int a = (ptNext.X - ptPrev.X);
            int b = (ptNext.Y - ptPrev.Y);
            double c = Math.Sqrt(a * a + b * b);

            // Compute how many dots need to be drawn within
            // this line
            int nSegments = (int)Math.Round(c / nDotSpacing);

            // Draw dots until the line's endpoint is reached
            Point ptCurr = new Point(ptPrev.X, ptPrev.Y);
            for (int i = 1; i <= nSegments; i++)
```

*(continued)*

**LassoUI.cs** *(continued)*

```
                {
                    double ratio = (double)i / nSegments;
                    ptCurr = new Point(
                        ptPrev.X + (int)Math.Round(a * ratio),
                        ptPrev.Y + (int)Math.Round(b * ratio));

                    // See if we need to bother drawing the dot
                    Rectangle rcDot = new Rectangle(
                        new Point(ptCurr.X - nDotSize/2,
                        ptCurr.Y - nDotSize/2),
                        new Size(nDotSize, nDotSize));
                    if (rcClip.IsEmpty ||
                        rcClip.IntersectsWith(rcDot))
                    {
                        DrawLassoDot(g, ptCurr);
                    }
                }

                ptPrev = ptNext;
            }
        }
    }

    // Get the current lasso polyline
    public Point[] Points
    {
        get
        {
            return (Point[])arrPts.ToArray(typeof(Point));
        }
    }

    // Get the current bounding rectangle of the dots drawn
    public Rectangle BoundingRect
    {
        get
        {
            Rectangle rcResult =
                new Rectangle(rcBounds.Location, rcBounds.Size);

            // Inflate the result by the dot size, taking into
            // account an odd-numbered size. i.e. if we just
            // performed an Inflate(nDotSize/2,nDotSize/2) and
            // the dot size were e.g. 5, the bounds would only
            // increase by 5/2*2 = 4. So we'll use our own
            // inflation method.
            rcResult.Offset(-nDotSize/2, -nDotSize/2);
```

```
                    rcResult.Width += nDotSize;
                    rcResult.Height += nDotSize;

                    return rcResult;
            }
    }

    // Get or set the dot spacing of the lasso
    public int DotSpacing
    {
        get
        {
            return nDotSpacing;
        }

        set
        {
            if (nDotSpacing < 1)
            {
                throw new ArgumentOutOfRangeException();
            }
            nDotSpacing = value;
        }
    }

    // Get or set the dot size of the lasso
    public int DotSize
    {
        get
        {
            return nDotSize;
        }

        set
        {
            if (nDotSize < 1)
            {
                throw new ArgumentOutOfRangeException();
            }
            nDotSize = value;
        }
    }

    // Get or set the brush used to draw the lasso dots
    public Brush DotBrush
    {
        get
```

*(continued)*

**LassoUI.cs** *(continued)*

```
        {
            return brDotColor;
        }

        set
        {
            brDotColor = value;
        }
    }

    // Render a single lasso dot
    private void DrawLassoDot(Graphics g, Point pt)
    {
        pt.Offset(-nDotSize/2, -nDotSize/2);
        g.FillEllipse(brDotColor,
            new Rectangle(pt, new Size(nDotSize, nDotSize)));
    }
  }
}
```

The class should be instantiated at the start of a lasso UI operation (for example, the start of a pen drag) and retained until the end of the operation (pen up). After creating the lasso class, the *Start* and *Continue* methods should be called to form the lasso polyline and draw the dots:

```
public void Start(Graphics g, Point ptStart)
public bool Continue(Graphics g, Point ptNew)
```

The lasso ink dots are drawn to the *Graphics* object *g*, and the points (specified in pixel coordinates) are filtered to reduce the complexity of the lasso polyline. The *Start* method should be called only at the start of a lasso because it initializes the polyline. The *Continue* method is called throughout, returning if a point was added to the lasso polyline—this is so a client of the class can conditionally perform a hit-test operation and avoid redundancy.

While a lasso is in progress, the input area might (and probably will) become invalidated as ink strokes rendered selected or unselected. The *Render* method should therefore be used in the input area's paint handler so that lasso ink dots that have already been drawn won't be erased:

```
public void Render(Graphics g)
public void Render(Graphics g, Rectangle rcClip)
```

The method draws the current lasso polyline to the *Graphics* object *g*, and the optional *rcClip* parameter results in only the dots contained in *rcClip* being rendered. This parameter should be supplied if the invalid area is known—typically the client's paint handler is provided a *PaintEventArgs* object containing a *ClipRectangle* property—so rendering performance is improved by avoiding redundant dot drawing.

During the lasso operation, the lasso polyline is obtained with the *Points* property:

```
public Point[] Points
```

The points returned are in pixels, so be sure to convert them to ink space before calling *HitTest*. To improve lasso hit test performance, the *Continue* method only adds points to the *Points* property when they are spaced far enough to matter. The *Continue* method does this by ignoring any points that are less than *DotSpacing* distance from the previous point captured.

When the lasso operation is complete, the *BoundingRect* property can be used to retrieve the region that should be invalidated for the lasso ink dots to disappear:

```
public Rectangle BoundingRect
```

Lastly, the LassoUI class provides some properties that are used to alter the look of the lasso ink dots:

```
public int DotSpacing
public int DotSize
public Brush DotBrush
```

The *DotSpacing* property gets or sets the distance (in pixels) between the dots, the *DotSize* property gets or sets the diameter (in pixels) of the dots, and the *DotBrush* property gets or sets the brush used to draw each dot. You shouldn't need to alter these under regular circumstances except for accessibility functionality (high contrast, for example).

Now that we understand how a lasso polyline is created, we can take a look at the sample application, which uses the *LassoUI* class.

**RealtimeLasso.cs**

```
//////////////////////////////////////////////////////////////////////////
//
// RealtimeLasso.cs
//
// (c) 2002 Microsoft Press
// by Rob Jarrett
//
// This program demonstrates an implementation of realtime selection
// user feedback for a "lasso" operation. It also illustrates how
// to render ink in a selected state.
//
//////////////////////////////////////////////////////////////////////////
```

*(continued)*

**RealtimeLasso.cs** *(continued)*

```csharp
using System;
using System.Collections;
using System.Drawing;
using System.Drawing.Drawing2D;
using System.Windows.Forms;
using Microsoft.Ink;
using MSPress.BuildingTabletApps;

public class frmMain : Form
{
    private int        nTapDistance = 4;
    private int        nSelThickness = 4;

    private InkInputPanel pnlInput;
    private Button        btnFormat;
    private ComboBox      cbxEditMode;
    private InkOverlay    inkOverlay;

    private bool         fSelectMode;
    private Stroke       strkCurr;
    private LassoUI      lasso;
    private Strokes      strksSelected;
    private Strokes      strksLassoed;

    // Entry point of the program
    [STAThread]
    static void Main()
    {
        Application.Run(new frmMain());
    }

    // Main form setup
    public frmMain()
    {
        SuspendLayout();

        // Create and place all of our controls
        pnlInput = new InkInputPanel();
        pnlInput.BackColor = Color.White;
        pnlInput.BorderStyle = BorderStyle.Fixed3D;
        pnlInput.Location = new Point(8, 8);
        pnlInput.Size = new Size(352, 192);
        pnlInput.Paint += new PaintEventHandler(pnlInput_Paint);

        btnFormat = new Button();
        btnFormat.Location = new Point(8, 204);
        btnFormat.Size = new Size(50, 20);
```

```
btnFormat.Text = "Format";
btnFormat.Click += new System.EventHandler(btnFormat_Click);

cbxEditMode = new ComboBox();
cbxEditMode.DropDownStyle = ComboBoxStyle.DropDownList;
cbxEditMode.Location = new Point(66, 204);
cbxEditMode.Size = new Size(72, 20);
cbxEditMode.SelectedIndexChanged +=
    new System.EventHandler(cbxEditMode_SelIndexChg);

// Configure the form itself
ClientSize = new Size(368, 236);
Controls.AddRange(new Control[] { pnlInput,
                                  btnFormat,
                                  cbxEditMode});
FormBorderStyle = FormBorderStyle.FixedDialog;
MaximizeBox = false;
Text = "RealtimeLasso";

ResumeLayout(false);

// Fill up the editing mode combobox
cbxEditMode.Items.Add(InkOverlayEditingMode.Ink);
cbxEditMode.Items.Add(InkOverlayEditingMode.Select);
cbxEditMode.Items.Add(InkOverlayEditingMode.Delete);

// Create a new InkOverlay, using pnlInput for the collection
// area
inkOverlay = new InkOverlay(pnlInput.Handle);
inkOverlay.AutoRedraw = false;
inkOverlay.EditingMode = InkOverlayEditingMode.Ink;

// Don't want select mode yet
fSelectMode = false;
strkCurr = null;
lasso = null;
strksSelected = inkOverlay.Ink.CreateStrokes();
strksLassoed = inkOverlay.Ink.CreateStrokes();

// Set up event handlers to deal with lasso selection
inkOverlay.CursorDown += new InkCollectorCursorDownEventHandler(
    inkOverlay_CursorDown);
inkOverlay.SystemGesture +=
    new InkCollectorSystemGestureEventHandler(
    inkOverlay_SystemGesture);
inkOverlay.NewPackets += new InkCollectorNewPacketsEventHandler(
    inkOverlay_NewPackets);
```

*(continued)*

**RealtimeLasso.cs** *(continued)*

```csharp
        inkOverlay.Stroke += new InkCollectorStrokeEventHandler(
            inkOverlay_Stroke);

        // Select the current editing mode in the combobox
        cbxEditMode.SelectedItem = inkOverlay.EditingMode;

        // We're now set to go, so turn on tablet input
        inkOverlay.Enabled = true;
    }


    // Handle the click of the format button
    private void btnFormat_Click(object sender, System.EventArgs e)
    {
        // Edit the current drawing attributes using our Format Ink
        // dialog class
        FormatInkDlg dlgFormat = new FormatInkDlg();
        dlgFormat.DrawingAttributes =
            inkOverlay.DefaultDrawingAttributes;
        if (dlgFormat.ShowDialog(this) == DialogResult.OK)
        {
            inkOverlay.DefaultDrawingAttributes =
                dlgFormat.DrawingAttributes;
        }
    }


    // Handle the selection change of the editing mode combobox
    private void cbxEditMode_SelIndexChg(object sender,
        System.EventArgs e)
    {
        // Clear the current selection
        UpdateStrokes(
            inkOverlay.Ink.CreateStrokes(), ref strksSelected);

        if ((InkOverlayEditingMode)cbxEditMode.SelectedItem ==
            InkOverlayEditingMode.Select)
        {
            // We want CursorDown, NewPackets, and Stroke events, but
            // don't want ink drawn - hence we'll change InkOverlay
            // into Ink mode but make the ink invisible. Then, we'll
            // make sure it's not added to the Ink object by cancelling
            // it in the Stroke event handler.
            inkOverlay.EditingMode = InkOverlayEditingMode.Ink;
            inkOverlay.DefaultDrawingAttributes.Transparency = 255;
            inkOverlay.DynamicRendering = false;
            inkOverlay.Cursor = System.Windows.Forms.Cursors.Cross;
            fSelectMode = true;
        }
```

```
      else
      {
          // Restore the InkOverlay to it's previous state
          fSelectMode = false;
          inkOverlay.Cursor = null;
          inkOverlay.DefaultDrawingAttributes.Transparency = 0;
          inkOverlay.DynamicRendering = true;

          // Set the current editing mode to the selection chosen
          // in the combobox
          inkOverlay.EditingMode =
              (InkOverlayEditingMode)cbxEditMode.SelectedItem;
      }
}


// Handle the pen going down
private void inkOverlay_CursorDown(object sender,
    InkCollectorCursorDownEventArgs e)
{
    // Since this or might become an invisible stroke we're
    // creating, we'll save it off so it can be removed from
    // upcoming hit-test results
    strkCurr = e.Stroke;
}


// Handle system gestures
private void inkOverlay_SystemGesture(object sender,
    InkCollectorSystemGestureEventArgs e)
{
    // If we're in ink mode and a right-tap or drag occurs, then
    // switch into our custom select mode
    if (!fSelectMode &&
        inkOverlay.EditingMode == InkOverlayEditingMode.Ink &&
        (e.Id == SystemGesture.RightDrag ||
        e.Id == SystemGesture.RightTap))
    {
        strkCurr.DrawingAttributes.Transparency = 255;
        cbxEditMode.SelectedItem = InkOverlayEditingMode.Select;
    }

    if (fSelectMode)
    {
        // Drag will start a lasso, tap will select
        if (e.Id == SystemGesture.Drag ||
            e.Id == SystemGesture.RightDrag)
```

*(continued)*

**RealtimeLasso.cs** *(continued)*

```
            {
                //TODO: a drag or right-drag inside the bounds of the
                // current selection (if any) triggers drag-n-drop

                // Clear the current selection
                UpdateStrokes(
                    inkOverlay.Ink.CreateStrokes(), ref strksSelected);

                // Create a new lasso UI object, and clear out the
                // in-progress lasso results
                lasso = new LassoUI();
                strksLassoed = inkOverlay.Ink.CreateStrokes();

                // Start up the lasso UI
                Point pt = new Point(e.Point.X, e.Point.Y);
                Graphics g = pnlInput.CreateGraphics();
                inkOverlay.Renderer.InkSpaceToPixel(g, ref pt);
                lasso.Start(g, pt);
                g.Dispose();
            }
            else if (e.Id == SystemGesture.Tap ||
                e.Id == SystemGesture.RightTap)
            {
                //TODO: a tap inside the bounds of the current selection
                // (if any) is a no-op and a right-tap triggers a
                // context menu

                // Compute the tap radius (i.e. how close the pen can be
                // to ink before it's considered hit)
                Point ptRadius = new Point(nTapDistance, nTapDistance);
                Graphics g = pnlInput.CreateGraphics();
                inkOverlay.Renderer.PixelToInkSpace(g, ref ptRadius);
                g.Dispose();

                // Do the hit test, removing the invisible stroke being
                // used for the tap itself, and select the result
                Strokes strks = inkOverlay.Ink.HitTest(
                    e.Point, ptRadius.X);
                strks.Remove(strkCurr);
                UpdateStrokes(strks, ref strksSelected);
            }
        }
    }

    // Handle new packets
    private void inkOverlay_NewPackets(object sender,
        InkCollectorNewPacketsEventArgs e)
```

```
{
    if (fSelectMode && lasso != null)
    {
        Graphics g = pnlInput.CreateGraphics();

        // Continue on with the lasso UI
        bool fUpdated = false;
        int nPktLength = e.PacketData.Length / e.PacketCount;
        int nIndex = 0;
        for (int i = 0; i < e.PacketCount; i++)
        {
            Point pt = new Point(
                e.PacketData[nIndex], e.PacketData[nIndex+1]);
            inkOverlay.Renderer.InkSpaceToPixel(g, ref pt);
            fUpdated = lasso.Continue(g, pt);
            nIndex += nPktLength;
        }

        Point [] pts = lasso.Points;
        if (fUpdated && pts.Length >= 3)
        {
            // Convert the points to ink space
            inkOverlay.Renderer.PixelToInkSpace(g, ref pts);

            // Perform the in-progress lasso hit-test
            Strokes strks = inkOverlay.Ink.HitTest(pts, 60);
            strks.Remove(strkCurr);
            UpdateStrokes(strks, ref strksLassoed);
        }

        g.Dispose();
    }
}

// Handle an ink stroke occurring
private void inkOverlay_Stroke(object sender,
    InkCollectorStrokeEventArgs e)
{
    // Don't need the in-progress stroke anymore
    strkCurr = null;

    if (fSelectMode)
    {
        // Erase the invisible ink stroke
        e.Cancel = true;
        inkOverlay.Ink.DeleteStroke(e.Stroke);
```

*(continued)*

**RealtimeLasso.cs** *(continued)*

```
        if (lasso != null)
        {
            // Clear out the in-progress lasso results
            strksLassoed = inkOverlay.Ink.CreateStrokes();

            Point [] pts = lasso.Points;

            // Erase the lasso UI
            Rectangle rcBounds = lasso.BoundingRect;
            lasso = null;
            pnlInput.Invalidate(rcBounds);

            if (pts.Length >= 3)
            {
                // Convert the points to ink space to perform the
                // hit-test operation
                Graphics g = pnlInput.CreateGraphics();
                inkOverlay.Renderer.PixelToInkSpace(g, ref pts);
                g.Dispose();

                // Perform the lasso hit-test resulting in a
                // selection change
                UpdateStrokes(inkOverlay.Ink.HitTest(pts, 60),
                    ref strksSelected);
            }
        }
    }
}

// Handle the ink input panel painting
private void pnlInput_Paint(object sender, PaintEventArgs e)
{
    // Compute selection ink thickness
    Point ptThk = new Point(nSelThickness, nSelThickness);
    inkOverlay.Renderer.PixelToInkSpace(e.Graphics, ref ptThk);

    Rectangle rcBounds;

    // Paint each stroke in inkOverlay.Ink
    foreach (Stroke s in inkOverlay.Ink.Strokes)
    {
        // Make sure we're not going to try to paint strokes that
        // have been deleted
        if (s.Deleted)
        {
            continue;
        }
```

```csharp
            // Should stroke be drawn selected?
            if (strksSelected.Contains(s) || strksLassoed.Contains(s))
            {
                GetBoundsInPixels(s, true, out rcBounds);
                if (e.ClipRectangle.IntersectsWith(rcBounds))
                {
                    RendererEx.DrawSelected(inkOverlay.Renderer,
                        e.Graphics, s);
                }
            }
            else
            {
                // Draw an unselected stroke
                GetBoundsInPixels(s, false, out rcBounds);
                if (e.ClipRectangle.IntersectsWith(rcBounds))
                {
                    inkOverlay.Renderer.Draw(e.Graphics, s);
                }
            }
        }

        // Paint any selection bounding box
        if (strksSelected.Count > 0)
        {
            GetBoundsInPixels(strksSelected, true, out rcBounds);
            if (e.ClipRectangle.IntersectsWith(rcBounds))
            {
                Pen p = new Pen(Color.DarkBlue);
                p.DashStyle = DashStyle.Dash;
                e.Graphics.DrawRectangle(p, rcBounds);
            }
        }

        // Paint any in-progress lasso UI
        if (lasso != null)
        {
            lasso.Render(e.Graphics, e.ClipRectangle);
        }
    }

    // Computes the bounds of strokes
    private void GetBoundsInPixels(Strokes strks, bool fSelected,
        out Rectangle rcBounds)
    {
        // Make sure the strokes collection has anything to measure
        if (strks == null || strks.Count == 0)
```

*(continued)*

**RealtimeLasso.cs** *(continued)*

```
        {
            rcBounds = Rectangle.Empty;
            return;
        }

        // First, get the bounds (in ink space)
        rcBounds = strks.GetBoundingBox();

        // Convert the bounds to pixels
        Graphics g = pnlInput.CreateGraphics();
        RendererEx.InkSpaceToPixel(inkOverlay.Renderer, g, ref rcBounds);
        g.Dispose();

        // Inflate the bounds by the selection thickness if needed
        if (fSelected)
        {
            rcBounds.Inflate(nSelThickness*2, nSelThickness*2);
        }
    }

    // Computes the bounds of a stroke
    private void GetBoundsInPixels(Stroke strk, bool fSelected,
        out Rectangle rcBounds)
    {
        GetBoundsInPixels(
            inkOverlay.Ink.CreateStrokes(new int [] {strk.Id}),
            fSelected, out rcBounds);
    }

    // Copy one stroke set to another - invalidating strokes that are
    // not common between the two
    private void UpdateStrokes(Strokes strksNew, ref Strokes strksCurr)
    {
        // If we're dealing with selection (rather than lasso), we
        // should invalidate the bounds of the entire current and new
        // stroke set so the outline UI is drawn properly
        if (strksCurr == strksSelected)
        {
            if (strksCurr.Count > 0)
            {
                Rectangle rcBounds;
                GetBoundsInPixels(strksCurr, true, out rcBounds);
                rcBounds.Width++;
                rcBounds.Height++;
                pnlInput.Invalidate(rcBounds);
            }
            if (strksNew.Count > 0)
```

```csharp
        {
            Rectangle rcBounds;
            GetBoundsInPixels(strksNew, true, out rcBounds);
            rcBounds.Width++;
            rcBounds.Height++;
            pnlInput.Invalidate(rcBounds);
        }

        strksCurr = strksNew;

        return;
    }


    // See if we need to continue - are the two stroke sets equal?
    if (strksNew.Count == strksCurr.Count)
    {
        bool fEqual = true;
        foreach (Stroke s in strksNew)
        {
            if (!strksCurr.Contains(s))
            {
                fEqual = false;
                break;
            }
        }
        if (fEqual)
        {
            return;
        }
    }


    // We'll use temporary variables since the invalidate calls may
    // cause the Paint handler to execute while we're in the middle
    // of this function
    Strokes s1 = strksCurr;
    Strokes s2 = strksNew;
    strksCurr = strksNew;

    // Invalidate the strokes that are not common
    foreach (Stroke s in s1)
    {
        if (!s2.Contains(s))
        {
            Rectangle rcBounds;
            GetBoundsInPixels(s, true, out rcBounds);
            pnlInput.Invalidate(rcBounds);
        }
```

*(continued)*

**RealtimeLasso.cs** *(continued)*

```
        }
        foreach (Stroke s in s2)
        {
            if (!s1.Contains(s))
            {
                Rectangle rcBounds;
                GetBoundsInPixels(s, true, out rcBounds);
                pnlInput.Invalidate(rcBounds);
            }
        }

        // Get the input panel to immediately redraw
        pnlInput.Update();
    }
}
```

This program uses an *InkOverlay* object rather than an InkControl because it implements its own custom Selection editing mode and the *InkControl* class has no provision for this. *InkOverlay*'s version of the mode doesn't facilitate the user performing real-time lasso operations very well, so I took the opportunity to also show a little of how a custom Selection mode might be implemented.

The application owns two *Strokes* collections—one used for the currently selected *Stroke* objects and the other used to track the *Stroke* objects that are currently enclosed by the lasso—in case we want to add any sort of *add to selection* capability. For example, many keyboard-based applications allow the selection to be extended if the user holds down the Ctrl key, and in fact Windows Journal provides this ability. Because a current selection that we want to preserve may be present while a lasso is occurring, it is prudent to use two separate *Strokes* collections.

A lasso is started when the application is in its custom Selection mode and either a *SystemGesture.Drag* or *SystemGesture.RightDrag* occurs. An instance of the *LassoUI* class is created and is used until the lasso stroke ends.

This application highlights the performance issues that percentage-based lasso enclosure brings. To see it for yourself, try writing a sentence in the inking area and then lasso the whole thing—you'll probably notice how the dots start to lag behind the pen toward the end of the lasso stroke. This is because of all the hit-testing computation and ink rendering going on, even though work was done to try to minimize it.

The *UpdateStrokes* method reduces the amount of rendering triggered while a lasso is in progress. Its purpose is to copy one *Strokes* collection to another and invalidate the bounding rectangles of any *Stroke* objects that are not in common between them. It could just invalidate the whole input area every time a stroke was added or removed from the current lasso selection set, but performance would suffer further because of all the redundant drawing going on.

The ideal implementation of real-time lasso selection should be multi-threaded: one thread receives tablet events and computes and renders the lasso polyline while another thread performs the hit-test operation and ink rendering. This is the implementation Windows Journal appears to use (or something similar), but it's a little beyond the scope of this book in its implementation.

# Splitting and Trimming Ink

We've covered most editing functions of ink strokes, including creation, deletion, drawing attributes, and transformation. One area in the Tablet PC Platform remains for which digital ink can be modified. In this section, we'll discuss the methods by which ink strokes are split into multiple pieces and clipped or trimmed outside a rectangle.

## Splitting Strokes

It is sometimes desirable to split an ink stroke into two or more separate pieces. For example, to implement point-erase we could compute the rectangle intersections of the eraser on the ink stroke and chop out the segments inside the rectangle, or we might want to support the user's ability to select only a portion of a stroke and perform operations such as moving. In this case, we would want to split the ink strokes at the selection boundary before performing any operation.

The Tablet PC Platform provides a method by which an ink stroke can be split into two pieces. It is accomplished with the *Stroke* class's *Split* method:

```
Stroke Stroke.Split(float index)
```

This method accepts a floating-point index that defines the point along a *Stroke* object for which the split will occur, and the newly created *Stroke* object that begins at the split point is returned. The *Stroke* object for which the method is called on is truncated up to the split point.

The $(X,Y)$ point along the *Stroke* at which the split occurs is inclusive to both strokes. In other words, the last point in the ink stroke that is split will always equal the first point of the newly created ink stroke.

> **Note**  The floating-point index used to specify the split point is based on the ink stroke's polyline representation. If an ink stroke employs curve fitting, a split operation might result in the ink appearing to jump very slightly while the curve fitting is updated to two separate strokes.

# Clipping/Trimming Strokes

Clipping ink strokes is similar to splitting them except that any ink outside the clipping area is deleted instead of preserved. *Ink* strokes can be clipped at the level of *Ink* object, *Strokes* collection, and *Stroke* object:

```
void Ink.Clip(Rectangle rectangle)
void Strokes.Clip(Rectangle rectangle)
void Stroke.Clip(Rectangle rectangle)
```

The rectangle's edge is inclusive of ink strokes and is specified in ink coordinates. In other words, any ink clipped by the rectangle will have at least one point on the rectangle's edge. Similar to the *Stroke* class's *Split* method, the *Clip* methods use the polyline representation of ink strokes to compute the split point—thus, the same issue mentioned for curve fitting will apply.

## Sample Application—StrokeChopper

The StrokeChopper sample application demonstrates splitting and trimming ink strokes by implementing erasing and clipping tools. The eraser can perform stroke-erase, cusp-erase, and point-erase, while the clipping tool allows the user to draw out a rectangle and have ink clipped either inside or outside it, depending on the user's choice.

The stroke-erase and point-erase functionality behave in the same manner as *InkOverlay*'s *InkOverlayEditingMode.Delete* mode does, but cusp-erase is functionality we haven't seen before. Cusp-based erase is kind of a hybrid of point-level and stroke-level erase—when the eraser targets a *Stroke* object, the ink segment defined by the cusps adjacent to the hit point is removed.

```
StrokeChopper.cs
/////////////////////////////////////////////////////////////////////
//
// StrokeChopper.cs
//
// (c) 2002 Microsoft Press
// by Rob Jarrett
//
// This program demonstrates an implementation of point-level erase
// as well as clipping strokes inside or outside of a rectangle.
//
/////////////////////////////////////////////////////////////////////

using System;
using System.Drawing;
using System.Windows.Forms;
using Microsoft.Ink;
using MSPress.BuildingTabletApps;
```

```
public class frmMain : Form
{
    // User interface
    private InkInputPanel              pnlInput;
    private Button                     btnFormat;
    private ComboBox                   cbxEditMode;
    private ComboBox                   cbxEraseMode;
    private CheckBox                   cbInside;
    private InkCollector               inkCollector;

    // Custom editing mode support
    private enum StrokeChopperEditingMode
    {
        Ink,
        Erase,
        Clip
    };
    private enum StrokeChopperEraseMode
    {
        Stroke,
        Cusp,
        Point
    };
    private StrokeChopperEditingMode   modeEditing;
    private StrokeChopperEraseMode     modeErase;
    private bool                       fClipInside;
    private Rectangle                  rcClip;

    // Entry point of the program
    [STAThread]
    static void Main()
    {
        Application.Run(new frmMain());
    }

    // Main form setup
    public frmMain()
    {
        SuspendLayout();

        // Create and place all of our controls
        pnlInput = new InkInputPanel();
        pnlInput.BackColor = Color.White;
        pnlInput.BorderStyle = BorderStyle.Fixed3D;
        pnlInput.Location = new Point(8, 8);
        pnlInput.Size = new Size(352, 192);
```

*(continued)*

**StrokeChopper.cs** *(continued)*

```csharp
btnFormat = new Button();
btnFormat.Location = new Point(8, 204);
btnFormat.Size = new Size(50, 20);
btnFormat.Text = "Format";
btnFormat.Click += new System.EventHandler(btnFormat_Click);

cbxEditMode = new ComboBox();
cbxEditMode.DropDownStyle = ComboBoxStyle.DropDownList;
cbxEditMode.Location = new Point(66, 204);
cbxEditMode.Size = new Size(72, 20);
cbxEditMode.SelectedIndexChanged +=
    new System.EventHandler(cbxEditMode_SelIndexChg);

cbxEraseMode = new ComboBox();
cbxEraseMode.DropDownStyle = ComboBoxStyle.DropDownList;
cbxEraseMode.Location = new Point(146, 204);
cbxEraseMode.Size = new Size(72, 20);
cbxEraseMode.SelectedIndexChanged +=
    new System.EventHandler(cbxEraseMode_SelIndexChg);

cbInside = new CheckBox();
cbInside.Location = new Point(146, 204);
cbInside.Size = new Size(96, 20);
cbInside.Text = "Clip Inside";
cbInside.Click += new System.EventHandler(cbInside_Click);

// Configure the form itself
ClientSize = new Size(368, 236);
Controls.AddRange(new Control[] { pnlInput,
                                  btnFormat,
                                  cbxEditMode,
                                  cbxEraseMode,
                                  cbInside});
FormBorderStyle = FormBorderStyle.FixedDialog;
MaximizeBox = false;
Text = "StrokeChopper";

ResumeLayout(false);

// Fill up the editing mode combobox
cbxEditMode.Items.Add(StrokeChopperEditingMode.Ink);
cbxEditMode.Items.Add(StrokeChopperEditingMode.Erase);
cbxEditMode.Items.Add(StrokeChopperEditingMode.Clip);

// Fill up the erase mode combobox
cbxEraseMode.Items.Add(StrokeChopperEraseMode.Stroke);
```

```
        cbxEraseMode.Items.Add(StrokeChopperEraseMode.Cusp);
        cbxEraseMode.Items.Add(StrokeChopperEraseMode.Point);

        // Hook up to mouse events to perform custom mode behaviors
        pnlInput.MouseDown += new MouseEventHandler(pnlInput_MouseDown);
        pnlInput.MouseMove += new MouseEventHandler(pnlInput_MouseMove);
        pnlInput.MouseUp += new MouseEventHandler(pnlInput_MouseUp);

        // Create a new InkCollector, using pnlInput for the collection
        // area
        inkCollector = new InkCollector(pnlInput.Handle);

        // Set up the initial mode settings
        modeEditing = StrokeChopperEditingMode.Ink;
        modeErase = StrokeChopperEraseMode.Stroke;
        fClipInside = true;

        // Update the UI with the mode settings
        cbxEditMode.SelectedItem = modeEditing;
        cbxEraseMode.SelectedItem = modeErase;
        cbInside.Checked = fClipInside;
}

// Handle the click of the format button
private void btnFormat_Click(object sender, EventArgs e)
{
    FormatInkDlg dlgFormat = new FormatInkDlg();
    dlgFormat.DrawingAttributes =
        inkCollector.DefaultDrawingAttributes;
    if (dlgFormat.ShowDialog(this) == DialogResult.OK)
    {
        inkCollector.DefaultDrawingAttributes =
            dlgFormat.DrawingAttributes;
    }
}

// Handle the selection change of the editing mode combobox
private void cbxEditMode_SelIndexChg(object sender, EventArgs e)
{
    modeEditing = (StrokeChopperEditingMode)cbxEditMode.SelectedItem;

    switch (modeEditing)
    {
        case StrokeChopperEditingMode.Ink:
            inkCollector.Enabled = true;
            break;
```

*(continued)*

**StrokeChopper.cs** *(continued)*

```csharp
            case StrokeChopperEditingMode.Erase:
                inkCollector.Enabled = false;
                pnlInput.Cursor = System.Windows.Forms.Cursors.Hand;
                break;

            case StrokeChopperEditingMode.Clip:
                inkCollector.Enabled = false;
                pnlInput.Cursor = System.Windows.Forms.Cursors.Cross;
                break;
        }

        // Update the UI as a result of the mode selection
        cbxEraseMode.Visible =
            (modeEditing == StrokeChopperEditingMode.Erase);
        cbInside.Visible =
            (modeEditing == StrokeChopperEditingMode.Clip);
    }

    // Handle the selection change of the erase mode combobox
    private void cbxEraseMode_SelIndexChg(object sender, EventArgs e)
    {
        modeErase = (StrokeChopperEraseMode)cbxEraseMode.SelectedItem;
    }

    // Handle the click of the clip inside checkbox
    private void cbInside_Click(object sender, EventArgs e)
    {
        fClipInside = cbInside.Checked;
    }

    // Handle mouse down in the input panel
    private void pnlInput_MouseDown(object sender, MouseEventArgs e)
    {
        if (modeEditing == StrokeChopperEditingMode.Clip)
        {
            // Start up clip tracking UI
            StartClip(e);
        }
    }

    // Handle mouse move in the input panel
    private void pnlInput_MouseMove(object sender, MouseEventArgs e)
    {
        if (modeEditing == StrokeChopperEditingMode.Erase &&
            e.Button == MouseButtons.Left)
        {
            // Perform erase mode
```

```
            ContinueErase(e);
        }
        else if (modeEditing == StrokeChopperEditingMode.Clip &&
            e.Button == MouseButtons.Left)
        {
            // Update clip tracking UI
            ContinueClip(e);
        }
    }


// Handle mouse up in the input panel
private void pnlInput_MouseUp(object sender, MouseEventArgs e)
{
    if (modeEditing == StrokeChopperEditingMode.Clip)
    {
        // Perform ink clip
        EndClip(e);
    }
}


// Perform erasing - dispatch to correct helper function
private void ContinueErase(MouseEventArgs e)
{
    Point ptHit = new Point(e.X, e.Y);

    switch (modeErase)
    {
        case StrokeChopperEraseMode.Stroke:
        {
            StrokeErase(ptHit);
            break;
        }

        case StrokeChopperEraseMode.Cusp:
        {
            CuspErase(ptHit);
            break;
        }

        case StrokeChopperEraseMode.Point:
        {
            PointErase(ptHit, 250);
            break;
        }
    }
}
```

*(continued)*

**StrokeChopper.cs** *(continued)*

```csharp
// Perform stroke-level erase
private void StrokeErase(Point ptHit)
{
    // Use a 2-pixel radius for the hit-area
    Point ptRadius = new Point(2, 2);

    // Convert hit point and radius to ink space
    Graphics g = pnlInput.CreateGraphics();
    inkCollector.Renderer.PixelToInkSpace(g, ref ptHit);
    inkCollector.Renderer.PixelToInkSpace(g, ref ptRadius);
    g.Dispose();

    // See what strokes are hit by the cursor
    Strokes strksHit = inkCollector.Ink.HitTest(ptHit, ptRadius.X);

    // Any strokes touched by the cursor are deleted
    foreach (Stroke s in strksHit)
    {
        DeleteStroke(s);
    }
}

// Perform cusp-level erase
private void CuspErase(Point ptHit)
{
    // Use a 2-pixel radius for the hit-area
    Point ptRadius = new Point(2, 2);

    // Convert hit point and radius to ink space
    Graphics g = pnlInput.CreateGraphics();
    inkCollector.Renderer.PixelToInkSpace(g, ref ptHit);
    inkCollector.Renderer.PixelToInkSpace(g, ref ptRadius);
    g.Dispose();

    // See what strokes are hit by the cursor
    Strokes strksHit = inkCollector.Ink.HitTest(ptHit, ptRadius.X);
    if (strksHit.Count > 0)
    {
        // Any strokes touched by the cursor will have the cusp
        // closest to the hit point removed and deleted
        foreach (Stroke s in strksHit)
        {
            int[] arrCusps = s.PolylineCusps;

            if (arrCusps.Length == 2)
```

```
                    {
                        // The stroke has no cusps so we'll erase the whole
                        // thing
                        DeleteStroke(s);
                    }
                    else
                    {
                        // Find out where along the stroke was hit
                        float fHit = s.NearestPoint(ptHit);

                        for (int i = 1; i < arrCusps.Length; i++)
                        {
                            if (arrCusps[i] >= fHit)
                            {
                                // Split off the 3rd segment
                                if (i < arrCusps.Length-1)
                                {
                                    s.Split(arrCusps[i]);
                                }

                                // Split off the preceding segment
                                if (i > 1)
                                {
                                    // There is a segment before so split
                                    // off the end of it
                                    DeleteStroke(s.Split(arrCusps[i-1]));
                                }
                                else
                                {
                                    // No preceding segment to split
                                    // so just erase the stroke
                                    DeleteStroke(s);
                                }
                                break;
                            }
                        }
                    }
                }
            }
        }
    }
}

// Perform point-level erase
private void PointErase(Point ptHit, int nEraserSize)
{
    // Convert hit point to ink space
    Graphics g = pnlInput.CreateGraphics();
    inkCollector.Renderer.PixelToInkSpace(g, ref ptHit);
```

*(continued)*

**StrokeChopper.cs** *(continued)*

```csharp
        g.Dispose();

        // Compute the rectangle to use for the eraser
        ptHit.Offset(-nEraserSize/2, -nEraserSize/2);
        Rectangle rcErase = new Rectangle(
            ptHit, new Size(nEraserSize, nEraserSize));

        // See if the eraser hits any strokes in the InkCollector
        foreach (Stroke s in inkCollector.Ink.Strokes)
        {
            StrokeIntersection[] si =
                s.GetRectangleIntersections(rcErase);

            // Walk through the hit results
            for (int i = si.Length-1; i >= 0; i--)
            {
                if (si[i].BeginIndex == si[i].EndIndex)
                {
                    if (si[i].BeginIndex == -1f)
                    {
                        // The entire stroke is contained within the
                        // rectangle, so delete the whole thing
                        DeleteStroke(s);
                        break;
                    }
                    else
                    {
                        // Only one point is intersecting the rectangle
                        // so we don't need to do anything
                        continue;
                    }
                }
                else if (si[i].BeginIndex > 0f && si[i].EndIndex > 0f)
                {
                    // A segment of the stroke segment is within the
                    // rectangle, so split it into three pieces,
                    // throwing away the middle one
                    s.Split(si[i].EndIndex);
                    DeleteStroke(s.Split(si[i].BeginIndex));
                }
                else if (
                    (si[i].BeginIndex == 0f || si[i].BeginIndex == -1f)
                    && si[i].EndIndex > 0f)
                {
                    // The stroke starts inside the rectangle and ends
                    // outside of it - split it into two and throw away
                    // the first half (i.e. what's inside the rect)
```

```
                        s.Split(si[i].EndIndex);
                        DeleteStroke(s);
                    }
                    else if (si[i].BeginIndex > 0f &&
                        (si[i].EndIndex == s.GetPoints().Length-1 ||
                        si[i].EndIndex == -1f))
                    {
                        // The stroke starts outside the rectangle and ends
                        // inside of it - split it into two parts and throw
                        // away the second half (i.e. what's inside the
                        // rect)
                        DeleteStroke(s.Split(si[i].BeginIndex));
                    }
                }
            }
        }
    }


    // Delete a stroke and invalidate the leftover area
    private void DeleteStroke(Stroke s)
    {
            Rectangle rcInvalid = inkCollector.Renderer.Measure(s);
            inkCollector.Ink.DeleteStroke(s);

            Graphics g = pnlInput.CreateGraphics();
            RendererEx.InkSpaceToPixel(
                inkCollector.Renderer, g, ref rcInvalid);
            g.Dispose();
            rcInvalid.Inflate(1, 1);


        pnlInput.Invalidate(rcInvalid);
    }


    // Start up clipping UI
    private void StartClip(MouseEventArgs e)
    {
        // Initialize tracking rectangle
        rcClip = new Rectangle(new Point(e.X, e.Y), new Size(0, 0));
    }


    // Continue the clipping UI
    private void ContinueClip(MouseEventArgs e)
    {
        // Erase the previous tracking rectangle
        Rectangle rcDraw = rcClip;
        rcDraw.Location = pnlInput.PointToScreen(rcClip.Location);
        ControlPaint.DrawReversibleFrame(
            rcDraw, BackColor, FrameStyle.Dashed);
```

*(continued)*

**StrokeChopper.cs** *(continued)*

```csharp
        // Update rectangle with new mouse location, constraining to
        // the input panel's bounds
        rcClip.Width = e.X - rcClip.X;
        if (rcClip.Left + rcClip.Width < 0)
        {
            rcClip.Width = -rcClip.X;
        }
        else if (rcClip.Right > pnlInput.ClientSize.Width)
        {
            rcClip.Width = pnlInput.ClientSize.Width - rcClip.X;
        }

        rcClip.Height = e.Y - rcClip.Y;
        if (rcClip.Top + rcClip.Height < 0)
        {
            rcClip.Height = -rcClip.Y;
        }
        else if (rcClip.Bottom > pnlInput.ClientSize.Height)
        {
            rcClip.Height = pnlInput.ClientSize.Height - rcClip.Y;
        }

        // Draw the new tracking rectangle
        rcDraw = rcClip;
        rcDraw.Location = pnlInput.PointToScreen(rcClip.Location);
        ControlPaint.DrawReversibleFrame(
            rcDraw, BackColor, FrameStyle.Dashed);
    }

    // End the clipping UI and perform the clip operation
    private void EndClip(MouseEventArgs e)
    {
        // Erase the previous tracking rectangle
        Rectangle rcDraw = rcClip;
        rcDraw.Location = pnlInput.PointToScreen(rcClip.Location);
        ControlPaint.DrawReversibleFrame(
            rcDraw, BackColor, FrameStyle.Dashed);

        // Compute the well-formed rectangle to use for clipping
        Point ptTopLeft =
            new Point(System.Math.Min(rcClip.X, rcClip.X + rcClip.Width),
            System.Math.Min(rcClip.Y, rcClip.Y + rcClip.Height));
        Point ptBottomRight =
            new Point(System.Math.Max(rcClip.X, rcClip.X + rcClip.Width),
            System.Math.Max(rcClip.Y, rcClip.Y + rcClip.Height));
```

```
Graphics g = pnlInput.CreateGraphics();
inkCollector.Renderer.PixelToInkSpace(g, ref ptTopLeft);
inkCollector.Renderer.PixelToInkSpace(g, ref ptBottomRight);
g.Dispose();

Rectangle rcClipInk =
    new Rectangle(ptTopLeft,
    new Size(ptBottomRight.X - ptTopLeft.X,
    ptBottomRight.Y - ptTopLeft.Y));

// Perform the clip operation
if (fClipInside)
{
    inkCollector.Ink.Clip(rcClipInk);
}
else
{
    inkCollector.Ink.ExtractStrokes(rcClipInk,
        ExtractFlags.RemoveFromOriginal);
}

// Update the display
pnlInput.Invalidate();
    }
}
```

The application provides three modes: Ink, Erase, and Clip. The Erase and Clip modes are custom modes that use mouse messages to trigger their functionality, although we just as easily could have used tablet events.

While in Erase mode, mouse movement with the left button down will call either the *StrokeErase*, *CuspErase*, or *PointErase* method to perform the chosen operation. These methods are fairly self-contained, each performing its respective erasing functionality.

The *StrokeErase* method uses the *Ink* class's *HitTest* method to compute the ink strokes within 2 pixels of the erase point; the strokes are then deleted. *CuspErase* also uses the *Ink* class's *HitTest* method to compute the strokes within 2 pixels of the erase point, and then it uses the *Stroke* class's *PolylineCusps* property and *NearestPoint* method to determine the segment of the ink strokes to delete. The *PointErase* method calls *GetRectangleIntersections* on every *Stroke* object to determine the segments of any ink strokes that must be deleted.

> **Note**   The *PointErase* method leverages the *Stroke* class's *GetRect-angleIntersections* to compute the segments of ink that need to be deleted. I first thought it would be nice to call *Ink.Extract-Strokes(rcErase, ExtractFlags.RemoveFromOriginal)*, but unfortunately the initial version 1 release of the Tablet PC Platform has a bug causing that version of *ExtractStrokes* to be overzealous in the extraction. If any edge of the extraction rectangle falls exactly on the first point of a stroke, the entire stroke will be extracted. I therefore found it unusable for point-erase. The rest of the *ExtractStrokes* functionality works wonderfully, though!

The clipping operation's functionality is found in the *StartClip*, *Continue-Clip*, and *EndClip* methods. *StartClip* and *ContinueClip* perform the rectangle UI animation, and *EndClip* cleans up the rectangle UI and also performs the clipping operation:

```
// Perform the clip operation
if (fClipInside)
{
    inkCollector.Ink.Clip(rcClipInk);
}
else
{
    inkCollector.Ink.ExtractStrokes(rcClipInk,
        ExtractFlags.RemoveFromOriginal);
}
```

Notice how the *ExtractStrokes* method is used without significant problems. The key difference here with respect to point-erase are the conditions under which the method is called. The user will rarely draw out a rectangle whose edge falls exactly on the first point of a stroke; with point-erase, however, it is very easy to expose the bug discussed in the preceding note because the mouse is dragged along pixel by pixel.

> **Note**   It would be a great exercise to write a bug-free version of *ExtractStrokes* based on the *PointErase* method.

# Serialization, the Clipboard, and Drag and Drop

All the cool functionality that we've been performing on ink won't do the user much good if he or she can't save or load data or have it interoperate with other applications via the clipboard or drag and drop. In this final section on the Ink Data Management API, we'll take a look at the platform's support for serialization, clipboard, and drag and drop functionality.

## Serialization

Ink data is always saved at the *Ink* object level, and it's accomplished with the *Ink* class's *Save* method:

```
byte[] Ink.Save()
byte[] Ink.Save(PersistenceFormat p)
byte[] Ink.Save(PersistenceFormat p, CompressionMode c)
```

This method produces a byte array in one of several formats. By default, the *Save* method will output the data in the Ink Serialized Format (ISF), which is the Tablet PC Platform's native binary format for ink data.

If the optional *PersistenceFormat* parameter is given, alternative formats can be generated. Table 6-2 lists all the formats that version 1 of the Tablet PC Platform supports.

**Table 6-2   The Values of the *PersistenceFormat* Enumeration**

| *PersistenceFormat* **Value** | **Description** |
| --- | --- |
| *Base64Gif* | The Graphics Interchange Format, which is then Base64-encoded, typically used for viewing ink via .mht files |
| *Base64InkSerializedFormat* | The ISF, which is then Base64-encoded, typically used for storing ink in XML |
| *Gif* | The Graphics Interchange Format, typically used for viewing ink in Web browsers |
| *InkSerializedFormat* | The Ink Serialized Format, typically used to save and load ink data |

Notice that there are really only two formats. You can choose to encode to Base64 or not. Encoding to the Base64 format doesn't even really have to be provided by the Tablet PC Platform because the Microsoft .NET Framework's *System.Convert.ToBase64String* method will do the same work. I believe the Base64 formats are a result of the managed API being built on top of the COM automation layer where .NET Framework functionality is not available.

The *Save* method's optional *CompressionMode* value is used when saving in *InkSerializedFormat*. Table 6-3 lists its values.

**Table 6-3** **The Values of the *CompressionMode* Enumeration**

| *CompressionMode* Value | Description |
| --- | --- |
| Default | The default compression mode—its value is Maximum |
| Maximum | The most compression possible (resulting in the smallest data size); also the most performance intensive |
| NoCompression | No compression occurs; the fastest performance |

As already mentioned, when no *CompressionMode* is provided to the *Save* method, the *CompressionMode.Default* value is used.

Once ink data has been saved, we'll need to reconstitute it into an *Ink* object. This is done with the *Ink* class's *Load* method:

```
void Ink.Load(byte[] inkData)
```

There is only one version of the method because the format and compression are automatically determined. The method has no return value, so if the byte array has some bad data in it or a problem otherwise occurs, the *Load* method will throw an exception. When no exception is thrown, you can assume the function has succeeded.

You cannot call *Load* on an *Ink* object that has ever contained an ink stroke—an exception will be thrown if you do! The reason is simple: when ink data is saved and loaded, stroke IDs are preserved. Recall from Chapter 5 that stroke IDs are unique only on a per–*Ink* object basis. An *Ink* object that has contained one or more ink strokes can have one or more *Strokes* collections referencing those ink strokes, even if all ink strokes have since been deleted. If data is then loaded into that *Ink* object and one or more stroke IDs match the references in a *Strokes* collection, the *Strokes* collection will dereference the wrong *Stroke* objects, possibly causing great harm. The solution to this problem is to always create a new *Ink* object before loading data into it.

To help us keep track of when to save ink data, the *Ink* class's *Dirty* property is set whenever any of its data is modified. It is very useful to track a document's dirty flag, a bit that is used to determine whether the document needs to be saved. This *Ink* class's *Dirty* property is a read-write property that is typically set to clean (or false) on file load and is queried on file save; if it's dirty (or true), the document is saved and the property is then set to clean.

## Persisting *Strokes* Collections

When ink data from an *Ink* object is saved, no existing *Strokes* collections will be saved by default. To persist a *Strokes* collection, it must be added to the *Ink* object's *CustomStrokes* property. This property is a collection of *Strokes* collections whose contents will be saved. It is useful for persisting relations of ink strokes, for example, layers, groups, and recognition data.

To keep track of which *Strokes* collection contains which data, *Strokes* collections are added to the *CustomStrokes* property along with a name of type *string*. To retrieve a *Strokes* collection, the name can be used as an argument to the *CustomStrokes* property's *operator[]*. Here's a hypothetical example showing the use of *CustomStrokes*:

```
// Make sure the strksTopLayer strokes collection is saved
ink.CustomStrokes.Add("TopLayer", strksTopLayer);

// Save the ink data
byte[] arrData = Ink.Save();

...

// Load the ink data into a new ink object
ink = new Ink();
ink.Load(arrData);

// Assign the top layer strokes collection to strksTopLayer
strksTopLayer = ink.CustomStrokes["TopLayer"];

// Remove it since it won't be used anymore
ink.CustomStrokes.Remove("TopLayer");
```

## Extended Property Data

The *CustomStrokes* property is handy for storing *Strokes* collections, but what about other types of data? We could write out our own custom data separately and read it back in, but that can take a lot of effort and is prone to errors. Fortunately, the Tablet PC Platform allows some arbitrary data to be persisted along with the ink data by using extended properties. An *extended property* is simply a name-value pair, where the name is a Guid and the value is any built-in type such as *int, string,* and *byte[ ]*.

The *Ink, Stroke,* and *DrawingAttributes* classes all possess an *Extended-Properties* property that is a collection of *ExtendedProperty* objects. The *Extended-Property* class has two properties: *Id,* which is a Guid value, and *Data,* which is an object of some kind. The *ExtendedProperties* property is found in the *Ink, Stroke,* and *DrawingAttributes* classes to satisfy saving data at any of those scopes. Use *Ink*'s *ExtendedProperties* for document-level data, *Stroke*'s for stroke-level data, and *DrawingAttributes*' for custom rendering settings.

## Sample Application—InkPersist

The InkPersist sample application shows just how easy it is to load and save ink data to a file. It supports loading, merging, and saving ink to an ISF file, as well as exporting ink data to a GIF file.

**InkPersist.cs**

```
/////////////////////////////////////////////////////////////////////
//
// InkPersist.cs
//
// (c) 2002 Microsoft Press
// by Rob Jarrett
//
// This program demonstrates how to use serialization API functions
// the TPG platform provides.
//
/////////////////////////////////////////////////////////////////////

using System;
using System.Drawing;
using System.IO;
using System.Windows.Forms;
using Microsoft.Ink;
using MSPress.BuildingTabletApps;

public class frmMain : Form
{
    private InkControl2 inkCtl;
    private MenuItem miNew;
    private MenuItem miOpen;
    private MenuItem miMerge;
    private MenuItem miSave;
    private MenuItem miExport;
    private MenuItem miExit;

    // Entry point of the program
    [STAThread]
    static void Main()
    {
        Application.Run(new frmMain());
    }

    // Main form setup
    public frmMain()
    {
```

```
SuspendLayout();

// Create the main menu
Menu = new MainMenu();

MenuItem miFile = new MenuItem("&File");
Menu.MenuItems.Add(miFile);

miNew = new MenuItem("&New", new EventHandler(miNew_Click));
Menu.MenuItems[0].MenuItems.Add(miNew);

Menu.MenuItems[0].MenuItems.Add(new MenuItem("-"));

miOpen =
    new MenuItem("&Open...", new EventHandler(miOpen_Click));
Menu.MenuItems[0].MenuItems.Add(miOpen);

miMerge =
    new MenuItem("&Merge...", new EventHandler(miMerge_Click));
Menu.MenuItems[0].MenuItems.Add(miMerge);

miSave =
    new MenuItem("Save &As...", new EventHandler(miSave_Click));
Menu.MenuItems[0].MenuItems.Add(miSave);

Menu.MenuItems[0].MenuItems.Add(new MenuItem("-"));

miExport =
    new MenuItem("&Export...", new EventHandler(miExport_Click));
Menu.MenuItems[0].MenuItems.Add(miExport);

Menu.MenuItems[0].MenuItems.Add(new MenuItem("-"));

miExit = new MenuItem("E&xit");
miExit.Click += new EventHandler(miExit_Click);
Menu.MenuItems[0].MenuItems.Add(miExit);

// Create and place all of our controls
inkCtl = new InkControl2();
inkCtl.Location = new Point(8, 8);
inkCtl.Size = new Size(352, 216);

// Configure the form itself
ClientSize = new Size(368, 232);
Controls.AddRange(new Control[] { inkCtl });
FormBorderStyle = FormBorderStyle.FixedDialog;
MaximizeBox = false;
```

*(continued)*

**InkPersist.cs** *(continued)*

```csharp
        Text = "InkPersist";

        ResumeLayout(false);

        // We're now set to go, so turn on tablet input
        inkCtl.InkOverlay.Enabled = true;
    }

    // Handle the "New" menu item being clicked
    private void miNew_Click(object sender, EventArgs e)
    {
        inkCtl.InkOverlay.Enabled = false;

        // Create a new ink object
        Ink newInk = new Ink();
        inkCtl.InkOverlay.Ink = newInk;
        inkCtl.InkInputPanel.Invalidate();

        // Show the new ink
        inkCtl.InkOverlay.Enabled = true;
    }

    // Handle the "Open..." menu item being clicked
    private void miOpen_Click(object sender, EventArgs e)
    {
        inkCtl.InkOverlay.Enabled = false;

        // Choose the file to open
        OpenFileDialog dlg = new OpenFileDialog();
        dlg.DefaultExt = "isf";
        dlg.Filter =
            "ISF binary files (*.isf)|*.isf|All files (*.*)|*.*";

        if (dlg.ShowDialog(this) == DialogResult.OK)
        {
            // Load the file into a new ink object
            Stream s = dlg.OpenFile();
            byte [] buf = new byte[s.Length];
            s.Read(buf, 0, buf.Length);
            Ink newInk = new Ink();
            newInk.Load(buf);
            inkCtl.InkOverlay.Ink = newInk;

            // Show the new ink
            inkCtl.InkInputPanel.Invalidate();
        }
```

```csharp
        inkCtl.InkOverlay.Enabled = true;
}

// Handle the "Merge..." menu item being clicked
private void miMerge_Click(object sender, EventArgs e)
{
    inkCtl.InkOverlay.Enabled = false;

    // Choose the file to merge
    OpenFileDialog dlg = new OpenFileDialog();
    dlg.DefaultExt = "isf";
    dlg.Filter =
        "ISF binary files (*.isf)|*.isf|All files (*.*)|*.*";

    if (dlg.ShowDialog(this) == DialogResult.OK)
    {
        // Load the file into a new ink object
        Stream s = dlg.OpenFile();
        byte [] buf = new byte[s.Length];
        s.Read(buf, 0, buf.Length);
        Ink newInk = new Ink();
        newInk.Load(buf);

        // Merge the ink into the current ink object
        inkCtl.InkOverlay.Ink.AddStrokesAtRectangle(
            newInk.Strokes, newInk.GetBoundingBox());

        // Show the new ink
        inkCtl.InkInputPanel.Invalidate();
    }

    inkCtl.InkOverlay.Enabled = true;
}

// Handle the "Save As..." menu item being clicked
private void miSave_Click(object sender, EventArgs e)
{
    inkCtl.InkOverlay.Enabled = false;

    // Choose the file to save
    SaveFileDialog dlg = new SaveFileDialog();
    dlg.DefaultExt = "isf";
    dlg.Filter =
        "ISF binary files (*.isf)|*.isf|All files (*.*)|*.*";

    if (dlg.ShowDialog(this) == DialogResult.OK)
```

*(continued)*

**InkPersist.cs**  *(continued)*

```
        {
            // Save the ink object to the file
            Stream s = dlg.OpenFile();
            byte [] buf = inkCtl.InkOverlay.Ink.Save(
                PersistenceFormat.InkSerializedFormat);
            s.Write(buf, 0, buf.Length);
        }

        inkCtl.InkOverlay.Enabled = true;
    }

    // Handle the "Export..." menu item being clicked
    private void miExport_Click(object sender, EventArgs e)
    {
        inkCtl.InkOverlay.Enabled = false;

        // Choose the file to export
        SaveFileDialog dlg = new SaveFileDialog();
        dlg.DefaultExt = "gif";
        dlg.Filter =
            "Graphics Interchange Format (GIF) files " +
            "(*.gif)|*.gif|All files (*.*)|*.*";

        if (dlg.ShowDialog(this) == DialogResult.OK)
        {
            // Export the ink object as a GIF image
            Stream s = dlg.OpenFile();
            byte [] buf =
                inkCtl.InkOverlay.Ink.Save(PersistenceFormat.Gif);
            s.Write(buf, 0, buf.Length);
        }

        inkCtl.InkOverlay.Enabled = true;
    }

    // Handle the "Exit" menu item being clicked
    private void miExit_Click(object sender, EventArgs e)
    {
        Application.Exit();
    }
}
```

Loading in ink is quite straightforward—the file is read into a byte array that is then passed to the *Load* method of a new *Ink* object. The *Ink* object is then assigned to the InkControl's *InkOverlay*:

```
// Load the file into a new ink object
Stream s = dlg.OpenFile();
byte [] buf = new byte[s.Length];
s.Read(buf, 0, buf.Length);
Ink newInk = new Ink();
newInk.Load(buf);
inkCtl.InkOverlay.Ink = newInk;
```

Merging a file requires almost the same set of operations as loading one except that instead of replacing the *InkOverlay*'s *Ink* object with the newly loaded ink, we use *AddStrokesAtRectangle* to copy the new ink into the existing *Ink* object:

```
// Load the file into a new ink object
Stream s = dlg.OpenFile();
byte [] buf = new byte[s.Length];
s.Read(buf, 0, buf.Length);
Ink newInk = new Ink();
newInk.Load(buf);

// Merge the ink into the current ink object
inkCtl.InkOverlay.Ink.AddStrokesAtRectangle(
    newInk.Strokes, newInk.GetBoundingBox());
```

Saving the ink data out to a file is even more straightforward than loading it in. The resulting byte array from the *Save* method is written to the target file:

```
// Save the ink object to the file
Stream s = dlg.OpenFile();
byte [] buf = inkCtl.InkOverlay.Ink.Save(
    PersistenceFormat.InkSerializedFormat);
s.Write(buf, 0, buf.Length);
```

Exporting ink to a .gif file is identical to saving except that it requires the *Save* method's *PersistenceFormat* value to be changed to *PersistenceFormat.Gif.*

---

**Note**   This sample doesn't use any exception handling, an omission I do *not* recommend, particularly when it comes to something as error prone as persistence code. Because the Tablet PC Platform doesn't introduce any issues that otherwise wouldn't occur in other persistence code, I chose to omit the exception handling for clarity. Please use exception handling in your own application.

# Using the Clipboard

Copying and pasting ink is almost a necessity if your ink application supports selection of some kind. Now that we know how to persist ink data, we can certainly write our own clipboard support—we put the byte array returned from the *Save* method into a data object and place the data object on the clipboard. However, this has a couple of drawbacks: the first is that we have to write all the code to perform the clipboard operations, and the second is that interoperating with other applications will be difficult if not impossible because the clipboard formats will have to match exactly.

Again, the Tablet PC Platform comes to the rescue by providing all the clipboard functionality we need. It has methods to cut, copy, paste, and query the clipboard for supported formats. Let's first take a look at how to cut and copy ink:

```
IDataObject Ink.ClipboardCopy(InkClipboardFormats formats, InkClipboardModes mo
des)
IDataObject Ink.ClipboardCopy(Strokes strokes, InkClipboardFormats formats, Ink
ClipboardModes modes)
IDataObject Ink.ClipboardCopy(Rectangle rectangle, InkClipboardFormats formats,
 InkClipboardModes modes)
```

The *ClipboardCopy* method can cut or copy ink data from an *Ink* object to the clipboard in many different formats. The *InkClipboardFormats* parameter indicates which formats should be created, and its values are found in Table 6-4.

**Table 6-4  The Values of the *InkClipboardFormats* Enumeration**

| *InkClipboardFormats* **Value** | **Description** |
| --- | --- |
| *Bitmap* | Equivalent to *CF_BITMAP* clipboard type; cannot be used to paste ink data |
| *CopyMask* | Equivalent to *Bitmap*, *EnhancedMetafile*, *InkSerializedFormat*, *Metafile*, *SketchInk*, and *TextInk* |
| *Default* | Equivalent to *CopyMask* |
| *EnhancedMetafile* | Equivalent to *CF_ENHMETAFILE* clipboard type; cannot be used to paste ink data |
| *InkSerializedFormat* | The Tablet PC Platform's binary format for ink persistence; can be used to paste ink data |
| *Metafile* | Equivalent to *CF_METAFILE* clipboard type; cannot be used to paste ink data |
| *None* | No clipboard formats |
| *PasteMask* | Equivalent to *InkSerializedFormat*, *SketchInk*, and *TextInk* |

**Table 6-4   The Values of the *InkClipboardFormats* Enumeration**   *(continued)*

| *InkClipboardFormats* Value | Description |
| --- | --- |
| *SketchInk* | Microsoft Office sketch ink ink-drawing format; can be used to paste ink data |
| *TextInk* | Microsoft Office text ink ink-word format; can be used to paste ink data |

The *InkClipboardFormats.Bitmap, InkClipboardModes.EnhancedMetafile, InkClipboardModes.InkSerializedFormat, InkClipboardModes.Metafile, InkClip-boardModes.SketchInk,* and *InkClipboardModes.TextInk* can be bitwise-ORed to produce various combinations of data formats on the clipboard. Common formats are found in the *InkClipboardModes.CopyMask* and *InkClipboard-Modes.PasteMask* values.

The *InkClipboardModes* parameter specifies how the ink data and *IDataObject* should be used. Table 6-5 lists its values.

**Table 6-5   The Values of the *InkClipboardModes* Enumeration**

| *InkClipboardModes* Value | Description |
| --- | --- |
| *Copy* | Puts the desired formats on the clipboard; leaves the ink data alone |
| *Cut* | Puts the desired formats on the clipboard; deletes the ink data from the *Ink* object |
| *Default* | Equivalent to *Copy* |
| *DelayedCopy* | Results in not executing the code to fill the *IDataObject* with data until it's first requested |
| *ExtractOnly* | Results in the Windows clipboard not being touched; instead just an *IDataObject* with the ink data is returned (for drag and drop) |

The *InkClipboardModes.Copy, InkClipboardModes.Cut,* and *InkClipboard-Modes.DelayedCopy* values are exclusive to the *InkClipboardModes.ExtractOnly* value. That is, you can bitwise-OR the *InkClipboardModes.ExtractOnly* value with the others. The *InkClipboardModes.ExtractOnly* value is used when performing a drag and drop operation. In the next section, we'll learn how to perform drag and drop.

Pasting ink from the clipboard or a data object is performed by the *Ink* class's *ClipboardPaste* method:

```
Strokes Ink.ClipboardPaste()
Strokes Ink.ClipboardPaste(Point point)
Strokes Ink.ClipboardPaste(Point point, object dataObject)
```

The default version of *ClipboardPaste* will try to read the supported data formats off the clipboard and merge it into the *Ink* object the method is called on, at location (0,0). An alternative position for pasting is specified by providing the *Point* argument. Performing a paste operation from a data object rather than from the Windows clipboard is accomplished by providing the *dataObject* parameter. The *ClipboardPaste* method returns a *Strokes* collection referencing the newly pasted ink data.

To determine whether a paste operation can occur, or if a data object supports any pasteable formats, the *CanPaste* method is used:

```
bool Ink.CanPaste()
bool Ink.CanPaste(object dataObject)
```

The *CanPaste* method returns true if pasting can occur and false if it can't. This method is useful for updating a Paste menu item or providing drop effect feedback during a drag and drop operation.

## Sample Application—InkClippy

This sample application shows how cut/copy/paste functionality can be implemented. It is named InkClippy to avoid confusion with the Tablet PC Platform SDK's sample named InkClipboard.

**InkClippy.cs**

```
/////////////////////////////////////////////////////////////////////
//
// InkClippy.cs
//
// (c) 2002 Microsoft Press
// by Rob Jarrett
//
// This program demonstrates how to use clipboard API functions the
// TPG platform provides.
//
/////////////////////////////////////////////////////////////////////

using System;
using System.Drawing;
using System.Windows.Forms;
using Microsoft.Ink;
using MSPress.BuildingTabletApps;

public class frmMain : Form
```

```
{
    private InkControl2 inkCtl;
    private MenuItem miCut;
    private MenuItem miCopy;
    private MenuItem miPaste;

    // Entry point of the program
    [STAThread]
    static void Main()
    {
        Application.Run(new frmMain());
    }

    // Main form setup
    public frmMain()
    {
        SuspendLayout();

        // Create the main menu
        Menu = new MainMenu();

        MenuItem miFile = new MenuItem("&File");
        Menu.MenuItems.Add(miFile);

        MenuItem miExit = new MenuItem("E&xit");
        miExit.Click += new EventHandler(miExit_Click);
        Menu.MenuItems[0].MenuItems.Add(miExit);

        MenuItem miEdit = new MenuItem("&Edit");
        miEdit.Popup += new EventHandler(miEdit_Popup);
        Menu.MenuItems.Add(miEdit);

        miCut = new MenuItem("Cu&t");
        miCut.Click += new EventHandler(miCut_Click);
        Menu.MenuItems[1].MenuItems.Add(miCut);

        miCopy = new MenuItem("&Copy");
        miCopy.Click += new EventHandler(miCopy_Click);
        Menu.MenuItems[1].MenuItems.Add(miCopy);

        miPaste = new MenuItem("&Paste");
        miPaste.Click += new EventHandler(miPaste_Click);
        Menu.MenuItems[1].MenuItems.Add(miPaste);

        // Create and place all of our controls
        inkCtl = new InkControl2();
        inkCtl.Location = new Point(8, 8);
```

*(continued)*

**InkClippy.cs** *(continued)*

```csharp
    inkCtl.Size = new Size(352, 216);

    // Configure the form itself
    ClientSize = new Size(368, 232);
    Controls.AddRange(new Control[] { inkCtl });
    FormBorderStyle = FormBorderStyle.FixedDialog;
    MaximizeBox = false;
    Text = "InkClippy";

    ResumeLayout(false);

    // We're now set to go, so turn on tablet input
    inkCtl.InkOverlay.Enabled = true;
}

// Handle the "Exit" menu item being clicked
private void miExit_Click(object sender, EventArgs e)
{
    Application.Exit();
}

// Handle the "Edit" submenu popping up
private void miEdit_Popup(object sender, EventArgs e)
{
    bool fSelectMode = (inkCtl.InkOverlay.EditingMode ==
        InkOverlayEditingMode.Select);

    // Enable or disable the various menu items
    miCut.Enabled = fSelectMode &&
        (inkCtl.InkOverlay.Selection.Count > 0);
    miCopy.Enabled = miCut.Enabled;
    miPaste.Enabled = fSelectMode &&
        inkCtl.InkOverlay.Ink.CanPaste();
}

// Handle the "Cut" menu item being clicked
private void miCut_Click(object sender, EventArgs e)
{
    if (inkCtl.InkOverlay.Selection.Count > 0)
    {
        // Cut the selected ink to the clipboard
        inkCtl.InkOverlay.Ink.ClipboardCopy(
            inkCtl.InkOverlay.Selection,
            InkClipboardFormats.CopyMask,
            InkClipboardModes.Cut);

        // Clear the selection
```

```
            inkCtl.InkOverlay.Selection =
                inkCtl.InkOverlay.Ink.CreateStrokes();

            // Update the display
            inkCtl.InkInputPanel.Invalidate();
        }
    }

    // Handle the "Copy" menu item being clicked
    private void miCopy_Click(object sender, EventArgs e)
    {
        if (inkCtl.InkOverlay.Selection.Count > 0)
        {
            // Copy the selected ink to the clipboard
            inkCtl.InkOverlay.Ink.ClipboardCopy(
                inkCtl.InkOverlay.Selection,
                InkClipboardFormats.CopyMask,
                InkClipboardModes.Copy);
        }
    }

    // Handle the "Paste" menu item being clicked
    private void miPaste_Click(object sender, EventArgs e)
    {
        if (inkCtl.InkOverlay.Ink.CanPaste())
        {
            Point ptOffset = new Point(0,0);

            // Do we need to replace any current selection?
            if (inkCtl.InkOverlay.Selection.Count > 0)
            {
                // Remember the offset of the selection so we can paste
                // the new data there
                ptOffset =
                    inkCtl.InkOverlay.Selection.GetBoundingBox().Location;

                // Delete the selection from the InkOverlay's Ink object
                inkCtl.InkOverlay.Ink.DeleteStrokes(
                    inkCtl.InkOverlay.Selection);

                // Clear the selection
                inkCtl.InkOverlay.Selection =
                    inkCtl.InkOverlay.Ink.CreateStrokes();
            }

            // Paste the data from the clipboard and select it
            inkCtl.InkOverlay.Selection =
```

*(continued)*

**InkClippy.cs** *(continued)*

```
            inkCtl.InkOverlay.Ink.ClipboardPaste(ptOffset);

        // Update the display
        inkCtl.InkInputPanel.Invalidate();
    }
}
}
```

The application allows cutting and copying if there is a current selection, and it allows pasting by deferring the decision to the value returned from *CanPaste*. The menu items' enabled state is updated in the *miEdit_Popup* event handler.

The cut operation uses the *ClipboardCopy* method to put the formats specified by *InkClipboardFormats.CopyMask* on the clipboard and results in the ink data being removed from the *Ink* object because of *InkClipboardModes.Cut* being used:

```
// Cut the selected ink to the clipboard
inkCtl.InkOverlay.Ink.ClipboardCopy(
    inkCtl.InkOverlay.Selection,
    InkClipboardFormats.CopyMask,
    InkClipboardModes.Cut);

// Clear the selection
inkCtl.InkOverlay.Selection =
    inkCtl.InkOverlay.Ink.CreateStrokes();
```

Once the ink data is on the clipboard, the selection is cleared because the ink strokes referenced by the selection don't exist anymore.

The copy operation is almost the same as cut except that *InkClipboard-Modes.Copy* is used and there is no need to clear the selection:

```
// Copy the selected ink to the clipboard
inkCtl.InkOverlay.Ink.ClipboardCopy(
    inkCtl.InkOverlay.Selection,
    InkClipboardFormats.CopyMask,
    InkClipboardModes.Copy);
```

Pasting is performed with the *ClipboardPaste* method, using a paste location computed to be the upper left of any current selection, or (0,0) otherwise:

```
// Paste the data from the clipboard and select it
inkCtl.InkOverlay.Selection =
    inkCtl.InkOverlay.Ink.ClipboardPaste(ptOffset);
```

If there is any existing selection, it is overwritten by the newly pasted data. This functionality isn't required, and you may not want to implement it in order to enable repeated pasting operations of the same data. Once the data has been pasted, it is also selected by utilizing the returned *Strokes* collection from the *ClipboardPaste* method.

## Implementing Drag and Drop

Drag and drop functionality is provided by the *InkOverlay* class in its select editing mode. However, it does not support dragging ink from one application to another—the user is only able to move ink around the inking area it was created in. The .NET Framework and Tablet PC Platform provide some great support for OLE drag and drop, which is the Windows standard way of drag and drop occurring between applications.

Recall that the *ClipboardCopy*, *CanPaste*, and *ClipboardPaste* methods provide variants to work only with data objects and not with the clipboard. It is this functionality that enables us to perform OLE drag and drop effectively and easily in an inking application.

### Sample Application—InkDragDrop

Let's take a look at a simple implementation of OLE drag and drop.

```
InkDragDrop.cs
///////////////////////////////////////////////////////////////////
//
// InkDragDrop.cs
//
// (c) 2002 Microsoft Press
// by Rob Jarrett
//
// This program demonstrates how to do OLE drag-drop using an Ink
// object as the source.
//
///////////////////////////////////////////////////////////////////

using System;
using System.Drawing;
using System.Windows.Forms;
using Microsoft.Ink;
using MSPress.BuildingTabletApps;

public class frmMain : Form
{
    // User interface
    private InkInputPanel            pnlInput;
    private CheckBox                 cbAllowDrag;
```

*(continued)*

**InkDragDrop.cs** *(continued)*

```
    private InkCollector              inkCollector;

    // Entry point of the program
    [STAThread]
    static void Main()
    {
        // Turn on OLE usage
        Application.OleRequired();

        // Start up using frmMain
        Application.Run(new frmMain());
    }

    // Main form setup
    public frmMain()
    {
        SuspendLayout();

        // Create and place all of our controls
        pnlInput = new InkInputPanel();
        pnlInput.BackColor = Color.White;
        pnlInput.BorderStyle = BorderStyle.Fixed3D;
        pnlInput.Location = new Point(8, 8);
        pnlInput.Size = new Size(352, 192);

        cbAllowDrag = new CheckBox();
        cbAllowDrag.Location = new Point(8, 204);
        cbAllowDrag.Size = new Size(96, 20);
        cbAllowDrag.Text = "Allow drag";
        cbAllowDrag.CheckedChanged +=
            new System.EventHandler(cbAllowDrag_CheckedChanged);

        // Configure the form itself
        ClientSize = new Size(368, 236);
        Controls.AddRange(new Control[] { pnlInput,
                                            cbAllowDrag});
        FormBorderStyle = FormBorderStyle.FixedDialog;
        MaximizeBox = false;
        Text = "InkDragDrop";

        ResumeLayout(false);

        // Hook up to mouse events so we can start drag-n-drop operation
        pnlInput.MouseDown += new MouseEventHandler(pnlInput_MouseDown);

        // Turn on drag-n-drop for the input area and hook up to events
        pnlInput.AllowDrop = true;
```

```
    pnlInput.DragEnter += new DragEventHandler(pnlInput_DragEnter);
    pnlInput.DragDrop += new DragEventHandler(pnlInput_DragDrop);

    // Create a new InkCollector, using pnlInput for the collection
    // area
    inkCollector = new InkCollector(pnlInput.Handle);

    // Update the UI with the settings
    cbAllowDrag.Checked = false;

    // We're now set to go, so turn on tablet input
    inkCollector.Enabled = true;
}

// Handle the click of the allow drag checkbox
private void cbAllowDrag_CheckedChanged(object sender, EventArgs e)
{
    // Enable/disable tablet input
    inkCollector.Enabled = !cbAllowDrag.Checked;
}

// Handle mouse down in the input panel
private void pnlInput_MouseDown(object sender, MouseEventArgs e)
{
    if (!inkCollector.Enabled)
    {
        // Start up drag-n-drop using a DataObject obtained from
        // the ClipboardCopy method
        pnlInput.DoDragDrop(
            inkCollector.Ink.ClipboardCopy(
                InkClipboardFormats.Default,
                InkClipboardModes.ExtractOnly),
            DragDropEffects.Copy);
    }
}

// Handle the drag enter of some data
private void pnlInput_DragEnter(object sender, DragEventArgs e)
{
    // Make sure the ink object supports the format
    if (inkCollector.Ink.CanPaste(e.Data))
    {
        // Additive only
        e.Effect = DragDropEffects.Copy;
    }
    else
```

*(continued)*

**InkDragDrop.cs** *(continued)*

```
        {
            // Format unsupported, reject the data
            e.Effect = DragDropEffects.None;
        }
    }

    // Handle the drag-drop event - data has been dropped!
    private void pnlInput_DragDrop(object sender, DragEventArgs e)
    {
        // Make sure the ink object supports the format
        if (inkCollector.Ink.CanPaste(e.Data))
        {
            // Convert the drop-point into ink coordinates
            Point pt = pnlInput.PointToClient(new Point(e.X, e.Y));
            Graphics g = pnlInput.CreateGraphics();
            inkCollector.Renderer.PixelToInkSpace(g, ref pt);
            g.Dispose();

            // Paste the data at the drop-point
            inkCollector.Ink.ClipboardPaste(pt, e.Data);
            e.Effect = DragDropEffects.Copy;

            // Update the ink area with the new ink
            pnlInput.Invalidate();
        }
        else
        {
            // Format unsupported, reject the data
            e.Effect = DragDropEffects.None;
        }
    }
}
```

The application provides a crude UI that enables the user to switch into drag mode, where any pen tap will start a drag and drop operation of all the ink in the inking area:

```
// Start up drag-n-drop using a DataObject obtained from
// the ClipboardCopy method
pnlInput.DoDragDrop(
    inkCollector.Ink.ClipboardCopy(
        InkClipboardFormats.Default,
        InkClipboardModes.ExtractOnly),
    DragDropEffects.Copy);
```

To facilitate dropping the ink in the same sample application, the *Allow-Drop* property of *pnlInput* is set to true, and its *DragEnter* and *DragDrop* events have handlers installed to deal with data being dragged over the input area.

The *DragEnter* handler checks whether the data object of the drag operation supports any ink data formats by using the *CanPaste* method:

```
// Make sure the ink object supports the format
if (inkCollector.Ink.CanPaste(e.Data))
{
    // Additive only
    e.Effect = DragDropEffects.Copy;
}
else
{
    // Format unsupported, reject the data
    e.Effect = DragDropEffects.None;
}
```

The *DragDrop* handler results in the data object being used in a call to *ClipboardPaste*:

```
// Paste the data at the drop-point
inkCollector.Ink.ClipboardPaste(pt, e.Data);
```

Once the data has been dropped, the inking area is invalidated to reflect the new ink.

# Summary

This chapter showed us a lot of functionality in the Tablet PC Platform. We learned about measuring ink strokes, retrieving and modifying the underlying point data of ink strokes, computing the various kinds of intersections, retrieving and using cusps, applying transformations, performing hit-testing, splitting and trimming ink strokes, and persisting ink data to memory or the clipboard. Wow, we've sure come a long way! I hope your head is spinning—in a good way—from all the cool ideas you're getting about your ink application!

We've now covered just about all there is to the ink data management functionality found in the Tablet PC Platform. I think the API is simple yet powerful—qualities that all developers want to find in a platform.

Next up, we'll be learning about the recognition of ink as both text and gestures—again, very cool stuff!

# 7

# Tablet PC Platform SDK: Ink Recognition

One of the most important design principles followed in developing software for the Tablet PC is to treat ink as a first-class data type. This means that whenever possible, ink should remain in a document as ink rather than be converted into another data type, such as a text string. However, the ability to translate electronic ink into a text string or a command can still be of great use to a tablet-enabled application. Interoperability with other applications, the repurposing of data into other forms such as an e-mail message or a schedule entry, and searching through notes are examples of the many tasks that benefit considerably from the conversion of electronic ink into a text string.

Gesture-based commands—ink strokes forming predefined shapes that trigger application behaviors—also streamline the usage model of ink-enabled applications. The process of ink recognition is therefore extremely important, and not in opposition to the ink as ink philosophy; in fact, it is complementary.

Until the Tablet PC Platform, the lack of accurate handwriting recognition had plagued most, if not all, pen-based computing systems. The Tablet PC boasts the most accurate handwriting recognition ever achieved in the industry, and it supports numerous languages, including English (both U.S. and U.K.), French, German, Chinese (both simplified and traditional), Japanese, and Korean. More are on the way, too—expect Spanish support to be released sometime in 2003.

This chapter discusses the various ways in which ink recognition can be performed and how the results can be interpreted. We'll start off by looking at the recognition architecture of the Tablet PC Platform and then discuss the different techniques by which ink recognition can be performed—from the simplest to the most complex. Methods and tips to improve the accuracy of the recognized results—maximizing the end-user experience—are included throughout the chapter.

# Recognizer Architecture

The Tablet PC Platform provides support for ink recognition using software libraries named *recognizers*—code that computes the textual or object representation of ink strokes for one or more languages. A *language* is any set of words or objects that is represented by writing. English, Chinese, German, and ink-based gestures are all considered languages. Each recognizer therefore includes a property denoting the languages for which it is capable of interpreting ink strokes.

Multiple recognizers can be installed and used in the system, with each recognizer residing in a DLL. It is perfectly valid for these DLLs to contain multiple recognizers. A recognizer supports one or more languages, although most often a recognizer will support only one language because the accuracy of results tends to decrease when recognizing multiple languages concurrently. More variability corresponds to a higher margin of error.

It is possible for you to write your own recognizer, but this is a somewhat specialized and usually rather difficult task. The Tablet PC Platform SDK documentation has more information on writing custom recognizers. This chapter covers the use of already existing recognizers.

With the ability for multiple recognizers to be installed in the system comes the *default recognizer*: this identifies the recognizer most suited to interpret ink given a specific *LCID* (locale identifier), usually obtained from the operating system's locale setting.

## Text vs. Object Recognition

Most recognizers available for the Tablet PC Platform perform ink recognition into text for languages. However, ink strokes can also be recognized as objects, representing things such as application commands, musical notes, Web site structure, and mathematical formulae. On the Tablet PC Platform, the most common type of object recognition is for *application gestures,* in which one or more ink strokes maps to a specific application command. This type of gesture contrasts to the system gestures we learned about in Chapter 4 in that application gestures are ink-based and trigger commands as a menu item or a toolbar button would. System gestures are not ink-based, and they typically translate into direct manipulation actions such as selection, moving, and resizing.

The Tablet PC Platform has great support for application gesture recognition built into the *InkCollector* and *InkOverlay* classes, as we'll soon see.

## Synchronous vs. Asynchronous Recognition

Performing ink recognition functionality is often a computationally intensive task. One of the main reasons high accuracy of results wasn't achievable until recently was because the computing power required to yield great recognition results just wasn't available on a wide scale. Even today, the amount of CPU power needed to recognize ink can be great enough to require the Tablet PC Platform to supply two usage models for performing recognition: synchronous and asynchronous.

*Synchronous recognition* occurs when the thread requesting recognition results blocks until computation is complete. *Asynchronous recognition* occurs when the thread requesting recognition results is allowed to continue immediately following the request and is later notified that computation is complete from an event.

---

### Reco Terminology

Synchronous and asynchronous recognition are more commonly referred to as *foreground recognition* and *background recognition*, respectively. "Recognition" is often shortened to "reco" (pronounced *reh-kôh*). For the most part, we'll be using the terms *foreground reco* and *background reco* throughout the rest of the chapter.

---

### Partial Recognition

Some recognizers possess a capability known as *partial recognition*, which refers to the occurrence of a recognition computation happening incrementally and on an alternative thread from the one working with the recognizer. Consider partial recognition a proactive approach a recognizer takes to the computation—it begins recognition as soon as any ink is given to it and incrementally adjusts the computation as ink is added or removed or recognition properties are changed. This way, when results are ultimately requested either synchronously or asynchronously, the recognition computation is already in progress or complete, resulting in much more timely results than if the computation were started at the time of the request.

### When to Use Foreground and Background Recognition

Foreground reco is more commonly used in ink-enabled applications since it is easier to code and generally meets the requirements most applications have for recognition. Because most recognizers that ship with the Tablet PC Platform support partial recognition, you can take steps that will result in little performance difference between foreground and background reco. This prompts the question, "Why use background reco if it's harder to code?"

Background reco is primarily useful for implementing timely application response to input—for example, if a user pastes a large number of strokes into his document, initiating synchronous recognition at that moment could block the application for many seconds, giving the appearance of a crash or a hang. Using asynchronous recognition yields recognition results without the computation getting in the user's way. Additionally, background recognition results are reported as soon as they're calculated; if your application makes use of the results (for example, the user interface shows the textual form of ink in tiny letters beneath the strokes) in a timely manner, the task becomes much easier to implement than if foreground reco were employed.

## Recognition Results

The results a recognizer returns comprise much more than just a text string. Information such as the recognizer's *confidence level* (the level of accuracy the software thinks it achieved in its computation), alternative results (in case the recognizer thinks more than one result applies), and association of strokes with the text in the string can all be extremely useful in the implementation of certain features. The most common use of recognition results, other than obtaining the recognized text string, is to provide the user with a UI capable of correcting any accuracy problems. This UI is referred to as a *correction UI*. The Tablet PC Platform exposes all the information required to build a correction UI while keeping the API simple and straightforward.

When ink is converted into words, the recognizer might be unsure of word breaking, otherwise known as the *segmentation* of ink, as well as the results for individual words. Consider this classic recognition example: a user writes the letters *t*, *o*, *g*, *e*, *t*, *h*, *e*, and *r*. They could mean one of many results, such as the word *together* or the phrases *to gather*, *tog ether*, or *to get her*. Each word in those segmentation alternates can itself have a number of alternate results. It is important to realize that recognition results encompass not only alternates for words but also alternates for their segmentation.

Many East Asian languages, such as Chinese, Japanese, and Korean, are based on the notion of a word being formed out of a set of discrete symbols or word segments. The possible combinations of all symbols or segments forming words are usually astronomical in size, so it is impractical to consider providing alternates for an entire word. It makes more sense to provide alternative results at the segment level. It is therefore not entirely correct to talk about a recognizer converting ink into words because recognizers actually convert ink into *segments*. For languages such as English and French, the boundary for segmentation happens to be the boundary between whole words.

Now that we've learned a little bit about the data a recognizer can return, let's jump into the Tablet PC Platform's support for using its great recognition functionality.

# Performing Simple Recognition

Some application features exploiting ink recognition need only simple results: searching a document for a text string, generating a default file name, and making application gestures such as Scratch-Out, for example. The results would become overly complex if we had to consider foreground or background reco, alternative segmentation, and the like. To solve this problem, the Tablet PC Platform provides some elegant support for obtaining recognition results in its basic form.

# Recognizing Text

The easiest way to perform recognition of ink into a text string is to use the *Strokes* class's *ToString* method. The stroke objects referenced in the collection are sent to the default recognizer, the recognition results are calculated, and the highest probability results obtained are then returned as a string. All this from one function—cool, huh?

### Sample Application—BasicReco

This first sample application demonstrates just how easy it is to obtain recognition results from a collection of ink strokes. An InkControl is used to collect and edit ink, and a menu item produces a message box containing the text string computed by the default recognizer. Figure 7-1 shows what the application looks like in action.

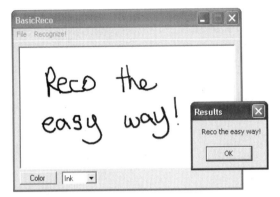

**Figure 7-1** The BasicReco sample application shows just how simple performing recognition can be.

## BasicReco.cs

```
/////////////////////////////////////////////////////////////////////
//
// BasicReco.cs
//
// (c) 2002 Microsoft Press
// by Rob Jarrett
//
// This program demonstrates the basic recognition capabilities of
// the Tablet PC Platform SDK.
//
/////////////////////////////////////////////////////////////////////

using System;
using System.Drawing;
using System.Windows.Forms;
using Microsoft.Ink;
using MSPress.BuildingTabletApps;

public class frmMain : Form
{
    private InkControl  inkCtl;

    // Entry point of the program
    [STAThread]
    static void Main()
    {
        // Check to see if any recognizers are installed by analyzing
        // the number of items in the Recognizers collection
        Recognizers recognizers = new Recognizers();
```

```
    if (recognizers.Count == 0)
    {
        MessageBox.Show("No recognizers are installed!",
            "Error", MessageBoxButtons.OK, MessageBoxIcon.Error);
    }
    else
    {
        Application.Run(new frmMain());
    }
}


// Main form setup
public frmMain()
{
    SuspendLayout();

    // Create the main menu
    Menu = new MainMenu();

    MenuItem miFile = new MenuItem("&File");
    Menu.MenuItems.Add(miFile);

    MenuItem miExit = new MenuItem("E&xit");
    miExit.Click += new EventHandler(miExit_Click);
    Menu.MenuItems[0].MenuItems.Add(miExit);

    MenuItem miReco = new MenuItem("&Recognize!");
    miReco.Click += new EventHandler(miReco_Click);
    Menu.MenuItems.Add(miReco);

    // Create and place all of our controls
    inkCtl = new InkControl();
    inkCtl.Location = new Point(8, 8);
    inkCtl.Size = new Size(352, 216);

    // Configure the form itself
    ClientSize = new Size(368, 232);
    Controls.AddRange(new Control[] { inkCtl });
    FormBorderStyle = FormBorderStyle.FixedDialog;
    MaximizeBox = false;
    Text = "BasicReco";

    ResumeLayout(false);

    // We're now set to go, so turn on tablet input
    inkCtl.InkOverlay.Enabled = true;
}
```

*(continued)*

**BasicReco.cs** *(continued)*

```
// Handle the "Exit" menu item being clicked
private void miExit_Click(object sender, EventArgs e)
{
    Application.Exit();
}

// Handle the Recognize! menu item being clicked
private void miReco_Click(object sender, EventArgs e)
{
    // Show the results via the Strokes.ToString method
    MessageBox.Show(this,
        inkCtl.InkOverlay.Ink.Strokes.ToString(), "Results");
}
}
```

The source listing contains almost nothing new, except for one line of code found in the *miReco_Click* event handler:

```
// Show the results via the Strokes.ToString method
MessageBox.Show(this,
    inkCtl.InkOverlay.Ink.Strokes.ToString(), "Results");
```

The *Strokes.ToString* method does a great job of providing the reco results with the highest confidence using the default recognizer. You should use *Strokes.ToString* with some restraint, however, because it implements recognition in an *end-to-end* fashion; that is to say, the method synchronously performs recognition from start to finish each time it is called. No results are cached, and no computation occurs in the background—therefore, be advised that the time taken for this call to execute can be considerable with even a few sentences of ink.

Another trade-off made when using the *Strokes.ToString* method is that no other information about the result besides the highest probability string can be obtained; alternates and confidence information get lost in the process. But if you don't need this information—maybe you're writing a forms-based application or want to include text on the clipboard or in drag-and-drop operations—using *Strokes.ToString* can mean that adding recognition to your application takes just one line of code!

# Recognizing Application Gestures

To recognize ink strokes as application gestures, we turn to the *InkCollector* and *InkOverlay* classes. Results of recognized application gestures are obtained through an event-based model rather than a synchronous query model like

*Strokes.ToString*. The reason for this is that application gestures represent commands, which are typically received from the keyboard, mouse, or user-interface elements such as menu and toolbar button clicks, all of which take the form of events.

## Specifying Application Gestures to Recognize

The *InkCollector* and *InkOverlay* classes provide application gesture recognition almost as simply as *Strokes.ToString* does. Recall from Chapter 4 that we can request the *Gesture* event to fire when an application gesture is recognized, optionally followed by a *Stroke* event (this depends on the value of the *Cancel* property of the *InkCollectorGestureEventArgs* object: if it is set to *true*, a *Stroke* event will fire; if it is *false*, the *Stroke* event will not fire). Setting the *InkCollector* or *InkOverlay* instance's *CollectionMode* property to either *Collection-Mode.InkAndGesture* or *CollectionMode.GestureOnly* activates the recognition of application gestures.

The *CollectionMode.GestureOnly* collection mode tells the *InkCollector* or *InkOverlay* to perform gesture recognition after a timeout has occurred from the last stroke drawn, allowing for multiple strokes to form one application gesture. The *Gesture* event will always be fired in this collection mode, regardless of the confidence level of the results.

The *CollectionMode.InkAndGesture* collection mode indicates a hybrid inking mode: the recognizer attempts to interpret every ink stroke as an application gesture. If a recognition result is computed, the *Gesture* event is fired. If no results are computed or if the *Gesture* event is cancelled by setting its *Ink-CollectorGestureEventArgs*'s *Cancel* property to *true*, the *Stroke* event is fired. This collection mode therefore yields a best-guess approach for ink strokes. When using this collection mode, the recognizable application gestures can comprise only a single stroke.

Once the collection mode has been set on the *InkCollector* or *InkOverlay*, the class's *SetGestureStatus* method is typically called to activate detection for the various application gestures requested. This is done to keep the set of recognized gestures as small as possible, thereby increasing accuracy results (the smaller the set of possibilities, the more likely the results will be correct). Values in the *ApplicationGesture* enumeration, listed in Tables 7-1, 7-2, and 7-3, identify the application gestures to be recognized.

Table 7-1 lists the application gestures for which there are recommended actions. These are operations for which an application gesture type has a well-defined behavior and hence should be considered a UI standard. Microsoft discourages deviating from this behavior if possible.

**Table 7-1   Listing of Application Gestures for Recommended Actions**

| Gesture Shape | ApplicationGesture Value | Action | Notes |
|---|---|---|---|
| | *ScratchOut* | Erase content | Must contain at least three horizontal back-and-forth movements. |
| | *Left* | Backspace | Horizontal line to the left. |
| | *Right* | Space | Horizontal line to the right. |
| | *UpRightLong* | Tab | Up and then right, two to four times as long as the up portion; should form a right angle. |
| | *DownLeftLong* | Enter | Down and then left, two to four times as long as the down portion; should form a right angle. |
| | *DownRightLong* | Space | Down and then right, two to four times as long as the down portion; should form a right angle. |
| | *UpDown* | Undo | Vertical line, up and then down, as straight and thin as possible |
| | *LeftRight* | Cut | Horizontal line, left and then right, as straight and thin as possible. |
| | *RightLeft* | Copy | Horizontal line, right and then left, as straight and thin as possible. |
| | *Curlicue* | Cut | Drawn at an angle from lower left to upper right, starting on the word to cut |
| | *DoubleCurlicue* | Copy | Drawn at an angle from the lower left to the upper right, starting on the word to copy. |
| | *DoubleCircle* | Paste | Two circles overlapping each other, drawn with one stroke. |

**Table 7-1    Listing of Application Gestures for Recommended Actions** *(continued)*

| Gesture Shape | ApplicationGesture Value | Action | Notes |
|---|---|---|---|
| ⌒ | *SemiCircleLeft* | Undo | Drawn from the right to the left, with the two ends of the arc lying on the same horizontal line. |
| ⌒ | *SemiCircleRight* | Redo | Drawn from the left to the right, with the two ends of the arc lying on the same horizontal line. |
| • | *Tap* | Left click | Must be short stroke with minimal area covered. |
| • | *DoubleTap* | Left double–click | Two taps as close to each other as possible. This multi-stroke gesture is not supported by *InkAndGesture* collection mode. |
| ⌐ | *RightUp* | Input Method Editor (IME) convert | Right and then up with same length as the right portion; should form a right angle. |

Table 7-2 contains the application gestures for which suggested actions should be taken. These are operations for which behavior is application-specific although predictable by the context in which they're used. In other words, the outcome is descriptively similar between applications, but the exact functionality is application-specific.

**Table 7-2    Listing of Application Gestures and Suggested Actions**

| Gesture shape | ApplicationGesture Value | Action | Notes |
|---|---|---|---|
| △ | *Triangle* | Insert | Must have the top pointing up |
| □ | *Square* | Action item | Must start at the upper left corner; can be drawn with one or two strokes |
| ☆ | *Star* | Action item | Must have exactly five points |

*(continued)*

**Table 7-2 Listing of Application Gestures and Suggested Actions** *(continued)*

| Gesture shape | ApplicationGesture Value | Action | Notes |
|---|---|---|---|
| ✓ | *Check* | Check a box or check off a list item | Must have the upward stroke two to four times as long as the smaller downward stroke |
| ∧ | *ChevronUp* | Paste, insert | Must have both sides be of equal length and have a sharp-angled point |
| ∨ | *ChevronDown* | Insert | Must have both sides be of equal length and have a sharp-angled point |

Table 7-3 lists the application gestures that are application-specific. These gestures can invoke commands that are specific to the application receiving them. There is no standard behavior associated with these gestures, and they can be used without restriction.

**Table 7-3 Listing of Application-Specific Application Gestures**

| Gesture shape | ApplicationGesture Value | Notes |
|---|---|---|
| ◯ | *Circle* | Must start and end at the topmost point. |
| < | *ChevronLeft* | Must have both sides be of equal length and have a sharp-angled point. |
| > | *ChevronRight* | Must have both sides be of equal length and have a sharp-angled point. |
| ↑ | *ArrowUp* | Must be drawn using either one or two strokes. For a single stroke, a full triangle-shaped head isn't supported, and for two strokes, one stroke must be the line and the other must be the arrowhead. |
| ↓ | *ArrowDown* | Must be drawn using either one or two strokes. For a single stroke, a full triangle-shaped head isn't supported, and for two strokes, one stroke must be the line and the other must be the arrowhead. |
| ← | *ArrowLeft* | Must be drawn using either one or two strokes. For a single stroke, a full triangle-shaped head isn't supported, and for two strokes, one stroke must be the line and the other must be the arrowhead. |

*(continued)*

**Table 7-3**  **Listing of Application-Specific Application Gestures**  *(continued)*

| Gesture shape | ApplicationGesture Value | Notes |
|---|---|---|
| → | *ArrowRight* | Must be drawn using either one or two strokes. For a single stroke, a full triangle-shaped head isn't supported, and for two strokes, one stroke must be the line and the other must be the arrowhead. |
| | *Up* | Vertical line upward. |
| | *Down* | Vertical line downward. |
| | *UpLeft* | Up and then left with same length as the up portion; should form a right angle. |
| | *UpRight* | Up and then right with same length as the up portion; should form a right angle. |
| | *DownLeft* | Down and then left with same length as the down portion; should form a right angle. |
| | *DownRight* | Down and then right with same length as the down portion; should form a right angle. |
| | *LeftUp* | Left and then up with same length as the left portion; should form a right angle. |
| | *LeftDown* | Left and then down with same length as the left portion; should form a right angle. |
| | *RightDown* | Right and then down with same length as the right portion; should form a right angle. |
| | *DownUp* | Vertical line, down and then up, as straight and thin as possible. |
| | *Exclamation* | Draw the dot soon after drawing the line and place it close to the line. This multistroke gesture is not supported by InkAndGesture collection mode. |

In addition to the entries listed in the preceding tables, two other values in the *ApplicationGesture* enumeration are worth mentioning here: *ApplicationGesture.AllGestures* and *ApplicationGesture.NoGesture*. *ApplicationGesture.AllGestures* is used with the *SetGestureStatus* method as a convenient shortcut to turn recognition for all application gestures on or off. *ApplicationGesture.NoGesture* is passed to the *Gesture* event when the application gesture recognizer believes there is no good result for the strokes the user entered.

## Receiving Application Gesture Events

The *Gesture* event's *InkCollectorGestureEventArgs* parameter provides a list of the application gestures that were detected by the gesture recognizer, along with their confidence and hot point. The confidence amount is specified with the *RecognitionConfidence* enumeration, whose values are listed in Table 7-4. The *hot point* of the gesture is the point in ink coordinates that the user targeted while drawing the gesture. The type of application gesture defines where the specific hot point is located in relation to the gesture shape.

**Table 7-4**  The *RecognitionConfidence* Enumeration

| Value | Description |
| --- | --- |
| *Strong* | Computed results are likely to be correct |
| *Intermediate* | Likelihood of correct results is fair |
| *Poor* | Computed results could likely be incorrect |

## Sample Application—GesturePad

This next sample application shows how gesture recognition is achieved using *InkCollector*'s *Gesture* event. The sample implements a crude interface to edit text in a TextBox—Cut, Copy, Paste, Delete, cursor navigation, Tab, Backspace, and Return.

**GesturePad.cs**

```
/////////////////////////////////////////////////////////////////////
//
// GesturePad.cs
//
// (c) 2002 Microsoft Press
// by Rob Jarrett
//
// This program demonstrates how to handle gesture events from the
// InkCollector class to implement gesture-based editing
// functionality.
//
/////////////////////////////////////////////////////////////////////

using System;
using System.Drawing;
using System.Windows.Forms;
using Microsoft.Ink;
```

```
public class frmMain : Form
{
    private TextBox        txtPad;
    private Panel          pnlInput;
    private Button         btnClose;
    private InkCollector   inkCollector;

    // Entry point of the program
    [STAThread]
    static void Main()
    {
        Application.Run(new frmMain());
    }

    // Main form setup
    public frmMain()
    {
        SuspendLayout();

        // Create and place all of our controls
        txtPad = new TextBox();
        txtPad.AcceptsReturn = true;
        txtPad.AcceptsTab = true;
        txtPad.Location = new System.Drawing.Point(8, 8);
        txtPad.Multiline = true;
        txtPad.ScrollBars = ScrollBars.Both;
        txtPad.Size = new System.Drawing.Size(280, 168);

        pnlInput = new Panel();
        pnlInput.BackColor = Color.White;
        pnlInput.BorderStyle = BorderStyle.Fixed3D;
        pnlInput.Location = new System.Drawing.Point(96, 184);
        pnlInput.Size = new System.Drawing.Size(104, 72);

        btnClose = new Button();
        btnClose.Location = new System.Drawing.Point(208, 232);
        btnClose.Text = "Close";
        btnClose.Click += new System.EventHandler(btnClose_Click);

        ClientSize = new System.Drawing.Size(296, 266);
        Controls.AddRange(new Control[] { btnClose,
                                          pnlInput,
                                          txtPad});
        FormBorderStyle = FormBorderStyle.FixedDialog;
        MaximizeBox = false;
        Text = "GesturePad";
```

*(continued)*

**GesturePad.cs** *(continued)*

```
        ResumeLayout(false);

        // Create an InkCollector object and put it in ink-and-gesture
        // collection mode
        inkCollector = new InkCollector(pnlInput.Handle);
        inkCollector.CollectionMode = CollectionMode.InkAndGesture;

        // Let the ink collector know which gestures we'd like
        // to have recognized
        inkCollector.SetGestureStatus(
            ApplicationGesture.Scratchout, true);
        inkCollector.SetGestureStatus(
            ApplicationGesture.Left, true);
        inkCollector.SetGestureStatus(
            ApplicationGesture.Right, true);
        inkCollector.SetGestureStatus(
            ApplicationGesture.UpRightLong, true);
        inkCollector.SetGestureStatus(
            ApplicationGesture.DownLeftLong, true);
        inkCollector.SetGestureStatus(
            ApplicationGesture.DownRightLong, true);
        inkCollector.SetGestureStatus(
            ApplicationGesture.LeftRight, true);
        inkCollector.SetGestureStatus(
            ApplicationGesture.RightLeft, true);
        inkCollector.SetGestureStatus(
            ApplicationGesture.ChevronDown, true);
        inkCollector.SetGestureStatus(
            ApplicationGesture.ArrowUp, true);
        inkCollector.SetGestureStatus(
            ApplicationGesture.ArrowDown, true);
        inkCollector.SetGestureStatus(
            ApplicationGesture.ArrowLeft, true);
        inkCollector.SetGestureStatus(
            ApplicationGesture.ArrowRight, true);

        // Hook up the gesture and stroke event handlers to inkCollector
        inkCollector.Gesture +=
            new InkCollectorGestureEventHandler(inkCollector_Gesture);
        inkCollector.Stroke +=
            new InkCollectorStrokeEventHandler(inkCollector_Stroke);

        // We're now set to go, so turn on gesture collection
        inkCollector.Enabled = true;
    }
```

```csharp
// InkCollector gesture event handler
private void inkCollector_Gesture(object sender,
    InkCollectorGestureEventArgs e)
{
    // If we're pretty sure about the gesture, perform the
    // operation — otherwise do nothing (to avoid doing
    // something wrong and frustrating the user!)
    if ((e.Gestures[0].Confidence ==
        RecognitionConfidence.Strong) ||
        (e.Gestures[0].Confidence ==
        RecognitionConfidence.Intermediate))
    {
        switch (e.Gestures[0].Id)
        {
            case ApplicationGesture.Scratchout:
                // Erase
                txtPad.Focus();
                SendKeys.Send("{DELETE}");
                break;

            case ApplicationGesture.Left:
                // Backspace
                txtPad.Focus();
                SendKeys.Send("{BACKSPACE}");
                break;

            case ApplicationGesture.Right:
            case ApplicationGesture.DownRightLong:
                // Space
                txtPad.Focus();
                SendKeys.Send(" ");
                break;

            case ApplicationGesture.UpRightLong:
                // Tab
                txtPad.Focus();
                SendKeys.Send("{TAB}");
                break;

            case ApplicationGesture.DownLeftLong:
                // Enter
                txtPad.Focus();
                SendKeys.Send("{ENTER}");
                break;
```

*(continued)*

**GesturePad.cs** *(continued)*

```csharp
                case ApplicationGesture.LeftRight:
                    // Cut
                    txtPad.Cut();
                    break;

                case ApplicationGesture.RightLeft:
                    // Copy
                    txtPad.Copy();
                    break;

                case ApplicationGesture.ChevronDown:
                    // Paste
                    txtPad.Paste();
                    break;

                case ApplicationGesture.ArrowUp:
                    // Cursor up
                    txtPad.Focus();
                    SendKeys.Send("{UP}");
                    break;

                case ApplicationGesture.ArrowDown:
                    // Cursor down
                    txtPad.Focus();
                    SendKeys.Send("{DOWN}");
                    break;

                case ApplicationGesture.ArrowLeft:
                    // Cursor left
                    txtPad.Focus();
                    SendKeys.Send("{LEFT}");
                    break;

                case ApplicationGesture.ArrowRight:
                    // Cursor right
                    txtPad.Focus();
                    SendKeys.Send("{RIGHT}");
                    break;

                default:
                    // We don't do anything otherwise
                    break;
            }
        }
```

```
        // Make sure the stroke gets deleted
        e.Cancel = false;
        pnlInput.Invalidate();
    }

    // InkCollector stroke event handler
    private void inkCollector_Stroke(object sender,
        InkCollectorStrokeEventArgs e)
    {
        // We never want to keep a stroke - this effectively means that
        // no gesture was recognized so we'll no-op.
        e.Cancel = true;
        pnlInput.Invalidate();
    }

    // Button close clicked handler
    private void btnClose_Click(object sender, System.EventArgs e)
    {
        Application.Exit();
    }
}
```

After creating an *InkCollector* instance, the application sets its collection mode to enable gesture recognition and then repeatedly calls the *SetGestureStatus* method to specify which gestures it's interested in. The *CollectionMode.InkAndGesture* mode is used because of the immediate response resulting from gesture recognition. The *CollectionMode.GestureOnly* mode requires a timeout to elapse once a gesture is drawn that cannot be altered, resulting in a rather painful waiting period while the user performs repeated operations such as cursor navigation. By using the ink-and-gesture mode, we get timely *Gesture* event firing, although we give up multistroke application gesture recognition; fortunately, however, most application gestures are formed by only a single stroke.

The *Gesture* event handler receives the computed results in the *InkCollectorGestureEventArgs* object, whose *Gestures* property is an array containing the computed results ordered by highest to lowest confidence. Because our application performs editing operations, only strong and intermediate confidence gestures are processed to avoid performing an unexpected action on the user's behalf:

```
// If we're pretty sure about the gesture, perform the
// operation - otherwise do nothing (to avoid doing
// something wrong and frustrating the user!)
if ((e.Gestures[0].Confidence ==
    RecognitionConfidence.Strong) ||
```

*(continued)*

```
    (e.Gestures[0].Confidence ==
    RecognitionConfidence.Intermediate))
{

    ....
```

It is entirely possible to have the *Gesture* event fired with *ApplicationGesture.NoGesture* and a confidence level of *RecognitionConfidence.Strong*. This occurs when the application gesture recognizer is certain that the strokes do not look like any active application gesture, and the collection mode is *CollectionMode.GestureOnly*.

A *Stroke* event handler is provided because of the ink-and-gesture collection mode the application uses. This event gets fired when no gesture is recognized and also when the *Gesture* event sets the *Cancel* property of the *InkCollectorGestureEventArgs* to *true*. To avoid having an ink stroke added to the *InkCollector*'s *Ink* object, the application's *Stroke* event sets the *Cancel* property of the *InkCollectorStrokeEventArgs* to *true*.

---

## Erasing Ink with the Scratch-Out Gesture

The Windows Journal, Tablet PC Input Panel, and Sticky Notes applications all support erasing ink with the *ApplicationGesture.Scratchout* gesture, akin to scribbling out the ink as one would on physical paper. Implementing this functionality is rather straightforward, although it is worthwhile pointing out a couple of issues.

The general algorithm for performing Scratch-Out erasing is as follows: for an application gesture of type *ApplicationGesture.Scratchout* with intermediate or greater confidence level, hit-test using the bounding box of the Scratch-Out stroke with a 60 percent tolerance. If no strokes other than the Scratch-Out are hit, keep the Scratch-Out stroke by setting the *InkCollectorGestureEventArgs*'s *Cancel* property to true. If one or more strokes other than the Scratch-Out are hit, delete them—including the Scratch-Out—from the document. Remember to take into account the granularity of selectable objects when hit-testing and deleting if it's appropriate for your application.

If your application supports undo, a Scratch-Out operation resulting in deletion should create two undo units: the first is the deletion of the hit object or objects including the Scratch-Out stroke, and the second is the addition of the Scratch-Out stroke to the document. Adding the second undo unit reduces user frustration if a stroke results in unintended Scratch-Out erasing.

# Using the Recognition Classes

While certainly convenient, the *Strokes* class's *ToString* method does have some shortcomings. Perhaps the most obvious is that the recognizer used to perform recognition cannot be specified; this means that only the default language of the system can be recognized. Another problem with the *ToString* recognition method is that no alternative results are provided in the event that the recognizer wasn't right the first time—nor is any other information provided, such as confidence level, stroke baseline, or associated strokes, for that matter. And lastly, the entire recognition computation is performed synchronously during the *ToString* method call, which can take up to several seconds depending on the amount of ink being recognized.

The Tablet PC Platform provides a set of recognition classes specifically designed for these issues while maintaining a simple design indicative of the rest of the Tablet PC Platform. The usage model for performing recognition with these classes is quite simple:

- Obtain a recognizer to use

- Initiate a recognition session with the recognizer

- Provide the strokes to recognize to the recognizer

- Collect the computed results

Let's take a closer look at each of these steps.

## Obtaining a Recognizer to Use

The first step in performing ink recognition is to obtain a reference to an instance of the *Recognizer* class. A *Recognizer* instance is the embodiment of a recognizer installed in the system; it therefore has properties reflecting the languages supported, its specific recognition capabilities, and name and vendor identification.

The *Recognizers* class encapsulates a collection of *Recognizer* objects, and the contents of the collection reflect the recognizers that are currently installed in the system. In this manner, the *Recognizers* collection is analogous to the *Tablets* collection we learned about in Chapter 4. An instance of the *Recognizers* class is obtained using the *new* operator and is enumerable with standard C# means; the only non-collection-related method on the class is *GetDefaultRecognizer*, which returns the default recognizer.

A recognizer's specific capabilities are obtained through a *Recognizer* instance's *Capabilities* property, a bitflag collection whose values are found in the *RecognizerCapbilities* enumeration, described in Table 7-5.

**Table 7-5**  **The *RecognizerCapabilities* Enumeration**

| *RecognizerCapabilities* enum Value | Description |
| --- | --- |
| *ArbitraryAngle* | The recognizer supports text written at any angle. |
| *BoxedInput* | The recognizer supports boxed input, meaning characters are entered in a box. |
| *CharacterAutoCompletionInput* | The recognizer supports character auto-complete. |
| *DownAndLeft* | The recognizer supports text flow as in Asian languages. |
| *DownAndRight* | The recognizer supports text flow as in the Chinese language. |
| *FreeInput* | The recognizer supports free input, meaning no guide is needed. |
| *Lattice* | The recognizer can return a lattice object, which is not used in the managed API. |
| *LeftAndDown* | The recognizer supports text flow as in Hebrew and Arabic languages. |
| *LinedInput* | The recognizer supports lined input, meaning text is written as it is on lined paper. |
| *Object* | Objects rather than text are recognized. |
| *RightAndDown* | The recognizer supports text flow as in Western and Asian languages. |

## Initiating a Recognition Session

Once a *Recognizer* instance has been obtained, a *recognizer context* (also referred to as a *reco context*) must be created to perform the recognition operation. This object represents a session of recognizer functionality; associated with it are the ink strokes to recognize, parameters such as the recognition mode, preferred words, content hints, and any recognition results as they are computed. Calling a *Recognizer*'s *CreateRecognizerContext* method creates a *RecognizerContext* object.

## The Recognition Mode

The reco context's *RecognitionFlags* property is used to control the *recognition mode*. This term refers to how the recognizer will treat the ink and compute the recognition results. The *RecognitionFlags* property is of the *RecognitionModes* enumeration type, the values for which are listed in Table 7-6.

**Table 7-6   The *RecognitionModes* Enumeration**

| Value | Description |
| --- | --- |
| *Coerce* | The recognizer will force the result to match the reco context's factoid. |
| *None* | No recognition mode (default). |
| *TopInkBreaksOnly* | Multiple segmentation results will not be returned—only the segmentation with highest confidence is computed. |
| *WordMode* | The recognizer will treat all the ink as a single word. |

The description for the *RecognitionModes.Coerce* flag in Table 7-6 refers to a factoid. Briefly, a *factoid* is a property on a reco context that describes the content of the strokes being recognized, thereby increasing accuracy. (For example, an e-mail address and a phone number are considered factoids.) If *RecognitionModes.Coerce* is not specified, the result returned might not match the factoid if the recognizer has a high enough confidence level—for example, if the factoid is an e-mail address but the recognizer is sure the ink is a phone number, it will return a phone number. Specifying the *Recognition-Modes.Coerce* flag ensures the results returned will match the factoid.

The *RecognitionModes.TopInkBreaksOnly* flag relates to the *together* segmentation issue covered earlier. Without this flag, the recognizer can compute different segmentations for the ink, so *together*, *to get her*, and *to gather* might be returned along with variations of each word, such as *colatter*, *to got hir*, and *to gopher*. Using *RecognitionModes.TopInkBreaksOnly* ensures that the recognizer will compute and return only one kind of segmentation. This helps performance and can simplify the user interface required for correcting the results.

*RecognitionModes.WordMode* tells the recognizer to treat all the ink it will recognize as a single word. This treatment improves accuracy when a user is required to enter only a single word of ink or when the application employs a Little Ink model. Recall the Big Ink vs. Little Ink discussion from Chapter 5, in which individual words being grouped into separate *Ink* objects is known as Little Ink, and all ink residing in one *Ink* object is known as Big Ink.

## Prefix and Suffix Strings

The recognizer context properties *Prefix* and *Suffix* are used to specify the text preceding and following the content to recognize. They can be useful when building Tablet PC Input Panel–style functionality because results adjacent to the word to recognize can be provided to the recognizer, and they are also useful in conjunction with the *RecognitionModes.WordMode* mode in providing proper context to the recognizer.

## The Character Auto-Complete Mode

The character auto-complete mode (sometimes referred to as the *CAC mode*) is useful in conjunction with Tablet PC Input Panel–style functionality for languages containing words that are made up of multiple segments, such as Chinese, Japanese, and Korean. As the user writes segments of a word, the recognizer will compute best-match whole word results rather than results for only the segments that have been entered up to that point. This allows for the provision of a user interface from which the user can choose from a list of completed possibilities, streamlining the text input process.

The *RecognizerContext* class's property *CharacterAutoCompletion* specifies the character auto-complete mode that the recognizer should use. Its type is of the *RecognizerCharacterAutoCompletionMode* enumeration; Table 7-7 lists the available modes.

**Table 7-7   The *RecognizerCharacterAutoCompletionMode* Enumeration**

| Value | Description |
|---|---|
| *Full* | Recognition occurs as if all strokes have been input (default). |
| *Prefix* | Recognition occurs for partial word with strokes input in a known order. |
| *Random* | Recognition occurs for partial word with strokes input in random order. |

The *Full* mode indicates that the recognizer won't perform character auto-completion. The *Prefix* mode indicates to the recognizer that auto-complete results should be computed by assuming the strokes were input in an order consistent with the correct way of writing the language. The *Random* value indicates that the order in which the strokes were input is random, and it happens to be the most computationally intensive. When using the character auto-complete functionality of a recognizer, it is recommended that a two-pass approach be implemented—the first pass displays results to the user from the *Prefix* mode because it is quicker, and the second pass displays more results with the *Random* mode because it is more accurate.

> **Note**   Using CAC functionality requires a recognizer guide be set on the reco context. We'll learn about recognizer guides later in the chapter, but for now they can be considered a hint to the recognizer about the layout of the strokes.

## Supplying Strokes to the Recognizer

Now that a recognizer context object has been created and configured, it is ready to begin recognizing ink data. The reco context needs to know what ink it should perform recognition on, which you indicate by setting its *Strokes* property.

Earlier we talked about *partial recognition*—the ability of the recognizer to incrementally perform recognition as ink is added to or removed from the context's *Strokes* collection. Partial recognition can reduce computation overhead significantly because the entire reco operation does not need to start over from the beginning when the user draws a new stroke or deletes one. If a completely new *Strokes* collection is assigned to the reco context's *Strokes* property, however, the recognition state is reset; this results in the entire recognition operation restarting.

If a recognizer does not support partial recognition, a special method must be called before trying to obtain any recognition results from the reco context. The *EndInkInput* method tells the recognizer that no more strokes will be added to or removed from the reco context, declaring it safe to perform the recognition operation. No result will be returned if *EndInkInput* is not called when using a recognizer that doesn't support partial recognition and an attempt is made to obtain recognition results.

Now let's restate the concepts of the past couple of paragraphs to make sure they're clear: if a recognizer supports partial recognition, when a reco context's *Strokes* collection is modified with *Strokes.Add* and/or *Strokes.Remove,* the reco results are incrementally computed. These results can be obtained at any time; there is no need to call *EndInkInput.* However, if a recognizer does not support partial recognition, once the reco context has been given the ink to recognize, the *EndInkInput* method must be called before reco results can be obtained. Subsequent modification of the *Strokes* collection with *Strokes.Add* and/or *Strokes.Remove* will result in a run-time error when recognition is attempted; the collection must be reassigned to an entirely new instance for new results to be obtained.

So if a recognizer supports partial recognition, is there ever a need to call *EndInkInput?* Yes, because querying for recognition results before calling

*EndInkInput* does not guarantee the recognizer will provide the most accurate results or the greatest number of them. The advantage in not calling *EndInkInput* is that much less computation takes place over the reco context's lifetime because the computation is all incremental. Once *EndInkInput* is called, the reco context's *Strokes* collection must be reassigned to a new collection for more recognition to occur; this results in the entire reco operation starting over.

Unfortunately, there is no easy way to query a recognizer to see whether it supports partial recognition. However, we'll discuss a manner in which partial recognition can be computed later in the chapter.

# Getting Results I: Easy Synchronous Recognition

Once a *RecognizerContext* object has been created and set up with the ink data to recognize, we request that the recognition operation be performed and then we obtain the results. We've discussed that the results of the recognition operation can be requested either synchronously or asynchronously; let's first take a look at the synchronous case.

The *Recognize* method of the *RecognizerContext* class is used to obtain recognition results synchronously. The method returns a *RecognitionResult* object, which is an encapsulation of the result data and includes alternates, confidence, and stroke association. The *out* parameter is the *RecognitionStatus* value, which is effectively a success code indicating any problems that the application might have encountered during the recognition operation.

> **Note**   Another term for an alternative result computation is *recognition alternate*, or just *alternate*.

## Sample Application—IntermediateReco

This sample application performs identically to the BasicReco application presented earlier in the chapter, but it's implemented using the recognition classes. The user enters some ink and chooses an application menu item to trigger recognition; a message box containing the recognition results is then displayed. The application uses the default recognizer for the recognition, and the recognition operation is performed all at once and in a synchronous fashion—exactly like the *Strokes.ToString* method.

## IntermediateReco.cs

```
///////////////////////////////////////////////////////////////////
//
// IntermediateReco.cs
//
// (c) 2002 Microsoft Press
// by Rob Jarrett
//
// This program shows how to perform recognition using the
// recognizer classes in a one-shot synchronous fashion.
//
///////////////////////////////////////////////////////////////////

using System;
using System.Drawing;
using System.Windows.Forms;
using Microsoft.Ink;
using MSPress.BuildingTabletApps;

public class frmMain : Form
{
    private InkControl2        inkCtl;
    private static Recognizers  recognizers = new Recognizers();

    // Entry point of the program
    [STAThread]
    static void Main()
    {
        // Check to see if any recognizers are installed by analyzing
        // the number of items in the Recognizers collection
        if (frmMain.recognizers.Count > 0)
        {
            Application.Run(new frmMain());
        }
        else
        {
            // None are, so display error message and exit
            MessageBox.Show("No recognizers are installed!",
                "Error", MessageBoxButtons.OK, MessageBoxIcon.Error);
        }
    }

    // Main form setup
    public frmMain()
    {
        SuspendLayout();
```

*(continued)*

**IntermediateReco.cs** *(continued)*

```
        // Create the main menu
        Menu = new MainMenu();

        MenuItem miFile = new MenuItem("&File");
        Menu.MenuItems.Add(miFile);

        MenuItem miExit = new MenuItem("E&xit");
        miExit.Click += new EventHandler(miExit_Click);
        Menu.MenuItems[0].MenuItems.Add(miExit);

        MenuItem miRecognize = new MenuItem("&Recognize!");
        miRecognize.Click += new EventHandler(miRecognize_Click);
        Menu.MenuItems.Add(miRecognize);

        // Create and place all of our controls
        inkCtl = new InkControl2();
        inkCtl.Location = new Point(8, 8);
        inkCtl.Size = new Size(352, 216);

        // Configure the form itself
        ClientSize = new Size(368, 232);
        Controls.AddRange(new Control[] { inkCtl });
        FormBorderStyle = FormBorderStyle.FixedDialog;
        MaximizeBox = false;
        Text = "IntermediateReco";

        ResumeLayout(false);

        // We're now set to go, so turn on tablet input
        inkCtl.InkOverlay.Enabled = true;
    }

    // Handle "Exit" menu item
    private void miExit_Click(object sender, EventArgs e)
    {
        Application.Exit();
    }

    // Handle Recognize! menu item
    private void miRecognize_Click(object sender, EventArgs e)
    {
        // Obtain the default recognizer
        Recognizer recognizer =
            frmMain.recognizers.GetDefaultRecognizer();
```

```
// Create a reco context, and add ink to it
RecognizerContext recoCtxt =
    recognizer.CreateRecognizerContext();
recoCtxt.Strokes = inkCtl.InkOverlay.Ink.Strokes;
recoCtxt.EndInkInput();

// Perform the recognition on the strokes
RecognitionStatus recoStatus;
RecognitionResult recoResult =
    recoCtxt.Recognize(out recoStatus);
if (recoStatus == RecognitionStatus.NoError)
{
    // Show the results
    MessageBox.Show(this, recoResult.TopString, "Results");
}
else
{
    // Problem; display error message
    MessageBox.Show(this, recoStatus.ToString(), "Error");
}
}
}
```

The application begins by checking whether any recognizers are installed in the system—we do this simply by checking the number of recognizer objects found in the *Recognizers* collection. If there are none, which is likely the case when running the sample on non–Windows XP Tablet PC Edition operating systems (discussed in Chapter 3), the application exits. If at least one recognizer is installed, the application creates a form with an InkControl along with a menu containing the Recognize! item, just as in the BasicReco sample.

What's different between this sample and the BasicReco application is the handler for the Recognize! menu item:

```
// Obtain the default recognizer
Recognizer recognizer =
    frmMain.recognizers.GetDefaultRecognizer();

// Create a reco context, and add ink to it
RecognizerContext recoCtxt =
    recognizer.CreateRecognizerContext();
recoCtxt.Strokes = inkCtl.InkOverlay.Ink.Strokes;
recoCtxt.EndInkInput();

// Perform the recognition on the strokes
RecognitionStatus recoStatus;
```

*(continued)*

```
RecognitionResult recoResult =
    recoCtxt.Recognize(out recoStatus);
if (recoStatus == RecognitionStatus.NoError)
{
    ...
```

Here, the default recognizer is obtained and a recognizer context is created. The reco context is told what ink it should perform recognition on by setting its *Strokes* property to reference all strokes in the InkControl's *Ink* object. Next the *EndInkInput* method is called on the reco context to signify that no more ink will be added to the *Strokes* collection. This makes it safe for the next step, calling the *Recognize* method on the reco context. If the recognition status indicates the method completed successfully, the returned *RecognitionResult* object's highest confidence result is displayed from the *TopString* property.

# Getting Results II: Electric Boogaloo (a.k.a. Harder Synchronous Recognition)

Performing recognition all at once is inefficient for most applications. Users will be frustrated if they invoke a command that triggers recognition and they're forced to wait for multiple seconds while the results are obtained synchronously. This problem can be overcome if the recognizer supports partial recognition and we keep the reco context in the loop regarding ink getting added to or removed from the document.

By keeping the reco context up-to-date on the strokes it will recognize, we gain the advantage of the recognizer incrementally performing the recognition operation. Thus, once results are finally requested, the computation operation is that much nearer to completion than it would be when starting from scratch. To let the reco context know whenever ink is added or removed, its *Strokes* collection should be modified accordingly. The Ink class's *InkAdded* and *InkDeleted* events are great for this purpose.

## Sample Application—AdvancedReco

This sample application shows how a recognizer context can be retained throughout the life of an ink document, keeping it up-to-date with the ink strokes in the document. In addition, instead of using only the default recognizer for recognition, the application fills the main menu with all installed recognizers. Users can then choose what recognizer they want to use when a recognition operation is performed.

The application creates the recognition context when a recognizer is chosen, and ink is added to or removed from the reco context's *Strokes* collection as it is added to and removed from the InkControl's *Ink* object. As you'll see, this greatly helps performance: by keeping the reco context up-to-date with the state of the ink, recognition occurs in the background while the user adds or deletes strokes, or pauses for some reason.

**AdvancedReco.cs**

```
/////////////////////////////////////////////////////////////////////
//
// AdvancedReco.cs
//
// (c) 2002 Microsoft Press
// by Rob Jarrett
//
// This program shows how to enumerate and use the installed
// recognizers in a synchronous manner.
//
/////////////////////////////////////////////////////////////////////

using System;
using System.Collections;
using System.Drawing;
using System.Windows.Forms;
using Microsoft.Ink;
using MSPress.BuildingTabletApps;

public class frmMain : Form
{
    private ArrayList            arrRecoMenu;
    private InkControl2          inkCtl;
    private RecognizerContext    recoCtxt;
    private StrokesEventHandler  evtInkAdded;
    private StrokesEventHandler  evtInkDeleted;
    private static Recognizers   recognizers = new Recognizers();

    // Entry point of the program
    [STAThread]
    static void Main()
    {
        // Check to see if any recognizers are installed by analyzing
        // the number of items in the Recognizers collection
        if (frmMain.recognizers.Count > 0)
        {
            Application.Run(new frmMain());
        }
```

*(continued)*

**AdvancedReco.cs** *(continued)*

```csharp
        else
        {
            // None are, so display error message and exit
            MessageBox.Show("No recognizers are installed!",
                "Error", MessageBoxButtons.OK, MessageBoxIcon.Error);
        }
    }
}

// Main form setup
public frmMain()
{
    SuspendLayout();

    // Create the main menu
    Menu = new MainMenu();

    MenuItem miFile = new MenuItem("&File");
    Menu.MenuItems.Add(miFile);

    MenuItem miExit = new MenuItem("E&xit");
    miExit.Click += new EventHandler(miExit_Click);
    Menu.MenuItems[0].MenuItems.Add(miExit);

    MenuItem miRecognizers = new MenuItem("&Recognizers");
    Menu.MenuItems.Add(miRecognizers);

    // Create a menu full of the installed recognizers
    arrRecoMenu = new ArrayList();
    foreach (Recognizer recognizer in frmMain.recognizers)
    {
        MenuItem miRecoInst = new MenuItem(recognizer.Name);
        miRecoInst.Click += new EventHandler(miRecoInst_Click);
        miRecoInst.RadioCheck = true;
        Menu.MenuItems[1].MenuItems.Add(miRecoInst);
        arrRecoMenu.Add(miRecoInst);
    }

    MenuItem miSeparator = new MenuItem("-");
    Menu.MenuItems[1].MenuItems.Add(miSeparator);

    MenuItem miRecognize = new MenuItem("Recognize!");
    miRecognize.Click += new EventHandler(miRecognize_Click);
    Menu.MenuItems[1].MenuItems.Add(miRecognize);
```

```
    // Create and place all of our controls
    inkCtl = new InkControl2();
    inkCtl.Location = new Point(8, 8);
    inkCtl.Size = new Size(352, 216);

    // Configure the form itself
    ClientSize = new Size(368, 232);
    Controls.AddRange(new Control[] { inkCtl });
    FormBorderStyle = FormBorderStyle.FixedDialog;
    MaximizeBox = false;
    Text = "AdvancedReco";

    ResumeLayout(false);

    // Start off using the default recognizer
    SwitchToRecognizer(frmMain.recognizers.GetDefaultRecognizer());

    // Get notification of ink being added and deleted so we'll know
    // when to add and remove ink from the reco context
    inkCtl.InkOverlay.Ink.InkAdded += new StrokesEventHandler(
        inkCtl_InkAdded);
    inkCtl.InkOverlay.Ink.InkDeleted += new StrokesEventHandler(
        inkCtl_InkDeleted);

    // Create event handlers so we can be called back on the correct
    // thread
    evtInkAdded = new StrokesEventHandler(inkCtl_InkAdded_Apt);
    evtInkDeleted = new StrokesEventHandler(inkCtl_InkDeleted_Apt);

    // We're now set to go, so turn on tablet input
    inkCtl.InkOverlay.Enabled = true;
}


// Sets up recognition using the given Recognizer instance
private void SwitchToRecognizer(Recognizer recognizer)
{
    // Create a recognizer context and set strokes on it
    recoCtxt = recognizer.CreateRecognizerContext();
    recoCtxt.Strokes = inkCtl.InkOverlay.Ink.Strokes;

    // Update the menu items with the new choice
    foreach (MenuItem miReco in arrRecoMenu)
    {
        miReco.Checked = miReco.Text.Equals(recognizer.Name);
    }
}
```

*(continued)*

**AdvancedReco.cs** *(continued)*

```
// Given a name, finds the Recognizer instance
private Recognizer FindRecognizer(string strName)
{
    foreach (Recognizer recognizer in frmMain.recognizers)
    {
        if (recognizer.Name.Equals(strName))
        {
            return recognizer;
        }
    }
    return null;
}


// Handle new ink being added
private void inkCtl_InkAdded(object sender, StrokesEventArgs e)
{
    // Make sure the event fires on the correct thread
    this.Invoke(evtInkAdded, new object[] { sender, e });
}
private void inkCtl_InkAdded_Apt(object sender, StrokesEventArgs e)
{
    // Update the strokes to recognize
    recoCtxt.Strokes.Add(
        inkCtl.InkOverlay.Ink.CreateStrokes(e.StrokeIds));
}


// Handle ink getting deleted
private void inkCtl_InkDeleted(object sender, StrokesEventArgs e)
{
    // Make sure the event fires on the correct thread
    this.Invoke(evtInkDeleted, new object[] { sender, e });
}
private void inkCtl_InkDeleted_Apt(object sender, StrokesEventArgs e)
{
    // Update the strokes to recognize - remove any that have been
    // deleted
    Strokes strksRemove = inkCtl.InkOverlay.Ink.CreateStrokes();
    foreach (Stroke strk in recoCtxt.Strokes)
    {
        if (strk.Deleted)
        {
            strksRemove.Add(strk);
        }
    }
    recoCtxt.Strokes.Remove(strksRemove);
}
```

```
// Handle "Exit" menu item
private void miExit_Click(object sender, EventArgs e)
{
    Application.Exit();
}


// Handle a recognizer menu item
private void miRecoInst_Click(object sender, EventArgs e)
{
    MenuItem miNewReco = sender as MenuItem;
    if (miNewReco != null)
    {
        SwitchToRecognizer(FindRecognizer(miNewReco.Text));
    }
}


// Handle Recognize! menu item
private void miRecognize_Click(object sender, EventArgs e)
{
    if (recoCtxt.Strokes.Count > 0)
    {
        // No more strokes will be input at this point
        recoCtxt.EndInkInput();

        // Obtain the recognition results
        RecognitionStatus recoStatus;
        RecognitionResult recoResult =
            recoCtxt.Recognize(out recoStatus);
        if (recoStatus == RecognitionStatus.NoError)
        {
            // Show the results
            MessageBox.Show(this, recoResult.TopString, "Results");
        }
        else
        {
            // Problem; display error message
            MessageBox.Show(this, recoStatus.ToString(), "Error");
        }

        // Reset the strokes to recognize for next time, "undoing"
        // what EndInkInput has done.
        recoCtxt.Strokes = inkCtl.InkOverlay.Ink.Strokes;
    }
}
}
```

Notice the event handlers for the *InkAdded* and *InkDeleted* events, and recall from Chapter 5 that they can be fired on a thread other than the application's main UI thread of execution. Therefore, to keep data access properly protected, the *Control* class's *Invoke* method is used to manually retrigger the event on the application's main thread.

The *InkAdded* handler simply adds the new strokes to the reco context's *Strokes* collection, and the *InkDeleted* handler removes the deleted strokes from the reco context. To remove the strokes from the reco context, the application computes a *Strokes* collection of the strokes that have their *Deleted* property set and then removes those strokes from the reco context's *Strokes* collection:

```
Strokes strksRemove = inkCtl.InkOverlay.Ink.CreateStrokes();
foreach (Stroke strk in recoCtxt.Strokes)
{
    if (strk.Deleted)
    {
        strksRemove.Add(strk);
    }
}
recoCtxt.Strokes.Remove(strksRemove);
```

The Recognize! menu item handler looks rather similar to the IntermediateReco application's version; the key differences here are that no recognizer instance is obtained nor is a recognizer context created because that has already occurred at application startup. In addition, once the recognized results have been displayed, the reco context's *Strokes* collection is reassigned. The reason for this reassignment is that we want to keep the reco context around for further use, and it needs to be reset for more strokes to be added to or removed from its collection because *EndInkInput* was called.

Contrast the performance of this application with the previous sample—write a couple of sentences, wait a few seconds, and choose the Recognize! command. The IntermediateReco sample will pause for a few seconds and then display the message box, whereas this sample should show the results in about half the time. This is partial recognition at work!

After dismissing the message box containing the results, quickly choose the Recognize! command again. The results take longer to appear because the recognition operation is reset by reassigning the reco context's *Strokes* collection after the call to the *Recognize* method. The application does this so that it can work regardless of whether the recognizer being used supports partial recognition. Although all the text recognizers in the Tablet PC Platform support partial recognition, future recognizers provided by Microsoft or third parties might not. This could be important for you to consider if you plan on your application supporting arbitrary recognizers. If you are certain that the recognizers your application uses support partial recognition, you can improve efficiency by not calling the *RecognizerContext.EndInkInput* method before *RecognizerContext.Recognize* and not reassigning the reco context's *Strokes* collection to avoid resetting the reco operation.

Now try the following modification to the sample in the Recognize! menu item handler:

```
if (recoCtxt.Strokes.Count > 0)
{
    // No more strokes will be input at this point
    //REMOVED: recoCtxt.EndInkInput();

    // Obtain the recognition results
    RecognitionStatus recoStatus;
    RecognitionResult recoResult =
        recoCtxt.Recognize(out recoStatus);
    if (recoStatus == RecognitionStatus.NoError)
    {
        // Show the results
        MessageBox.Show(this, recoResult.TopString, "Results");
    }
    else
    {
        // Problem; display error message
        MessageBox.Show(this, recoStatus.ToString(), "Error");
    }

    // Reset the strokes to recognize for next time, "undoing"
    // what EndInkInput has done.
    //REMOVED: recoCtxt.Strokes = inkCtl.InkOverlay.Ink.Strokes;
}
```

This modification is targeted toward recognizers that support partial recognition. When using a recognizer that supports partial recognition, the results will be returned quickly no matter how soon subsequent recognition operations are triggered. If the recognizer used does not support partial recognition, you will encounter an error when the *Recognize* method is called.

---

**Note**   The *Recognize* method can be used to determine whether a recognizer supports partial recognition or not, given that a *Recognizer* object, a reco context, an *Ink* object, and a *Stroke* object can be programmatically created and a recognition attempt can be made on the ink without calling *EndInkInput*. If an error occurs from calling the reco context's *Recognize* method, the recognizer does not support partial recognition.

## Using the Microsoft Gesture Recognizer

The Microsoft Gesture Recognizer cannot be used from the recognition classes because there is currently no way to specify what application gestures are desired, as there is for the *InkCollector* and *InkOverlay* classes (the *SetGestureStatus* method). Hence, if your application requires gesture recognition, you will have to use either the *InkCollector* or *InkOverlay* class and its *Gesture* event. However, there is nothing preventing a custom-developed gesture recognizer from being used with the recognition API; the issue being discussed here applies only to the Microsoft Gesture Recognizer.

# Getting Results III: The Final Chapter (a.k.a. Asynchronous Recognition)

Obtaining recognition results by the *Recognize* method can be time-consuming, even when the recognizer being used supports partial recognition and the reco context's *Strokes* collection is kept up-to-date at all times. For some application features it is useful to receive notification that recognition results have been computed rather than block while waiting for *Recognize* to return. Asynchronous recognition is the answer to this problem—instead of waiting for a method to return while the recognition results are being computed, the method to request recognition results returns immediately and the results are provided later from an event.

To perform asynchronous recognition, either of the *RecognizerContext* class's methods, *BackgroundRecognize* or *BackgroundRecognizeWithAlternates,* is called. Whichever one is called returns immediately, and when recognition results are computed then either the *Recognition* or *RecognitionWithAlternates* event is fired. The difference between the two methods is how much information is computed and supplied in their respective event: the *BackgroundRecognize* method provides only the top string from the *Recognition* event, whereas *BackgroundRecognizeWithAlternates* provides a full *RecognitionResult* instance to the *RecognitionWithAlternates* event. The methods are rather like asynchronous versions of *Strokes.ToString* and *RecognizerContext.Recognize*, respectively.

If the recognizer being used supports partial recognition and the recognition context is kept up-to-date with ink, it is actually a little more efficient to perform recognition asynchronously than it is to do so synchronously. The utility of requesting recognition results in an asynchronous manner is that the requesting thread is not blocked while waiting for the computation, allowing for further user input.

## Sample Application—AsyncReco

This sample application, shown in Figure 7-2, illustrates how asynchronous recognition can be performed. As strokes are added to and removed from an *Ink-Control*'s *Ink* object, the recognition results are updated in real time in an edit box—effectively forming a log of results.

**Figure 7-2**   The AsyncReco application displays recognition results as they're calculated.

### AsyncReco.cs

```
///////////////////////////////////////////////////////////////////////
//
// AsyncReco.cs
//
// (c) 2002 Microsoft Press
// by Rob Jarrett
//
// This program demonstrates using asynchronous recognition.
//
///////////////////////////////////////////////////////////////////////

using System;
using System.Drawing;
using System.Windows.Forms;
using Microsoft.Ink;
using MSPress.BuildingTabletApps;
```

*(continued)*

**AsyncReco.cs** *(continued)*

```
public class frmMain : Form
{
    private InkControl2        inkCtl;
    private TextBox            txtResults;
    private RecognizerContext  recoCtxt;
    private StrokesEventHandler evtInkAdded;
    private StrokesEventHandler evtInkDeleted;
    private RecognizerContextRecognitionEventHandler evtRecognition;

    // Entry point of the program
    [STAThread]
    static void Main()
    {
        // Check to see if any recognizers are installed
        if ((new Recognizers()).Count > 0)
        {
            Application.Run(new frmMain());
        }
        else
        {
            // None are, so display error message and exit
            MessageBox.Show("No recognizers are installed!",
                "Error", MessageBoxButtons.OK, MessageBoxIcon.Error);
        }
    }

    // Main form setup
    public frmMain()
    {
        SuspendLayout();

        // Create and place all of our controls
        inkCtl = new InkControl2();
        inkCtl.Location = new Point(8, 8);
        inkCtl.Size = new Size(352, 216);

        txtResults = new TextBox();
        txtResults.Location = new Point(8, 232);
        txtResults.Multiline = true;
        txtResults.ReadOnly = true;
        txtResults.ScrollBars = ScrollBars.Vertical;
        txtResults.Size = new Size(352, 72);

        // Configure the form itself
        ClientSize = new Size(368, 312);
```

```
        Controls.AddRange(new Control[] { inkCtl,
                                          txtResults});
        FormBorderStyle = FormBorderStyle.FixedDialog;
        MaximizeBox = false;
        Text = "AsyncReco";

        ResumeLayout(false);

        // Get the default recognizer
        Recognizer reco = (new Recognizers()).GetDefaultRecognizer();

        // Create a recognizer context
        recoCtxt = reco.CreateRecognizerContext();
        recoCtxt.Strokes = inkCtl.InkOverlay.Ink.CreateStrokes();

        // Get notification of ink being added and deleted so we'll know
        // when to stop and start background recognition
        inkCtl.InkOverlay.Ink.InkAdded += new StrokesEventHandler(
            inkCtl_InkAdded);
        inkCtl.InkOverlay.Ink.InkDeleted += new StrokesEventHandler(
            inkCtl_InkDeleted);

        // Get notification of recognition occurring to display the
        // current results
        recoCtxt.Recognition +=
            new RecognizerContextRecognitionEventHandler(
            recoCtxt_Recognition);

        // Create event handlers so we can be called back on the correct
        // thread
        evtInkAdded = new StrokesEventHandler(inkCtl_InkAdded_Apt);
        evtInkDeleted = new StrokesEventHandler(inkCtl_InkDeleted_Apt);
        evtRecognition = new RecognizerContextRecognitionEventHandler(
            recoCtxt_Recognition_Apt);

        // We're now set to go, so turn on tablet input
        inkCtl.InkOverlay.Enabled = true;
    }


// Handle new ink being added
private void inkCtl_InkAdded(object sender, StrokesEventArgs e)
{
    // Make sure the event fires on the correct thread
    this.Invoke(evtInkAdded, new object[] { sender, e });
}
private void inkCtl_InkAdded_Apt(object sender, StrokesEventArgs e)
```

*(continued)*

**AsyncReco.cs** *(continued)*

```csharp
{
    // Stop any current background recognition
    recoCtxt.StopBackgroundRecognition();

    // Update the strokes to recognize
    recoCtxt.Strokes.Add(
        inkCtl.InkOverlay.Ink.CreateStrokes(e.StrokeIds));

    // No more strokes will be input at this point
    recoCtxt.EndInkInput();

    // Restart background recognition
    recoCtxt.BackgroundRecognize();
}

// Handle ink being deleted
private void inkCtl_InkDeleted(object sender, StrokesEventArgs e)
{
    // Make sure the event fires on the correct thread
    this.Invoke(evtInkDeleted, new object[] { sender, e });
}
private void inkCtl_InkDeleted_Apt(object sender, StrokesEventArgs e)
{
    // Stop any current background recognition
    recoCtxt.StopBackgroundRecognition();

    // Figure out which strokes have been deleted
    Strokes strksRemove = inkCtl.InkOverlay.Ink.CreateStrokes();
    foreach (Stroke strk in recoCtxt.Strokes)
    {
        if (strk.Deleted)
        {
            strksRemove.Add(strk);
        }
    }

    // Update the strokes to recognize
    recoCtxt.Strokes.Remove(strksRemove);

    // Check if we can restart background recognition
    if (recoCtxt.Strokes.Count > 0)
    {
        // No more strokes will be input at this point
        recoCtxt.EndInkInput();
```

```
                        // Restart background recognition
                        recoCtxt.BackgroundRecognize();
                    }
                    else
                    {
                        // No strokes left, so empty results
                        txtResults.Text = "";
                    }
                }


        // Handle recognition results being computed
        private void recoCtxt_Recognition(
            object sender, RecognizerContextRecognitionEventArgs e)
        {
            // Make sure the event fires on the correct thread
            this.Invoke(evtRecognition, new object[] { sender, e });
        }
        private void recoCtxt_Recognition_Apt(
            object sender, RecognizerContextRecognitionEventArgs e)
        {
            if (e.RecognitionStatus == RecognitionStatus.NoError)
            {
                // Display the result
                txtResults.AppendText(e.Text + "\r\n");
            }
            else
            {
                // Display the recognition status
                txtResults.AppendText("Problem: RecoStatus=");
                txtResults.AppendText(e.RecognitionStatus.ToString());
                txtResults.AppendText("\r\n");
            }

            // Reset the strokes to recognize for next time, "undoing"
            // what EndInkInput has done.
            recoCtxt.Strokes = inkCtl.InkOverlay.Ink.Strokes;
        }
    }
```

The first part of the application is similar to what we've seen in the Inter-mediateReco and AdvancedReco samples—at least one recognizer is confirmed to be installed for the application to run. After creating a form with an InkControl and a TextBox, a *RecognizerContext* is created from the default recognizer.

The *Recognition* event has a handler installed for it in the same fashion as *InkAdded* and *InkDeleted* do because the *Recognition* event can be fired on a thread other than the main application thread.

The handling of the *InkAdded* and *InkDeleted* events is similar to, but not quite the same as, the other samples that keep the reco context up-to-date with ink. Let's take a look at the logic found in the *InkAdded* event handler:

```
// Stop any current background recognition
recoCtxt.StopBackgroundRecognition();

// Update the strokes to recognize
recoCtxt.Strokes.Add(
    inkCtl.InkOverlay.Ink.CreateStrokes(e.StrokeIds));

// No more strokes will be input at this point
recoCtxt.EndInkInput();

// Restart background recognition
recoCtxt.BackgroundRecognize();
```

The *RecognizerContext.StopBackgroundRecognition* method results in the cancellation of any in-progress asynchronous recognition operation. We'll see shortly why we'd want to call that method at the top of the event handler. The modification of the reco context's *Strokes* collection is straightforward; it simply adds the new ink strokes to the collection. The *EndInkInput* method is then called because a recognition operation is about to be requested—namely, the *BackgroundRecognize* method. This is why the call to *StopBackgroundRecognition* is needed at the top of the function. If ink strokes are added in rapid succession, it's quite possible that an asynchronous recognition operation is still in progress when the reco context's *Strokes* collection is about to be modified with the new ink. To avoid this run-time error condition we therefore cancel any recognition operation by calling *StopBackgroundRecognition* before touching the reco context's *Strokes* collection.

The *Recognition* event handler receives a *RecognizerContextRecognition-EventArgs* object containing the result of asynchronous recognition. The event arguments provide no other information other than the recognition status and an optional object reference passed into *BackgroundRecognize*. To get a *RecognitionResult* instance from an asynchronous recognition operation, we need to call *BackgroundRecognizeWithAlternates*. In this case, the *RecognitionWith-*

*Alternate* event's *RecognizerContextRecognitionWithAlternatesEventArgs* class contains a property named *Result* that holds the computed *RecognitionResult*.

## Working with Recognition Results

Now that we know how to get hold of a *RecognitionResult* instance, what exactly can it be used for? As mentioned earlier, we know the class encapsulates recognized result data such as text, alternative results, and confidence level. This section discusses how to work with that information to deliver the best possible user experience from an ink-enabled application.

Recognition result data is compiled from a complex data structure containing all the possible results for ink data that has been recognized. Known as a *lattice*, it is a matrix-like structure produced by a recognizer when a recognition operation has been completed. You can imagine it to be something like a large table whose columns define the segmentation of ink and whose rows define the possible results. The data in a lattice comprises cells containing recognized text, confidence level, ink segmentation, line information, and stroke association with the recognized text. *Alternates* define a path through cells of the lattice from adjacent columns. Don't fret if this isn't making much sense at this point—just keep in mind that alternates represent the recognition results for consecutive segments of ink.

A *RecognitionResult* instance has what's known as a *top alternate*; this is the path through the lattice that has the highest confidence. We saw from the IntermediateReco and AdvancedReco samples that the *RecognitionResult* class's *TopString* property returns the text string with highest confidence. Similarly, the *TopConfidence* property indicates the confidence level of the top alternate. Because the top alternate can be (and usually is) made up of multiple segments, each containing a confidence value, the *TopConfidence* property is actually an average of values.

The *TopAlternate* property of the *RecognitionResult* class provides the top alternate for the result, returning an instance of the *RecognitionAlternate* class. To access other alternates from a *RecognitionResult* instance, the *GetAlternates-FromSelection* method returns a collection of *RecognitionAlternate* instances by way of the *RecognitionAlternates* class. The method can optionally accept a start position and length of text from the result string in order to drill down into the results. The CorrectionUI sample later in this chapter makes use of this method to display the alternative results for an arbitrary selection.

## The *RecognitionAlternate* Class

Once a *RecognitionAlternate* instance has been obtained from a *RecognitionResult*, we can access the data the recognizer has computed as well as further explore the recognition results. Table 7-8 lists some common properties found on a *RecognitionAlternate* instance.

**Table 7-8   Common Properties of the *RecognitionAlternate* Class**

| Value | Type | Description |
|-------|------|-------------|
| *Ascender* | Line | The ascender line computed for the strokes drawn; the upper boundary of the characters |
| *Baseline* | Line | The baseline computed for the strokes drawn; equivalent to the underline of the characters |
| *Confidence* | RecognitionConfidence | The confidence level for the entire alternate; an average of the confidence values of the referenced lattice cells |
| *Descender* | Line | The descender line computed for the strokes drawn; the lower boundary of the characters |
| *LineNumber* | Int | The line number the strokes were computed on; 0 = first, 1 = second, etc. |
| *Midline* | Line | The midline computed for the strokes drawn; lies between the baseline and ascender |
| *Strokes* | Strokes | The strokes associated with this alternate |

The *ConfidenceAlternates* property of the *RecognitionAlternate* class returns a *RecognitionAlternates* collection, effectively subdividing the alternate into consecutive pieces that share the same confidence level. For example, if the segments in the sentence, *I'm an operator of my pocket calculator,* had confidence levels of high, high, poor, intermediate, intermediate, intermediate, and high respectively, four alternates corresponding to *I'm an, operator, of my pocket,* and *calculator* would be returned from the *ConfidenceAlternates* property.

Similarly, the *LineAlternates* property subdivides an alternate into pieces that share the same line. Ink can be entered on multiple lines, of course, so this property is handy in order to find out what strokes lie on what line.

## Querying Line-Based Properties

Querying the *Ascender, Baseline, Descender, LineNumber,* and *Midline* properties will throw a run-time exception if the alternate spans multiple lines of ink. This is because the properties are *line-based,* meaning their value applies to a specific line. To ensure it is safe to query them, you can either check that the count of alternates returned from the *LineAlternates* property is 1, or iterate over each alternate returned from the *LineAlternates* property, querying each one.

It can be useful to match ink strokes to character positions in the recognized text string and vice versa; correction UI and word-based selection, for instance, benefit greatly from this functionality. The *GetStrokesFromTextRange, GetTextRangeFromStrokes,* and *GetStrokesFromStrokeRanges* methods are used to accomplish this. The *GetStrokesFromTextRange* method computes the *Strokes* collection that references the ink strokes forming the segments specified by the character position and length in the recognized text. Likewise, the *GetTextRangeFromStrokes* method computes the character position and length in the recognized text that is formed by the specified strokes. A useful feature of these functions is that they automatically snap to a segment boundary, meaning the data provided to the methods doesn't have to contain all strokes or characters forming a word.

The *GetStrokesFromStrokeRanges* method is a combination of *GetTextRangeFromStrokes* and *GetStrokesFromTextRange.* Given one or more *Strokes* collections, this method returns the *Strokes* collection for those segments that are spanned. You can get the same value by calling *GetTextRangeFromStrokes* and then passing the return value from that method to *GetStrokesFromTextRange. GetStrokesFromStrokeRanges* is a handy method for performing word selection, as we're about to see.

### Sample Application—WordSelect

The WordSelect sample application shows how we can make use of recognition results to perform word-based selection. If you compare the selection behavior of Windows Journal and the *InkOverlay* class, you'll notice that tapping on a word in Windows Journal results in the entire word being selected, whereas *InkOverlay* selects only the single stroke hit by the tap.

By taking advantage of the *GetStrokesFromStrokeRanges* method of the *RecognitionAlternate* class, we can easily change *InkOverlay*'s behavior to select the entire word.

**WordSelect.cs**

```
///////////////////////////////////////////////////////////////////
//
// WordSelect.cs
//
// (c) 2002 Microsoft Press
// by Rob Jarrett
//
// This program demonstrates how to select full words based on
// recognition results.
//
///////////////////////////////////////////////////////////////////

using System;
using System.Drawing;
using System.Windows.Forms;
using Microsoft.Ink;
using MSPress.BuildingTabletApps;

public class frmMain : Form
{
    private InkControl2          inkCtl;
    private TextBox              txtResults;
    private RecognizerContext    recoCtxt;
    private RecognitionResult    recoResult;
    private StrokesEventHandler  evtInkAdded;
    private StrokesEventHandler  evtInkDeleted;
    private RecognizerContextRecognitionWithAlternatesEventHandler
                                 evtRecognitionWithAlternates;

    // Entry point of the program
    [STAThread]
    static void Main()
    {
        // Check to see if any recognizers are installed
        if ((new Recognizers()).Count > 0)
        {
            Application.Run(new frmMain());
        }
        else
        {
            // None are, so display error message and exit
```

```
            MessageBox.Show("No recognizers are installed!",
                "Error", MessageBoxButtons.OK, MessageBoxIcon.Error);
        }
    }

    // Main form setup
    public frmMain()
    {
        SuspendLayout();

        // Create and place all of our controls
        inkCtl = new InkControl2();
        inkCtl.Location = new Point(8, 8);
        inkCtl.Size = new Size(352, 216);

        txtResults = new TextBox();
        txtResults.HideSelection = false;
        txtResults.Location = new Point(8, 232);
        txtResults.ReadOnly = true;
        txtResults.ScrollBars = ScrollBars.Vertical;
        txtResults.Size = new Size(352, 20);

        // Configure the form itself
        ClientSize = new Size(368, 260);
        Controls.AddRange(new Control[] { inkCtl,
                                          txtResults});
        FormBorderStyle = FormBorderStyle.FixedDialog;
        MaximizeBox = false;
        Text = "WordSelect";

        ResumeLayout(false);

        // Get the default recognizer
        Recognizer reco = (new Recognizers()).GetDefaultRecognizer();

        // Create a recognizer context
        recoCtxt = reco.CreateRecognizerContext();
        recoCtxt.RecognitionFlags = RecognitionModes.TopInkBreaksOnly;
        recoCtxt.Strokes = inkCtl.InkOverlay.Ink.CreateStrokes();

        // Get notification of ink being added and deleted so we'll know
        // when to stop and start background recognition
        inkCtl.InkOverlay.Ink.InkAdded += new StrokesEventHandler(
            inkCtl_InkAdded);
        inkCtl.InkOverlay.Ink.InkDeleted += new StrokesEventHandler(
            inkCtl_InkDeleted);
```

*(continued)*

**WordSelect.cs** *(continued)*

```csharp
        // Get notification of selection changing so we can tweak the
        // result if needed
        inkCtl.InkOverlay.SelectionChanging +=
            new InkOverlaySelectionChangingEventHandler(
            inkCtl_SelectionChanging);

        // Get notification of recognition occurring to display the
        // current results
        recoCtxt.RecognitionWithAlternates +=
            new RecognizerContextRecognitionWithAlternatesEventHandler(
            recoCtxt_RecognitionWithAlternates);

        // Create event handlers so we can be called back on the correct
        // thread
        evtInkAdded = new StrokesEventHandler(inkCtl_InkAdded_Apt);
        evtInkDeleted = new StrokesEventHandler(inkCtl_InkDeleted_Apt);
        evtRecognitionWithAlternates =
            new RecognizerContextRecognitionWithAlternatesEventHandler(
            recoCtxt_RecognitionWithAlternates_Apt);

        // We're now set to go, so turn on tablet input
        inkCtl.InkOverlay.Enabled = true;
    }


// Handle new ink being added
private void inkCtl_InkAdded(object sender, StrokesEventArgs e)
{
    // Make sure the event fires on the correct thread
    this.Invoke(evtInkAdded, new object[] { sender, e });
}
private void inkCtl_InkAdded_Apt(object sender, StrokesEventArgs e)
{
    // Stop any current background recognition
    recoCtxt.StopBackgroundRecognition();

    // Update the strokes to recognize
    recoCtxt.Strokes.Add(
        inkCtl.InkOverlay.Ink.CreateStrokes(e.StrokeIds));

    // No more strokes will be input at this point
    recoCtxt.EndInkInput();

    // Restart background recognition
    recoCtxt.BackgroundRecognizeWithAlternates();
}
```

```csharp
// Handle ink getting deleted
private void inkCtl_InkDeleted(object sender, StrokesEventArgs e)
{
    // Make sure the event fires on the correct thread
    this.Invoke(evtInkDeleted, new object[] { sender, e });
}
private void inkCtl_InkDeleted_Apt(object sender, StrokesEventArgs e)
{
    // Stop any current background recognition
    recoCtxt.StopBackgroundRecognition();

    // Figure out which strokes have been deleted
    Strokes strksRemove = inkCtl.InkOverlay.Ink.CreateStrokes();
    foreach (Stroke strk in recoCtxt.Strokes)
    {
        if (strk.Deleted)
        {
            strksRemove.Add(strk);
        }
    }

    // Update the strokes to recognize
    recoCtxt.Strokes.Remove(strksRemove);

    // Check if we can restart background recognition
    if (recoCtxt.Strokes.Count > 0)
    {
        // No more strokes will be input at this point
        recoCtxt.EndInkInput();

        // Restart background recognition
        recoCtxt.BackgroundRecognizeWithAlternates();
    }
    else
    {
        // No strokes left, so empty results
        txtResults.Text = "";
    }
}

// Handle ink getting selected
private void inkCtl_SelectionChanging(
    object sender, InkOverlaySelectionChangingEventArgs e)
{
    // Stop any current background recognition to make sure we
    // have stable results
    recoCtxt.StopBackgroundRecognition();
```

*(continued)*

**WordSelect.cs** *(continued)*

```csharp
    if ((e.NewSelection.Count > 0) && (recoResult != null))
    {
        // Select the strokes comprising a full word using the
        // GetStrokesFromStrokeRanges method

        // Just using this method would cause an entire range to
        // always be selected, breaking expected lasso behavior
        //e.NewSelection.Add(
        //    recoResult.TopAlternate.GetStrokesFromStrokeRanges(
        //    e.NewSelection));

        // Select the full words that contain the selected stroke(s)
        Strokes strksToSelect =
            inkCtl.InkOverlay.Ink.CreateStrokes();
        foreach (Stroke s in e.NewSelection)
        {
            if (strksToSelect.Contains(s))
            {
                continue;
            }
            Strokes strksStroke =
                inkCtl.InkOverlay.Ink.CreateStrokes(
                new int[] { s.Id } );
            Strokes strksWord =
                recoResult.TopAlternate.GetStrokesFromStrokeRanges(
                strksStroke);
            strksToSelect.Add(strksWord);
        }
        e.NewSelection.Clear();
        e.NewSelection.Add(strksToSelect);

        // Select the text in the results textbox corresponding
        // to the new selection — since the textbox doesn't support
        // multi-ranged selection, we'll have to select the entire
        // range of words defined by the new selection
        int nStart = 0, nLength = 0;
        recoResult.TopAlternate.GetTextRangeFromStrokes(
            e.NewSelection, ref nStart, ref nLength);
        txtResults.Select(nStart, nLength);
    }
    else
    {
        // Clear the selection in the textbox
        txtResults.Select(0, 0);
    }
}
```

```csharp
// Handle recognition results being computed
private void recoCtxt_RecognitionWithAlternates(object sender,
    RecognizerContextRecognitionWithAlternatesEventArgs e)
{
    // Make sure the event fires on the correct thread
    this.Invoke(
        evtRecognitionWithAlternates, new object[] { sender, e });
}
private void recoCtxt_RecognitionWithAlternates_Apt(object sender,
    RecognizerContextRecognitionWithAlternatesEventArgs e)
{
    if (e.RecognitionStatus == RecognitionStatus.NoError)
    {
        // Check to see if these reco results are needed - if there
        // are no strokes in the recognition context, then these
        // results are stale
        if (recoCtxt.Strokes.Count > 0)
        {
            // Store the result for later
            recoResult = e.Result;

            // Display the result
            txtResults.Text = e.Result.TopString;
        }
        else
        {
            // Clear the displayed results
            txtResults.Text = "";
        }
    }
    else
    {
        // Clear the stored result
        recoResult = null;

        // Display the recognition status
        txtResults.Text =
            "Problem: RecoStatus=" + e.RecognitionStatus.ToString();
    }

    // Reset the strokes to recognize for next time, "undoing"
    // what EndInkInput has done.
    recoCtxt.Strokes = inkCtl.InkOverlay.Ink.Strokes;
}
}
```

Similar to the AsyncReco sample we saw earlier, background recognition is used to display the current recognition result in real time. Instead of using *BackgroundRecognize*, however, we use *BackgroundRecognizeWithAlternates* to obtain a *RecognitionResult* instance. This recognition result is saved each time the *RecognitionWithAlternates* event fires so that the application always has up-to-date results from which to query.

When stroke selection occurs, the strokes being selected are used as the argument to the saved recognition result's top alternate's *GetStrokesFromStrokeRanges* method. The strokes constituting both the words and the text in the results textbox are then selected. Because only the top alternate is used from the recognition result, we need only one set of segmentation, so for efficiency we can specify the *RecognitionModes.TopInkBreaksOnly* flag to the recognition context.

Word selection is achieved with the following code in the *SelectionChanging* event handler:

```
// Select the full words that contain the selected stroke(s)
Strokes strksToSelect =
    inkCtl.InkOverlay.Ink.CreateStrokes();
foreach (Stroke s in e.NewSelection)
{
    if (strksToSelect.Contains(s))
    {
        continue;
    }
    Strokes strksStroke =
        inkCtl.InkOverlay.Ink.CreateStrokes(
        new int[] { s.Id } );
    Strokes strksWord =
        recoResult.TopAlternate.GetStrokesFromStrokeRanges(
        strksStroke);
    strksToSelect.Add(strksWord);
}
e.NewSelection.Clear();
e.NewSelection.Add(strksToSelect);
```

Each stroke to be selected is given individually to *GetStrokesFromStrokeRanges*, which effectively performs a word-by-word calculation. The resulting *Strokes* collections are then added to one master *Strokes* collection, and finally the *InkOverlaySelectionChangingEventArgs*'s *NewSelection* property is set to this master collection.

You might think that instead of this sequence, *GetStrokesFromStrokeRanges* could just be called with the entire contents of the *NewSelection* property. However, this would result in incorrect lasso selection behavior when multiple words were selected. For example, if the user wrote two lines of text such as *My name is* and *Rico Suavé* and then tried to lasso select only the words *My* and *Rico*, the words *My name is Rico* would get selected because *Get-StrokesFromStrokeRanges* returns not only the strokes for the two words, but for all the words in between.

## Sample Application—CorrectionUI

This next sample application shows how a user can edit a *RecognitionResult* instance from a correction UI. The sample implements a dialog enabling the user to choose alternate recognition results and then copy the recognized text to the clipboard. For convenience, the implementation of the dialog is found in the BuildingTabletApps helper library introduced in Chapter 4. Figure 7-3 shows what the CorrectionUI application looks like.

**Figure 7-3**   The CorrectionUI sample application provides the user with the ability to alter the top alternate result.

### CorrectionUI.cs

```
///////////////////////////////////////////////////////////////////////
//
// CorrectionUI.cs
//
// (c) 2002 Microsoft Press
// by Rob Jarrett
//
// This program shows how to display correction UI for a "Copy As
// Text" menu item.
//
///////////////////////////////////////////////////////////////////////
```

*(continued)*

**CorrectionUI.cs** *(continued)*

```csharp
using System;
using System.Drawing;
using System.Windows.Forms;
using Microsoft.Ink;
using MSPress.BuildingTabletApps;

public class frmMain : Form
{
    private InkControl2        inkCtl;
    private RecognizerContext  recoCtxt;
    private StrokesEventHandler evtInkAdded;
    private StrokesEventHandler evtInkDeleted;

    // Entry point of the program
    [STAThread]
    static void Main()
    {
        // Check to see if any recognizers are installed by analyzing
        // the number of items in the Recognizers collection
        Recognizers recognizers = new Recognizers();
        if (recognizers.Count > 0)
        {
            Application.Run(new frmMain());
        }
        else
        {
            // None are, so display error message and exit
            MessageBox.Show("No recognizers are installed!",
                "Error", MessageBoxButtons.OK, MessageBoxIcon.Error);
        }
    }

    // Main form setup
    public frmMain()
    {
        SuspendLayout();

        // Create the main menu
        Menu = new MainMenu();

        MenuItem miFile = new MenuItem("&File");
        Menu.MenuItems.Add(miFile);

        MenuItem miExit = new MenuItem("E&xit");
        miExit.Click += new EventHandler(miExit_Click);
        Menu.MenuItems[0].MenuItems.Add(miExit);
```

```
        MenuItem miEdit = new MenuItem("&Edit");
        Menu.MenuItems.Add(miEdit);

        MenuItem miCopyAsText = new MenuItem("&Copy As Text");
        miCopyAsText.Click += new EventHandler(miCopyAsText_Click);
        Menu.MenuItems[1].MenuItems.Add(miCopyAsText);

        // Create and place all of our controls
        inkCtl = new InkControl2();
        inkCtl.Location = new Point(8, 8);
        inkCtl.Size = new Size(352, 216);

        // Configure the form itself
        ClientSize = new Size(368, 232);
        Controls.AddRange(new Control[] { inkCtl });
        FormBorderStyle = FormBorderStyle.FixedDialog;
        MaximizeBox = false;
        Text = "CorrectionUI";

        ResumeLayout(false);

        // Get the default recognizer
        Recognizer reco = (new Recognizers()).GetDefaultRecognizer();

        // Create a recognizer context and hook up to recognition event
        recoCtxt = reco.CreateRecognizerContext();
        recoCtxt.Strokes = inkCtl.InkOverlay.Ink.CreateStrokes();

        // Get notification of ink being added and deleted so we'll know
        // when to add and remove ink from the reco context
        inkCtl.InkOverlay.Ink.InkAdded += new StrokesEventHandler(
            inkCtl_InkAdded);
        inkCtl.InkOverlay.Ink.InkDeleted += new StrokesEventHandler(
            inkCtl_InkDeleted);

        // Create event handlers so we can be called back on the correct
        // thread
        evtInkAdded = new StrokesEventHandler(inkCtl_InkAdded_Apt);
        evtInkDeleted = new StrokesEventHandler(inkCtl_InkDeleted_Apt);

        // We're now set to go, so turn on tablet input
        inkCtl.InkOverlay.Enabled = true;
    }

// Handle new ink being added
private void inkCtl_InkAdded(object sender, StrokesEventArgs e)
```

*(continued)*

**CorrectionUI.cs** *(continued)*

```
{
    // Make sure the event fires on the correct thread
    this.Invoke(evtInkAdded, new object[] { sender, e });
}
private void inkCtl_InkAdded_Apt(object sender, StrokesEventArgs e)
{
    // Update the strokes to recognize
    recoCtxt.Strokes.Add(
        inkCtl.InkOverlay.Ink.CreateStrokes(e.StrokeIds));
}


// Handle ink getting deleted
private void inkCtl_InkDeleted(object sender, StrokesEventArgs e)
{
    // Make sure the event fires on the correct thread
    this.Invoke(evtInkDeleted, new object[] { sender, e });
}
private void inkCtl_InkDeleted_Apt(object sender, StrokesEventArgs e)
{
    // Update the strokes to recognize - remove any that have been
    // deleted
    Strokes strksRemove = inkCtl.InkOverlay.Ink.CreateStrokes();
    foreach (Stroke strk in recoCtxt.Strokes)
    {
        if (strk.Deleted)
        {
            strksRemove.Add(strk);
        }
    }
    recoCtxt.Strokes.Remove(strksRemove);
}


// Handle "Exit" menu item
private void miExit_Click(object sender, EventArgs e)
{
    Application.Exit();
}


// Handle "Copy As Text" menu item
private void miCopyAsText_Click(object sender, EventArgs e)
{
    if (recoCtxt.Strokes.Count > 0)
    {
        // No more strokes will be input at this point
        recoCtxt.EndInkInput();
```

```
            // Obtain the recognition results
            RecognitionStatus recoStatus;
            RecognitionResult recoResult =
                recoCtxt.Recognize(out recoStatus);
            if (recoStatus == RecognitionStatus.NoError)
            {
                // Show correction UI dialog
                CopyAsTextDlg dlg = new CopyAsTextDlg();
                dlg.RecognitionResult = recoResult;
                dlg.ShowDialog(this);
            }
            else
            {
                // Problem; display error message
                MessageBox.Show(this, "Error: " + recoStatus);
            }

            // Reset the strokes to recognize for next time, "undoing"
            // what EndInkInput has done.
            recoCtxt.Strokes = inkCtl.InkOverlay.Ink.Strokes;
        }
    }
}
```

This first file is the main program that calls the dialog implementation found in the BuildingTabletApps library. It is similar to the AdvancedReco application in that it keeps the reco context up-to-date with the ink to recognize—the "Copy As Text" menu item handler obtains the reco results synchronously by a call to *Recognize*. The *RecognitionResult* value returned is then provided as the argument to the *CopyAsTextDlg* class, which performs all the neat editing functionality.

The implementation of *CopyAsTextDlg* is presented here:

**CopyAsTextDlg.cs**
```
/////////////////////////////////////////////////////////////////////////
//
// CopyAsTextDlg.cs
//
// (c) 2002 Microsoft Press
// by Rob Jarrett
//
// This class implements a dialog which provides correction and
// clipboard copying of reco results via a RecognitionResults object.
//
/////////////////////////////////////////////////////////////////////////
```

*(continued)*

**CopyAsTextDlg.cs** *(continued)*

```csharp
using System;
using System.Collections;
using System.Drawing;
using System.Windows.Forms;
using Microsoft.Ink;

namespace MSPress.BuildingTabletApps
{
    public class CopyAsTextDlg : Form
    {
        private TextBox            txtResults;
        private ListBox            lbAlternates;
        private InkInputPanel      pnlInk;
        private Button             btnCopy;
        private Button             btnClose;
        private RecognitionResult  recoResult;
        private Strokes            strksDisplay;

        // Dialog setup
        public CopyAsTextDlg()
        {
            SuspendLayout();

            // Create and place all of our controls
            txtResults = new TextBox();
            txtResults.HideSelection = false;
            txtResults.Location = new Point(8, 8);
            txtResults.Multiline = true;
            txtResults.ReadOnly = true;
            txtResults.ScrollBars = ScrollBars.Vertical;
            txtResults.Size = new Size(384, 96);

            lbAlternates = new ListBox();
            lbAlternates.Location = new Point(8, 112);
            lbAlternates.Size = new Size(188, 96);

            pnlInk = new InkInputPanel();
            pnlInk.BackColor = Color.White;
            pnlInk.BorderStyle = BorderStyle.Fixed3D;
            pnlInk.Location = new Point(204, 112);
            pnlInk.Size = new Size(188, 96);

            btnCopy = new Button();
            btnCopy.DialogResult = DialogResult.OK;
            btnCopy.Location = new Point(264, 226);
            btnCopy.Size = new Size(60, 20);
            btnCopy.Text = "Copy";
```

```
    btnClose = new Button();
    btnClose.DialogResult = DialogResult.OK;
    btnClose.Location = new Point(332, 226);
    btnClose.Size = new Size(60, 20);
    btnClose.Text = "Close";

    // Configure the form itself
    AcceptButton = btnClose;
    CancelButton = btnClose;
    ClientSize = new Size(400, 256);
    Controls.AddRange(new Control[] { txtResults,
                                      lbAlternates,
                                      pnlInk,
                                      btnCopy,
                                      btnClose});
    FormBorderStyle = FormBorderStyle.FixedDialog;
    MinimizeBox = false;
    MaximizeBox = false;
    Text = "Copy As Text";

    ResumeLayout(false);

    // Get notification of user input occuring in the "Results"
    // TextBox so we can update the "Alternates" ListBox
    txtResults.KeyUp += new KeyEventHandler(txtResults_KeyUp);
    txtResults.MouseUp +=
        new MouseEventHandler(txtResults_MouseUp);

    // Get notification of an alternate getting chosen so we
    // can alter the result
    lbAlternates.SelectedIndexChanged +=
        new EventHandler(lbAlternates_SelectedIndexChanged);

    // Paint the preview of the strokes making up the selection
    pnlInk.Paint += new PaintEventHandler(pnlInk_Paint);

    // Perform copying of the text
    btnCopy.Click += new EventHandler(btnCopy_Click);
}

// Get or set the RecognitionResult object being used for the
// correction
public RecognitionResult RecognitionResult
{
    get
    {
        return recoResult;
    }
```

*(continued)*

CopyAsTextDlg.cs  *(continued)*

```
        set
        {
            recoResult = value;
            if (recoResult != null)
            {
                // Display the current result
                txtResults.Text = recoResult.TopString;
                txtResults.SelectionStart = 0;
                txtResults.SelectionLength = 0;
                SelectionChanged();
            }
        }
    }

    private void FillListbox(RecognitionAlternates recoAlternates)
    {
        // Clear out any current items in the listbox
        lbAlternates.BeginUpdate();
        lbAlternates.Items.Clear();

        // Fill up the listbox with each alternate
        foreach (RecognitionAlternate recoAlternate in recoAlternates)
        {
            lbAlternates.Items.Add(recoAlternate);
        }
        lbAlternates.EndUpdate();
    }

    // The selection in the results textbox has changed, so figure
    // out what word(s) were selected, "snap" the selection to them
    // if needed, fill the listbox, and update the preview with the
    // ink being used
    private void SelectionChanged()
    {
        // Figure out the best text range in the "Results" TextBox
        // to use in obtaining the alternates
        int nStart = txtResults.SelectionStart;
        int nLength = txtResults.SelectionLength;
        if (nLength == 0)
        {
            if (nStart < txtResults.Text.Length &&
                txtResults.Text.Length > 0)
            {
                nLength = 1;
            }
```

```
                    else if (nStart > 0)
                    {
                        nStart--;
                        nLength = 1;
                    }
            }

            // If we still have no selection, no need to do anything
            if (nLength == 0)
            {
                return;
            }

            // Select the strokes that represent the selection in the
            // "Results" Textbox
            strksDisplay =
                recoResult.TopAlternate.GetStrokesFromTextRange(
                ref nStart, ref nLength);
            txtResults.Select(nStart, nLength);
            pnlInk.Invalidate();

            // Show the list of alternates for the selection
            FillListbox(
                recoResult.GetAlternatesFromSelection(nStart, nLength));
        }

// Handle a key being released
private void txtResults_KeyUp(object sender, KeyEventArgs e)
{
    // Selection probably changed, so update the alternates listbox
    SelectionChanged();
}

// Handle a mouse button being released
private void txtResults_MouseUp(object sender, MouseEventArgs e)
{
    // Selection probably changed, so update the alternates listbox
    SelectionChanged();
}

// Handle an alternate getting selected
private void lbAlternates_SelectedIndexChanged(
    object sender, EventArgs e)
{
    // Get the alternate that was selected
    RecognitionAlternate recoAlternate =
        (RecognitionAlternate)lbAlternates.SelectedItem;
```

*(continued)*

**CopyAsTextDlg.cs** *(continued)*

```
        // Adjust the current reco results with it
        recoResult.ModifyTopAlternate(recoAlternate);

        // Update selected text
        int nStart = txtResults.SelectionStart;
        int nLength = txtResults.SelectionLength;
        recoResult.TopAlternate.GetTextRangeFromStrokes(
            strksDisplay, ref nStart, ref nLength);

        // Update the results edit box
        txtResults.Text = recoResult.TopString;
        txtResults.Select(nStart, nLength);

        // Show the list of alternates for the selection
        FillListbox(
            recoResult.GetAlternatesFromSelection(nStart, nLength));
    }

    // Handle painting the preview of ink
    private void pnlInk_Paint(object sender, PaintEventArgs e)
    {
        if (strksDisplay != null)
        {
            Renderer r = new Renderer();

            // Offset the ink to be drawn so it will display in
            // the top-left of the preview window
            Rectangle rcBounds = strksDisplay.GetBoundingBox();
            r.Move(-rcBounds.Left, -rcBounds.Top);

            // Figure out how much the ink needs to be scaled in
            // order for it all to fit within the preview window
            float fScaleWidth = 1, fScaleHeight = 1;

            Misc.InkSpaceRectToPixels(r, e.Graphics, ref rcBounds);
            if (pnlInk.ClientSize.Width < rcBounds.Width)
            {
                fScaleWidth =
                    (float)pnlInk.ClientSize.Width / rcBounds.Width;
            }
            if (pnlInk.ClientSize.Height < rcBounds.Height)
            {
                fScaleHeight =
                    (float)pnlInk.ClientSize.Height / rcBounds.Height;
            }
            float fScaleBy = Math.Min(fScaleWidth, fScaleHeight);
            r.Scale(fScaleBy, fScaleBy);
```

```
                    // Now we can draw the ink
                    r.Draw(e.Graphics, strksDisplay);
            }
        }


        // Handle copying the current result to the clipboard
        private void btnCopy_Click(object sender, EventArgs e)
        {
            Clipboard.SetDataObject(txtResults.Text);
        }
    }
}
```

The dialog consists of a read-only TextBox containing the recognized text for the current top alternate, a ListBox containing alternates for the current selection, and a Panel where the strokes constituting the current selection is drawn. As the selection is changed in the TextBox, the alternates and stroke preview are updated. If an alternate is selected, the text in the TextBox is updated accordingly.

The ListBox of alternates is filled with *RecognitionAlternate* instances obtained from the *GetAlternatesFromSelection* method:

```
// Fill up the listbox with each alternate
foreach (RecognitionAlternate recoAlternate in recoAlternates)
{
    lbAlternates.Items.Add(recoAlternate);
}
```

When an alternate is selected, the real functionality of the sample is exhibited. The *ModifyTopAlternate* method of the *RecognitionResult* class allows the top alternate to be overridden, in essence correcting it. No matter what the granularity of the alternate (be it multiple words or a single segment), *Modify-TopAlternate* adjusts the recognition result accordingly:

```
// Get the alternate that was selected
RecognitionAlternate recoAlternate =
    (RecognitionAlternate)lbAlternates.SelectedItem;

// Adjust the current reco results with it
recoResult.ModifyTopAlternate(recoAlternate);
```

When the "Copy" button is clicked, the recognition result text is placed onto the clipboard and the dialog is closed. If the user chooses the "Copy To Clipboard" menu item again, the dialog will show the modified *RecognitionResult* instance, ready for further use or correction.

If ink is added to or removed from the document, a new *RecognitionRe-sult* instance is generated by the recognizer—this means that any previous user modifications to the top alternative are lost. This is an understandable but unfortunate reality, but it is possible to overcome it. One method is to remember the top alternative string and match it against the new reco result; unfortunately, this is a complex algorithm, and it would likely be too performance intensive. Another way is to use a capability of the *Strokes* collection—it can be tagged with recognition results. If you are able to divide your document into separate *Strokes* collections (perhaps by every line or paragraph), only the results directly affected by adding or removing ink will be reset. The question then arises, "How do we associate recognition result instances to *Strokes* collections?" The next section explains how.

## Storing Recognition Results

Once a recognition result instance has been obtained and optionally modified by the user, it can be useful to persist those results along with the *Ink* object that contains the recognized strokes. Alternatively, it can be useful to associate a *Strokes* collection to a recognition result instance for a variety of reasons, including splitting an ink document into pieces to preserve edited recognition results and maintaining recognition results for multiple languages simultaneously.

The *Strokes* collection class possesses a *RecognitionResult* property, used to reference a *RecognitionResult* instance. It is set from the *SetStrokesResult* method found on the *RecognitionResult* class. Using explicit assignment to set the *RecogitionResult* property on a *Strokes* collection will cause an exception to be thrown. Only the *SetStrokesResult* method is able to alter the property's value, in order to ensure consistency between the strokes referenced by the collection and the *RecognitionResult*.

After setting the *RecognitionResult* property of a *Strokes* collection, an application will typically hang onto that *Strokes* collection for future use—perhaps as long as the recognition results are needed. You might think this is not necessary because subsequent *Strokes* collections that reference the same ink strokes as a *Strokes* collection with a *RecognitionResult* instance will reference the *RecognitionResult*. This is not so! The reference is kept only on a per-instance basis of a *Strokes* collection. Consider the following code:

```
// Recognize all ink on the page
RecognizerContext recoCtxt = recognizer.CreateRecognizerContext();
recoCtxt.Strokes = inkCtl.InkOverlay.Ink.Strokes;
recoCtxt.EndInkInput();
RecognitionResult recoResult = recoCtxt.Recognize();
```

```
// Set the results on the recoCtxt's RecognitionResult property
recoResult.SetStrokesResult();
RecognitionResult recoResult2 =
    inkCtl.InkOverlay.Ink.Strokes.RecognitionResult;
```

The *recoCtxt.Strokes.RecognitionResult* will reference the same *RecognitionResult* instance as *recoResult* because of *SetStrokesResult* being called. However, the *recoResult2* reference will be null and definitely not equivalent to *recoResult*. Recall from Chapter 5 that the *Strokes* property of the *Ink* class always returns a copy of the collection, so the *RecognitionResult* property would not be set.

The contents of a *RecognitionResults* instance can be persisted by adding a *Strokes* collection referencing the recognition results to the *CustomStrokes* collection on the *Ink* class. Storing recognition results is useful for at least two reasons: recognition results don't have to be recomputed when a file loads—avoiding the application freezing during synchronous reco or not behaving optimally during asynchronous reco—and down-level support—machines that don't have a recognizer installed can still view the alternates that were computed.

## Recognition Properties

You've seen how quite a lot of data can be extracted from a recognition result by using the computed alternates. Even more data can be obtained by using APIs supporting recognition properties. *Recognition properties* are *Guid* values that represent various data found in a recognition alternate and provide a generic means of accessing and specifying data. The *RecognitionProperty* class contains the values, listed in Table 7-9, of the supported recognition properties.

**Table 7-9   Recognition Property Types in the *RecognitionProperty* Class**

| Value | Description |
| --- | --- |
| ConfidenceLevel | The confidence level the recognizer has in the recognition result |
| *HotPoint* | The hot point of the recognition; typically used by gesture recognizers |
| *LineMetrics* | The line metrics of the recognition result |
| *LineNumber* | The line number of the result; not supported for recognizers of East Asian characters |
| *MaximumStrokeCount* | The maximum stroke count for the recognition result |
| *PointsPerInch* | The points-per-inch metric for the recognition result |
| *Segmentation* | The ink fragment or unit the recognizer used to produce the recognition result |

The *RecognitionAlternate* class's *AlternatesWithConstantPropertyValues* method chops an alternate into one or more alternates that are grouped by the same specific property value. It accepts a *RecognitionProperty Guid* value and returns a *RecognitionAlternates* collection containing the appropriate *RecognitionAlternate* instances.

Using the *AlternatesWithConstantPropertyValues* method can yield some cool information. For example, it becomes easy to underline inked words in colors according to the recognized confidence level by chopping an alternate into the segments as computed by the recognizer. A green underline can indicate strong confidence, yellow intermediate, and red poor. The code would look something like:

```
// Underline words in a color according to their confidence
// Green - strong, Yellow - intermediate, Red - poor
Graphics g = inkCtl.InkInputPanel.CreateGraphics();
foreach (RecognitionAlternate alt in
    recoResult.TopAlternate.AlternatesWithConstantPropertyValues(
    RecognitionProperty.Segmentation))
{
    // Skip over any whitespace
    if (alt.Strokes.Count == 0)
    {
        continue;
    }

    // Get start point of the segment's baseline
    Point ptStart = alt.Baseline.BeginPoint;
    RendererEx.InkSpaceToPixel(r, e.Graphics, ref ptStart);

    // Get end point of the segment's baseline
    Point ptEnd = alt.Baseline.EndPoint;
    inkCtl.InkOverlay.Renderer.InkSpaceToPixel(g, ref ptEnd);

    // Draw the baseline in a color according to confidence
    Pen pen = null;
    switch (alt.Confidence)
    {
        case RecognitionConfidence.Strong:
            pen = Pens.Green;
            break;
        case RecognitionConfidence.Intermediate:
            pen = Pens.Gold;
            break;
```

```
        case RecognitionConfidence.Poor:
            pen = Pens.Red;
            break;
    }
    g.DrawLine(pen, ptStart, ptEnd);
}
g.Dispose();
```

You can see this functionality in action by modifying any of the samples that maintain a *RecognitionResult* instance, and then overriding the *InkInput-Panel's Paint* event handler. The information can be a handy visual indicator of results that don't have a high confidence, letting users know they should double-check the result from the correction UI.

The results of calling *AlternatesWithConstantPropertyValues* with *RecognitionProperty.ConfidenceLevel* and *RecognitionProperty.LineNumber* are exposed through the *ConfidenceAlternates* and *LineAlternates* properties, respectively. They are provided as properties solely for convenience.

Some of the recognition properties don't make much sense for use with the *AlternatesWithConstantPropertyValues* method—for example, the *RecognitionProperty.MaximumStrokeCount* and *RecognitionProperty.PointsPerInch* properties. They are meant to be used with the other method that supports recognition properties, namely the *GetPropertyValue* method. This is used to serialize recognition data to a byte array.

# Improving Recognition Results

Recognition accuracy can be improved by giving the recognizer information about the expected input. The Tablet PC Platform supports this information in two forms: hints about the content and hints about the layout or positioning of the ink.

## Factoids—Content Hint

As mentioned earlier in the chapter, factoids are content hints given to the recognizer so that it can bias its results and achieve greater accuracy. Sometimes the context or type of information being entered is known by an application—for example, asking the user to enter a phone number. By specifying to the recognizer that the ink it will perform recognition on probably represents a phone number, the application can assume a certain format and distinguish between letters and numbers (such as *0* or *O*, and *1* or *l*).

## A Factoid About Factoids

Norman Mailer first coined the term *factoid* in his biography of Marilyn Monroe. In the biography, Mailer intended factoid to mean a false piece of information that everyone assumes is true because it appears in print. In Marilyn Monroe's case, the press would often invent factoids about her to create drama and interest.

Factoid is a misnomer as used by the Tablet PC Platform SDK. When used during ink recognition, a factoid is really a *factette*: a small piece of interesting trivia.

The Tablet PC Platform supports numerous kinds of factoids, which are listed in Table 7-10. Different languages can have different conventions for the content format—for example, phone numbers in North America and in Europe, and country postal codes. Some recognizers don't support some factoids, as noted in the table.

The *Factoid* property of the *RecognizerContext* class is used to specify the factoids the recognizer should use. Factoids are specified by a string, the values as seen in the left-hand column of Table 7-10. Multiple factoids are specified by separating them with a pipe character ("|"). Some examples of setting factoids are thus:

```
// Recognize a date
recoCtxt.Factoid = "DATE";

// Recognize an email address or URL
recoCtxt.Factoid = "EMAIL|WEB";

// Restore the factoid back to default behavior
recoCtxt.Factoid = "DEFAULT";
```

**Table 7-10   Factoid Listing**

| Factoid Value | Description | Example/Notes |
| --- | --- | --- |
| *DIGIT* | Bias toward single digits | 0, 1, 2, 3, etc. |
| *EMAIL* | Bias toward e-mail addresses | *jimmy@adatum.com* |
| *WEB* | Bias toward URLs | *http://www.microsoft.com* *www.microsoft.com/tabletpc* |

**Table 7-10  Factoid Listing**  *(continued)*

| Factoid Value | Description | Example/Notes |
| --- | --- | --- |
| *DEFAULT* | Returns the recognizer to default settings | n/a |
| *NONE* | Disables all factoids, dictionary, and language model | n/a |
| *FILENAME* | Bias toward file name path | C:\ Chapter7.doc \\robstablet\public\*.* |
| *SYSDICT* | Enables the system dictionary | n/a |
| *WORDLIST* | Enables the word list (see the following section) | n/a |
| *CURRENCY* | Bias toward currency: dollars, euros, yen, pounds, etc. | $100.00 25¢ €1.00 ¥7 |
| *DATE* | Bias toward dates | 11/7/03 November 7, 2003 11-07-2003 Thursday, Nov. 7, 2003 |
| *NUMBER* | Bias toward numbers, including math symbols, ordinals, suffixes such as KB and MB, and the TIME and CURRENCY factoids | 456 100 MB 2nd #1 11-7-02 8*8+5 |
| *ONECHAR* | Bias toward a single ANSI character | A, B, C, D, 0, 1, 2, \, ", #, $, %, &, etc. |
| *PERCENT* | Bias toward a number followed by the percent symbol | 100 % 3.14 % |
| *POSTALCODE* | Bias toward postal codes | 98052 |
| *TELEPHONE* | Bias toward telephone numbers | 555-2368 (425)555-2368 |
| *TIME* | Bias toward time | 3:38 pm 8:35:23 14:00:00 |
| *UPPERCHAR* | Bias toward a single uppercase character | A, B, C, D, etc. |
| *KANJI_COMMON* | Bias toward Kanji characters; depends on language for exact set | *East Asian only* |

*(continued)*

**Table 7-10  Factoid Listing**    *(continued)*

| Factoid Value | Description | Example/Notes |
|---|---|---|
| *JPN_COMMON* | Bias toward KANJI_COMMON, HIRAGANA, KATAKANA, alphanumeric, standard punctuation, and symbol characters | *Japanese only* |
| *CHS_COMMON* | Bias toward KANJI_COMMON, alphanumeric, standard punctuation, and symbol characters | *Chinese (simplified) only* |
| *CHT_COMMON* | Bias toward KANJI_COMMON, BOPOMOFO, alphanumeric, standard punctuation, and symbol characters | *Chinese (traditional) only* |
| *KOR_COMMON* | Bias toward KANJI_COMMON, JAMO, HANGUL_COMMON, alphanumeric, standard punctuation, and symbol characters | *Korean only* |
| *HIRAGANA* | Bias toward Hiragana characters | *Japanese only* |
| *KATAKANA* | Bias toward Katakana characters | *Japanese only* |
| *BOPOMOFO* | Bias toward Taiwanese phonetic characters | *Chinese (traditional) only* |
| *JAMO* | Bias toward Jamo characters | *Korean only* |
| *HANGUL_COMMON* | Bias toward Hangul characters | *Korean only* |

You can consult the Tablet PC Platform SDK documentation for more details on what exact formats and characters are allowed for various languages.

## Word Lists—Content Hint

Factoids do a great job for common types of data, but what about application-specific types, for example, coworkers' names or parking lot section numbers? Table 7-10 lists a factoid type named *WORDLIST* that instructs the recognizer to use a predefined set of words that are likely to appear in the recognized text. The *RecognizerContext* class's property *WordList* is a collection of strings the recognizer should bias toward. Like other factoids, word lists can either be suggested or forced; by default, word lists are suggested, but if the recognizer context flag *RecognitionModes.Coerce* is specified the results are forced to match the word list contents.

## Determining if a Word Is Supported

After setting up a factoid, you might want to determine whether the recognizer context is in a state to recognize a specific word. The *RecognizerContext* class method *IsStringSupported* provides this information.

## Guides—Spatial Hint

The hints we've been discussing so far have been content related. *Recognizer guides* specify the layout or positioning of ink. An electronic form might have boxes in which to enter characters of a name. Text entry UI such as the Tablet PC Input Panel has a well-defined area in which to draw ink. Recognizer guides allow an application to tell the recognizer where to expect ink characters or words to be drawn.

The *RecognizerContext* class's property *Guide* is used to specify an instance of *RecognizerGuide* to use. The constructor of the *RecognizerGuide* class is given the number of rows and columns in the guide, the midline height for ink (the distance between the baseline and the middle of a character), the writing area rectangle, and the drawing area rectangle. Figure 7-4 illustrates how these properties relate to one another.

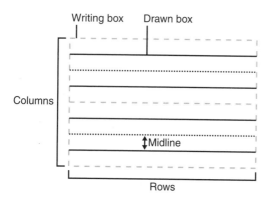

**Figure 7-4**    *RecognizerGuides* provide the ability to indicate the layout of text that is entered. This example shows two rows by one column of text.

Character auto-complete functionality requires a guide to be set for it to function properly. This is because the recognizer needs to know the positioning and scale of strokes as they are entered in order to provide the best results.

# Summary

The ink recognition services the Tablet PC Platform offers can provide some of the most compelling end-user functionality a Tablet PC–based application has. Text and objects can be recognized, with the *Strokes.ToString* method and the *InkCollector* and *InkOverlay* classes' *Gesture* event offering the most convenient level of access to recognition.

If more data or functionality is needed, a *Recognizer* instance must be obtained, and a recognizer context created from it. The recognizer context supplies recognition results either synchronously or asynchronously, and if the recognizer supports partial recognition it is recommended that the recognizer context be kept up-to-date with the ink strokes to be recognized in order to improve efficiency.

Recognition results are composed of alternates. These alternates consist of pathways through the recognizer's lattice of all possible results computed by the recognizer. Alternates can be split up by factors such as segmentation, line number, and confidence level. The top alternate of a recognition result can be modified by a user from a correction UI.

Programmers can improve recognition results by taking into account content hints such as factoids, word lists, and prefix and suffix text, and also by providing layout hints (such as a recognizer guide) to the end user.

As someone once said, "We've come a long way, baby!" You have reached a milestone in learning about the Tablet PC Platform because all major areas have now been covered: the Tablet Input API, the Ink Data Management API, and the Ink Recognition API. We hope you've gained enough knowledge to set out and write some great tablet applications of your own!

We're not done with learning about the Tablet PC Platform, however. The next chapter covers the ink controls, and if you're going to want any ink input in a dialog box or a Windows Forms application, that chapter is definitely for you.

# 8

# Ink Controls

Now that you're familiar with most of the Tablet PC Platform, let's take a look at two of the higher-level classes in the SDK. InkEdit and InkPicture combine aspects of tablet input, ink data management, and recognition into easy-to-use controls. They make it simple to add digital ink features to an application because they capture, manipulate, and store ink without much intervention. Forms developers especially will find them useful. Simply dropping InkEdit or InkPicture controls onto a form might be all that your application needs!

## Achtung Baby

Your deep understanding of the platform-managed APIs will help you pick up the ink controls quickly because they expose some of the same interfaces. Before diving into the individual controls, we'll mention a few short but important caveats that apply to both controls.

■ **The functionality of these controls is limited on machines not running Microsoft Windows XP Tablet PC Edition.** You'll probably recall these limitations, which we first mentioned in Chapter 3. The gist is that the two ink controls will not capture, edit, or recognize ink when running on other versions of Windows. A notable exception is that InkPicture captures ink as long as the Tablet PC Platform SDK is installed. But if you deploy your application onto machines running other non-tablet versions of Windows, the controls will lose their ink capture, edit, and recognition capabilities.

■ **You must create and use the controls on your application's main thread.**    Both InkEdit and InkPicture will misbehave if they are not created and used on the main thread. This will not be a problem in typical applications since the main thread most often uses UI elements. All Windows Forms controls, for instance, have this restriction as well.

■ **The controls have differing capabilities depending on their version.**    There are managed, Microsoft ActiveX, and Microsoft Win32 versions of InkEdit, but there are only managed and ActiveX versions of InkPicture. Variations between the controls are small and are mostly due to differences between Microsoft .NET and ActiveX. For instance, the ActiveX version of InkEdit supplies a *BorderStyle-Constants* enumeration that's unnecessary in the managed version, which instead uses *System.Windows.Forms.BorderStyle*. On the other hand, only the managed version of both controls has public constructors since ActiveX controls do not have publicly callable constructors.

> **Important**    A practical implication of these limitations is that the InkEdit samples in this chapter will capture ink only if you run the samples on Windows XP Tablet PC Edition. On all other operating systems, the InkEdit samples will not capture ink.

Other than what we've just listed, the ink controls behave pretty much like other .NET or ActiveX controls. You can drag them onto forms using Microsoft Visual Studio's form designer or create them programmatically. You can even reference them from a Web page using Microsoft JScript or Microsoft Visual Basic Scripting Edition (VBScript).

More than likely, you are going to add the controls to your application by dragging them onto forms in Visual Studio. However, in the interests of clarity we will continue to programmatically create them in our code listings so that stand-alone C# files are sufficient to compile and run the listings.

# InkEdit

The InkEdit control is a superset of standard text boxes in Windows. As such, it is meant to replace edit controls in an ink-aware application. Instead of accepting only text input, InkEdit also captures digital ink, optionally converting it into text. The managed version of InkEdit is a superset of RichTextBox, while the ActiveX and Win32 versions are supersets of RichEdit. RichEdit and its .NET counterpart, RichTextBox, supply advanced text-editing features for text boxes in Windows. These features include support for entering complex scripts, saving in Rich Text Format (RTF), and editing bidirectional text. Perhaps the most notable exposure of RichEdit is in Windows WordPad, whose text features are all implemented by its underlying RichEdit control.

InkEdit offers a superset of RichEdit functionality, which immediately makes it much more than just a simple digital ink capture and display control. Through InkEdit, you can access all the functionality of RichEdit. However, in this chapter we will be focusing only on the new features that InkEdit adds. For more information about the RichEdit and RichTextBox functionality, please see *Programming Microsoft Windows with C#,* by Charles Petzold (Microsoft Press, 2002).

## InkEdit Basics

The Tablet PC team designed InkEdit with pen-based data entry scenarios in mind. Applications that require the user to enter text by means of text boxes can use an InkEdit control to make data entry a seamless experience for the user. Instead of having to bring up the Tablet PC Input Panel whenever entering text, the user can simply write directly into an InkEdit control, which takes care of converting the written ink into text.

The sample application that follows shows how you can integrate InkEdit into a Windows Forms application. This form gathers basic information to register college students, requiring that students enter their name, identification number, and phone number, and allowing them to add optional comments. It uses InkEdit controls without any customization, preferring the default behavior that's supplied by the controls. This means that on a non-tablet Windows machine, you won't get an inking cursor. The application is shown running in Figure 8-1.

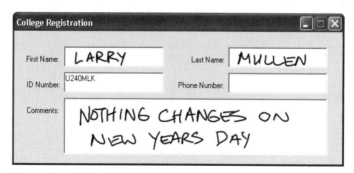

**Figure 8-1**   The CollegeBasic application running with both ink and text in its InkEdit fields.

**CollegeBasic.cs**

```csharp
//////////////////////////////////////////////////////////////////////
// CollegeBasic.cs
// (c) 2002 Microsoft Press, by Philip Su
// This program demonstrates basic usage of InkEdit controls
//////////////////////////////////////////////////////////////////////
using System;
using System.Drawing;
using System.Windows.Forms;
using Microsoft.Ink;

public class CollegeBasic : Form
{
    private InkEdit m_editFirst;      // First name
    private InkEdit m_editLast;       // Last name
    private InkEdit m_editID;         // Student ID
    private InkEdit m_editPhone;      // Phone number
    private InkEdit m_editComment;    // Any comments
    private Label m_labelFirst;
    private Label m_labelLast;
    private Label m_labelID;
    private Label m_labelPhone;
    private Label m_labelComments;

    [STAThread]
    static void Main()
    {
        Application.Run(new CollegeBasic());
    }

    public CollegeBasic()
    {
        InitializeComponent();
    }

    private void InitializeComponent()
    {
        SuspendLayout();

            // Create the InkEdit controls and labels
        InitializeEdit(ref m_editFirst, new Point(80, 24),
                    new Size(160, 32), false);
        InitializeEdit(ref m_editLast, new Point(344, 24),
                    new Size(160, 32), false);
        InitializeEdit(ref m_editID, new Point(80, 64),
                    new Size(160, 32), false);
        InitializeEdit(ref m_editPhone, new Point(344, 64),
                    new Size(160, 32), false);
```

```
        InitializeEdit(ref m_editComment, new Point(80, 104),
                    new Size(424, 88), true);   // Multiline!
        InitializeLabel(ref m_labelFirst, new Point(-8, 32),
                    new Size(88, 23), "First Name:");
        InitializeLabel(ref m_labelLast, new Point(256, 32),
                    new Size(88, 23), "Last Name:");
        InitializeLabel(ref m_labelID, new Point(-8, 72),
                    new Size(88, 23), "ID Number:");
        InitializeLabel(ref m_labelPhone, new Point(256, 72),
                    new Size(88, 23), "Phone Number:");
        InitializeLabel(ref m_labelComments, new Point(-8, 112),
                    new Size(88, 23), "Comments:");

        // Configure the form itself
        this.AutoScaleBaseSize = new Size(5, 13);
        this.ClientSize = new Size(528, 206);
        this.Controls.AddRange(new Control[] {
            m_labelComments, m_labelPhone, m_labelID,
            m_labelLast, m_labelFirst, m_editFirst,
            m_editLast, m_editID, m_editPhone, m_editComment
                                 });
        this.FormBorderStyle = FormBorderStyle.FixedDialog;
        this.MaximizeBox = false;
        this.Text = "College Registration";

        ResumeLayout(false);
    }

    // Helper function to create an InkEdit control
    private void InitializeEdit(ref InkEdit io_edit, Point in_pt,
                            Size in_size, bool in_fMultiline)
    {
        io_edit = new InkEdit();
        io_edit.Location = in_pt;
        io_edit.Size = in_size;
        io_edit.Multiline = in_fMultiline;
    }

    // Helper function to create a label
    private void InitializeLabel(ref Label io_label, Point in_pt,
                            Size in_size, string in_strText)
    {
        io_label = new Label();
        io_label.Location = in_pt;
        io_label.Size = in_size;
        io_label.Text = in_strText;
        io_label.TextAlign = ContentAlignment.MiddleRight;
    }
}
```

As you can see from running the CollegeBasic application, InkEdit controls have all the keyboard-based text-editing facilities available to standard edit controls. You can use the keyboard to type in the control, move the cursor, and copy and paste text. InkEdit controls, just like the RichTextBox control, can be either multiline or single line. By default, both types of controls are multiline.

You probably noticed right away that, although there are a lot of similarities, the InkEdit control uses a different screen cursor from RichTextBox when you hover the pen or mouse over it. It's a round black dot, reflecting the type of ink that would be created if you wrote with the pen into the control. Using default settings, you can ink into the control only with a pen. The mouse behaves as it normally does in a RichTextBox control—so you can use it to select text and position the insertion caret.

Try inking into the InkEdit controls. If you're on a Tablet PC, the ink you've written is converted (after a slight pause) into text and inserted at the position of the caret. You can change the position of the caret by tapping where you want the caret. With a little practice, you can also select text by pressing and holding at the start of your selection. If you hold the pen down long enough, the cursor turns into a selection cursor, at which point you can drag to select underlying text. These basic text-editing features are all accessible using the pen.

The InkEdit control was designed so that most of its default behavior would be acceptable for everyday use. In the following sections, we'll talk about some settings you should be aware of when customizing an InkEdit control.

## Basic Properties

*InkMode* is a key property of InkEdit. Using *InkMode*, you can choose whether the InkEdit control accepts ink and possibly gestures as well. By default, *Ink-Mode* is set to *InkAndGesture*, allowing the control to accept both ink and gestures. The InkEdit control supports several one-stroke gestures that make it possible to Return, Tab, Space, and Backspace directly within the control. The Tablet PC Platform SDK documentation gives details on how to trigger these gestures. You can also set *InkMode* to *Ink*, which will disable gestures but still allow the capture of digital ink. To turn off both ink and gestures entirely, set *InkMode* to *Disabled*. Even if *InkMode* is *Disabled*, contents of the InkEdit control can still be modified just like a standard RichTextBox. The *InkMode* property controls only whether digital ink will be captured and whether gestures will be recognized.

You can query InkEdit for its read-only *Status* property, which tells you whether it's currently *Idle*, *Collecting*, or *Recognizing* ink. The most common reason for checking the *Status* property is to fulfill requirements imposed by the SDK. Specifically, there are a number of InkEdit properties and methods that can be changed or called only when the control is *Idle*. It's somewhat of a drag that InkEdit has this requirement because it amounts to requiring a *while* loop whenever you want to change some properties or call some methods. For instance, you can set *InkMode* only when the *Status* property is *Idle*, requiring code such as the following:

```
while (edit.Status != InkEditStatus.Idle)
{
    // Wait a little while for user input and/or recognition to
    // end before trying again
    System.Threading.Thread.Sleep(100);
}
edit.InkMode = InkMode.Disabled;
```

Even this code isn't satisfactory, since the platform doesn't offer any guarantees that it won't change *Status* from another thread. Thus there is no bulletproof way to fulfill the platform's requirement that *Status* be *Idle* when modifying *InkMode*. Worse yet, if *Status* isn't *Idle* when you change *InkMode*, an exception is thrown. An equally unsavory alternative is possible:

```
bool fStatusIsSet = false;
while (!fStatusIsSet)
{
    try
    {
        edit.InkMode = InkMode.Disabled;
        fStatusIsSet = true;
    }
    catch (Exception)
    {
        // Wait a little while for user input and/or recognition to
        // end before trying again
        System.Threading.Thread.Sleep(100);
    }
}
```

The preceding code keeps attempting to set *InkMode* until it is successful. If the code sets *InkMode* while the user is entering ink or the control is recognizing ink, the control will throw an exception. To recover, we catch the exception and repeat the process. The purpose of *Sleep* is to give the user or the control some time to stop inking or recognizing ink before we attempt to set *InkMode* again.

Whichever way you choose, be aware that some properties and methods require that *Status* be *Idle* before they are changed or called. The SDK documentation is usually pretty good at calling out this requirement, but unfortunately it offers no suggestion as to how the requirement should be fulfilled.

The *InkInsertMode* property affects whether ink is inserted into the control as text or ink. The default setting is *InsertAsText*. However, if you want digital ink to be inserted as ink into InkEdit, set *InkInsertMode* to *InsertAsInk*. Upon recognition, the ink will be inserted as ink unless you later change it to text manually. We'll see how to convert ink manually into text later in the chapter. There are two caveats concerning *InkInsertMode*. The first is that *InkInsertMode* can be modified only when InkEdit is running on Windows XP Tablet PC Edition. On all other operating systems, changes to the value will have no effect. The second caveat is that InkEdit will change the size of inserted ink when *InkInsertMode* is *InsertAsInk*. InkEdit tries to make inserted ink match the characteristics of nearby text. To do so, it changes the ink's height to match the font height of text at the insertion point. If you find the inserted ink is too small, increase the font size of the InkEdit control.

You can change the appearance of ink that's drawn in InkEdit by changing the control's *DrawingAttributes* property. When setting this property, you should consider making the ink thick enough to be easily visible but not so thick as to take over the control's area. You can set *Color*, *PenTip*, *Transparency*, and any other properties on *DrawingAttributes* as well. The default results in a black round-tipped pen. By setting *DrawingAttributes*, the on-screen pen cursor is updated automatically to reflect the type of ink that is produced.

## Mouse-Related Properties

There are two mouse-related properties in InkEdit. The first is the *UseMouseForInput* property, and with it you can control whether InkEdit interprets mouse movements and mouse actions as if they originated from a pen. In practice, this is equivalent to controlling whether the mouse can create ink in the control. By default, *UseMouseForInput* is *false*, ensuring that the mouse behaves as it does in regular *RichTextBox* controls (that is, it can move the caret and select text). If you set *UseMouseForInput* to *true*, the mouse will create digital ink when you click and drag it over InkEdit. When *UseMouseForInput* is *true*, you can still use the mouse to set the caret position and to select text—you'll just have to imitate the pen in doing those actions by clicking for the former and holding-and-dragging for the latter.

> **Note**   Setting *UseMouseForInput* will not affect the pen's ability to generate ink. A pen can always write into an InkEdit control (assuming the current InkMode setting allows it).

InkEdit also has a *Cursor* property. Unlike most of the Tablet PC Platform's managed API, this cursor refers to the on-screen representation of the mouse location. By setting this property, you change the cursor that is used when the mouse hovers over InkEdit. You can set this property to any object of type *System.Windows.Forms.Cursor*, although you most often will set it to one of the static cursors available through the *System.Windows.Forms.Cursors* collection (such as *IBeam*). You cannot change the pen's on-screen cursor through the *Cursor* property or any other property. Thus, the pen's cursor will always reflect the type of ink that will be drawn. By default, the *Cursor* property is *null*, making the mouse cursor the same as the pen's cursor when hovering over InkEdit. (An exception is that if *InkMode* is *Disabled*, the *null Cursor* results in an I-beam cursor.)

At this point, if you've been keeping up with the default mouse-related properties, you're probably asking yourself a couple of good questions: Why would *UseMouseForInput* default to *false* and *Cursor* default to *null* at the same time? Wouldn't that lead to the mouse being unable to ink while having a cursor that indicates inking ability? Indeed, the default mouse-related settings are in conflict with one another. On one hand, the mouse defaults to *not* generating ink. This makes sense for most applications, in which a user would not want the mouse to ink within the control. On the other hand, by leaving *Cursor null*, the mouse cursor appears to be a pen tip when hovering over InkEdit, leading the user to believe that the mouse will behave like a pen. For almost all imaginable purposes, you should not leave these two defaults as they are. Instead, you should set one or the other so that they are not in conflict. You will probably set *Cursor* to *IBeam* and leave *UseMouseForInput* as *false* in most scenarios.

## Basic Properties Example

Now that we have a better understanding of the basic properties that are settable on InkEdit, we can look at a more complete example of the CollegeBasic application. The following CollegeFull application shows how you might use the basic properties and mouse-related properties to enhance CollegeBasic.

## CollegeFull.cs

```
/////////////////////////////////////////////////////////////////////
// CollegeFull.cs
// (c) 2002 Microsoft Press, by Philip Su
// This program demonstrates usage of InkEdit controls
/////////////////////////////////////////////////////////////////////
using System;
using System.Drawing;
using System.Windows.Forms;
using Microsoft.Ink;

public class CollegeFull : Form
{
    private InkEdit m_editFirst;    // First name
    private InkEdit m_editLast;     // Last name
    private InkEdit m_editID;       // Student ID
    private InkEdit m_editPhone;    // Phone number
    private InkEdit m_editComment;  // Any comments
    private Label m_labelFirst;
    private Label m_labelLast;
    private Label m_labelID;
    private Label m_labelPhone;
    private Label m_labelComments;

    [STAThread]
    static void Main()
    {
        Application.Run(new CollegeFull());
    }

    public CollegeFull()
    {
        InitializeComponent();
    }

    private void InitializeComponent()
    {
        SuspendLayout();

            // Create the InkEdit controls and labels
        InitializeEdit(ref m_editFirst, new Point(80, 24),
                    new Size(160, 32), false);
        InitializeEdit(ref m_editLast, new Point(344, 24),
                    new Size(160, 32), false);
        InitializeEdit(ref m_editID, new Point(80, 64),
                    new Size(160, 32), false);
        InitializeEdit(ref m_editPhone, new Point(344, 64),
                    new Size(160, 32), false);
```

```
InitializeEdit(ref m_editComment, new Point(80, 104),
               new Size(424, 88), true);   // Multiline!
InitializeLabel(ref m_labelFirst, new Point(-8, 32),
               new Size(88, 23), "First Name:");
InitializeLabel(ref m_labelLast, new Point(256, 32),
               new Size(88, 23), "Last Name:");
InitializeLabel(ref m_labelID, new Point(-8, 72),
               new Size(88, 23), "ID Number:");
InitializeLabel(ref m_labelPhone, new Point(256, 72),
               new Size(88, 23), "Phone Number:");
InitializeLabel(ref m_labelComments, new Point(-8, 112),
               new Size(88, 23), "Comments:");

    // Configure the form itself
this.AutoScaleBaseSize = new Size(5, 13);
this.ClientSize = new Size(528, 206);
this.Controls.AddRange(new Control[] {
    m_labelComments, m_labelPhone, m_labelID,
    m_labelLast, m_labelFirst, m_editFirst,
    m_editLast, m_editID, m_editPhone, m_editComment
                            });
this.FormBorderStyle = FormBorderStyle.FixedDialog;
this.MaximizeBox = false;
this.Text = "College Registration";

    // This is new!  We now customize some InkEdits.
CustomizeEditControls();

ResumeLayout(false);
}


// Helper function to create an InkEdit control
private void InitializeEdit(ref InkEdit io_edit, Point in_pt,
                        Size in_size, bool in_fMultiline)
{
io_edit = new InkEdit();
io_edit.Location = in_pt;
io_edit.Size = in_size;
io_edit.Multiline = in_fMultiline;

    // Choose ONE of the two following lines.  Either
    // let the mouse ink in the control, or show the
    // IBeam cursor when the mouse hovers over.
io_edit.Cursor = System.Windows.Forms.Cursors.IBeam;
//  io_edit.UseMouseForInput = true;
}
```

*(continued)*

**CollegeFull.cs** *(continued)*

```
        // Helper function to create a label
private void InitializeLabel(ref Label io_label, Point in_pt,
                               Size in_size, string in_strText)
{
    io_label = new Label();
    io_label.Location = in_pt;
    io_label.Size = in_size;
    io_label.Text = in_strText;
    io_label.TextAlign = ContentAlignment.MiddleRight;
}


        // Customizes some of the edit controls
private void CustomizeEditControls()
{
    DrawingAttributes da = new DrawingAttributes();

    da.Color = Color.Red;
    da.PenTip = PenTip.Rectangle;
    da.Width = 10;

        // Change the First Name field to red ink
    m_editFirst.DrawingAttributes = da;

        // Disable inking in the Last Name field
    while (m_editLast.Status != InkEditStatus.Idle)
    {
        System.Threading.Thread.Sleep(100);
    }
    m_editLast.InkMode = InkMode.Disabled;

        // Keep ink as ink in the Comment field
    m_editComment.InkInsertMode = InkInsertMode.InsertAsInk;
}
}
```

CollegeFull contains a few small changes from CollegeBasic. In *Initialize-Edit*, we set *Cursor* to an I-beam cursor and leave *UseMouseForInput false*:

```
        // Choose ONE of the two following lines.  Either
        // let the mouse ink in the control, or show the
        // IBeam cursor when the mouse hovers over.
    io_edit.Cursor = System.Windows.Forms.Cursors.IBeam;
//      io_edit.UseMouseForInput = true;
```

We also introduce a new function, *CustomizeEditControls*. It sets the First Name field to use a red rectangle-tipped pen:

```
DrawingAttributes da = new DrawingAttributes();

da.Color = Color.Red;
da.PenTip = PenTip.Rectangle;
da.Width = 10;

    // Change the First Name field to red ink
m_editFirst.DrawingAttributes = da;
```

It then disables the Last Name field from accepting ink or gestures:

```
    // Disable inking in the Last Name field
while (m_editLast.Status != InkEditStatus.Idle)
{
    System.Threading.Thread.Sleep(100);
}
m_editLast.InkMode = InkMode.Disabled;
```

Finally it prevents automatic conversion of ink into text in the Comment field:

```
    // Keep ink as ink in the Comment field
m_editComment.InkInsertMode = InkInsertMode.InsertAsInk;
```

The CollegeFull application serves as an example of basic InkEdit use. We'll turn our attention to more advanced ways to use InkEdit in the following sections.

# Working with Ink

Up to this point, we have seen how to change the behavior of InkEdit in some simple ways. But we have not yet been able to work with any ink generated by the user. Now we will consider two properties that deal with the ink within an InkEdit control.

## Accessing Ink with *SelInks*

The *SelInks* property gets or sets the selected ink in an InkEdit control. When you read from the *SelInks* property, it returns *clones* of all the ink objects in the selection. Changes to these clones will not affect the ink that is in the selection. If you want to change the selected ink, you need to explicitly set the *SelInks* property (you can set the *SelInks* property only on Windows XP Tablet PC Edition):

```
Ink[] rgink = m_edit.SelInks;
foreach (Ink ink in rgink)
{
    ink.DeleteStroke(ink.Strokes[0]);
}
m_edit.SelInks = rgink; // Set the ink back into the control
```

One oddity of the InkEdit control is that it never accepts any changes to *DrawingAttributes*. For instance, the following code will not change the color of selected ink:

```
Ink[] rgink = m_edit.SelInks;
foreach (Ink ink in rgink)
{
    foreach (Stroke stroke in ink.Strokes)
    {
        stroke.DrawingAttributes.Color = Color.Red;
    }
}
m_edit.SelInks = rgink;   // Set the ink back into the control
```

InkEdit refuses to allow you to change the appearance of the ink using *DrawingAttributes* on the selected *Ink* objects because it wants the ink to look like the text around it. InkEdit will scale ink according to the font size of nearby text and will also change ink color to match the color of nearby text. The only way to affect the visual appearance of ink in an InkEdit control is to change the ink's *text* properties. As an example, the following code changes any selected ink to red:

```
m_edit.SelectionColor = Color.Red;
```

This might cause you to wonder why the *SelInks* property is settable at all, given that you cannot use it to change the appearance of selected ink. You can, however, use it to change other ink properties. For instance, you can use the *SelInks* property to insert custom data into the selected ink objects' *Extended-Properties* collections.

## Toggling Ink Display with *SelInksDisplayMode*

By default, InkEdit inserts all ink as text upon recognition. However, if you set *InkInsertMode* to *InsertAsInk*, InkEdit inserts *Ink* objects instead of text. One of the resulting benefits of this is that the inserted *Ink* objects can toggle between displaying themselves as ink and displaying themselves as text. *Ink* objects in an InkEdit control maintain all their properties even when they are displayed as text.

You can toggle the *SelInksDisplayMode* property between *InkDisplay-Mode.Ink* and *InkDisplayMode.Text*. When you change the *SelInksDisplayMode* property, you change how InkEdit displays the selected ink. The following code will toggle how selected *Ink* objects display themselves:

```
if (m_edit.SelInksDisplayMode == InkDisplayMode.Ink)
{
    m_edit.SelInksDisplayMode = InkDisplayMode.Text;
}
```

```
else
{
    m_edit.SelInksDisplayMode = InkDisplayMode.Ink;
}
```

If the selection contains mixed ink and text, *SelInksDisplayMode* will return *InkDisplayMode.Ink*. Keep in mind when setting *SelInksDisplayMode* to *InkDisplayMode.Text* that *SelInks* will not return any *Ink* objects that are displayed as text. This anomaly in *SelInks*' behavior means there is no way to detect the presence of *Ink* objects in a selection if those *Ink* objects are set to display themselves as text. The following code illustrates this problem:

```
m_edit.SelInksDisplayMode = InkDisplayMode.Text;
if (m_edit.SelInks.Length > 0)
{
    // This if statement will NEVER be true in InkEdit
}
```

# Recognizing Ink and Gestures

An InkEdit control will automatically capture and recognize ink as well as gestures. But what if you want to fine-tune its recognition in some way? Fortunately, you can change both the timing and the nature of ink recognition. You can also modify InkEdit's built-in set of gestures. This flexibility makes InkEdit fairly customizable to your application's needs.

## Changing Recognition

One major way to affect the results obtained from InkEdit's ink recognition is to change the *Recognizer* it uses. This capability is particularly useful if your application accepts input in multiple languages. If left unmodified, InkEdit uses the default recognizer obtainable through *Recognizers.GetDefaultRecognizer*. Most often, you will be perfectly happy with the recognizer that's used, but you will want to give it some hints to improve its accuracy. We introduced *Factoids* in Chapter 7 as a means to offer hints to a recognizer. By supplying a *Factoid* based on contextual clues known only to you (the application developer), you can improve recognition accuracy significantly. *Factoids* are particularly important in InkEdit fields, where there is often little or no outside context on which the recognizer can rely. You should set the *Factoid* property in InkEdit whenever there is an appropriate *Factoid* that will help narrow the recognizer's context.

The following CollegeFact application shows how factoids improve recognition accuracy. The *SetFactoids* method applies the *Number* and *Telephone* factoids to the Student ID and Phone Number fields, respectively. In addition, it sets the First Name and Last Name *Factoid* property to *None* so that unique

names are not coerced into dictionary words. Other than these modifications,
CollegeFact is largely based on CollegeBasic.

**CollegeFact.cs**

```
/////////////////////////////////////////////////////////////////////
// CollegeFact.cs
// (c) 2002 Microsoft Press, by Philip Su
// This program demonstrates Factoid usage in InkEdit controls
/////////////////////////////////////////////////////////////////////
using System;
using System.Drawing;
using System.Windows.Forms;
using Microsoft.Ink;

public class CollegeFact : Form
{
    private InkEdit m_editFirst;      // First name
    private InkEdit m_editLast;       // Last name
    private InkEdit m_editID;         // Student ID
    private InkEdit m_editPhone;      // Phone number
    private InkEdit m_editComment;    // Any comments
    private Label m_labelFirst;
    private Label m_labelLast;
    private Label m_labelID;
    private Label m_labelPhone;
    private Label m_labelComments;

    [STAThread]
    static void Main()
    {
        Application.Run(new CollegeFact());
    }

    public CollegeFact()
    {
        InitializeComponent();
    }

    private void InitializeComponent()
    {
        SuspendLayout();

        // Create the InkEdit controls and labels
        InitializeEdit(ref m_editFirst, new Point(80, 24),
                    new Size(160, 32), false);
```

```
        InitializeEdit(ref m_editLast, new Point(344, 24),
                    new Size(160, 32), false);
        InitializeEdit(ref m_editID, new Point(80, 64),
                    new Size(160, 32), false);
        InitializeEdit(ref m_editPhone, new Point(344, 64),
                    new Size(160, 32), false);
        InitializeEdit(ref m_editComment, new Point(80, 104),
                    new Size(424, 88), true);   // Multiline!
        InitializeLabel(ref m_labelFirst, new Point(-8, 32),
                    new Size(88, 23), "First Name:");
        InitializeLabel(ref m_labelLast, new Point(256, 32),
                    new Size(88, 23), "Last Name:");
        InitializeLabel(ref m_labelID, new Point(-8, 72),
                    new Size(88, 23), "ID Number:");
        InitializeLabel(ref m_labelPhone, new Point(256, 72),
                    new Size(88, 23), "Phone Number:");
        InitializeLabel(ref m_labelComments, new Point(-8, 112),
                    new Size(88, 23), "Comments:");


        // Configure the form itself
        this.AutoScaleBaseSize = new Size(5, 13);
        this.ClientSize = new Size(528, 206);
        this.Controls.AddRange(new Control[] {
            m_labelComments, m_labelPhone, m_labelID,
            m_labelLast, m_labelFirst, m_editFirst,
            m_editLast, m_editID, m_editPhone, m_editComment
                                    });
        this.FormBorderStyle = FormBorderStyle.FixedDialog;
        this.MaximizeBox = false;
        this.Text = "College Registration";

        // Set the Factoids that will be used
        SetFactoids();

        ResumeLayout(false);
    }


    // Helper function to create an InkEdit control
    private void InitializeEdit(ref InkEdit io_edit, Point in_pt,
                            Size in_size, bool in_fMultiline)
    {
        io_edit = new InkEdit();
        io_edit.Location = in_pt;
        io_edit.Size = in_size;
        io_edit.Multiline = in_fMultiline;
    }
```

*(continued)*

**CollegeFact.cs** *(continued)*

```
        // Helper function to create a label
    private void InitializeLabel(ref Label io_label, Point in_pt,
                                     Size in_size, string in_strText)
    {
        io_label = new Label();
        io_label.Location = in_pt;
        io_label.Size = in_size;
        io_label.Text = in_strText;
        io_label.TextAlign = ContentAlignment.MiddleRight;
    }


        // Set our factoids according to what's expected.
    private void SetFactoids()
    {
        m_editFirst.Factoid = Factoid.None;
        m_editLast.Factoid = Factoid.None;
        m_editID.Factoid = Factoid.Number;
        m_editPhone.Factoid = Factoid.Telephone;
    }
}
```

## Recognition Timing

When inking in a typical InkEdit control, you'll notice that it recognizes ink and turns it into text when one of two things happens—either the InkEdit control loses focus or some time passes since you've last written into the control.

You can control the amount of time that passes before InkEdit converts the ink into text by changing the *RecoTimeout* property. You can set the number of milliseconds you want InkEdit to wait before beginning recognition through this property:

```
m_edit.RecoTimeout = 5000;    // Wait for 5 seconds before reco!
```

Setting *RecoTimeout* to too short an interval risks interrupting the user in the middle of a multistroke word, whereas making the interval too long risks boring the user. You can also set *RecoTimeout* to zero, which does *not* mean that ink gets recognized immediately when you lift the pen. Zero actually means infinite in this case. If *RecoTimeout* is zero, automatic recognition simply will not happen.

But even if *RecoTimeout* is zero, you can manually force recognition to occur at any time by calling *Recognize*. The *Recognize* call is synchronous, so it will not return until the recognition and conversion to text has been completed. One point to remember is that *Recognize* will convert only freshly added ink into text. It will not convert any previously inserted ink added when *InkInsertMode* was *InsertAsInk*, for instance.

The following sample program shows how *RecoTimeout* and *Recognize* can work together to make InkEdit recognize ink on demand. It sets *RecoTimeout* to zero and calls *Recognize* only when the Recognize Now button is clicked.

**DelayedReco.cs**

```
//////////////////////////////////////////////////////////////////
// DelayedReco.cs
// (c) 2002 Microsoft Press, by Philip Su
// This program demonstrates delayed recognition with InkEdit
//////////////////////////////////////////////////////////////////
using System;
using System.Windows.Forms;
using System.Drawing;
using Microsoft.Ink;

public class DelayedReco : Form
{
    private InkEdit m_edit;
    private Label   m_label;
    private Button  m_btnReco;

    [STAThread]
    static void Main()
    {
        Application.Run(new DelayedReco());
    }

    public DelayedReco()
    {
        InitializeComponent();
        m_edit.RecoTimeout = 0;      // Prevent automatic recognition
    }

    // Handle the click of the Recognize Now button
    private void RecoBtnClick(object sender, EventArgs e)
    {
        m_edit.Recognize();
    }

    private void InitializeComponent()
    {
        SuspendLayout();

        // Create the InkEdit control and label
        m_edit = new InkEdit();
```

*(continued)*

**DelayedReco.cs** *(continued)*

```
        m_edit.Location = new Point(65, 24);
        m_edit.Size = new Size(424, 88);
        m_edit.Cursor = System.Windows.Forms.Cursors.IBeam;

        m_label = new Label();
        m_label.Location = new Point(0, 24);
        m_label.Size = new Size(60, 23);
        m_label.Text = "Ink Here:";
        m_label.TextAlign = ContentAlignment.MiddleRight;

        m_btnReco = new Button();
        m_btnReco.Location = new Point(65, 120);
        m_btnReco.Size = new Size(100, 23);
        m_btnReco.Text = "Recognize Now";
        m_btnReco.Click += new EventHandler(RecoBtnClick);

            // Configure the form itself
        this.AutoScaleBaseSize = new Size(5, 13);
        this.ClientSize = new Size(528, 150);
        this.Controls.AddRange(new Control[] {
            m_label, m_edit, m_btnReco });
        this.FormBorderStyle = FormBorderStyle.FixedDialog;
        this.MaximizeBox = false;
        this.Text = "InkEdit Delayed Recognition";

        ResumeLayout(false);
    }
}
```

Whether you call *Recognize* programmatically or InkEdit calls it automatically, the control always fires the *Recognition* event. You can attach a delegate to receive this event, which fires immediately after recognition but before InkEdit inserts the recognized text. Unfortunately, you cannot change the text that will be inserted into the control by calling *ModifyTopAlternate* on the *RecognitionResult* passed in the event's *InkEditRecognitionEventArgs* parameter. On Windows XP Tablet PC Edition, calling *ModifyTopAlternate* on an InkEdit's *RecognitionResult* will have no effect.

### Gestures in InkEdit

You have limited control over gestures in an InkEdit control. You can toggle the detection of gestures and you can respond to the *Gesture* event. The following gestures are on by default:

| Gesture | Action |
|---|---|
| DownLeft, DownLeftLong | Return |
| UpRight, UpRightLong | Tab |
| Right | Space |
| Left | Backspace |

Let's dive right into the Gesticulator sample program. Gesticulator has an InkEdit control that responds to two additional gestures: Scratch-Out and Star.

**Gesticulator.cs**

```
///////////////////////////////////////////////////////////////////
// Gesticulator.cs
// (c) 2002 Microsoft Press, by Philip Su
// This program demonstrates gestures in InkEdit
///////////////////////////////////////////////////////////////////
using System;
using System.Drawing;
using System.Windows.Forms;
using Microsoft.Ink;

public class Gesticulator : Form
{
    private InkEdit m_edit;
    private Label m_label;

    [STAThread]
    static void Main()
    {
        Application.Run(new Gesticulator());
    }

    public Gesticulator()
    {
        InitializeComponent();
        RegisterForGestures();       // Here's where the action's at!
    }

    private void InitializeComponent()
    {
        SuspendLayout();
```

*(continued)*

**Gesticulator.cs** *(continued)*

```csharp
        // Create the InkEdit control and label
    m_edit = new InkEdit();
    m_edit.Location = new Point(65, 24);
    m_edit.Size = new Size(424, 88);
    m_edit.Cursor = System.Windows.Forms.Cursors.IBeam;

    m_label = new Label();
    m_label.Location = new Point(0, 24);
    m_label.Size = new Size(60, 23);
    m_label.Text = "Ink Here:";
    m_label.TextAlign = ContentAlignment.MiddleRight;

        // Configure the form itself
    this.AutoScaleBaseSize = new Size(5, 13);
    this.ClientSize = new Size(528, 125);
    this.Controls.AddRange(new Control[] {
        m_label, m_edit });
    this.FormBorderStyle = FormBorderStyle.FixedDialog;
    this.MaximizeBox = false;
    this.Text = "Gesticulator";

    ResumeLayout(false);
}


    // Let the InkEdit control know which additional
    // gestures to inform us of
private void RegisterForGestures()
{
        // SetGestureStatus requires us to be idle
    while (m_edit.Status != InkEditStatus.Idle)
    {
        System.Threading.Thread.Sleep(100);
    }
    m_edit.SetGestureStatus(ApplicationGesture.Scratchout,
                            true);
    m_edit.SetGestureStatus(ApplicationGesture.Star,
                            true);
    m_edit.Gesture += new InkEditGestureEventHandler(
                            GestureHandler);
}

private void GestureHandler(object in_sender,
    InkEditGestureEventArgs in_args)
{
```

```
switch (in_args.Gestures[0].Id)
{
case ApplicationGesture.Scratchout:
    m_edit.Clear();      // Remove all text
    break;
case ApplicationGesture.Star:
    m_edit.SelectedText = "*";  // Insert an asterisk
    break;
}
    }
}
```

The Gesticulator constructor first initializes its components and then calls *RegisterForGestures*. The actual registration for gestures is a simple two-step process. First you express your interest in detecting a particular gesture by calling *SetGestureStatus* (the second parameter determines whether you'd like to hear about the gesture):

```
m_edit.SetGestureStatus(ApplicationGesture.Scratchout,
                        true);
m_edit.SetGestureStatus(ApplicationGesture.Star,
                        true);
```

In this case, we've expressed interest in both the *Scratchout* and *Star* gestures. You can call *SetGestureStatus* only while InkEdit is idle, so the program goes through the familiar idle-detection loop prior to the code shown here. Once you've expressed interest, the control will start to detect these two additional gestures. The second step in the process is to register for the gesture event:

```
m_edit.Gesture += new InkEditGestureEventHandler(
                      GestureHandler);
```

The *GestureHandler* function does the real work of responding to any triggered gestures. In it, we look for and process the two gestures of interest:

```
switch (in_args.Gestures[0].Id)
{
case ApplicationGesture.Scratchout:
    m_edit.Clear();      // Remove all text
    break;
case ApplicationGesture.Star:
    m_edit.SelectedText = "*";  // Insert an asterisk
    break;
}
```

When we receive the *Scratchout* gesture, we remove all text from the InkEdit control (it inherits the *Clear* function from its ancestor class, *TextBox-Base*). The *Star* gesture ends up either inserting an asterisk at the caret or replacing the selection with an asterisk, depending on whether you've got text selected. There's really nothing else to Gesticulator!

You've probably realized that even though *GestureHandler* deals only with two gestures, the default InkEdit gestures still work when executed. This is because InkEdit has a gesture handler registered with the *Gesture* event, independent of anything we've done. This might make you wonder whether you can turn a few of the default InkEdit gestures off. The good news is that you can—just call *SetGestureStatus* with *false* as the second parameter for any default InkEdit gestures that you want to turn off. Those gestures will no longer trigger any unwanted behaviors.

If you're interested in finding out whether a gesture is currently turned on, call *GetGestureStatus*. This method returns whether a given application gesture is being watched for (*true*) or not watched for (*false*) by the gesture recognizer. Gestures can also have more than one handler, each performing a different task when InkEdit detects the gesture.

> **Note** Remember that a gesture that's enabled is only being listened for; it doesn't necessarily have to have a handler that does something with it.

## InkEdit Parting Thoughts

So far in this chapter we've shown you how easy it is to integrate InkEdit into application user interfaces. You've also seen how InkEdit can be reasonably accommodating to customization of its appearance, behavior, and recognition. These characteristics make InkEdit an ideal candidate to help enhance your application's ink awareness, particularly in its ability to accept direct ink input into its dialog box edit controls.

Despite its flexibility, InkEdit has certain limitations. Its biggest one is that it does not expose an *InkCollector* or *InkOverlay* interface. Thus, you cannot control specifics about how InkEdit collects ink. For instance, what if you wanted to prevent the user from inking over existing text in the control? Or if you wanted to stop ink from being captured when it flows outside the boundaries of the control? These are things you simply cannot do with InkEdit. Another limitation is that InkEdit does not expose the *RecognizerContext* it uses to perform recognition. Without access to the *RecognizerContext* you cannot fine-tune ink recognition. For example, you might want to enforce that recognition adhere to a given *Factoid* by using the *RecognitionFlags* value *Coerce*, which we learned about in Chapter 7. However, because there is no reco context available, there is no *RecognitionMode* property to set.

We end our exploration into InkEdit with some thoughts about usability. Strictly speaking, on a tablet there is no need for the InkEdit control at all. After all, the Tablet PC Input Panel is able to inject text into regular edit boxes. However, the InkEdit control offers a more direct way for the tablet user to interact with your application without needing to bring up the Input Panel. Successful integration of InkEdit controls goes beyond simply adding these controls to our applications. Usability demands that we answer two questions:

- How does the user know that an edit control is inkable?

- Is the writing area of the InkEdit control big enough to write in comfortably?

The Tablet PC Platform, unfortunately, does not answer the first question. InkEdit controls are visually indistinguishable from their *RichTextBox* counterparts. It's true that while hovering a pen over InkEdit, the user can look for a cursor that's not an I-beam. But this minor distinction is arguably too small to be considered usable as the primary means of determining whether to attempt to write directly in an edit box. Given that it's not at all easy to visually distinguish InkEdit controls from standard TextBox controls, we offer one important piece of advice:

*Do not mix InkEdit with plain edit boxes in your application!*

Doing so will cause a usability nightmare since the user will need to memorize the edit boxes that are ink aware and those that are not. Instead, if you plan to add even a single InkEdit to your application, consider making all your application's edit controls InkEdit.

You control the answer to the second question—whether the InkEdit controls are big enough to write in. Plain edit boxes are typically tall enough to display 10-point fonts, which is not that tall at all (especially compared to handwriting). You can provide a better user experience if you make your InkEdit controls big enough to write in. Sizing the InkEdit controls is a tough balancing act, though. If you make them too big, non-tablet users will wonder what all that space is for. There will also no doubt be the familiar challenges from designers regarding the visual appearance of large edit boxes juxtaposed with small text labels.

All things considered, the InkEdit control is a useful tool in your Tablet PC development arsenal. In cases where your application needs an ink-aware control for data entry, InkEdit is the clear choice.

# InkPicture

InkPicture is the second control available for use in the Tablet PC Platform SDK. Its intended use focuses narrowly around inking on images. In fact, the InkPicture control offers little value over the *InkOverlay* class, as we'll soon see. Unlike InkEdit, InkPicture supports only managed and ActiveX flavors—it does not have a Win32 interface.

The InkPicture control is essentially a combination of the *InkOverlay* class and the .NET Framework's PictureBox control. If you do a method-by-method, event-by-event, property-by-property comparison of InkPicture and *InkOverlay*, you will find that they are similar. In addition, because InkPicture derives from the PictureBox, it includes and exposes all the functionality of the PictureBox control.

> **Note**    Chapter 4 covered the *InkOverlay* class extensively. InkPicture retains almost 100 percent of the *InkOverlay* interface, so your knowledge of *InkOverlay* should transfer nicely to InkPicture. The PictureBox control is comprehensively covered in MSDN and books such as *Programming Microsoft Windows with C#*, so we won't delve into it too deeply.

Now let's dive right into an InkPicture sample. The following program lets a user ink over any image file by first loading it into the InkPicture control and then capturing the user's ink. When the user saves, we combine the image and the ink together in one file. Subsequently, the user can reload a saved file to continue working on it. Figure 8-2 shows the application in action.

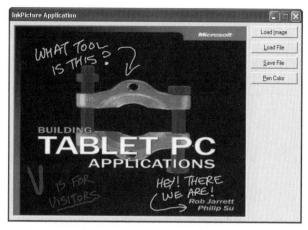

**Figure 8-2**   InkPictureApp supports inking on loaded images and saves image and ink together in ISF files.

**InkPictureApp.cs**

```
/////////////////////////////////////////////////////////////////////
// InkPictureApp.cs
// (c) 2002 Microsoft Press, by Philip Su
// This program uses InkPicture to collect ink over an image.  It
// supports saving and loading of ink along with the image.
/////////////////////////////////////////////////////////////////////
using System;
using System.Drawing;
using System.Windows.Forms;
using System.Collections;
using System.IO;
using Microsoft.Ink;
using System.Runtime.Serialization.Formatters.Binary;

public class InkPictureApp : Form
{
        // File filters for load / save dialogs
    private const string strFileFilter = "ISF files (*.isf)|*.isf|" +
        "All files (*.*)|*.*";
    private const string strImageFilter = "Image files " +
        "(*.bmp; *.gif; *.jpg; *.png)|*.bmp;*.gif;*.jpg;*.png|" +
        "All files (*.*)|*.*";
```

*(continued)*

**InkPictureApp.cs** *(continued)*

```csharp
        // Store images in the ink object using a custom property
        // with this guid
private static Guid guidImage =
    new Guid("{B3BF218B-2923-4d8a-9675-D36FA38EF17D}");

private InkPicture      m_inkpict;
private Button          m_btnLoadImage;
private Button          m_btnLoad;
private Button          m_btnSave;
private Button          m_btnColor;

    // Entry point of the program
static void Main()
{
    Application.Run(new InkPictureApp());
}

    // Main form setup
public InkPictureApp()
{
    CreateUI();

        // Stretch images to fit
    m_inkpict.SizeMode = PictureBoxSizeMode.StretchImage;
}

    // Load Image button handler — loads an image
private void OnLoadImage(object sender, EventArgs e)
{
    OpenFileDialog opendlg = new OpenFileDialog();

        // Show the Open File dialog
    opendlg.Filter = strImageFilter;
    if (opendlg.ShowDialog() == DialogResult.OK)
    {
        try
        {
            m_inkpict.Image = Image.FromFile(opendlg.FileName);
        }
        catch (Exception)
        {
            MessageBox.Show(this, "Unable to load the image!",
                                  "Load error");
        }
    }
}

    // Load button handler — uses the system Load dialog
```

```
private void OnLoad(object sender, EventArgs e)
{
    OpenFileDialog opendlg = new OpenFileDialog();

        // Show the Open File dialog
    opendlg.Filter = strFileFilter;
    if (opendlg.ShowDialog() == DialogResult.OK)
    {
        Stream stream = opendlg.OpenFile();

        if (stream != null && stream.Length > 0)
        {
            byte[] rgb = new byte[stream.Length];
            int cbRead = 0;

                // Read in the ISF into rgb
            cbRead = stream.Read(rgb, 0, rgb.Length);
            if (cbRead == stream.Length)
            {
                Ink ink = new Ink();

                ink.Load(rgb);  // Load the ISF

                    // Set the loaded ink into m_inkpict.  To do
                    // so, we must disable inking in m_inkpict
                    // before setting its Ink property.
                m_inkpict.InkEnabled = false;
                m_inkpict.Ink = ink;
                m_inkpict.InkEnabled = true;

                    // Load an image, if it exists, into the
                    // control.
                m_inkpict.Image = LoadImageFromInk(ink);

                    // Update our UI
                m_inkpict.Invalidate();
            }
            stream.Close();
        }
    }
}

private Image LoadImageFromInk(Ink ink)
{
    if (ink.ExtendedProperties.Contains(guidImage))
    {
        byte[] rgbImage =
```

*(continued)*

**InkPictureApp.cs** *(continued)*

```
                (byte[])ink.ExtendedProperties[guidImage].Data;
        MemoryStream    ms  = new MemoryStream(rgbImage);
        BinaryFormatter bf  = new BinaryFormatter();

            // Convert the memory stream of bytes into an image
        return (Image)bf.Deserialize(ms);
    }
    else
    {
        return null;
    }
}


    // Save button handler -- uses the system Save dialog
private void OnSave(object sender, EventArgs e)
{
    SaveFileDialog savedlg = new SaveFileDialog();

        // Initialize and show the Save dialog
    savedlg.Filter = strFileFilter;
    if (savedlg.ShowDialog() == DialogResult.OK)
    {
        Stream stream = savedlg.OpenFile();

            // Prepare to write the ISF.
        if (stream != null)
        {
            byte[] rgbISF;

                // Save the image as an extended property
            if (m_inkpict.Image != null)
            {
                SaveImageInInk(m_inkpict.Image, m_inkpict.Ink);
            }

                // Now save it all
            rgbISF = m_inkpict.Ink.Save();
            stream.Write(rgbISF, 0, rgbISF.Length);
            stream.Close();
        }
    }
}

private void SaveImageInInk(Image image, Ink ink)
{
    MemoryStream    ms  = new MemoryStream();
    BinaryFormatter bf  = new BinaryFormatter();
    byte[]          rgbImage;
```

```
            // Convert the image to a memory stream of bytes
        bf.Serialize(ms, image);
        rgbImage = ms.GetBuffer();

            // Add the image's data as an extended property
        ink.ExtendedProperties.Add(guidImage, rgbImage);
    }

        // Color button handler -- uses system color dialog
    private void OnColor(object sender, EventArgs e)
    {
        ColorDialog colordlg = new ColorDialog();

        if (colordlg.ShowDialog() == DialogResult.OK)
        {
            DrawingAttributes drawattrs;

            drawattrs = m_inkpict.DefaultDrawingAttributes;
            drawattrs.Color = colordlg.Color;
        }
    }

    private const int cSpacing = 8; // Space between controls

    private void CreateUI()
    {
        int x = cSpacing;
        int y = cSpacing;

        SuspendLayout();

            // Create and place all of our controls
        m_inkpict = new InkPicture();
        m_inkpict.BorderStyle = BorderStyle.Fixed3D;
        m_inkpict.Location = new Point(x, y);
        m_inkpict.Size = new Size(500, 400);
        m_inkpict.BackColor = Color.White;
        x += m_inkpict.Bounds.Width + cSpacing;

        y = CreateButton(out m_btnLoadImage, x, y, 100, 24,
                        "Load &Image",
                        new EventHandler(OnLoadImage));
        y = CreateButton(out m_btnLoad, x, y, 100, 24, "&Load File",
                        new EventHandler(OnLoad));
        y = CreateButton(out m_btnSave, x, y, 100, 24, "&Save File",
                        new EventHandler(OnSave));
```

*(continued)*

**InkPictureApp.cs** *(continued)*

```
    y = CreateButton(out m_btnColor, x, y, 100, 24, "&Pen Color",
                        new EventHandler(OnColor));


        // Configure the form itself
    x += m_btnColor.Bounds.Width + cSpacing;
    y = m_inkpict.Bounds.Height + (2 * cSpacing);
    AutoScaleBaseSize = new Size(5, 13);
    ClientSize = new Size(x, y);
    Controls.AddRange(new Control[] { m_inkpict, m_btnLoadImage,
                                      m_btnLoad, m_btnSave,
                                      m_btnColor });
    FormBorderStyle = FormBorderStyle.FixedDialog;
    MaximizeBox = false;
    Text = "InkPicture Application";


    ResumeLayout(false);
}


    // Creates a button and suggests the next y value to use
private int CreateButton(out Button btn, int x, int y,
                int cWidth, int cHeight,
                    string strName, EventHandler eh)
{
    btn = new Button();
    btn.Location = new Point(x, y);
    btn.Size = new Size(cWidth, cHeight);
    btn.Text = strName;
    btn.Click += eh;
    return y + btn.Bounds.Height + cSpacing;   // Suggest next y
}
}
```

*CreateUI* (called from the constructor) creates an InkPicture control just as you would create any other control. It sets a border around the InkPicture control and also makes its background white:

```
m_inkpict = new InkPicture();
m_inkpict.BorderStyle = BorderStyle.Fixed3D;
m_inkpict.Location = new Point(x, y);
m_inkpict.Size = new Size(500, 400);
m_inkpict.BackColor = Color.White;
```

InkPicture inherits a *SizeMode* setting from *PictureBox*, which determines how a loaded image is sized relative to the control. We decided that it would be nice to have images stretched to fit the control.

```
m_inkpict.SizeMode = PictureBoxSizeMode.StretchImage;
```

Loading the image is also straightforward. After using the standard *Open-FileDialog* to choose an image, we load it using *Image's FromFile*. Then we assign the resulting *Image* to the *Image* property on InkPicture:

```
m_inkpict.Image = Image.FromFile(opendlg.FileName);
```

If we stopped right here, we would already have an application that is capable of inking on top of loaded images. But to increase the fun, we added two more features: ink color and load/save capability. For color, we rely on the standard color dialog to let the user choose a color, and then set the chosen color into InkPicture's *DefaultDrawingAtttributes*:

```
drawattrs = m_inkpict.DefaultDrawingAttributes;
drawattrs.Color = colordlg.Color;
```

Now for the interesting part—loading and saving the image along with the ink. InkPicture will not save them together automatically, so you'll need a strategy of your own if you'd like the image and ink saved together. The strategy in our sample application is simple: we save the image as an extended property in the *Ink* object, which is then streamed out with the ink into Ink Serialized Format (ISF). Let's take a look at *SaveImageInInk* first:

```
MemoryStream     ms  = new MemoryStream();
BinaryFormatter bf  = new BinaryFormatter();
byte[]          rgbImage;

    // Convert the image to a memory stream of bytes
bf.Serialize(ms, image);
rgbImage = ms.GetBuffer();

    // Add the image's data as an extended property
ink.ExtendedProperties.Add(guidImage, rgbImage);
```

Because *Image* supports *ISerializable*, *BinaryFormatter* does all the magic of converting it into a stream of bytes. We add the array of bytes to the *ExtendedProperties* collection, associating it with a *Guid* we chose for all such embedded images. This effectively assures that the *Image* will remain with the ink when we save and load, since all extended properties are automatically saved and loaded from ISF. Using the *ExtendedProperties* collection is just one of many ways in which ink can be tied together in a file format with an image. We chose this as our strategy for its relative ease and clarity.

You might be wondering why we need to go through all the trouble of using *BinaryFormatter* to save the ink. After all, shouldn't the following work?

```
ink.ExtendedProperties.Add(guidImage, image); // Throws!
```

Unfortunately, this code will throw an exception. The *ExtendedProperties* collection does not accept just any object that implements *ISerializable*. Instead, it is quite limited in being able to store only built-in types (such as *int*, *float*, *double*, *bool*, *byte*[], or *string*). So if you need to store an extended property that is not a built-in type, serialize it into a byte array prior to calling *Add*.

In *LoadImageFromInk*, we search for an extended property with the same *Guid* as when we saved. Using *BinaryFormatter*, we convert the stream of bytes back into the original image:

```
if (ink.ExtendedProperties.Contains(guidImage))
{
    byte[] rgbImage =
        (byte[])ink.ExtendedProperties[guidImage].Data;
    MemoryStream    ms  = new MemoryStream(rgbImage);
    BinaryFormatter bf  = new BinaryFormatter();

        // Convert the memory stream of bytes into an image
    return (Image)bf.Deserialize(ms);
}
```

Up to this point, nothing we've done with InkPicture should be new. All the functionality that we've been using so far in InkPicture is exactly the same as what's available in the related *InkOverlay* and *PictureBox* classes.

However, InkPicture has an *InkEnabled* property that is not available in either related class. InkPicture's *InkEnabled* property is analogous to *InkOverlay's Enabled* property. It was merely renamed to distinguish it from the Picture-Box control's *Enabled* property (inherited from *System.Windows.Forms.Control*). In InkPicture, changing the *Enabled* property will enable or disable the control as a whole. However, changing the *InkEnabled* property turns ink capture on and off, just as it does in *InkOverlay*.

It's worth mentioning again that the Tablet PC Platform SDK requires that you turn off ink capture before changing the *Ink* property. This is true for *Ink-Overlay*, and it remains true for InkPicture. After loading an image from the ISF, we carefully set the image into InkPicture:

```
m_inkpict.InkEnabled = false;
m_inkpict.Ink = ink;
m_inkpict.InkEnabled = true;
```

It's important to set *InkEnabled* to *false* prior to assigning a new *Ink* object into InkPicture. Given the tremendous similarity between *InkOverlay* and Ink-Picture, it is all too easy to do the following by habit:

```
m_inkpict.Enabled = false;    // Wrong!
m_inkpict.Ink = ink;
m_inkpict.Enabled = true;     // Wrong!
```

This code compiles, but it will throw a mysterious exception when run. Remembering this subtle difference between InkPicture and *InkOverlay* will save you precious debugging time!

## Summary

In this chapter, we looked at the two ink controls available in the Tablet PC Platform SDK: InkEdit and InkPicture. We first discussed InkEdit, which adds inking ability to *RichTextBox*, the standard system textbox control. InkEdit's primary purpose is to enable the user to write directly in textboxes. Without InkEdit, pen users need to bring up the Tablet PC Input Panel to enter text data into your application. InkEdit gives you the choice between automatic ink-to-text conversion, where ink is recognized after a pause in the user's writing, and manual conversion, where your application calls *Recognize* when appropriate. It also detects some basic gestures while letting your application listen for other gestures of interest.

We then took a brief look at InkPicture. We showed you that InkPicture combines what's available through *InkOverlay* and *PictureBox*. The only caveat concerned the difference between the *Enabled* and *InkEnabled* properties. Ink-Picture does not automatically save an image and ink together. Instead, you will have to devise your own scheme for saving both image and ink if your application needs to do so.

This concludes our technical investigation into the Tablet PC Platform SDK. Through the last five chapters we have made a lot of progress, moving from tablet input to ink data management, ink recognition, and ink controls. You are now a fully outfitted Tablet PC developer!

Write some code and create some great Tablet PC applications! And share your best work with us.

# Part III

# Advanced Tablet PC Topics

# 9

# Updating Existing Applications

Up to now, our investigation into the Tablet PC Platform SDK has not concerned itself with whether you're writing a new application or retrofitting an existing one for the Tablet PC. However, we will now change our focus to examine the specific issues involved with updating an existing application to leverage the Tablet PC Platform. You will find when using the SDK that there are some important considerations unique to working with an existing application.

In this chapter we will cover the reasons you might want to update your application to work on the Tablet PC Platform. We will also explore the reasons why, depending on the characteristics of your application, you might not need to use the SDK at all. We then delve into several practical considerations of integrating the SDK in terms of its effect on both application design and performance.

## Even Better than the Real Thing

A majority of existing applications work just fine on the Tablet PC, indicating that integration with the Tablet PC Platform isn't necessarily a requirement for a great tablet application. After all, a major design goal of the Tablet PC Platform was that legacy applications would work without modification, using the platform's mouse emulation and the Tablet PC Input Panel for mouse and keyboard input.

However, the fact that you're reading this book is an indicator that your application is most likely different from the ones just mentioned. You probably already suspect that your application might benefit from tighter integration with the Tablet PC Platform. Let's get right into the reasons why your application might be better off leveraging the platform, and what level of integration is appropriate for your needs.

# User Benefits of Integration

A user who purchases a Tablet PC will reap all the hardware-related benefits of the device, such as its portability and pen-based mouse emulation, *without any intervention from your software*. The question of whether to change your application to work better on the Tablet PC instead revolves around two issues: pen-friendly user interfaces and digital ink features.

## Pen-Friendly User Interfaces

Even if your application will not support digital ink, there are significant user interface challenges that you must surmount in order to make it truly usable on a Tablet PC. The pen is great as a natural and intuitive manipulator—users are adept at directly interacting with the visible user interface elements in an application. However, you can add functionality to your application that the pen can take advantage of to fully realize its value as a direct manipulator. Some of the problems that existing user interfaces might pose were discussed in Chapter 2, and included:

- **Inadequate control size**   Controls that are several pixels wide are simply too hard to target with a pen.

- **Parallax**   The difference between where the user thinks the pen is and where the system thinks it is can be significant.

- **Physical obscuration**   The user's hand and the pen itself will often block large portions of the user interface.

- **Hover sensitivity**   Features relying on the user to hold the cursor still, such as tool tips, are problematic when using a pen.

When updating an existing application for use on a Tablet PC, these user interface issues need to be addressed. However, it's not all bad news! Pens also open up a new world of possibilities for your application's user interface, including:

- **Advanced pen features**   Many Tablet PCs support querying some pretty fancy pen features, such as hover distance, rotation, tilt, and pressure. This allows your application to pioneer new, more intuitive user interfaces. For instance, a 3-D modeling application might use a pen's rotation and tilt to decide how to orient an object in space. It might even use pressure and hover distance to determine how far into a scene an object should be placed. The possibilities are quite exciting given these new axes of freedom.

- **Pen buttons and tips**   A Tablet PC pen might also have barrel buttons and even sensitivity on both tips (ends). Their availability opens the door to more natural user interfaces. Perhaps the best example of this is using the tail end of a pen as the eraser, but there are many other opportunities (such as using tips and buttons for highlighter or selection functions).

You should decide which of these user interface problems and possibilities to tackle and exploit in your application. You can usually overcome problems in your applications without having to use the Tablet PC Platform SDK because control size, parallax, physical obscuration, and hover sensitivity do not involve Tablet PC Platform–specific APIs. However, you can often capitalize on opportunities to use the new pen capabilities through the Tablet PC Platform SDK.

## Digital Ink Features

If you want digital ink features, updating your application to work with the Tablet PC Platform SDK is the right way to go. The platform and the SDK take care of a host of ink-related problems for you, making your job much easier. Here are a few ways in which your application might use digital ink:

- **As a replacement for physical ink**   Perhaps one of the greatest draws of digital ink is its ability to replace physical pen and paper. Currently, annotating, note taking, and transcribing are largely done on paper. However, the ease with which digital ink is manipulated, searched, and stored outmatches traditional paper in many usage scenarios.

- **As an alternative input methodology**   The pen and digital ink are intuitive alternatives for entering data. For instance, a parcel carrier might find it easier to fill out forms with a pen instead of a keyboard while on a route. A graphic designer might prefer sketching logo ideas using a pen instead of constructing them slowly with a mouse. A musician might want to draw notes on a digital staff. There are many other applications that could profit from allowing digital ink as a natural method of input.

And what if your application already supports digital ink? This is not that far-fetched of a possibility because there have been many tablet-like PC devices before Microsoft's Tablet PC. Furthermore, some niche market applications have long been using pens and digitizer tablets as their primary input device. If your application currently accepts digital ink, the remaining question is whether it would be better off converting its features' implementations to use the Tablet PC Platform SDK. This is a difficult question only you can answer, but we aim to provide you with the necessary information to make a knowledgeable decision. Benefits of using the platform with the SDK include:

- **Standardization**   Using the SDK will automatically afford basic interoperability (by means of the Clipboard, for instance) with other applications that support digital ink.

- **Effortless improvements**   As further advances are made in areas such as handwriting recognition, new platform binaries will automatically improve your application without requiring it to be changed.

- **Built-in features**   Bézier curve fitting, antialiased ink, high-throughput pen data, and ink recognition are just a few of the advanced features that come bundled in the Tablet PC Platform. Chances are good that replicating these features would require a significant investment of time on your part.

## Business Benefits of Integration

Now that we've explored some possible user benefits of integrating your application with the Tablet PC Platform, we'll turn our attention to the business-driven reasons why you might want your application to shine on the Tablet PC. As this is a book meant for programmers, not for marketers, we'll keep the business reasoning simple. Three basic factors that affect the decision to invest in building Tablet PC features in your application are:

- **Business cost**   How many developers and testers will it take to integrate pen and ink features? This cost will fluctuate depending on how pen-friendly and ink-ready your application is currently.

- **User benefit**   Earlier we discussed the various user benefits of applications designed for the Tablet PC. Your application's purpose and usage scenarios will influence the amount your users will benefit.

- **Tablet PC adoption rate**   The number of Tablet PCs sold and the speed at which they're sold are important factors that unfortunately you have little control over (unless, of course, you write the killer application that single-handedly drives sales of Tablet PCs through the roof). A more accurate forecast of the adoption rate can be given only after Tablet PCs start selling in many markets worldwide.

The specifics of cost and user benefit will depend on your business. Intimate knowledge of your own situation will help you to choose correctly for your application.

# Technical Considerations

Now that we're done with the reasons you might want to revise your application to leverage the Tablet PC Platform, we're ready to evaluate the technical considerations involved with using the SDK. These considerations are grouped into the two broad categories of application design and performance.

# Application Design

Successful integration of Tablet PC Platform features will require some planning in regard to an application's design. Several key design issues are surveyed in the following sections. You might find that while some of these issues might not concern your application, others might dramatically affect how you end up implementing your pen and digital ink features.

### *InkCollector* and *InkOverlay*

Assimilating either an *InkCollector* object or an *InkOverlay* object into an application can be easy, depending on what you have in mind. For the purposes of this discussion, we will assume that you are using *InkOverlay*, though everything in this section applies to *InkCollector* as well. The simplest type of application that integrates *InkOverlay* is one in which there is both a mode and an area that accepts ink. For instance, if an application has an Insert Inking Surface feature that inserts a window that collects ink only when it's selected and activated, it is fairly straightforward to use *InkOverlay* with that window. Similarly, if an application has an annotation mode that collects ink annotations over a document, it is easy to enable and disable *InkOverlay* as needed.

However, one of the challenges of integrating *InkOverlay* comes in making the boundary between inking and other operations modeless. There are a few obstacles to overcome if you want there to be no explicit mode switching between the user inking and doing other things (for instance, selecting or bringing up a context menu).

One such obstacle is that tablet input events and mouse messages come in an unpredictable order. The reasons for this were described in detail in Chapter 4. The effect, nonetheless, is that your application's existing input message handler might need to be made aware of tablet input events (and their unpredictable order) to respond correctly to user action. There might be a variety of cases in which the mixture of input messages and tablet input events yield unexpected behavior in your application, and some of them might be tricky to debug.

Another potential hurdle when implementing modeless inking is that you will most likely want to respond to many of the events sent by *InkOverlay* in order to override or cancel them. For instance, when the user touches the pen to the window, you'll want to first decide whether the pen might be targeting a UI element such as a selection handle. If so, you'll likely cancel the stroke in progress (by making it transparent and later discarding it when the *Stroke* event fires, for example) and instead track the dragging of the handle. There are many other cases in which you might need to listen to tablet input events in order to override or augment the default behavior.

In the end, you might find that it's easier to control both when and where the user can ink by supplying an explicit inking mode and an inking window or area. A modeless interface is more difficult to get right, and it can even be frustrating if it's not tweaked to respond well to the average user's expectations.

## Storage

Your application probably already stores its data in a particular way. Depending on how closely compatible it is with your existing format, it shouldn't be too difficult for you to integrate the Tablet PC Platform's digital ink storage format into your application. The Tablet PC stores digital ink in four flavors: Ink Serialized Format (ISF), Graphics Interchange Format (GIF), and Base64-encoded variants of both.

ISF is the default format for storing digital ink on the Tablet PC Platform. It is an opaque (not publicly documented) binary format that stores all the relevant data from an *Ink* object so that the same ink can be reconstituted later. It is also the standard format by which digital ink is exchanged between applications from the Clipboard on Tablet PCs. ISF supports two modes of compression in order to reduce the size of the resulting binary stream.

GIF is the once-popular 256-color image format supported by all Internet browsers and most image applications. You might be struck by the seeming oddity of the Tablet PC Platform supporting GIF, of all things, for storage. GIF was chosen as the down-level compatibility solution for digital ink (that is, the solution for the problem of how non-Tablet PC users can view digital ink created on a Tablet PC). Two characteristics make GIF a good solution: its widespread support and its ability to embed arbitrary metadata. ISF is actually embedded in GIF's metadata section, thereby making it possible to recapture the original ink by using the SDK to load such a GIF.

Base64 is a method of encoding binary streams into text. The Tablet PC Platform supports saving of its ISF and GIF formats in Base64-encoded flavors, thereby making it possible to embed the streams into text-based formats such as XML and HTML. We will analyze the amount of bloat that Base64 encoding introduces in the upcoming section on performance.

In all likelihood your application data is already being stored in some convenient binary or text format. It should be straightforward to store digital ink alongside your current data using the Tablet PC Platform's *Ink.Save* method.

One final thing to think about is versioning of the storage format, which the Tablet PC Platform documentation does not explicitly address. The problem is with both backward compatibility (future versions reading current formats) and forward compatibility (current versions reading future formats) because the platform guarantees neither. Although it might seem reasonable to expect that at least backward compatibility will be preserved, lack of an explicitly stated policy or guarantee should make you wary. Do not assume that future revisions of the platform will handle versioning transparently! If your application needs to guarantee backward or forward compatibility, you might need to provide that functionality yourself by storing version information, for example.

## Clipboard

Your application probably interacts with the Clipboard to interoperate with other applications. There are three ways in which you can incorporate digital ink into your existing Clipboard code:

- **Embed it into your custom Clipboard format**   If you put a custom data format on the Clipboard specific to your application, you can embed ISF (either binary or Base64) as part of that format. Your application will presumably be responsible for both sides of the interchange (putting the custom format on the Clipboard and reading it off).

- **Embed it into a well-known Clipboard format**   HTML, RTF, WMF, BMP, and Unicode are just some of the many well-known Clipboard formats that popular applications expect. When embedding digital ink in HTML, use the GIF format supported by the platform to maximize interoperability. WMF and BMP can be generated simply by drawing the ink using the appropriate Graphics object, while Unicode can be obtained from a *RecognitionResult*'s *TopAlternate* property. Whether your application reads these well-known formats is up to you.

- **Put it directly on the Clipboard**   *Ink* objects themselves will interact with the Clipboard if you want them to. Using methods such as *ClipboardCopy*, *CanPaste*, and *ClipboardPaste*, you can easily put digital ink on the Clipboard and read it off as well. This makes for an easy way to get up and running with the Clipboard from the Tablet PC Platform.

> **Note** One caveat concerning putting ink directly on the Clipboard: the *IDataObject* created by *ClipboardCopy* cannot have other data formats added to it! If you want the Clipboard to have native ink data as well as some of your application's own data on it, you'll have to create an *IDataObject* of your own.

## Undo

The ability to undo actions has become standard across applications, and most users assume its existence as a matter of course. Undo is one of those features that seems harmless and simple at the outset, but often turns out to be tremendously complicated to implement correctly. Unfortunately, the Tablet PC Platform SDK offers almost no help whatsoever to make the task of implementing undo any easier. Let's take a moment to first understand the problem.

Applications that support undo functionality typically support either single-level undo or multilevel undo. Single-level undo allows the undoing of only one action—the one most recently performed—and might support redoing of that same action once undone. Multilevel undo, on the other hand, allows undoing of more than one action in sequence, usually back to the last point you saved or to when you first launched the application.

In addition to supporting either single-level or multilevel undo, advanced applications might also support undoing of actions across control or process boundaries. For instance, if you type a sentence in Microsoft Word, embed a Microsoft Excel spreadsheet into the document, and edit the spreadsheet as well, you'll find that you can actually sequentially undo actions performed across both Word and the embedded Excel *in the order you performed them*. This is natural and expected, until you actually try to figure out what's going on! How is it that Word tells Excel when to undo an action? How does Excel's undo information live in Word, since they're different applications running in different processes? The answer, perhaps surprisingly, is *not* that "it's a Microsoft thing." In fact, there is nothing proprietary going on. Both Word and Excel (among many other applications and Microsoft ActiveX controls) support the Object Linking and Embedding (OLE) Undo standard, which defines a protocol for applications to share undo information with each other. Whenever a user action is performed, the application is responsible for generating the undo information, called an *undo unit*, required to fully undo that action. These undo units are then stored by the host application and executed during an undo operation. Any application supporting OLE Undo can thus embed and undo the actions of any other OLE Undo-compatible control or application that it might interact with, thereby creating a seamless undo experience for the user. Figure 9-1 gives an example of what such an undo stack might look like.

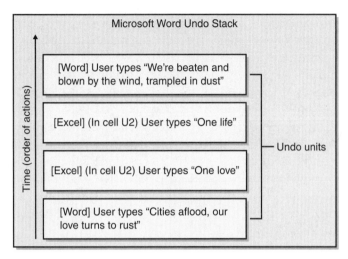

**Figure 9-1**   One possible way to visualize the undo units in Microsoft Word's undo stack.

Other than the InkPicture control, which has an *Undo* method supporting single-level undo, the Tablet PC Platform SDK is entirely without undo functionality. In fact, in some ways the SDK even makes implementing your own undo support difficult.

The heart of the problem is that the SDK does not generate undo units. "Well," you astutely remark, "I'll just generate my own!" If only it were so easy. You could generate undo units yourself *if you knew what information to put in them*. For some of the methods in the SDK, the required information is readily available. For example, if you create a stroke from *CreateStroke*, it's easy enough to store away the resulting *Stroke* so that during undo you can call *DeleteStroke* on it. However, other methods in the SDK make it difficult, and sometimes impossible, to deduce the necessary information to cleanly undo an action. Take, for instance, the *Transform* method. You can apply an arbitrary transform to a set of strokes, but what if you wanted to restore its original transform during an undo? What *was* the original transform? The SDK does not give you a way to determine it once it's been changed from identity (the default transform)! In this case, you'd have to separately remember the transforms you've applied to an ink object in case you ever have to undo them. It might not at first strike you as tedious, but in trying to work around these deficiencies you will soon discover that there is a lot that needs to be done. When calling

*Ink.ExtractStrokesAtRectangle*, how do you determine which original strokes were affected so that you can later reassemble them? How would you undo a *Clip* operation? Many of these issues are surmountable, but most only with reasonable difficulty.

"Ah!" you conclude, "I'll just clone *Ink* objects whenever I change them so that I can reinstitute their clones when undoing an action." Indeed, this is a viable solution, particularly if your application only needs single-level undo. It's also fairly simple to implement, once you've isolated all the code that modifies *Ink* objects directly (or indirectly through *Strokes* or other means). With good design this is doable. The solution can also be extended to support multilevel undo by creating as many clones as necessary whenever *Ink* objects are changed. Before latching onto this solution, however, the outstanding issues of performance and resources need to be resolved. Cloning *Ink* objects during modification can be both slow and memory intensive if not done with restraint. Particularly when *Ink* objects contain a lot of strokes, the amount of time and memory required can be prohibitive. The situation is further exacerbated if you require multilevel undo.

There is no easy solution to the problem of undo. We recommend that you fully investigate and understand the implications of any solution you consider because many snares lie in wait for the unsuspecting! Later in the chapter we present a sample application that implements a simple undo architecture by cloning *Ink* objects.

## Ink Architecture

When designing your application, the question of its underlying ink architecture will undoubtedly arise. By *ink architecture*, we mean the way in which you will represent ink internally in your application's data structures. One of the decisions to be made is whether you will have one *Ink* object containing all the digital ink in the document or whether you will instead have a set of smaller *Ink* objects each containing a portion of the total ink. Recall from Chapter 5 that this was referred to as Big Ink vs. Little Ink. In some cases, the choice between these two architectures will fall naturally out of the ink features themselves. For instance, if you want the user to be able to attach ink annotations to various objects in your document, it might make a lot of sense to have each annotation consist of its own *Ink* object. Or you might have one big *Ink* object if instead your application has a dedicated scribbling area for the user.

The choice between using one big *Ink* object versus many little *Ink* objects might be inconsequential given your needs, in which case you should pick the architecture that's most convenient. It's usually easy to transfer strokes between *Ink* objects or to operate only on select strokes, further diminishing the distinction between the architectures. Sometimes, however, one architecture will have clear advantages over the other. If you support multilevel undo by cloning *Ink* objects, having a set of little *Ink* objects might be the right design to reduce memory usage because you would then have to clone only the *Ink* objects that are actually changed by a particular operation. Alternatively, if you have a simple inking surface that doesn't support undo, using one big *Ink* object might be easiest. Other contributing factors specific to your application are likely to influence your architecture as well.

### Accessibility

One final issue to consider is that of accessibility. In particular, ink should respect the high contrast settings in Windows. Fortunately, the *InkPicture*, *InkCollector*, and *InkOverlay* classes all support high contrast mode through their *SupportHighContrastInk* property (which defaults to *true*). When using these objects, nothing additional needs to be done to comply with accessibility requirements—ink strokes will automatically paint in high contrast (usually white on a black background, or whatever the system-defined high contrast colors are). However, the *Renderer* class doesn't have built-in support for high contrast. Unfortunately, this means that if you ever draw ink using a *Renderer* object (which is all too likely if you use *Ink* objects at all), you'll have to manually specify *DrawingAttributes* appropriately prior to rendering to achieve high contrast and accessibility compliance. This will require that you determine the system's high contrast colors if high contrast is turned on, and set the appropriate color in the *DrawingAttributes* passed to *Renderer.Draw*.

## Performance

No discussion on integrating Tablet PC Platform features would be complete without considering performance. Digital ink is captured by the platform at high resolution and rendered with a fair degree of realism. These and other features of the platform come with a performance cost that you should be aware of. At the same time, with a good understanding of the platform's various performance trade-offs you will be able to strike the right balance between the features you need and the performance you want.

We divide our analysis of performance into two dimensions: time and space. First we consider how fast (or slow) various key operations on the platform are. Next we take a look at how much memory and disk space various platform features require. In the following sections we provide a simple framework in which performance in a few key areas can be tested. You will no doubt want to independently analyze performance characteristics specific to your application.

The performance analysis given here is minimal and in many cases imprecise. One point to keep in mind is that the code samples used to collect this performance data are designed foremost for clarity. There are many complex issues (such as cache latency, paging/swapping, and video memory) that have been intentionally ignored in our analysis. The performance numbers are best used as ballpark figures to aid in decision making. They are perhaps most reliable as measurements of relative performance between features of the platform, not as absolute gauges of performance you should expect on all Tablet PCs.

## Speed of Common Operations

As an introduction to the performance characteristics of the managed API, we include the LoadSaveRenderPerf application that tests the speed of loading, saving, and rendering of digital ink. Some simplifying assumptions have been made in the application in order to keep the code as lucid as possible. We will discuss these assumptions after presenting the code. Figure 9-2 shows the application just after profiling rendering.

**Figure 9-2**   The LoadSaveRenderPerf application tests the performance of loading, saving, and rendering using the managed API.

### LoadSaveRenderPerf.cs

```
/////////////////////////////////////////////////////////////////////////
// LoadSaveRenderPerf.cs
//
// (c) 2002 Microsoft Press, by Philip Su
//
// This program measures load, save, and render performance
/////////////////////////////////////////////////////////////////////////
using System;
using System.Drawing;
```

```
using System.Windows.Forms;
using System.IO;
using Microsoft.Ink;

public class LoadSaveRenderPerf : Form
{
    private Panel  m_pnlRender;
    private Button m_btnLoad;
    private Button m_btnSave;
    private Button m_btnRender;
    private Button m_btnRenderBasic;
    private Label  m_label;
    private Ink    m_ink;           // Cached ink, once loaded
    private int    m_cStrokes;      // Number of strokes in m_ink
    private int    m_cAvgPoints;    // Avg num points per stroke

    struct RenderParams            // Parameters for the Render
    {                              // perf runs.
        public Renderer renderer;
        public Graphics graphics;
        public Ink      ink;
    };

        // Name of the ISF file we will load our data from.  Be
        // sure that this file is in the directory that this
        // application executes from!
    const string s_strFileName = "PerfInk.isf";

        // Entry point of the program
    static void Main()
    {
        Application.Run(new LoadSaveRenderPerf());
    }

        // Main form setup
    public LoadSaveRenderPerf()
    {
        bool fLoadSuccessful = false;

        CreateUI();     // Create our dialog

            // Now that the dialog is up and running, attempt
            // to load our ISF file.
        try
        {
            FileStream fs;
            int cbRead = 0; // Count of bytes read
            byte[] rgb;     // Our ISF bytes from disk
```

*(continued)*

**LoadSaveRenderPerf.cs** *(continued)*

```
                // Attempt to load the ISF file.  Make sure that
                // this file is in the directory you run this
                // application from!
            fs = new FileStream(s_strFileName, FileMode.Open);
            rgb = new byte[fs.Length];
            cbRead = fs.Read(rgb, 0, rgb.Length);   // Read ISF
            if (cbRead == fs.Length)
            {
                m_ink = new Ink();
                m_ink.Load(rgb);         // Load the ISF into ink
                CalcInkStatistics();     // Figure out our stats
                fLoadSuccessful = true;
            }
            fs.Close();
        }
        catch (FileNotFoundException)
        {
        }

        if (!fLoadSuccessful)
        {
            MessageBox.Show("File " + s_strFileName +
                            " not loaded successfully.  Please " +
                            "make sure it is in the same " +
                            "directory as this program.",
                            "Load error");
            m_ink = null;
        }
    }


    // Instead of throwing in the constructor when loading
    // fails, we simply wait for the dialog to be shown, at
    // which point we close if loading failed.
    protected override void OnVisibleChanged(EventArgs e)
    {
        if (m_ink == null)       // Must not have loaded it!
            Close();
    }


    // Load button handler.
    private void OnLoad(object sender, EventArgs e)
    {
        const int kcReps = 50;   // Number of times to repeat
        double sec = 0.0;        // Total time
        byte[] rgb;              // The bytes we should load from

            // Generate our bytes to load from m_ink
        rgb = m_ink.Save();
```

```
            // Run the perf test
        sec = TestPerf(new RunSingle(LoadRunSingle), kcReps, rgb);
        ShowResults("loads", kcReps, sec);
    }


        // Save button handler.
    private void OnSave(object sender, EventArgs e)
    {
        const int kcReps = 50;  // Number of times to repeat
        double sec = 0.0;       // Total time

        sec = TestPerf(new RunSingle(SaveRunSingle), kcReps, null);
        ShowResults("saves", kcReps, sec);
    }


        // Render button handler.
    private void OnRender(object sender, EventArgs e)
    {
            // Render smooth ink (passing true for fSmooth)
        TestRenderPerf(GetRenderingInk(true));
    }


        // Render Basic button handler.
    private void OnRenderBasic(object sender, EventArgs e)
    {
            // Render simple ink (passing false for fSmooth)
        TestRenderPerf(GetRenderingInk(false));
    }


        // Display the results from a particular run of cReps
        // repetitions lasting sec seconds.
    private void ShowResults(string strWhat, int cReps, double sec)
    {
        m_label.Text = string.Format("{0} {1} of {2} strokes " +
                    "averaging {3} points each took {4:0.00} " +
                    "seconds \n({5:0.} strokes/sec)", cReps,
                    strWhat, m_cStrokes, m_cAvgPoints, sec,
                    (m_cStrokes * cReps) / sec);
    }


        // Stores the number of ink strokes into m_cStrokes, and
        // calculates the average number of points per stroke.
    private void CalcInkStatistics()
    {
        int cTotalPoints = 0;

        m_cStrokes = m_ink.Strokes.Count;
        if (m_cStrokes > 0)
```

*(continued)*

**LoadSaveRenderPerf.cs** *(continued)*

```
    {
        foreach (Stroke s in m_ink.Strokes)
            cTotalPoints += s.PacketCount;

        m_cAvgPoints = cTotalPoints / m_cStrokes;
    }
    else
    {
        m_cAvgPoints = 0;
    }
}


    // Tests rendering perf.  Sets up the RenderParams
    // with a Renderer and a Graphics object, as well as
    // the ink object that should be rendered.
private void TestRenderPerf(Ink ink)
{
    const int kcReps = 10;  // Number of times to repeat
    double sec = 0.0;        // Total time
    RenderParams rp;

    rp = new RenderParams();
    rp.renderer = new Renderer();
    rp.graphics = m_pnlRender.CreateGraphics();
    rp.ink = ink;
    sec = TestPerf(new RunSingle(RenderRunSingle), kcReps, rp);
    rp.graphics.Dispose();       // Clean up our graphics object

    ShowResults("renders", kcReps, sec);
}


    // Clones m_ink and changes all drawing attributes to be
    // either smooth or not.  "Smooth" is defined as being both
    // antialiased and Bezier curve fitted.  Also scales the
    // ink to fit within m_pnlRender;
private Ink GetRenderingInk(bool fSmooth)
{
    Ink ink = m_ink.Clone();    // Make a copy of the ink

        // Modify each stroke's drawing attributes accordingly
    foreach (Stroke s in ink.Strokes)
    {
        DrawingAttributes drawattrs = s.DrawingAttributes;

        drawattrs.AntiAliased = fSmooth;
        drawattrs.FitToCurve = fSmooth;

        s.DrawingAttributes = drawattrs;
```

```
        }

            // Scale the ink to fit within m_pnlRender
        if (ink.Strokes.Count > 0)
        {
            Renderer renderer = new Renderer();
            Graphics graphics = m_pnlRender.CreateGraphics();
            Point ptExtent = new Point(m_pnlRender.Bounds.Size);
            Rectangle rcInk;    // The new rectangle for ink to fit

            renderer.PixelToInkSpace(graphics, ref ptExtent);
            rcInk = new Rectangle(0, 0, ptExtent.X, ptExtent.Y);
            ink.Strokes.ScaleToRectangle(rcInk);

            graphics.Dispose(); // Free our graphics resources
        }

        return ink;
    }


        // Our delegate allows all four perf tests to use the
        // same timing function TestPerf().  Each RunSingle
        // delegate is responsible for doing a single iteration
        // of the perf test (whether it be load, save, or render)
    private delegate void RunSingle(object o);

    private void LoadRunSingle(object o)
    {
        byte[] rgb = (byte[])o;    // We're passed a byte array
        Ink ink = new Ink();       // See text for important note!

        ink.Load(rgb);
    }

    private void SaveRunSingle(object o)
    {
        m_ink.Save();
    }

    private void RenderRunSingle(object o)
    {
        RenderParams rp = (RenderParams)o;

            // Clear ourselves first so that progress is visible.
            // This impacts the resulting timing negligibly.
        m_pnlRender.Invalidate();
        m_pnlRender.Update();
```

*(continued)*

**LoadSaveRenderPerf.cs** *(continued)*

```csharp
            rp.renderer.Draw(rp.graphics, rp.ink.Strokes);
    }


        // The heart of our performance testing.  Runs cReps
        // repetitions of "single", the delegate that actually
        // performs the profiled functionality.
    private double TestPerf(RunSingle single, int cReps,
                            object oParam)
    {
        DateTime dtStart;

            // Set our "running" text.  Need to Update() right
            // away, otherwise the form is too busy to repaint.
        m_label.Text = "Testing performance — please wait...";
        m_label.Invalidate();
        m_label.Update();

        dtStart = DateTime.UtcNow;  // Record starting time

            // Run the tests on our delegate's method
        for (int i = 0; i < cReps; i++)
            single(oParam);

            // Return the time delta since we began
        return (DateTime.UtcNow - dtStart).TotalSeconds;
    }

    const int cSpacing = 8;        // Spacing between controls

    private void CreateUI()
    {
        int x = cSpacing;                // Position of next control
        int y = cSpacing;

        SuspendLayout();

            // Create and place all of our controls.  You may
            // wish to experiment with setting m_pnlRender.Size
            // to something bigger, like 900x650, since it
            // greatly affects render performance.
        m_pnlRender = new Panel();
        m_pnlRender.BorderStyle = BorderStyle.FixedSingle;
        m_pnlRender.Location = new Point(x, y);
        m_pnlRender.Size = new Size(400, 192);
//      m_pnlRender.Size = new Size(900, 650);
        y += m_pnlRender.Bounds.Height + cSpacing;

        CreateButton(ref m_btnLoad, ref x, y, 50, 24, "&Load",
```

```
                               new EventHandler(OnLoad));
        CreateButton(ref m_btnSave, ref x, y, 50, 24, "&Save",
                        new EventHandler(OnSave));
        CreateButton(ref m_btnRender, ref x, y, 70, 24, "&Render",
                        new EventHandler(OnRender));
        CreateButton(ref m_btnRenderBasic, ref x, y, 100, 24,
                        "Render &Basic",
                        new EventHandler(OnRenderBasic));

        x = cSpacing;
        y += m_btnRenderBasic.Height + cSpacing;
        m_label = new Label();
        m_label.BorderStyle = BorderStyle.FixedSingle;
        m_label.Location = new Point(x, y);
        m_label.Size = new Size(m_pnlRender.Width, 32);
        m_label.Text = "Press any button to begin";

            // Configure the form itself
        AutoScaleBaseSize = new Size(5, 13);
        ClientSize = new Size(m_label.Right + cSpacing,
                              m_label.Bottom + cSpacing);
        Controls.AddRange(new Control[] { m_pnlRender, m_btnLoad,
                                    m_btnSave, m_btnRender,
                                    m_btnRenderBasic,
                                    m_label });
        FormBorderStyle = FormBorderStyle.FixedDialog;
        MaximizeBox = false;
        Text = "Load, Save, Render Performance";

        ResumeLayout(false);
    }

        // Creates a button, updating the x location for the next
        // button.
    private void CreateButton(ref Button btn, ref int x, int y,
                              int cWidth, int cHeight,
                              string strName, EventHandler eh)
    {
        btn = new Button();
        btn.Location = new Point(x, y);
        btn.Size = new Size(cWidth, cHeight);
        btn.Text = strName;
        btn.Click += eh;
        x += btn.Width + cSpacing;
    }
}
```

A large chunk of this code sets up the user interface, but we will focus on the non-UI elements of the application in our discussion. First, the application tests the performance of *Ink.Load*, *Ink.Save*, and *InkRenderer.Draw* using delegate methods that each performs one iteration of the functionality being probed (*LoadRunSingle*, *SaveRunSingle*, and *RenderRunSingle*). The application gets the ink from a specific file, PerfInk.isf, which is available in the companion content. This file is provided merely for your convenience—in fact, you can create your own ink and use it for these tests if you want. The one that comes with the companion content is basic, consisting of about 1300 black ink strokes of various lengths stored in ISF format. Make sure when running the application that PerfInk.isf is in the same directory as the executable file so that the ink can be successfully loaded. When the application starts, it loads the ink from PerfInk.isf and uses it for all the tests.

When the user taps a button, the application runs a number of iterations of the particular function being tested. You should feel free to modify the number of iterations to your liking. The default iterations were chosen to last between 10–20 seconds on an average 1-GHz Pentium 4 to give the trials the amount of time needed to get consistent results.

Lastly, the application tests both regular rendering and basic rendering, neither of which uses pressure data. The difference between these two modes is that basic rendering turns off antialiasing and curve fitting. With these two appearance enhancing features turned off, performance of rendering varies dramatically. Although you will likely keep antialiasing and curve fitting on when rendering ink, you might want to investigate the performance consequences of these features.

Enough about the application—time to analyze the results! The following numbers were obtained on a 1.4-GHz Pentium 4 (Dell Dimension 8100) with 128-MB RAM running Windows XP Professional. The performance of the Tablet PC Platform SDK was as follows:

■ **Load: 18000 strokes per second** This number is somewhat affected by the code, which creates a new *Ink* object every time that *Ink.Load* is called. Unfortunately, there is no way to call *Load* multiple times on an *Ink* object because the SDK allows loading ink only into pristine (never dirtied) *Ink* objects. This result was thus obtained in tandem with creating 50 *Ink* objects (one per iteration). In addition, the ISF being loaded was saved using the platform defaults, which is normal compression. Surprisingly, loading both maximally compressed and uncompressed ink is neither faster nor slower than normal compression.

- **Save: 8500 strokes per second**   *Ink.Save* is much slower than *Ink.Load* using normal compression. Maximum compression has no effect on *Save* speed. On the other hand, if you use no compression, *Save* is twice as fast (19,000 strokes per second).

- **Render: 600 strokes per second**   Thin black ink was rendered with both antialiasing and curve fitting turned on, using an *m_pnlRender* size of 900 x 650 (instead of the code listing's 400 x 192). The larger size was used to simulate full-screen rendering because the size of the rendering surface is intimately tied to resulting performance. This result should be used only as a relative gauge of how long rendering takes. In addition to rendering surface size, the speed with which ink is rendered also depends greatly on factors such as the *DrawingAttributes.PenTip* used (*Ball* or *Rectangle*), whether pressure is available, and whether any transparency is used. You might want to investigate rendering speed using the type of digital ink expected by your application (incorporating factors such as width, average length, transparency, and pen tip) because there is such wide variance based on ink characteristics. Incidentally, the type of hardware on which you test rendering performance is also critical to the results, so choose carefully! Rendering hardware will greatly affect performance on Tablet PCs, especially if you're running in portrait mode. It's best to verify your application's rendering performance on a Tablet PC before finalizing your design.

- **Basic render: 1200 strokes per second**   Without antialiasing and curve fitting, the same ink renders twice as fast (while keeping the larger 900 x 650 *m_pnlRender size*). The dramatic difference in turning off the two ink-smoothing features might come as a surprise, but this result is typical on many hardware configurations. Antialiasing is often slower because it needs to read from video memory (an inherently slow operation on most hardware because video hardware is optimized for *writing to*, not *reading from*). Curve fitting fundamentally requires a greater number of calculations in order to find the Bézier control points needed for rendering a smoother curve. Although you will typically retain these two ink-smoothing features for aestheticism, in the most dire performance situations you might want to revisit the decision.

By now you're probably thinking, "What do these numbers mean? How much writing is, say, 1000 strokes' worth?" The answer depends on several variables, including the language being written as well as the handwriting style of the writer. In typical English, expect printed handwriting to be somewhere on the order of 6 strokes per word (about 170 words per 1000 strokes), while cursive writing is closer to around 1.6 strokes per word (or 625 words per 1000 strokes). Although there is much variance between these two ends of the English handwriting spectrum, note that the average cursive stroke is often around five times longer than the average printed stroke. This, in effect, brings both cursive and print to about the same number of packets per word. The performance estimates given above were obtained using printed handwriting strokes. Using those initial estimates, we'd expect the same machine to render around 133 printed words per second. As a point of reference, a wide-rule 8.5-by-11-inch sheet of paper has around 30 lines. If each line has on average 10 words, rendering such a page will take a little over two seconds on the machine used in the preceding example. This ballpark estimate might be of great interest to you if you plan to develop an application that will support the user writing pages and pages of ink because it might feel quite slow flipping through such an application's document at two seconds a page.

In stark contrast to English, the 2965 most commonly used traditional Chinese characters have a weighted average of 9.1 strokes each. An average wide-rule line can easily accommodate 20 Chinese characters, further worsening the situation. All else being equal, we'd expect a page of Chinese to take about *seven seconds* to render on the same machine used in the preceding example (disregarding its obviously shorter average stroke length). Toss in some transparency with pressure-variant ink and you've got a real problem on your hands!

**Note** Shih-Kun Huang (Institute of Information Science, Academia Sinica, Taiwan) and Chih-Hao Tsai (Council for Cultural Planning and Development, Taiwan) compiled the statistics in 1993 and 1994 regarding traditional Chinese characters. You can find other parts of the same study at *http://www.geocities.com/hao510/charfreq/*.

Fortunately, neither loading nor saving should be an issue because they are much faster and occur less often than rendering. Even several pages full of ink should, at these rates, take only a second or two to load or save. The performance trials were run by loading from and saving to memory so that speed of writing to the hard disk or other storage medium was not factored in. When deploying your application, the time required to access a hard disk might be significant and should be factored in.

Ink recognition is orders of magnitude slower than loading, saving, or rendering because it involves several sophisticated and computationally intensive algorithms. The English ink recognizer works at the pace of about 12 words per second. A full page of ink, using the familiar wide-rule 10 words per page assumption, will thus take on the order of 25 seconds to recognize — a rather disconcerting conclusion. Figure 9-3 is a screenshot of the ink used to obtain these estimates (cursive writing yielded about the same performance). You can run the following sample application only on a machine running Windows XP Tablet PC Edition because handwriting recognition requires the presence of recognizers.

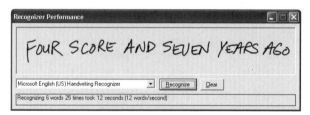

**Figure 9-3**   The RecoPerf application in action, recognizing several words from the Gettysburg Address.

## RecoPerf.cs

```
/////////////////////////////////////////////////////////////////////
// RecoPerf.cs
//
// (c) 2002 Microsoft Press, by Philip Su
//
// This program measures ink recognition performance
/////////////////////////////////////////////////////////////////////
using System;
using System.Drawing;
using System.Windows.Forms;
using Microsoft.Ink;

public class RecoPerf : Form
{
    private Panel          m_pnlInput;     // The inking surface
    private ComboBox       m_comboReco;    // Which engine to use
    private Button         m_btnReco;      // Recognize button
    private Button         m_btnClear;     // Clear button
    private Label          m_label;        // Text
    private InkCollector   m_inkCollector; // Ink collector object

    static void Main()
    {
```

**RecoPerf.cs** *(continued)*

```csharp
        Application.Run(new RecoPerf());
}

public RecoPerf()
{
    CreateUI();

        // Create a new InkCollector using m_pnlInput
        // for the collection area and turn on ink
        // collection.
    m_inkCollector = new InkCollector(m_pnlInput.Handle);
    m_inkCollector.Enabled = true;
}

    // Handle the click of the Recognize button
private void BtnRecoClick(object sender, EventArgs e)
{
    const int cReps = 25;    // Repeat the test 25 times

    Recognizer reco = (Recognizer)m_comboReco.SelectedItem;
    RecognizerContext context;
    RecognitionResult recoresult;
    RecognitionStatus recostatus;
    DateTime dtStart;
    int cSeconds = 0;
    int cWords = 0;
    string strResult;
    string strOutput;
    char[] rgchWhitespace = " \n\r\t".ToCharArray();

    if (reco == null)
    {
        m_label.Text = "No recognizer selected!";
        return;
    }

        // First recognize it once for our label's text
    context = reco.CreateRecognizerContext();
    context.Strokes = m_inkCollector.Ink.Strokes;
    context.EndInkInput();
    recoresult = context.Recognize(out recostatus);
    if (recostatus != RecognitionStatus.NoError)
    {
        m_label.Text = "There was an error while recognizing!";
        return;
    }
    strResult = recoresult.ToString();
```

```
        // First set text for user before testing reco speed
    m_label.Text = "Recognizing '" + strResult + "' " + cReps +
                   " times...";
    m_label.Invalidate();
    m_label.Update();

        // Run the actual recognition cReps times
    dtStart = DateTime.UtcNow;  // Record starting time
    for (int i = 0; i < cReps; i++)
    {
        context.Recognize(out recostatus);
    }
    cSeconds = (int)(DateTime.UtcNow - dtStart).TotalSeconds;

        // A fairly simplistic calculation of the number of
        // words in the recognized string (western languages)
    cWords = strResult.Split(rgchWhitespace).Length;
    strOutput = string.Format("Recognizing {0} words {1} " +
                   "times took {2} seconds", cWords, cReps,
                   cSeconds);
    if (cSeconds > 0)
    {
        strOutput += " (" + (cWords * cReps) / cSeconds +
                     " words/second)";
    }
    m_label.Text = strOutput;
}


    // Handle the click of the Clear button
private void BtnClearClick(object sender, EventArgs e)
{
    m_inkCollector.Ink.DeleteStrokes();
    m_pnlInput.Invalidate();
}


    // Populate the recognizer combo box with all the
    // available recognizers
private void LoadComboWithRecognizers()
{
    Recognizers recos = new Recognizers();
    Recognizer recoDefault = recos.GetDefaultRecognizer();

    m_comboReco.BeginUpdate();
    foreach (Recognizer r in recos)
    {
        m_comboReco.Items.Add(r);

            // Auto-select the default recognizer.
```

*(continued)*

**RecoPerf.cs** *(continued)*

```
                    // Unfortunately, Recognizer objects do not
                    // implement Equals in a meaningful way, so we'll
                    // live with comparing names.
            if (r.Name == recoDefault.Name)
            {
                    m_comboReco.SelectedItem = r;
            }
        }
    m_comboReco.EndUpdate();
}

private void CreateUI()
{
    SuspendLayout();

        // Create and place all of our controls
    m_pnlInput = new Panel();
    m_pnlInput.BorderStyle = BorderStyle.Fixed3D;
    m_pnlInput.Location = new Point(8, 8);
    m_pnlInput.Size = new Size(600, 100);

    m_comboReco = new ComboBox();
    m_comboReco.Location = new Point(8, 116);
    m_comboReco.Size = new Size(300, 24);
    m_comboReco.DropDownStyle = ComboBoxStyle.DropDownList;
    LoadComboWithRecognizers();

    m_btnReco = new Button();
    m_btnReco.Location = new Point(316, 116);
    m_btnReco.Size = new Size(80, 24);
    m_btnReco.Text = "&Recognize";
    m_btnReco.Click += new EventHandler(BtnRecoClick);

    m_btnClear = new Button();
    m_btnClear.Location = new Point(404, 116);
    m_btnClear.Size = new Size(50, 24);
    m_btnClear.Text = "&Clear";
    m_btnClear.Click += new EventHandler(BtnClearClick);

    m_label = new Label();
    m_label.Location = new Point(8, 148);
    m_label.Size = new Size(600, 24);
    m_label.BorderStyle = BorderStyle.FixedSingle;
```

```
        // Configure the form itself
    AutoScaleBaseSize = new Size(5, 13);
    ClientSize = new Size(616, 180);
    Controls.AddRange(new Control[] { m_pnlInput, m_comboReco,
                                      m_btnReco, m_btnClear,
                                      m_label });
    FormBorderStyle = FormBorderStyle.FixedDialog;
    MaximizeBox = false;
    Text = "Recognizer Performance";


    ResumeLayout(false);
    }
}
```

## Memory and Storage of Ink

In addition to speed, another key consideration of any performance analysis is the problem of memory and storage requirements. When it comes to memory, the Tablet PC Platform can be surprisingly demanding. This makes a clear understanding of digital ink's memory requirements imperative to making design decisions regarding your application. Fortunately, the platform can be efficient in how it stores ink. We will look at and compare the size requirements of various storage formats for ink.

First, let's take a look at digital ink's memory usage. The MemoryPerf application allows some basic investigation of memory consumption. It loads an ISF file and subsequently replicates the strokes in the file quite a few times. These replications are meant to produce a significant number of strokes in total, in an effort to asymptotically minimize the amount of non-ink-related memory overhead. In particular, making sure the strokes themselves compose the bulk of consumed memory should reduce the effects of platform (and application) memory overhead not directly related to the ink strokes. After replicating the strokes, MemoryPerf gives the user a chance to take another memory measurement. The difference between the pre-replication memory and the post-replication memory is thus a fair estimate of the amount of memory actually used.

MemoryPerf does not provide its own method of measuring memory because there is no simple piece of code that would yield a reasonable measurement. Instead, you should use another tool to gauge the amount of memory consumed. One such tool is the Windows Task Manager, which, though not always strictly accurate, offers a good first-order approximation of the memory used by any application.

> **Note**  You might be tempted to use *GC.GetTotalMemory*, a compelling function provided by the Microsoft .NET garbage collector. However, in the case of the Tablet PC Platform, any figure obtained from *GC.GetTotalMemory* would be grossly understating the actual memory usage because it tracks only memory allocated in managed code (using the .NET Framework). The Tablet PC Platform managed API was largely implemented as a set of .NET-compatible wrappers around classic C/C++ code, whose memory usage is not tracked by the .NET garbage collector.

The code for MemoryPerf is listed here and is also available in the companion content.

**MemoryPerf.cs**

```
/////////////////////////////////////////////////////////////////////
// MemoryPerf.cs
//
// (c) 2002 Microsoft Press, by Philip Su
//
// This program measures memory performance
/////////////////////////////////////////////////////////////////////
using System;
using System.IO;
using System.Drawing;
using Microsoft.Ink;

class MemoryPerf
{
    public static void Main(string[] args)
    {
        Ink ink;

        if (args.Length == 0)
        {
            Console.WriteLine("Usage: MemoryPerf.exe [file.ISF]");
            return;
        }

        LoadInk(args[0], out ink);
        if (ink != null)
        {
            RunTest(ink);
```

```
        }
    }
    private static void RunTest(Ink ink)
    {
        const int cCopies = 150;   // Copies of ink to make
        Strokes strokes = ink.Strokes;
        Rectangle rc = strokes.GetBoundingBox();
        int cStrokes = strokes.Count;
        int cPoints = 0;
        foreach (Stroke s in strokes)
        {
            cPoints += s.PacketCount;
        }
        Console.WriteLine("(measure memory and press return)");
        Console.ReadLine();
        for (int i = 0; i < cCopies; i++)
        {
            ink.AddStrokesAtRectangle(strokes, rc);
        }
        Console.Write("{0} strokes and {1} points total ",
                      cStrokes * cCopies, cPoints * cCopies);
        Console.WriteLine("(measure memory and press return)");
        Console.ReadLine();
    }

    private static void LoadInk(string strFile, out Ink ink)
    {
        ink = null;

        try
        {
            FileStream fs;
            int cbRead = 0; // Count of bytes read
            byte[] rgb;     // Our ISF bytes from disk

                // Attempt to load the ISF file.  Make sure that
                // this file is in the directory you run this
                // application from!
            fs = new FileStream(strFile, FileMode.Open);
            rgb = new byte[fs.Length];
            cbRead = fs.Read(rgb, 0, rgb.Length);   // Read ISF
            if (cbRead == fs.Length)
            {
                ink = new Ink();
                ink.Load(rgb);          // Load the ISF into ink
            }
            fs.Close();
        }
```

*(continued)*

**MemoryPerf.cs** *(continued)*

```
        catch (FileNotFoundException)
        {
            Console.WriteLine(strFile + " not found!");
        }
    }
}
```

Table 9-1 presents a heavy usage scenario involving a large set of plain strokes.

**Table 9-1   Sample Memory Usage Data Obtained with the *MemoryPerf* Application**

| | |
|---|---|
| Total Strokes | 32,850 |
| Total Packets (Points) | 671,400 |
| Average Packets per Stroke | 46 |
| Packet Size | 12 bytes |
| Total Memory Used | 20 Mb |
| Average Memory per Stroke | 620 bytes |
| Average Memory per Packet | 31 bytes |

First, it's important to recognize that 32,000+ strokes of ink equate to about 68 pages of wide-ruled paper filled with cursive writing (or about 18 pages of print). This might be a lot of ink compared to scenarios you're thinking about. However, the critical figure in the table is the average memory per stroke, which is about 620 bytes in this scenario. Using this figure, you can arrive at some rough estimates about the memory requirements of your ink-enabled application (a page of cursive might be about 300 Kb, for example).

However, the average memory per stroke is heavily dependent on two things: the average stroke packet count and the packet size. Both of these variables can vary quite dramatically depending on the situation. The stroke packet count varies with the amount of time the pen is down as well as the sampling rate of the hardware being used. Typical Tablet PC hardware might capture 120+ points per second or beyond. Assuming that a typical cursive stroke takes on the order of two seconds, the average stroke packet count you deal with might be quite higher than that in Table 9-1. The other factor that might further inflate these figures is the packet size you choose. By requesting more information per packet (for example, pressure or tilt), each packet's memory requirements go up. If you want each packet to contain a lot of information, be prepared for a lot of memory to be used. When you compound average stroke packet count and packet size, it can cause a serious memory usage concern, so investigate your ink feature needs a bit before finalizing a design.

You might be wondering why the average memory per packet is almost triple the packet size. This is likely due to per-stroke implementation overheads of the platform, but there is no concrete evidence. What matters most, though, is not what the platform says the packet size is—instead, the empirically measured memory consumption is all that matters when it comes to estimating how much memory your application will need.

We would be remiss in our discussion of memory requirements not to reiterate the implications of undo. If your application supports undo, users will expect to be able to undo ink modifications as well. However, as we discussed earlier in the chapter, the Tablet PC Platform SDK provides no native support for undoing modifications. In fact, the design of the managed API makes it downright hard in certain cases to implement undo without cloning each *Ink* object as it's modified. If you implement undo by cloning, the memory requirements of your application might rise dramatically as the amount of ink being worked with increases. Imagine that you have a page of writing housed in one *Ink* object, which might use somewhere on the order of several hundred kilobytes of memory. As the user enters new ink strokes, you might have to clone the *Ink* object with each additional stroke in order to support undoing of the strokes. This process quickly becomes unwieldy if you support multilevel undo and begs for a smarter solution. Depending on whether and how you plan to support undo, you might need to design around this fundamental limitation of the platform by either partitioning ink into smaller *Ink* objects or by implementing a smarter undo. You can investigate the undo issue further by experimenting with the InkPadJunior sample application presented later in this chapter—it implements multilevel undo by cloning *Ink* objects as they change.

> **Note**   If you monitor memory usage as you enter more and more ink in the application, you will witness the unfortunate $O(n^2)$ memory consumption of such an implementation. For each ink stroke added, all previous ink strokes must be cloned; therefore, given the $n^{th}$ ink stroke, each previous stroke must be cloned $n$-1 times.

The good news is that the size of digital ink is much smaller when persisted than when it's in memory. A typical storage requirement breakdown is presented in Table 9-2, followed by the source code used to generate the data. The source code is simply a different implementation of the *RunTest* function in the MemoryPerf application. The code for the entire application is available as the StoragePerf solution in the companion content.

**Table 9-2    Sample Persisted Size of Ink Using the StoragePerf Application**

| | |
|---|---|
| Total Strokes | 1344 |
| Total Packets (Points) | 62,550 |
| Average Packets per Stroke | 46 |
| Packet Size | 12 bytes |
| No Compression ISF | 277 Kb (211 bytes per stroke / 4.5 bytes per packet) |
| Default Compression ISF | 156 Kb (119 bytes per stroke / 2.5 bytes per packet / 56% of uncompressed) |
| Maximum Compression ISF | 156 Kb (119 bytes per stroke / 2.5 bytes per packet / 56% of uncompressed) |
| GIF (Default ISF) | 165 Kb (105% of default ISF) |
| Base64 (Default ISF) | 208 Kb (133% of default ISF) |

```
private static void RunTest(Ink ink)
{
    int cStrokes = ink.Strokes.Count;
    int cPoints = 0;
    int cbNone = 0;
    int cbNormal = 0;
    int cbMaximum = 0;
    int cbGIF = 0;
    int cbBase64 = 0;
    byte[] rgb;

    foreach (Stroke s in ink.Strokes)
    {
        cPoints += s.PacketCount;
    }
    Console.WriteLine("{0} strokes and {1} points total:",
                    cStrokes, cPoints);

    rgb = ink.Save(PersistenceFormat.InkSerializedFormat,
                CompressionMode.NoCompression);
    cbNone = rgb.Length;
    rgb = ink.Save(PersistenceFormat.InkSerializedFormat,
                CompressionMode.Default);
    cbNormal = rgb.Length;
    rgb = ink.Save(PersistenceFormat.InkSerializedFormat,
                CompressionMode.Maximum);
```

```
        cbMaximum = rgb.Length;
        rgb = ink.Save(PersistenceFormat.Gif);
        cbGIF = rgb.Length;
        rgb = ink.Save(PersistenceFormat.Base64InkSerializedFormat);
        cbBase64 = rgb.Length;

        Console.WriteLine("No compression: {0} bytes", cbNone);
        Console.WriteLine("Default compression: {0} bytes " +
                    "({1}% of no compression size)",
                    cbNormal, cbNormal * 100 / cbNone);
        Console.WriteLine("Maximum compression: {0} bytes " +
                    "({1}% of no compression size)",
                    cbMaximum, cbMaximum * 100 / cbNone);
        Console.WriteLine("GIF (default ISF): {0} bytes " +
                    "({1}% of default ISF)",
                    cbGIF, cbGIF * 100 / cbNormal);
        Console.WriteLine("Base64 (default ISF): {0} bytes " +
                    "({1}% of default ISF)",
                    cbBase64, cbBase64 * 100 / cbNormal);
    }
```

Using our handy 30-line, 10-words-per-line approximation of a page, we see that the data in Table 9-2 pertains to about 4–5 pages of ink. Under default compression, each page of ink should take about 36 Kb of storage, which is not bad at all. Remember that the amount of data per packet will affect results.

Most of the storage performance data is self-explanatory, with a few notable anomalies that we'll discuss. First, notice that even without compression, we needed only 4.5 bytes on average to store each 12-byte packet. This is surprising indeed! The only explanation we've been able to surmise is that perhaps the platform removes duplicate points (say, if the pen didn't move between two samples) even in "no compression" mode. In any case, this result is startling. Another exception that we need to bring up is that the overhead for the GIF output format does not seem to grow with the number of strokes or packets stored. This makes some sense because the only overhead that should be incurred is the GIF-related headers and tags. Another consequence of this observation is that even the smallest ink object will take several kilobytes (upwards of 10) to store in the GIF format due to this overhead. Finally, Base64's 33 percent bloat is exactly as expected because the Base64 algorithm turns every 3 binary bytes into 4 characters.

# InkPadJunior

We'll bring this chapter to a close by presenting InkPadJunior, a simple inking application that you can use to generate files with which to run your own tests, as shown in Figure 9-4. It supports loading and saving ISF files, as well as using various colors of ink. As a special bonus, it also supports a simple undo/redo mechanism based on cloning ink objects whenever they change. The undo functionality is included as a starting point to explore the many possibilities of how you might implement undo in your own application.

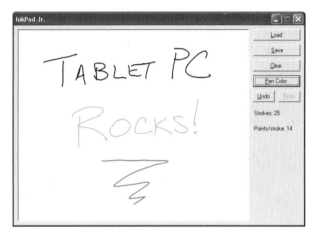

**Figure 9-4**  InkPadJunior supports loading, saving, capturing, and undoing ink.

**InkPadJunior.cs**

```
/////////////////////////////////////////////////////////////////////
// InkPadJunior.cs
//
// (c) 2002 Microsoft Press, by Philip Su
//
// This program collects, loads, and saves ink.  It also calculates
// the number of strokes and average points per stroke.  Finally, it
// supports undoing and redoing of strokes.
/////////////////////////////////////////////////////////////////////
using System;
using System.Drawing;
using System.Windows.Forms;
using System.Collections;
using System.IO;
using Microsoft.Ink;

public class InkPadJunior : Form
{
    private Panel          m_pnlPad;
    private Button         m_btnLoad;
    private Button         m_btnSave;
    private Button         m_btnClear;
```

```
private Button          m_btnColor;
private Button          m_btnUndo;
private Button          m_btnRedo;
private Label           m_labelCount;    // Stroke count
private Label           m_labelAvgPts;   // Avg. points / stroke
private InkCollector    m_inkcoll;
private Stack           m_stackUndo;     // Undo stack of ink
private Stack           m_stackRedo;     // Redo stack

const string strFileFilter = "ISF files (*.isf)|*.isf|" +
                             "All files (*.*)|*.*";

    // Entry point of the program
static void Main()
{
    Application.Run(new InkPadJunior());
}

    // Main form setup
public InkPadJunior()
{
    m_stackUndo = new Stack();
    m_stackRedo = new Stack();

    CreateUI();

        // Set up m_inkcoll to collect from m_pnlPad and
        // also to send Stroke events to OnStroke
    m_inkcoll = new InkCollector(m_pnlPad.Handle);
    m_inkcoll.Enabled = true;
    m_inkcoll.Stroke += new InkCollectorStrokeEventHandler(
                        OnStroke);

    UpdateUI();
}

    // Load button handler -- uses the system Load dialog
private void OnLoad(object sender, EventArgs e)
{
    OpenFileDialog opendlg = new OpenFileDialog();

        // Show the Open File dialog
    opendlg.Filter = strFileFilter;
    if (opendlg.ShowDialog() == DialogResult.OK)
    {
        Stream stream = opendlg.OpenFile();

        if (stream != null && stream.Length > 0)
```

*(continued)*

**InkPadJunior.cs** *(continued)*

```
        {
            byte[] rgb = new byte[stream.Length];
            int cbRead = 0;

                // Read in the ISF into rgb
            cbRead = stream.Read(rgb, 0, rgb.Length);
            if (cbRead == stream.Length)
            {
                Ink ink = new Ink();

                ink.Load(rgb);  // Load the ISF

                    // Set the loaded ink into m_inkcoll.  To do
                    // so, we must disable m_inkcoll before
                    // setting its Ink property.
                m_inkcoll.Enabled = false;
                m_inkcoll.Ink = ink;
                m_inkcoll.Enabled = true;

                    // Our undo/redo stacks should be cleared
                m_stackUndo.Clear();
                m_stackRedo.Clear();

                    // Update our UI
                m_pnlPad.Invalidate();
                OnStroke(null, null);
            }
            stream.Close();
        }
    }
}


    // Save button handler -- uses the system Save dialog
private void OnSave(object sender, EventArgs e)
{
    SaveFileDialog savedlg = new SaveFileDialog();

        // Initialize and show the Save dialog
    savedlg.Filter = strFileFilter;
    if (savedlg.ShowDialog() == DialogResult.OK)
    {
        Stream stream = savedlg.OpenFile();

            // Now write the ISF stream to the file
        if (stream != null)
        {
            byte[] rgb = m_inkcoll.Ink.Save();
```

```
                    stream.Write(rgb, 0, rgb.Length);
                    stream.Close();
            }
        }
    }


    // Clear button handler — deletes all strokes
private void OnClear(object sender, EventArgs e)
{
        // Have to invalidate for the changes to be shown
    m_inkcoll.Ink.DeleteStrokes();
    m_pnlPad.Invalidate();

    m_stackUndo.Clear();    // Clear our stacks as well
    m_stackRedo.Clear();
    UpdateUI();
}


    // Color button handler — uses system color dialog
private void OnColor(object sender, EventArgs e)
{
    ColorDialog colordlg = new ColorDialog();

    if (colordlg.ShowDialog() == DialogResult.OK)
    {
        DrawingAttributes drawattrs;

        drawattrs = m_inkcoll.DefaultDrawingAttributes;
        drawattrs.Color = colordlg.Color;
    }
}


    // Undo button handler — Restores a previous ink object
private void OnUndo(object sender, EventArgs e)
{
    Ink inkCurrent = ReplaceInk((Ink)m_stackUndo.Pop());

        // Now that we've instituted the previous ink object,
        // store the original "current" one in the redo stack
    m_stackRedo.Push(inkCurrent);
    UpdateUI();
}


    // Redo button handler
private void OnRedo(object sender, EventArgs e)
{
    Ink inkUndo = ReplaceInk((Ink)m_stackRedo.Pop());
```

*(continued)*

**InkPadJunior.cs** *(continued)*

```csharp
                // Now that we've redone the previous ink object,
                // store the replaced ink into the undo stack
            m_stackUndo.Push(inkUndo);
            UpdateUI();
        }


            // Replaces m_inkcoll.Ink with inkNew, returning the
            // original ink
        private Ink ReplaceInk(Ink inkNew)
        {
            Ink inkOld = m_inkcoll.Ink; // Save the old ink to return

            m_inkcoll.Enabled = false;  // Must disable to replace ink
            m_inkcoll.Ink = inkNew;
            m_inkcoll.Enabled = true;   // Re-enable collection

            m_pnlPad.Invalidate();      // Have to see the new ink

            return inkOld;
        }


            // Handles the Stroke event from m_inkcoll when a new
            // stroke has just been added to m_inkcoll.Ink
        private void OnStroke(object sender,
                            InkCollectorStrokeEventArgs e)
        {
            Ink inkUndo = m_inkcoll.Ink.Clone();
            int cStrokes = m_inkcoll.Ink.Strokes.Count;

                // Arrange our undo stack and clear the redo.
                // We need to remove the most recently added stroke
                // to have to ink we should add to the undo stack.
            inkUndo.DeleteStroke(inkUndo.Strokes[cStrokes - 1]);
            m_stackUndo.Push(inkUndo);
            m_stackRedo.Clear();      // User action means no redo!

            UpdateUI();
        }

        const int cSpacing = 8; // Space between controls

        private void CreateUI()
        {
            int x = cSpacing;
            int y = cSpacing;

            SuspendLayout();
```

```
      // Create and place all of our controls
m_pnlPad = new Panel();
m_pnlPad.BorderStyle = BorderStyle.Fixed3D;
m_pnlPad.Location = new Point(x, y);
m_pnlPad.Size = new Size(500, 400);
m_pnlPad.BackColor = Color.White;
x += m_pnlPad.Bounds.Width + cSpacing;


y = CreateButton(out m_btnLoad, x, y, 100, 24, "&Load",
                  new EventHandler(OnLoad));
y = CreateButton(out m_btnSave, x, y, 100, 24, "&Save",
                  new EventHandler(OnSave));
y = CreateButton(out m_btnClear, x, y, 100, 24, "&Clear",
                  new EventHandler(OnClear));
y = CreateButton(out m_btnColor, x, y, 100, 24, "&Pen Color",
                  new EventHandler(OnColor));
CreateButton(out m_btnUndo, x, y, 46, 24, "&Undo",
                  new EventHandler(OnUndo));
CreateButton(out m_btnRedo,
              x + m_btnUndo.Bounds.Width + cSpacing, y,
              46, 24, "&Redo", new EventHandler(OnRedo));
x = m_btnUndo.Bounds.X;
y += m_btnRedo.Bounds.Height + (2 * cSpacing);


m_labelCount = new Label();
m_labelCount.Location = new Point(x, y);
m_labelCount.Size = new Size(100, 24);
y += m_labelCount.Bounds.Height + cSpacing;


m_labelAvgPts = new Label();
m_labelAvgPts.Location = new Point(x, y);
m_labelAvgPts.Size = new Size(100, 24);
y += m_labelAvgPts.Bounds.Height + cSpacing;


      // Configure the form itself
x += m_labelAvgPts.Bounds.Width + cSpacing;
y = m_pnlPad.Bounds.Height + (2 * cSpacing);
AutoScaleBaseSize = new Size(5, 13);
ClientSize = new Size(x, y);
Controls.AddRange(new Control[] { m_pnlPad, m_btnLoad,
                                  m_btnSave, m_btnClear,
                                  m_btnColor, m_btnUndo,
                                  m_btnRedo, m_labelCount,
                                  m_labelAvgPts });
FormBorderStyle = FormBorderStyle.FixedDialog;
MaximizeBox = false;
Text = "InkPad Jr.";
```

*(continued)*

**InkPadJunior.cs** *(continued)*

```
        ResumeLayout(false);
    }


    // Creates a button and suggests the next y value to use
    private int CreateButton(out Button btn, int x, int y,
                             int cWidth, int cHeight,
                             string strName, EventHandler eh)
    {
        btn = new Button();
        btn.Location = new Point(x, y);
        btn.Size = new Size(cWidth, cHeight);
        btn.Text = strName;
        btn.Click += eh;
        return y + btn.Bounds.Height + cSpacing;  // Suggest next y
    }


    // Update our stroke statistics as well as the Undo/Redo
    // button states according to m_inkcoll.Ink
    private void UpdateUI()
    {
        int cStrokes = m_inkcoll.Ink.Strokes.Count;
        int cTotalPoints = 0;
        int cAvgPtsPerStroke = 0;

        // Calculate the average by counting all the points
        // and dividing by the number of strokes
        if (cStrokes > 0)
        {
            foreach (Stroke s in m_inkcoll.Ink.Strokes)
            {
                cTotalPoints += s.PacketCount;
            }
            cAvgPtsPerStroke = cTotalPoints / cStrokes;
        }
        m_labelCount.Text = "Strokes: " + cStrokes;
        m_labelAvgPts.Text = "Points/stroke: " + cAvgPtsPerStroke;

        // These buttons are enabled/disabled depending on
        // whether their stacks are empty
        m_btnUndo.Enabled = m_stackUndo.Count > 0;
        m_btnRedo.Enabled = m_stackRedo.Count > 0;
    }
}
```

InkPadJunior is an example of a basic ink-aware application. The most complicated thing it does is implement an undo stack and redo stack by cloning ink objects. The basic idea behind undo and redo stacks is that every change in the document adds an entry to one of the stacks. If the action was a normal user action, you add its entry to the undo stack. If, however, the action was an undo, you add its entry to the redo stack. When the user does an undo, you pull the top entry off the undo stack, undo the action, and place its entry on the redo stack. Similarly, when you redo, you pull the top entry off the redo stack, redo the action, and place its entry on the undo stack again. When all is said and done, the user has unlimited undo and redo functionality. The only caveat is that you should always clear the redo stack whenever a normal user action occurs; this prevents user errors such as inking followed by redo, which makes no sense.

Other than undo, InkPadJunior doesn't exhibit much fancy behavior. It loads and saves data in much the same way we always have, taking care to clear the undo and redo stacks when a new file is loaded. It also responds to new strokes by adding them to the undo stack, clearing the redo stack, and finally calculating some statistics during *UpdateUI*. The amount of functionality you can get out of the Tablet PC Platform SDK with such little work is amazing!

## Summary

We started this chapter by considering the benefits of updating an existing application to leverage the Tablet PC Platform's features. We found that in doing so, we had many technical challenges to overcome. We discussed some of these challenges as well as a few potential solutions. We then turned our attention to the issue of performance, which we analyzed from the perspectives of speed and size.

The topic of how to update an existing Tablet PC application to be pen-aware or ink-aware is a potentially complex one. In this chapter we introduced you to some of the basic issues that you can take into account when deciding how to implement the first Tablet PC version of your application.

# Part IV

# Appendixes

# Appendix A

# BuildingTabletApps Library Reference

This appendix is a complete reference to the BuildingTabletApps utility library found on this book's companion content. The library's primary purpose is to provide a set of functionality to augment the Tablet PC Platform. This functionality should be useful for developers working on Tablet PC applications.

The full source code to the library can be found on the companion content in the C:\Program Files\Microsoft Press Books\Building Tablet PC Applications\BuildingTabletPCApps folder and is installed locally along with the rest of the sample applications. The BuildingTabletApps library is not registered in the Microsoft .NET global assembly cache, so to use it in your own application you must choose the "Add References" menu item in Microsoft Visual Studio .NET and then select the *BuildingTabletApps.dll* file name from the "Browse" option.

The library uses the namespace *MSPress.BuildingTabletApps* and contains numerous classes we hope you'll find helpful in exploring the Tablet PC Platform. The following sections describe these classes.

## The *InkInputPanel* Class

The *InkControl* and *InkControl2* classes use the *InkInputPanel* class for their ink input area. It is derived from *Panel*, hence it is a control, with the only change in functionality being the support for double-buffered rendering to reduce redraw flicker. The InkInputPanel control is also useful for acting as a preview window for ink, especially if animation is involved (for example, scrolling).

### *InkInputPanel*

```
public InkInputPanel()
```
The class constructor.

# The *InkControl* and *InkControl2* Classes

These two classes provide a quick and dirty user interface to most of the *Ink-Overlay* class's functionality and are mainly useful for exploring API behavior. Derived from the *Control* class, the *InkControl* and *InkControl2* classes require no host window to use them. They are almost identical to one another, with one subtle difference: the *InkControl* class allows changing ink color only using the .NET Framework's *ColorDialog* class. The *InkControl2* class provides more control over ink formatting using the utility library's *FormatInkDlg* class.

> **Note**    The two classes are provided for reader reference—the book starts out using *InkControl*, but once the appropriate material is covered we switch over to the *InkControl2* class. The use of these controls in production-level applications isn't recommended.

## *InkControl*

```
public InkControl()
```

Class constructor.

## *InkControl2*

```
public InkControl2()
```

Class constructor.

## *InkOverlay*

```
public InkOverlay InkOverlay
```

This property returns the *InkOverlay* instance the control is using. There is no restriction on altering any of the instance's properties, calling its methods, or responding to its events.

## *InkInputPanel*

```
public InkInputPanel InkInputPanel
```

This property returns the *InkInputPanel* instance the control is using.

# The *FormatInkDlg* Class

The *FormatInkDlg* class implements a dialog box used to edit an instance of the *DrawingAttributes* class. It allows the user to view and alter all the instance's properties.

To use the *FormatInkDlg* class, create an instance using the *new* operator, set the *DrawingAttributes* property to a valid instance of the *DrawingAttributes* class, and then call *ShowDialog*. The result returned from the *ShowDialog* method is either *DialogResult.OK* or *DialogResult.Cancel. DialogResult.OK* means the user clicked the OK button, typically indicating that the *Drawing-Attributes* instance should be applied or stored.

The initial *DrawingAttributes* instance assigned to the *DrawingAttributes* property will not be modified, regardless of the user's interaction with the dialog box.

## FormatInkDlg

```
public FormatInkDlg()
```

Class constructor.

## DrawingAttributes

```
public DrawingAttributes DrawingAttributes
```

This property gets or sets the *DrawingAttributes* instance the dialog box uses. When setting the value, the source instance will not be modified in any way.

# The *InkEx* Class

This class can be thought of as an extension of the *Ink* class. It comprises one static method.

## AddStrokesAtRectangle

```
public static Strokes AddStrokesAtRectangle
        (Ink ink, Strokes strokes, Rectangle rectDestination)
```

This method provides the same functionality as the *Ink* class's *AddStrokes-AtRectangle*, except that it returns a *Strokes* collection that references the newly added ink.

# The *RendererEx* Class

The *RendererEx* class provides rendering functionality and can be thought of as an extension of the *Renderer* class. It comprises static methods, most of which take a *Renderer* object for their first parameter.

## InkSpaceToPixel

```
public static void InkSpaceToPixel
        (Renderer renderer, Graphics g, ref Rectangle rcRect)
```

This method is exactly like the *Renderer* class's *InkSpaceToPixel* method, except that it operates on a *Rectangle* object.

## PixelToInkSpace

```
public static void PixelToInkSpace
        (Renderer renderer, Graphics g, ref Rectangle rcRect)
```

This method works like the *Renderer* class's *PixelToInkSpace* method, except that it operates on a *Rectangle* object.

## DrawSelected

```
public static void DrawSelected
        (Renderer renderer, Graphics g, Strokes strokes)
```

```
public static void DrawSelected
        (Renderer renderer, Graphics g, Stroke s)
```

These methods render ink strokes to appear outlined or with a halo style, as seen in *InkOverlay*'s select mode and in Windows Journal. The halo style usually indicates that the ink is selected. These methods are useful in implementing a custom selection mode or real-time lasso selection.

## DrawStrokeIds

```
public static void DrawStrokeIds
        (Graphics g, Font font, Ink ink)
```

```
public static void DrawStrokeIds
        (Renderer renderer, Graphics g, Font font, Strokes strokes)
```

These methods draw each stroke ID value at the beginning point of each stroke in the specified *Ink* object or *Strokes* collection.

A *Font* object can be specified to alter the style of the rendering.

## DrawBoundingBoxes

```
public static void DrawBoundingBoxes(Graphics g, Ink ink)

public static void DrawBoundingBoxes
        (Renderer renderer, Graphics g,
        Strokes strokes, Pen pen, BoundingBoxMode mode)
```

These methods draw the bounding boxes of each stroke contained in the specified *Ink* object or *Strokes* collection. Use the *BoundingBoxMode* enumeration to specify the computation method of the bounding box.

A *Pen* object can be specified to alter the style of the rendering.

## DrawPoints

```
public static void DrawPoints(Graphics g, Ink ink)

public static void DrawPoints
        (Renderer renderer, Graphics g, Strokes strokes,
        Brush brush, StrokePointType type)

public static void DrawPoints
        (Renderer renderer, Graphics g,
        Stroke stroke, Brush brush, StrokePointType type)
```

These methods draw the points making up each specified stroke. The type of the points to use for display is specified with a *StrokePointType* enumeration:

```
public enum StrokePointType
{
    Polyline,
    Bezier,
    FlattenedBezier
}
```

Specify a *Brush* object to alter the color of the rendering.

## DrawIntersections

```
public static void DrawIntersections(Graphics g, Ink ink)

public static void DrawIntersections
        (Renderer renderer, Graphics g, Strokes strokes,
        Pen pen, StrokeIntersectionType type)
```

These methods draw the intersections of the strokes specified in the *Ink* object or *Strokes* collection. The type of intersection is specified with the *StrokeIntersectionType* enumeration:

```
public enum StrokeIntersectionType
{
    Self,
    Stroke,
    BoundingBox
}
```

A *Pen* object can be specified to alter the style of the rendering.

## *DrawCusps*

```
public static void DrawCusps(Graphics g, Ink ink)

public static void DrawCusps
        (Renderer renderer, Graphics g, Strokes strokes,
        Pen pen, StrokeCuspType type)

public static void DrawCusps
        (Renderer renderer, Graphics g, Stroke stroke,
        Pen pen, StrokeCuspType type)
```

These methods draw the cusps computed in each specified stroke. The type of cusp is specified with the *StrokeCuspType* enumeration:

```
public enum StrokeCuspType
{
    Bezier,
    Polyline
}
```

A *Pen* object can be specified to alter the style of the rendering.

# The *LassoUI* Class

This class is useful if you're implementing a custom selection mode or a real-time lasso selection. It implements the lasso dots seen in *InkOverlay* and Windows Journal.

To use the *LassoUI* class, create an instance using the *new* operator, call the *Start* method with the initial starting point of the lasso, and then repeatedly call the *Continue* method for subsequent points of the lasso. No calculation is required to measure distance or drop points to achieve the evenly spaced lasso dots—the class handles this automatically. To obtain the array of points constituting the lasso, query the *Points* property.

## LassoUI

```
public LassoUI()
```

Class constructor.

## Start

```
public void Start(Graphics g, Point ptStart)
```

This method indicates the start of a lasso, typically called in response to an *InkCollector* or *InkOverlay*'s *CursorDown* or *SystemGesture.DragStart* event. The *ptStart* parameter is specified in pixels.

## Continue

```
public bool Continue(Graphics g, Point ptNew)
```

This method indicates the continuation of a lasso, typically called in response to an *InkCollector* or *InkOverlay*'s *Packets* event. The *ptNew* parameter is specified in pixels.

## Render

```
public void Render(Graphics g)
```

```
public void Render(Graphics g, Rectangle rcClip)
```

These methods will draw the entire in-progress lasso, typically called in the *Paint* handler for the window being used to capture the lasso data. The *rcClip* parameter can be used to avoid the redundant painting of lasso dots and thus increase rendering performance.

## Points

```
public Point[] Points
```

This property returns the array of points used to draw the lasso. This array should be used as the basis for the point array specified in the hit-testing computation. The values returned are in pixels, so make sure to convert them into ink space coordinates if they are to be used with the *Ink.HitTest* method.

## BoundingRect

```
public Rectangle BoundingRect
```

This property returns the boundaries of the lasso currently in progress and is specified in pixels.

## *DotSpacing*

```
public int DotSpacing
```

This property gets or sets the spacing between lasso dots and is specified in pixels.

## *DotSize*

```
public int DotSize
```

This property gets or sets the size of each lasso dot and is specified in pixels.

## *DotBrush*

```
public Brush DotBrush
```

This property gets or sets the brush used to draw lasso dots. By setting this property, you can alter the lasso color.

# The *CopyAsTextDlg* Class

This class is used to edit an instance of the *RecognitionResult* class. It's a handy dialog box commonly used in conjunction with the "Copy As Text" command, and it's similar in functionality to the user interface seen in Windows Journal.

To use the *CopyAsTextDlg* class, create an instance using the *new* operator, set the *RecognitionResult* property, and then call *ShowDialog*. The *RecognitionResult* instance that is supplied to the dialog box *will* be modified as a result of any user interactions.

## *CopyAsTextDlg*

```
public CopyAsTextDlg()
```

Class constructor.

## *RecognitionResult*

```
public RecognitionResult RecognitionResult
```

This property gets or sets the *RecognitionResult* instance the dialog box uses. When setting the value, any user interaction with the dialog box will modify the source instance.

# Appendix B

# Tablet PC Hardware Guidelines

The following Microsoft Tablet PC hardware guidelines are provided as reference. They are fairly technical and especially relevant for hardware manufacturers. However, knowing the set of hardware features that must be supported by all Tablet PCs will help you to make informed decisions as you design your application. These requirements are subject to change, and any updates can be found at *http://www.microsoft.com/WINDOWSXP/tabletpc/developer/hdwreq.asp*.

## Windows XP Tablet PC Edition Hardware Requirements

Microsoft has established unique hardware requirements for manufacturers designing hardware for Windows XP Tablet PC Edition. Every effort was made to balance the need to deliver a positive end-user experience in key scenarios while maintaining maximum flexibility in the hardware manufacturers' ability to innovate and differentiate their products based on this platform. Please send an e-mail message to tpc_hreq@microsoft.com if you have any questions about these requirements. In addition to the hardware requirements listed below, it is highly recommended that PC manufacturers design their systems to comply with the "Designed for Windows XP" guidelines (available at Windows Logo Program for Hardware, *http://www.microsoft.com/winlogo/hardware/*).

## Digitizer:

- **D1.** The digitizer must report X and Y stylus position coordinates accurately when the stylus tip is within 5 millimeters of the writing surface anywhere within the active display area. Physical contact must not be required to determine the stylus location.

■ **D2.** When the digitizer is active, it must report position coordinates and stylus tip up/down status at least 100 times per second. The sample rate may be reduced to conserve power upon inactivity, but must increase to at least 100 samples per second anytime the pen is in contact with the display surface. Using active sample rates of 133 samples per second is recommended.

■ **D3.** The digitizer resolution must be at least five times greater than the LCD pixel density, but must not be less than 600 points per inch. Although lower digitizer resolutions are permitted, using digitizer resolutions of 1,000 points per inch is recommended. Example: For a 10.4-inch XGA (1024 x 768) display panel, LCD pixel density is 123 points per inch, and therefore the minimum digitizer resolution must be at least 615 points per inch (5 x 123).

■ **D4.** The cursor position must be within 3 millimeters of the point of contact between the stylus tip and the display surface anywhere within the active display area. While rapid response and accurate positioning regardless of varying pen tilt-angles should be designed for, the stylus can be held motionless and orthogonal to the display surface during the screen calibration test.

## Power States:

■ **P1.** Resume from S3 to S0 must reliably complete in less than 5 seconds. Resume time is measured by BootVis.exe (available at Fast Boot/Fast Resume for the Windows Platform, *http://www.microsoft.com/hwdev/platform/performance/fastboot/default.asp*) and includes the sum of "Bios Wake + Device init + Apps init." No applications are required to be running during the BootVis test, and the test must be executed with the Tablet PC configured as it's expected to ship. Any applications or services that will run automatically out-of-the-box (such as tray applications provided by the hardware manufacturer, not run-once applications such as end-user registration) must be running during the test. No external peripherals are required to be connected, but all built-in devices must be enabled during the test.

■ **P2.** On a single fully charged battery, S3 must be reliably maintained for at least 72 hours without any external power source.

- **P3.**   Automatic transition from S3 to S4 upon low battery is highly recommended to prevent the potential loss of unsaved user data. The S3 to S4 transition should use an intermediate step at S0. Therefore, it is recommended that if a design provides automatic S3 to S4 transition, the low-battery trigger should be set so that there is sufficient power for the S3 to S0 to S4 transition.

For more complete definitions of S3 and S4 low-power states, please refer to Advanced Configuration and Power Interface Specification Revision 2.0 (ACPI - Advanced Configuration and Power Interface, *http://www.acpi.info/ index.html*). In brief, S3 ("sleep mode") is a low-latency sleep state where memory context is typically maintained by placing the system RAM into a low-power auto-refresh mode while most other system devices are completely powered down. S4 ("hibernate mode") is a higher latency but extremely low-power sleep state in which RAM contents are stored to hard disk and restored quickly when the system wakes up. S0 ("awake mode") is the normal system working state.

## Viewing Mode:

- **V1.**   Switching the display between full-screen, native-resolution landscape and portrait orientations without reboot must be supported. For example, a tablet with a 1024 x 786 XGA display must allow switching to portrait mode (768 x 1024) without requiring a reboot.

## Removal from Dock:

- **R1.**   If a Tablet PC supports docking, surprise removal must be allowed. Removal of the Tablet PC from the docking station without prior notification must not cause any system instability, and any devices contained in or attached to the dock must enumerate and function properly when the Tablet PC is redocked.

- **R2.**   When the unit is redocked, any device enumeration must be automatic and not require a reboot or other elaborate process.

## Legacy-Free:

- **L2.**  Designs must be legacy-free as defined for mobiles in the Microsoft Windows System and Device Requirements 2.0 (available at Technical Requirements for Hardware - Windows Logo Program, *http://www.microsoft.com/winlogo/hardware/tech.asp*).

## CTRL+ALT+DEL or Equivalent Functionality:

- **C1.**  A Tablet PC without an attached keyboard must support a single, dedicated, non-overloaded hardware mechanism for generating the Secure Attention Sequence (SAS), also known as "CTRL+ALT+DEL" or "CAD."

- **C2.**  If the SAS button is implemented as a Human Interface Device (HID), the HID-compliant button driver must provide a keyboard collection to report the SAS event.

# Index

Send feedback about this index to *mspindex@microsoft.com*

# Rob Jarrett

Rob Jarrett works as a Software Design Engineer in the Tablet PC group designing and implementing tablet input, real-time inking, and the ink interaction model for Windows Journal and the Windows shell. He has worked on the Tablet PC since he joined Microsoft in August 2000, relocating to Washington from Toronto, Ontario, Canada. For the previous seven years of his professional career, Rob worked on various commercial Windows software packages, ranging in focus from multimedia-based presentations to rapid Web-application design. Areas of interest for Rob include music composition (his work has

been heard on radio, television, and film), audio production and engineering, riding his motorcycle, playing classic arcade games, and watching really bad films. Rob graduated with a Bachelor of Science honors degree from McMaster University (Hamilton, Ontario) in 1992.

# Philip Su

Philip Su is a Lead Developer at Microsoft in the Tablet PC group working on integration of the Tablet PC Platform into Windows Journal software. Previously, he worked as a Lead Developer on Microsoft Money and as a Software Design Engineer on Microsoft Word. Philip is also the founder and CEO of Sonetics Software, LLC, a company that specializes in digital audio software. Philip has won numerous awards, including the prestigious National Science Foundation Graduate Fellowship as well as the Maryland Technical Invention of the Year Award. His areas of interest include discrete digital audio processing, multimodal

user interfaces, and digital media. He holds dual Bachelor of Science degrees in Computer Science and Neurobiology, graduating summa cum laude from the University of Maryland.

## Steel-Nibbed Pen

As the size of writing became smaller, the quill replaced the reed pen. Although quill pens can be made from the outer wing feathers of any bird, those of goose, swan, crow, and (later) turkey were preferred. The quill pen was the principal writing implement for nearly 1300 years. To make a quill pen, a wing feather is first hardened by heating or letting it dry out gradually. The hardened quill is then cut to a broad edge with a special penknife. The writer had to recut the quill pen frequently to maintain its edge. The sixteenth-century Spanish calligrapher Juan de Yciar mentions brass pens for very large writing in his 1548 writing manual, but the use of metal pens did not become widespread until the early part of the nineteenth century. English engineer Bryan Donkin made the first patented steel-nibbed pen in 1803. In 1884 Lewis Waterman, a New York insurance agent, patented the first practical fountain pen containing its own ink reservoir. Waterman invented a mechanism that fed ink to the pen point by capillary action, allowing ink to flow evenly while writing. By the 1920s the fountain pen was the chief writing instrument in the West and remained so until the introduction of the ballpoint pen after World War II.*

At Microsoft Press, we use tools to illustrate our books for software developers and IT professionals. Tools simply and powerfully symbolize human inventiveness. They're a metaphor for people extending their capabilities, precision, and reach. From simple calipers and pliers to digital micrometers and lasers, these stylized illustrations give a visual identity to each book and a personality to the series. With tools and knowledge, there's no limit to creativity and innovation. Our tag line says it all: *the tools you need to put technology to work.*

---

*Microsoft Encarta Reference Library 2002. © 1993-2001 Microsoft Corporation. All rights reserved.

---

The manuscript for this book was prepared and galleyed using Microsoft Word. Microsoft Press composed the pages using Adobe FrameMaker+SGML for Microsoft Windows, with text in Garamond and display type in Helvetica Condensed. Composed pages were delivered to the printer as electronic prepress files.

| | |
|---|---|
| Cover Designer: | Methodologie, Inc. |
| Interior Graphic Designer: | James D. Kramer |
| Principal Compositor: | Paula Gorelick |
| Electronic Artist: | Michael Kloepfer |
| Principal Copy Editor: | Sandi Resnick |
| Indexer: | Seth Maislin |

# The definitive
## one-stop resource
### for developing on the revolutionary
## .NET platform

**U.S.A.** **$59.99**
Canada $86.99
ISBN: 0-7356-1376-1

This core reference for Microsoft® .NET provides everything you need to know to build robust, Web-extensible applications for the revolutionary Microsoft development platform. Leading Windows® programming authority Jeff Prosise masterfully distills this new Web-enabled programming paradigm and its Framework Class Library—easily one of the most complex collections ever assembled—into a conversational, easy-to-follow programming reference you can repeatedly visit to resolve specific .NET development questions. Prosise clearly explains all the critical elements of application development in the .NET environment, including Windows Forms, Web Forms, and XML Web services—illustrating key concepts with inline code examples and many complete sample programs. All the book's sample code and programs—most of them written in C#—appear on the companion CD-ROM so you can study and adapt them for your own Web-based business applications.

**Microsoft**®
microsoft.com/mspress

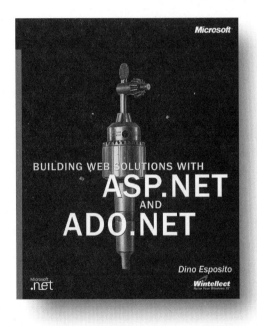

Get a **Free**
e-mail newsletter, updates,
special offers, links to related books,
and more when you

# register on line!

Register your Microsoft Press® title on our Web site and you'll get a FREE subscription to our e-mail newsletter, *Microsoft Press Book Connections.* You'll find out about newly released and upcoming books and learning tools, online events, software downloads, special offers and coupons for Microsoft Press customers, and information about major Microsoft® product releases. You can also read useful additional information about all the titles we publish, such as detailed book descriptions, tables of contents and indexes, sample chapters, links to related books and book series, author biographies, and reviews by other customers.

## Registration is easy. Just visit this Web page and fill in your information:

*http://www.microsoft.com/mspress/register*

**Microsoft**®

---

# MICROSOFT LICENSE AGREEMENT

Book Companion CD

**IMPORTANT—READ CAREFULLY:** This Microsoft End-User License Agreement ("EULA") is a legal agreement between you (either an individual or an entity) and Microsoft Corporation for the Microsoft product identified above, which includes computer software and may include associated media, printed materials, and "online" or electronic documentation ("SOFTWARE PRODUCT"). Any component included within the SOFTWARE PRODUCT that is accompanied by a separate End-User License Agreement shall be governed by such agreement and not the terms set forth below. By installing, copying, or otherwise using the SOFTWARE PRODUCT, you agree to be bound by the terms of this EULA. If you do not agree to the terms of this EULA, you are not authorized to install, copy, or otherwise use the SOFTWARE PRODUCT; you may, however, return the SOFTWARE PRODUCT, along with all printed materials and other items that form a part of the Microsoft product that includes the SOFTWARE PRODUCT, to the place you obtained them for a full refund.

## SOFTWARE PRODUCT LICENSE

The SOFTWARE PRODUCT is protected by United States copyright laws and international copyright treaties, as well as other intellectual property laws and treaties. The SOFTWARE PRODUCT is licensed, not sold.

1. **GRANT OF LICENSE.** This EULA grants you the following rights:

   a. **Software Product.** You may install and use one copy of the SOFTWARE PRODUCT on a single computer. The primary user of the computer on which the SOFTWARE PRODUCT is installed may make a second copy for his or her exclusive use on a portable computer.

   b. **Storage/Network Use.** You may also store or install a copy of the SOFTWARE PRODUCT on a storage device, such as a network server, used only to install or run the SOFTWARE PRODUCT on your other computers over an internal network; however, you must acquire and dedicate a license for each separate computer on which the SOFTWARE PRODUCT is installed or run from the storage device. A license for the SOFTWARE PRODUCT may not be shared or used concurrently on different computers.

   c. **License Pak.** If you have acquired this EULA in a Microsoft License Pak, you may make the number of additional copies of the computer software portion of the SOFTWARE PRODUCT authorized on the printed copy of this EULA, and you may use each copy in the manner specified above. You are also entitled to make a corresponding number of secondary copies for portable computer use as specified above.

   d. **Sample Code.** Solely with respect to portions, if any, of the SOFTWARE PRODUCT that are identified within the SOFTWARE PRODUCT as sample code (the "SAMPLE CODE"):

      i. **Use and Modification.** Microsoft grants you the right to use and modify the source code version of the SAMPLE CODE, *provided* you comply with subsection (d)(iii) below. You may not distribute the SAMPLE CODE, or any modified version of the SAMPLE CODE, in source code form.

      ii. **Redistributable Files.** Provided you comply with subsection (d)(iii) below, Microsoft grants you a nonexclusive, royalty-free right to reproduce and distribute the object code version of the SAMPLE CODE and of any modified SAMPLE CODE, other than SAMPLE CODE, or any modified version thereof, designated as not redistributable in the Readme file that forms a part of the SOFTWARE PRODUCT (the "Non-Redistributable Sample Code"). All SAMPLE CODE other than the Non-Redistributable Sample Code is collectively referred to as the "REDISTRIBUTABLES."

      iii. **Redistribution Requirements.** If you redistribute the REDISTRIBUTABLES, you agree to: (i) distribute the REDISTRIBUTABLES in object code form only in conjunction with and as a part of your software application product; (ii) not use Microsoft's name, logo, or trademarks to market your software application product; (iii) include a valid copyright notice on your software application product; (iv) indemnify, hold harmless, and defend Microsoft from and against any claims or lawsuits, including attorney's fees, that arise or result from the use or distribution of your software application product; and (v) not permit further distribution of the REDISTRIBUTABLES by your end user. Contact Microsoft for the applicable royalties due and other licensing terms for all other uses and/or distribution of the REDISTRIBUTABLES.

2. **DESCRIPTION OF OTHER RIGHTS AND LIMITATIONS.**

   - **Limitations on Reverse Engineering, Decompilation, and Disassembly.** You may not reverse engineer, decompile, or disassemble the SOFTWARE PRODUCT, except and only to the extent that such activity is expressly permitted by applicable law notwithstanding this limitation.

   - **Separation of Components.** The SOFTWARE PRODUCT is licensed as a single product. Its component parts may not be separated for use on more than one computer.

   - **Rental.** You may not rent, lease, or lend the SOFTWARE PRODUCT.

- **Support Services.** Microsoft may, but is not obligated to, provide you with support services related to the SOFTWARE PRODUCT ("Support Services"). Use of Support Services is governed by the Microsoft policies and programs described in the user manual, in "online" documentation, and/or in other Microsoft-provided materials. Any supplemental software code provided to you as part of the Support Services shall be considered part of the SOFTWARE PRODUCT and subject to the terms and conditions of this EULA. With respect to technical information you provide to Microsoft as part of the Support Services, Microsoft may use such information for its business purposes, including for product support and development. Microsoft will not utilize such technical information in a form that personally identifies you.

- **Software Transfer.** You may permanently transfer all of your rights under this EULA, provided you retain no copies, you transfer all of the SOFTWARE PRODUCT (including all component parts, the media and printed materials, any upgrades, this EULA, and, if applicable, the Certificate of Authenticity), **and** the recipient agrees to the terms of this EULA.

- **Termination.** Without prejudice to any other rights, Microsoft may terminate this EULA if you fail to comply with the terms and conditions of this EULA. In such event, you must destroy all copies of the SOFTWARE PRODUCT and all of its component parts.

3. **COPYRIGHT.** All title and copyrights in and to the SOFTWARE PRODUCT (including but not limited to any images, photographs, animations, video, audio, music, text, SAMPLE CODE, REDISTRIBUTABLES, and "applets" incorporated into the SOFTWARE PRODUCT) and any copies of the SOFTWARE PRODUCT are owned by Microsoft or its suppliers. The SOFTWARE PRODUCT is protected by copyright laws and international treaty provisions. Therefore, you must treat the SOFTWARE PRODUCT like any other copyrighted material **except** that you may install the SOFTWARE PRODUCT on a single computer provided you keep the original solely for backup or archival purposes. You may not copy the printed materials accompanying the SOFTWARE PRODUCT.

4. **U.S. GOVERNMENT RESTRICTED RIGHTS.** The SOFTWARE PRODUCT and documentation are provided with RESTRICTED RIGHTS. Use, duplication, or disclosure by the Government is subject to restrictions as set forth in subparagraph (c)(1)(ii) of the Rights in Technical Data and Computer Software clause at DFARS 252.227-7013 or subparagraphs (c)(1) and (2) of the Commercial Computer Software—Restricted Rights at 48 CFR 52.227-19, as applicable. Manufacturer is Microsoft Corporation/One Microsoft Way/Redmond, WA 98052-6399.

5. **EXPORT RESTRICTIONS.** You agree that you will not export or re-export the SOFTWARE PRODUCT, any part thereof, or any process or service that is the direct product of the SOFTWARE PRODUCT (the foregoing collectively referred to as the "Restricted Components"), to any country, person, entity, or end user subject to U.S. export restrictions. You specifically agree not to export or re-export any of the Restricted Components (i) to any country to which the U.S. has embargoed or restricted the export of goods or services, which currently include, but are not necessarily limited to, Cuba, Iran, Iraq, Libya, North Korea, Sudan, and Syria, or to any national of any such country, wherever located, who intends to transmit or transport the Restricted Components back to such country; (ii) to any end user who you know or have reason to know will utilize the Restricted Components in the design, development, or production of nuclear, chemical, or biological weapons; or (iii) to any end user who has been prohibited from participating in U.S. export transactions by any federal agency of the U.S. government. You warrant and represent that neither the BXA nor any other U.S. federal agency has suspended, revoked, or denied your export privileges.

## DISCLAIMER OF WARRANTY

**NO WARRANTIES OR CONDITIONS.** MICROSOFT EXPRESSLY DISCLAIMS ANY WARRANTY OR CONDITION FOR THE SOFTWARE PRODUCT. THE SOFTWARE PRODUCT AND ANY RELATED DOCUMENTATION ARE PROVIDED "AS IS" WITHOUT WARRANTY OR CONDITION OF ANY KIND, EITHER EXPRESS OR IMPLIED, INCLUDING, WITHOUT LIMITA-TION, THE IMPLIED WARRANTIES OF MERCHANTABILITY, FITNESS FOR A PARTICULAR PURPOSE, OR NONINFRINGEMENT. THE ENTIRE RISK ARISING OUT OF USE OR PERFORMANCE OF THE SOFTWARE PRODUCT REMAINS WITH YOU.

**LIMITATION OF LIABILITY.** TO THE MAXIMUM EXTENT PERMITTED BY APPLICABLE LAW, IN NO EVENT SHALL MICROSOFT OR ITS SUPPLIERS BE LIABLE FOR ANY SPECIAL, INCIDENTAL, INDIRECT, OR CONSEQUENTIAL DAM-AGES WHATSOEVER (INCLUDING, WITHOUT LIMITATION, DAMAGES FOR LOSS OF BUSINESS PROFITS, BUSINESS INTERRUPTION, LOSS OF BUSINESS INFORMATION, OR ANY OTHER PECUNIARY LOSS) ARISING OUT OF THE USE OF OR INABILITY TO USE THE SOFTWARE PRODUCT OR THE PROVISION OF OR FAILURE TO PROVIDE SUPPORT SERVICES, EVEN IF MICROSOFT HAS BEEN ADVISED OF THE POSSIBILITY OF SUCH DAMAGES. IN ANY CASE, MICROSOFT'S ENTIRE LIABILITY UNDER ANY PROVISION OF THIS EULA SHALL BE LIMITED TO THE GREATER OF THE AMOUNT ACTUALLY PAID BY YOU FOR THE SOFTWARE PRODUCT OR US$5.00; PROVIDED, HOWEVER, IF YOU HAVE ENTERED INTO A MICROSOFT SUPPORT SERVICES AGREEMENT, MICROSOFT'S ENTIRE LIABILITY REGARDING SUPPORT SERVICES SHALL BE GOVERNED BY THE TERMS OF THAT AGREEMENT. BECAUSE SOME STATES AND JURISDICTIONS DO NOT ALLOW THE EXCLUSION OR LIMITATION OF LIABILITY, THE ABOVE LIMITATION MAY NOT APPLY TO YOU.

## MISCELLANEOUS

This EULA is governed by the laws of the State of Washington USA, except and only to the extent that applicable law mandates govern-ing law of a different jurisdiction.

Should you have any questions concerning this EULA, or if you desire to contact Microsoft for any reason, please contact the Microsoft subsidiary serving your country, or write: Microsoft Sales Information Center/One Microsoft Way/Redmond, WA 98052-6399.